CARVING *as* CRAFT

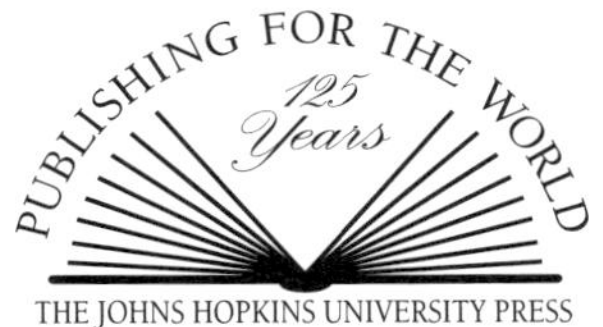

CARVING *as* CRAFT

PALATINE EAST *and* the GRECO-ROMAN BONE *and* IVORY CARVING TRADITION

ARCHER ST. CLAIR

THE JOHNS HOPKINS UNIVERSITY PRESS

BALTIMORE AND LONDON

The Johns Hopkins University Press
2715 North Charles Street
Baltimore, Maryland 21218-4363
www.press.jhu.edu

Library of Congress Cataloging-in-Publication Data

St. Clair, Archer.
    Carving as craft : Palatine east and the Greco-Roman bone and ivory
carving tradition / Archer St. Clair.
        p.   cm
Includes bibliographical references and index.
    ISBN 0-8018-7261-8 (hardcover : alk. paper)
1. Ivories, Ancient—Italy—Rome. 2. Ivory carving—Italy—Rome.
3. Bone carving—Italy—Rome. 4. Ivories—Italy—Palatine Hill.
5. Palatine Hill (Italy)—Antiquities, Roman. I. Title.
    NK5860 .S7 2003
736′.62′09376—dc21
                                                         2002012552

A catalog record for this book is available from the British Library.

CONTENTS

CHAPTER ILLUSTRATIONS

ACKNOWLEDGMENTS

This study owes its inception to Eric Hostetter, director of the Palatine East Excavation, who invited me to study the bone and ivory remains and encouraged me to undertake a monographic study of the material. Throughout this project I relied on his expertise, sound advice, and generous support. The excavation was a collaborative undertaking of the Soprintendenza Archeologica di Roma and the American Academy in Rome. Special thanks go to Professor Adriano La Regina, Soprintendente, Soprintendenza Archeologica di Roma, who invited the collaboration, and to Dr. I. Jacopi and G. Tedone for their assistance in all aspects of the project. At the American Academy in Rome, Adele Chatfield Taylor, Joseph Connors, and Caroline Bruzelius, as well as the institution's staff, supported all aspects of this project over a number of seasons. Their generous allocation of space and facilities for processing and analysis of excavated material made this study possible. Funding for the excavation was provided by the Alexander Abraham Foundation, the Samuel H. Kress Foundation, the Emily and John Harvey Foundation, the Norwegian Research Council for the Humanities, Rutgers University, and the University of Illinois at Urbana–Champaign. Research on the ivory and bone remains was supported by a Dumbarton Oaks/Harvard University Project Grant and by the Rutgers University Research Council. I am grateful to the Ephoreia of Classical Antiquities at Olympia and the Deutsches Archäologisches Institut at Athens for allowing me to study the remains associated with Pheidias's workshop at Olympia.

This project would have been impossible without the support and assistance of numerous colleagues and students who participated in the excavation over six active seasons. It is impossible to name them all, but thanks are especially due to J. Rasmus Brandt, associate director of the excavation; Theodore Peña, pottery specialist; and David Reese, faunal remains specialist, who generously shared his vast expertise on bone with me. Others include Danae Thimme, conservator; Laura Flusche, and Bradley Ault, sector supervisors and metal specialists; and

Maryline Parca, epigraphy specialist, who was a fund of knowledge and gracious support throughout the excavation.

To our great benefit, numerous students participated in the excavation. Especially helpful to me were Julia Lenaghan, Stephanie Smith, Marice Rose, and Abigail Berler, who were involved in the processing and analysis of finds. A large number of students and professionals drew and photographed objects of bone and ivory. Special thanks go to Tracy Scott, Mark Cameron, Linda Robbenolt, and especially Michelle Trageser, who inked the drawings for this book. Technical assistance at later stages was supplied by John and Joan Emerick and Tara Kolb.

Visiting and resident scholars at the American Academy in Rome, including Lawrence Richardson, Russell Scott, Malcolm Bell, and Elizabeth Fentress, provided valuable assistance and expertise throughout the excavation period, as did visiting specialists such as Dale Kinney. My greatest debt, however, is to Anthony Cutler, whose expertise in ivory carving is matched only by his generosity in sharing his broad knowledge, and whose scholarship on the subject of ivory has been an inspiration.

This study is dedicated to my husband, Tom, without whom nothing would have been possible.

INTRODUCTION

The bone and ivory remains that are the focus of this study constitute the largest and most varied collection unearthed in the city of Rome and possibly the entire western Mediterranean area and document the existence of a bone- and ivory-carving industry that functioned over several centuries. The remains came to light during excavations carried out in two major trenches on the northeast slope of the Palatine Hill from 1989 to 1994 under the joint sponsorship of the American Academy in Rome and the Soprintendenza Archeologica di Roma and directed by E. Hostetter.*

The major architectural features of the site, which lies immediately southwest of the Arch of Constantine, are what appears to be an extensive late antique *domus* and ancillary structures that occupy a roughly triangular area, stretching on its longest side approximately 110 meters behind the row of shops that faced the street under the present day Via di San Gregorio. The *domus* rests on and incorporates mid- and late republican remains, including a series of late republican structures, as well as wall fragments of probable Neronian and Flavian date. Later Antonine and Severan structures, including a frescoed room of the first half of the third century, were enclosed in the construction of the large *domus,* which is assigned to the second half of the third century A.D. (before Diocletian) and is distinguished by a large apsidal reception hall, or *aula.* Beginning at the end of the third century, rooms to the south of the apsidal hall were deliberately filled in, but parts of the complex, including the apsidal hall itself, remained in use, and there is evidence of continued late antique and medieval occupation, including varied structural additions and alterations.

Upslope and to the northwest of the *domus* complex proper, a second smaller trench, opened in 1991 (Sector D), revealed remains of late republican and early

---

*For preliminary reports of the excavation see Hostetter et al. 1990, 1991, 1993, 1994.

imperial constructions beneath fourth- and fifth-century deposits, including a fountain complex.

Bone and ivory remains, which include both finished objects and significant amounts of manufacturing debris, were present in both areas. The heaviest concentrations of material were in deposits of mixed debris dating from the first through early second century and mid-third through fifth century that were used as fill over and around earlier structures.

The decision to examine these remains within the broader context of the Greco-Roman tradition came about as the result of my examination of the carving debris associated with the so-called workshop of Pheidias at Olympia, distant in time from but in some ways remarkably similar to the material from Palatine East. Although this debris is associated with a dramatically different location and class of object—the great fifth-century B.C. chryselephantine statue of Zeus—one is struck by the similarity of the remains and hence by what appears to be the remarkable continuity of carving traditions over a broad geographical and temporal expanse. Both ancient and modern authors have traditionally separated ivory from bone carving, elevating ivory carving to a higher realm, but physical evidence in the form of manufacturing debris and finished objects points clearly to the close association of the two materials at the workshop level, and perhaps to a less rigid notion of material value than often supposed. Casting a broader, although necessarily selective, net permits us to test the hypothesis of a shared and long-lived "Mediterranean" vocabulary of form and technique that embraced both materials, while at the same time allowing us to examine changing fashions and varying responses at particular times and places and to identify the audiences for whom these artisans worked. It allows us as well, armed with recently obtained archaeological data, to reevaluate long-held assumptions concerning the location of carving centers that are based solely on stylistic groupings or findspots, and to bring to bear on these issues our growing understanding of patterns of trade and consumption within the broader Mediterranean context. It is hoped that this multifaceted approach to the Palatine East remains will be of value to art historians as well as to others interested in broader cultural issues of the period.

It should be emphasized, however, that this brief volume is in no way comprehensive, either in its examination of the past, from which it draws upon a small sample of material, or in its recording of the present, specifically the admirable studies, particularly of bone carving, being carried out at present in association with numerous archaeological excavations.

CARVING *as* CRAFT

1

THE MATERIALS

Bone and ivory were major carving mediums in the ancient world, yet the notion that bone is merely a poor substitute for ivory is prevalent in both ancient and modern literature. The material remains, however, provide a more nuanced picture. Ample evidence shows that carvers recognized and appreciated structural differences between the two and that these differences influenced the choice of one material over the other, even when both were available. The extensive remains from Palatine East, which include a wide range of objects and manufacturing debris in both bone and ivory, clearly illustrate these differences and provide insights into each material's strengths and weaknesses. For this reason, a brief overview of the structure and mechanical properties of bone and ivory is presented here, illustrated by examples from Palatine East, with an emphasis on understanding why one material was chosen over the other when both were available within the same setting.[1]

BONE

Although superficially similar to ivory, bone possesses particular qualities that made it the material of choice for a variety of objects in antiquity. Bone tissue is composed of inorganic and organic material. The organic elements are collagen, which constitutes about 40–60% of adult bone, and polysaccharide complexes, which attach to the collagen fibrils. Inorganic mineral crystals, composed mainly of calcium and phosphate, surround and bond to the collagen fibers. The elasticity and tensile strength of bone are a function of the collagen bundles, whereas bone's characteristic hardness, rigidity, and compressive strength are due to the mineral crystals.

Its composite structure gives bone a distinct advantage over other materials. In bending strength and elasticity, for example, bone is superior to ivory.[2] A related advantage is its resistance to stress fractures and cracking. Acting as an interface between the inorganic mineral crystals, the collagenous matrix functions as a "crack stopper," preventing fractures from running through an entire structure.[3] These qualities are amply demonstrated among the Palatine East remains, particularly in utensils, where, in contrast to the few poorly preserved ivory examples, numerous bone examples survive intact.

Mature bone is characterized as either cancellous or compact, a distinction visible to the naked eye (Pl. 3c). Cancellous tissue forms the inner substance of most bones and consists mainly of intersecting units that give the bone its characteristic spongy or open character, forming a network of support. The spaces between the units are filled with blood vessels, marrow, and connective tissue. The depth to which any bone can be carved is limited by the presence of cancellous tissue on its interior, and cancellous tissue is frequently visible on blanks and even on finished objects (Pls. 10a,b, 11a,e, 25b). Compact tissue forms the outer layer of bone and is the area suitable for carving. In general, the highest concentration of compact bone is associated with the appendicular skeleton. It is smooth, dense, and hard. The only gaps in its structure are foramina— or passages for nerves and nutritive blood vessels, which often appear as black dots or holes on its worked surfaces (Pls. 13, 24d).

Bones that were used for carving were basically the waste from butchered animals, particularly cattle, sheep, and goats, but also pigs, donkey, deer, horse, and camel, among others.[4] At Palatine East, as elsewhere, the bones of larger animals were preferred, and cattle was the predominant species.[5] The most commonly used bone was the straight and relatively solid metapodial or cannon bone, either from the front (metacarpus) or the rear (metatarsus) leg (Illus. 1.1). Generally, carvers preferred the more circular metatarsus. The second most commonly utilized bone was the radius, often with its associated fused ulna, followed by the tibia. The fused bones of mature animals provided the largest and densest material. Flattened bones, such as the scapula, mandible, and ribs, were carved as

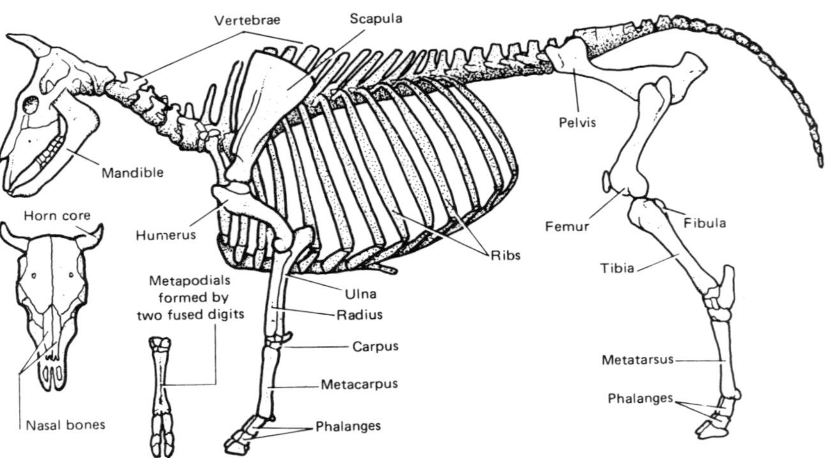

1.1.
Cattle skeleton (MacGregor 1985, 8, Fig. 7)

well; their sandwich-like structure of cancellous tissue between thin layers of compact bone can sometimes be recognized in finished objects.[6] Scapula and ribs were particularly useful for veneers (see, e.g., Figs. 5a,b, 9a,c; Pls. 4c,d, 14c,g). Smaller bones, such as astragali (knuckle bones) and phalangeal bones, were used but often only minimally worked.

The nature of the raw material limited the size and shape of objects carved in bone. By analyzing raw material and finished objects from Gallo-Roman sites now in Marseille and Lyon, Jourdan and Béal calculated the average length of a bovine metatarsal to be 0.224 meter, with an average diameter of 0.0469 by 0.0496 at its proximal end and of 0.0306 by 0.0542 at its distal end. The average for the metacarpal was 0.198 meter in length, with a diameter of 0.0362 by 0.0585 at its proximal end and 0.0284 by 0.0542 at its distal end. Once the articular ends were removed, a carvable length of approximately 0.160 was left for the metatarsal and 0.130 for the metacarpal. Béal's analysis of the Roman worked bone from the Musée de la Civilisation Gallo-Romaine at Lyon revealed that objects rarely exceeded 0.100 meter in length.[7] Although the size of bones varies according to species and diet, a more casual examination of objects from the Greco-Roman period suggests that, with few exceptions, Greek and Roman artisans faced similar constraints.[8]

Next to size, the greatest constraint for the carver is the thickness of the compact bone layer, which determines the depth to which the bone can be carved. Objects carved from the compact layer of metapodials rarely exceed 0.015 meter in thickness, the thickest encountered in Béal's analyses being a blank of 0.018.[9] Scapulae and ribs provided a much thinner layer of carvable material. The limitations of the material in this respect are visible on objects from Palatine East that incorporate or inadvertently expose cancellous material (Fig.13c; Pl. 25b). In one case, the carver appears to have mistakenly carved through a layer of compact bone that was particularly thin; as a result, the intended intaglio plaque featuring a horse became a discard in the manufacturing process (Fig. 15c; Pl. 21a).

The shape and structure of bone sometimes limited the carver; the natural longitudinal depression on the external surface of the metapodials, for example, appears as a defect on a domed gaming piece (Fig. 45a; Pl. 55b). However, makers of hinges used the depression to line up the holes for dowels,[10] a technique that makers of flutes and whistles similarly exploited (Fig. 47d); for carvers of bone statuettes, the depression sometimes defined the space between legs.[11] Carvers also exploited the central medullary cavity of metapodials when making mounts, hinges, pyxides, and utensil handles (Figs. 13c, 16h, 17a, 40a; Pls. 25a,b, 28, 48a), although they plugged the cavity when necessary to create a solid object. Objects ranging from sculpture in the round to dice and other gaming pieces, for example, were frequently carved from horizontal sections of metapodials. The central cavity was filled by a bone plug or in the case of larger objects by two plugs, one at the top and another at the bottom (Fig. 45; Pl. 56).

Use of the scapula and ribs, rather than metapodials, for veneer and strip mounts reduced the preparatory work of the carver by offering a natural profile closer to that of the finished object.[12] Once split, the thin top layer of compact bone provided the veneer's surface, while the web of cancellous tissue on the back surface, even when smoothed with a file, gave the veneer strength and discouraged cracking and splitting. In addition, the cancellous surface provided a naturally roughened surface for gluing to the wooden frame.

Although carvers may have worked some bones immediately after slaughter of the animal, it is unlikely that this took place on a regular basis. There has been considerable debate, especially among archaeologists in Poland, concerning methods by which bone and antler were softened for shaping or decorating. Various acid solutions have been proposed, but according to MacGregor they result in structural impairment that makes such processes undesirable, especially for the manufacture of implements. He suggests that softening in water would in most cases be sufficient and less deleterious.[13]

IVORY

Elephant ivory is recognizable because of its unique dentine structure. Tusks comprise approximately 60% dentine and 40% pulp and cementum. Dentine, which is the carvable part of the tusk, is approximately 30% organic material, mainly collagen and water, and 70% inorganic material.[14] In cross section, the tiny intersecting tubules that make up the vascular system of the tusk appear as intersecting curving arcs or hatching (Fig. 41d; Pls. 7e, 35e, 50a,b). In longitudinal section the alternating patterns of light and dark striations appear in the form of curves or ellipses laid down as the dentine is deposited (Figs. 10g, 40d; Pl. 7d). In cross section the concentric rings corresponding to the growth layers originating in the pulp cavity are visible (Pl. 7e). Like long bones, elephant tusks are not solid; a pulp cavity extends part way along the tusk's length, and a nerve canal extends from the tip of the cavity to the tip of the tusk (illus. 1.2).

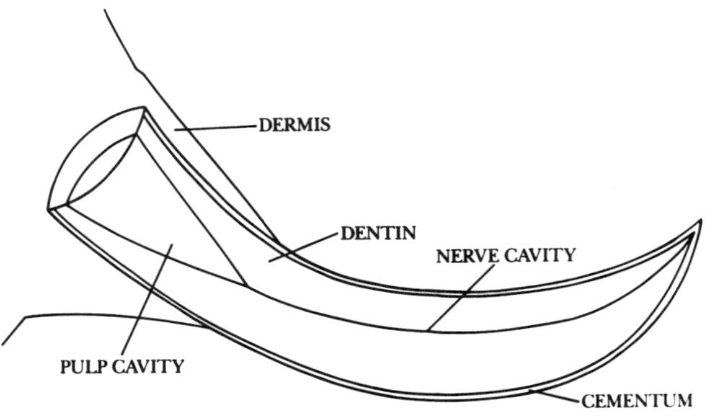

1.2.
Diagram of elephant tusk (St. Clair and McLachlan 1989, 3, Fig. 2)

CARVING AS CRAFT

Elephant ivory was preferred in antiquity, although walrus and hippopotamus ivory were used as well. Pausanius mentions the image of a goddess from Proconnesus, for example, whose face was made from hippopotamus teeth.[15] Males of the Indian, and both males and females of the African species of elephant produce tusks, which can grow to more than 3.050 meters in length and weigh more than 74 kilograms.[16] A pair preserved in the British Museum was reported to weigh 84.343 and 88.075 kilograms, and to measure 3.505 and 3.048 meters in length.[17] Mammoths, extinct relatives of the Asiatic elephant, produced tusks as long as three meters and weighing more that 111 kilograms. They were undoubtedly carved in areas in which the fossilized material survived.[18]

By virtue of their size, tusks allowed for the creation of larger objects than bone, as well as for relief carving in greater depth. At its base a mature elephant tusk often exceeds 0.160 meter in diameter; the existence of pyxides up to 0.145 in diameter, of plaques up to 0.409 in length and 0.123 wide, and of a late antique box with walls up to 0.013 thick testifies clearly to the advantages of ivory over bone as a medium for carving.[19] Portions of the tusk were uncarvable, however, including the outermost older and more friable dentine and the material closest to the pulp cavity, which is relatively soft. Like the marrow cavity of bone, the pulp cavity was exploited for cylindrical containers (which are cut from horizontal sections of tusk), utilizing the natural cavity for the interior.

Despite ivory's apparent advantages, comparative studies of the mechanical properties of bone, antler, and ivory carried out by Currey and MacGregor indicate that both the bending strength and modulus of elasticity of ivory are inferior to those of bone and antler, making it a less desirable material for many classes of objects.[20] The association of ivory with luxury and hence wealth, however, determined its choice even when it was structurally less desirable. For example, its inferior bending strength and elasticity in comparison with bone or antler made ivory far less practical for implements such as combs and pins, which nonetheless were produced in large numbers when the material was available. The common practice of attaching ivory heads to shafts of bronze or bone (nos. 451, 455, 460–462) may well reflect recognition of this weakness.[21]

Ivory is inherently more delicate in other ways as well. It has a tendency to delaminate with time and in an adverse environment, and it is especially vulnerable to changes of temperature, which affect color and chemical composition, and to desiccation, which causes surface cracks and decomposition.[22] Baer and colleagues document a progressive color change from white at the lowest temperature, through shades of yellow, brown, and black, to gray-blue at the highest temperature. A black and gray-blue fragmentary handle from Palatine East (Fig. 40c) provides an example of damage caused by burning. A gaming piece (Fig. 44a; Pl. 53a) and a pin (Fig. 31f; Pl. 36e) provide excellent examples of the tendency of ivory to crack and delaminate.[23] In the latter case, not only adverse climatic conditions but the stress created by insertion of the shaft into the head were factors. In sharp contrast to bone, ivory recovered from Palatine East was invariably in poor condition, usually fragmentary, and in various stages of decomposition, a situation aggravated by the inevitable disturbance caused by excavation. It is likely that a good deal of material, especially carving debris, disintegrated underground.

Although the natural properties of ivory make it a highly desirable carving medium, there are references to preliminary softening both from antiquity and the Middle Ages. Recent experiments in softening undertaken by Lapatin, while not scientifically rigorous, demonstrated that thin strips can be softened by soaking in vinegar and bent.[24] Methods for "unscrolling" elephant tusks to create large thin pieces, which must have involved preliminary softening, were patented in the nineteenth century, but whether they were known in antiquity remains open to question.[25]

CARVING AS CRAFT

2

LITERARY EVIDENCE

Despite its superiority as a carving medium over ivory under certain conditions, bone is seldom mentioned in this regard in Greek or Roman literature. In dramatic contrast, ivory is celebrated both as a material and as a carving medium for a wide variety of objects. When bone *is* mentioned, it is generally in association with simple utilitarian objects such as pins or implements such as fruit knives, grafting tools, boxes for medicaments, and flutes.[1] Pliny the Elder indicates that it was used for loftier purposes as well, such as the decoration of furniture, but only as a last resort: "[R]ecently owing to our poverty even the bones have begun to be cut into layers in as much as an ample supply of tusks is now rarely obtained except from India, all the rest of the world having succumbed to luxury."[2] Juvenal, writing in the second century, further expands the repertory, but in a similarly negative vein. "So destitute am I of ivory that neither my dice nor my counters are made of it: even my knife handles are bone."[3] There is even greater reticence concerning the craftspeople and the craft, although Plutarch states that bone that had been softened by soaking in cinders and vinegar could be cut with a thread.[4]

Ivory, on the other hand, is a frequent topic. References to the material and trade are common, as are references to objects carved, ranging from works of art of the highest order to the simplest artifacts.[5] The reason for this discrepancy is obvious. Whereas bone was cheap and readily available, ivory was a rare and valuable commodity and, even in times of plenty, a potent symbol of prestige. In the form of tusks, intricately fashioned works of art, or even on the hoof, ivory was hoarded, paraded, exhibited, and even burned as a sign of wealth and status. Its primary value lay not in its structural or mechanical properties, or even in its beauty, but rather in its perceived value as a commodity. Whether the reference is to the 1,231 tusks that accompanied Lucius Cornelius Scipio on his triumphant return from Syria in 189 B.C., or to the 500 tripod tables with ivory legs reportedly owned by Seneca in the first century A.D., it is the material itself that conveys status.[6]

This means of flaunting wealth was not without detractors. The first-century poet and consul Silius Italicus complained that "even the images of deities were made from trees before men had yet thought of paying a price for the corpses of huge animals, or arranged that inasmuch as the privilege of luxury had originated from the gods, we should behold the countenances of the deities and the legs of our tables made of ivory."[7] For the most part, however, criticism appears to have fallen on deaf ears. The ownership of ivory, in whatever form, remained one way of defining the wealthy citizen of the Greek and Roman worlds.

Given this focus on ivory as a commodity, it is not surprising that little information is conveyed concerning the craft of ivory carving, or that much of the information that is conveyed appears to belong more to the realm of myth than to reality. The often-debated issue of softening ivory as a preliminary procedure provides an example. Although both ancient and medieval writers mention the process, there is little agreement on whether or how softening was achieved. According to an apparently skeptical Seneca, for example, it was Democritus who "discovered how ivory could be softened, how, by boiling, a pebble could be transformed into an emerald."[8] Fire, water, beer, and mandrake root are among the agents mentioned by others, but overall the descriptions inspire little confidence in the authors' direct knowledge of such a procedure.[9] Some may reflect a confusion of ivory with more common horn working, where boiling and heating were standard procedures used to soften and unscroll the horn from its core in order to create thin sheets.[10]

Despite this apparent lack of interest in, or direct knowledge of, ivory as a carving medium, valuable evidence for a carving industry can be gleaned from these sources, especially when they are viewed in conjunction with material remains. Greek and Roman accounts of the trade in ivory document the fluctuating supply, as well as the vagaries of fashion that affected the demand for objects made not only of ivory but of bone as well. The innumerable accounts of specific objects carved from ivory are also valuable, not because they provide a reliable picture—like their modern counterparts, ancient authors undoubtedly on occasion mistook bone for ivory—but because they document an industry that, as material remains clearly indicate, embraced both materials.

Evidence for the fluctuating supplies, and hence cost, of ivory is provided by a variety of sources, especially from the Hellenistic and Roman periods.[11] In the third century B.C., for example, the dumping of African ivory on the market by Ptolemy Philadelphus supposedly led to the reduction in the price of ivory to one-fifteenth of what it was in the previous century.[12] In contrast, Pliny the Elder's and Juvenal's remarks suggest that, at least in some parts of the empire, ivory was no longer widely available in the first century A.D. and scarce in the second. A mid-second-century papyrus records its value at only slightly less than its weight in silver.[13] By the beginning of fourth century, however, the supply was once again abundant. The value of ivory was calculated in Diocletian's Edict of Maximum Prices at one-fortieth its weight in silver, considerably below the value of silk, thanks to a plentiful supply of ivory from East Africa and North Africa.[14]

From at least the third century B.C., the lucrative trade included elephants as well as tusks, the former valued as war machines and, by the Romans, as parade and circus animals. Both the animals and their tusks were flaunted as booty and tribute. The Roman general Metellus, after defeating Hasdrubel in Sicily in 250 B.C., brought back 140 elephants, which were exhibited in his triumph and then slain; a half century later, as noted above, Lucius Cornelius Scipio exhibited tusks as booty on his return from Syria.[15] Their value was evident in late antiquity as well. In A.D. 573 a delegation of the Macurrae, from Mauretania Caesariensis, presented Justin II with elephant tusks as a token of friendship.[16] Such public displays undoubtedly influenced patterns of consumption by introducing ivory to a far wider audience than those who could afford its purchase, stimulating a fashion for objects in ivory as well as in its more readily available alternative. As we shall see, material remains reveal that it is at just such times that bone and ivory industries flourished in tandem.

Raw ivory was also hoarded in temples and tombs. In 54 B.C. Ptolemy XII Auletes presented thirty tusks weighing either 11.942 or 14.928 kilograms each to the temple of Apollo Didyma.[17] Both Cicero and Pliny remark on its presence in temples, and Plutarch reports that Cleopatra hoarded ivory along with other precious materials in a tomb.[18]

References to ivory in association with statuary, which was similarly displayed in temples and shrines, provide occasional hints concerning the craft and its practitioners, although material remains suggest that they are far less reliable than references to tusks as to the actual materials involved. According to Pausanius, the artists Dipoenus and Scyllis, who were probably active in the early sixth century B.C., used ivory in combination with ebony to create human figures, while Endoeus was the first to carve an entire figure of ivory, for the temple of Athena Alea at Tegea in the late sixth century B.C.[19] Acro-elephantine statues, in which the flesh parts were created in ivory and the rest of the statue in wood, stone, or other materials—including gold in the case of chryselephantine statues—allowed a new level of monumentality, impossible with ivory alone. The Athena Parthenos and the seated Zeus at Olympia, which reached heights of 12.87 and 12.38 meters, respectively,[20] are the best-known examples of an art form that must have considerably impacted the carving industry, bringing to the fore carvers and joiners more closely allied to furniture makers than to sculptors in stone or wood. By the fourth century the technique was employed to depict historical figures as well. The more than two dozen chryselephantine statues in Greek temples and shrines recorded by Pausanius included portraits by Leochares of Phillip II, his parents, and his son, Alexander the Great, in the Philippeion at Olympia.[21] In the third century B.C., Ptolemy Philadelphus reportedly commissioned chryselephantine statues of his parents.[22]

Roman ivory or chryselephantine images included statues of Jupiter in the temple of Jupitor Stator and in the Capitoline temple of Jupiter, replacing a terra-cotta version in the latter, and statues of Julius Caesar, Germanicus, and Britannicus, recorded as being carried in triumphs or on display.[23] Pliny mentions an ivory statue of Saturn that was filled with olive oil to prevent decay.[24] Chryselephantine nikai were reportedly carried in the triumphal procession celebrating the victory of Titus and Vespasian over Judea in A.D. 70.[25] On a more private level, Pliny the Younger mentions the commission of ivory portraits, testifying to the fashion for ivory at other levels of society.[26] In the second century, Hadrian commissioned a colossal chryselephantine cult figure of Zeus for the temple of the Olympian Zeus at Athens, and Herodes Atticus commissioned ivory and chryselephantine statues for Athens and Isthmia.[27] By the time of Constantine the Great there were said to be more than seventy ivory statues in Rome.[28]

References to doors, furniture, and other objects decorated with ivory indicate that it was a material of choice for a wide variety of both utilitarian and luxury objects, frequently in combination with wood or metal.[29] Ivory doors, presumably created by applying ivory veneer to a wooden framework, are recorded at the late fifth- or early fourth-century B.C. temple of Asklepios; in the first century B.C. by Diodorus Siculus in the land of Panchaeitis; and by Propertius at the temple of Apollo on the Palatine in Rome.[30] Cicero reports that ivory doors were among the treasures looted from Syracuse by Verres.[31] References to ivory couches and chairs, tables with ivory legs, and ivory boxes suggest a flourishing furniture industry. Like statuary, furniture was publicly displayed in temples and in triumphal and funerary processions, bringing it before a wide audience and stimulating the fashion for imitations. According to Pausanius, a wooden chest decorated with ivory, gold, and cedar wood figures that was associated with Cypselus, the seventh-century B.C. ruler of Corinth, was displayed in the temple of Hera at Olympia along with an ivory and gold table created by Kolotes, reportedly a pupil of Pheidias who produced chryselephantine statuary as well.[32] The fourth-century B.C. Heraion in Samos included an ivory couch and table among its treasures, and the third-century B.C. festival in Alexandria offered by Ptolemy Philadelphus featured thrones constructed of ivory and gold.[33] Aristophanes, who headed the Alexandrian Library at the beginning of the second century B.C., mentions furniture legs decorated with ivory and amber.[34] Plautus refers to beds in ivory and bronze associated with the triumph of Gnaeus Manlius Vulso in 187 B.C.[35] Herodian mentions that ivory couches were used as funeral biers, which were burned along with the wax image of the deceased emperor on pyres decorated with ivory figures and other precious materials.[36]

Suetonius confirms that the funerary couch of Julius Caesar was ivory, and the practice has a long subsequent history.[37] Dio Cassius mentions ivory and gold funerary couches, not only in association with the emperor Augustus (A.D. 14), but in his own day in association with the funeral of Pertinax (A.D. 193), where it was placed within an aedicula of the same materials and topped with a wax image of the emperor.[38] According to Herodian, the apotheosis ceremony of Septimius Severus was similar, featuring an ivory funerary couch set within a structure that included golden drapery, ivory statues, and paintings.[39]

More casual references to furniture adorned with, or made from, ivory suggest that such furniture was fashionable and available to a broader audience.[40] Propertius, for example, rejects the notion of elaborate funerary rites for himself that would include a funerary couch decorated with ivory, implying that, like the five hundred tripod tables with ivory legs purportedly owned by Seneca, such luxuries were not limited to emperors.[41] In the fourth century Clement of Alexandria and John Chrysostom denounced the luxury of ivory furniture,[42] but Cyril, the late fifth-century patriarch of Alexandria, apparently had no qualms about sending gifts that included eight stools and fourteen chairs purportedly of this material to Constantinople.[43]

Whether these reports are reliable, especially as to the materials involved, is open to question, but they are clear indicators of a fashion that stimulated both the ivory and bone industries, as well as a particular type of craftsmanship, during this period. Ivory is mentioned, although less frequently, in association with other types of objects as well. Demosthenes mentions that ivory was used for the manufacture of swords, and Diogenes Laertius reports that in the third century A.D. only the ivory veneer of a shield dedicated by Menelaos survived at the temple of Apollo at Didyma.[44] On a smaller scale, ivory objects ranging from scepters to writing tablets and letters of the alphabet, from jewelry to back scratchers and gaming pieces, are recorded by Roman authors and testify to a widespread fashion for the material.[45] Ivory diptychs, perhaps the best-known witness to the conspicuous consumption of ivory in late antiquity, were singled out in a law of A.D. 384 addressed to the Senate of Constantinople forbidding all but ordinary consuls to distribute them.[46]

With the exception of the few Greek artists who are associated with ivory or chryselephantine statuary, artists are rarely named. More generic references are scattered and imprecise. Seven inscriptions from Rome, dated between the first century B.C. and the first century A.D. mention individual *eborarii,* all of whom were freedmen.[47] The term *faber eborarius* is more common, but *politor eborarius* is used as well.[48] One inscription mentions an *eborarius "ab Hercule Primog(enio)."*[49] It is possible that this implies a connection between the carver and a cult, but equally likely that the statue or building mentioned was simply a convenient topographical marker, indicating the location of the craftsperson or workshop. The individuals mentioned in these inscriptions are male, but Pliny mentions a woman, Iaia of Cyzicus, who engraved images on ivory in addition to working as a painter at Rome.[50] Ivory workers are designated by the term ελεφαντοῦργός in a second-century A.D. papyrus,[51] and Oppian refers to ελεφαντοτόμος in the third, perhaps in reference to cutters of inlay.[52] An inscription in the catacomb of Comodilla refers to a certain Olympius as an *elefantarius*.[53] An industrial fraternity or collegium, which included *negotiatores eborarii et citrarii* (workers in citrus wood), existed in Trastevere by the time of Hadrian.[54] An edict of A.D. 337 in the Theodosian Code includes ivory workers among a group of artisans exempted from public service in order to improve their skills and instruct their children.[55]

References as to where or how these ivory workers practiced their craft are scarce and often ambiguous. Writing in the third century A.D., Philostratus reports that the first-century philosopher Apollonius of Tyana, who was denied passage on a cargo ship carrying statues of the gods in gold and stone, or gold and ivory, expressed his disapproval of the trade: "But the image-makers of old behaved not in this way, nor did they go round the cities selling their gods. All they did was to export their own hands and their tools for working stone and ivory; and they provided the raw materials and plied their handicraft in the temples themselves."[56] The implication that in "olden times" artists gathered at sanctuaries where their services were in demand is borne out by both literary evidence and material remains. The more secular model presented by the fourth-century B.C. Greek orator Demosthenes, however, is no doubt accurate as well. He states that his father owned two factories, one for the manufacture of couches decorated with ivory, which employed twenty slaves, the other for swords, which employed thirty-two or thirty-three slaves. According to his calculations, the furniture factory easily consumed two minae of ivory per month, in addition to wood, and the weapons factory consumed as much or more ivory, in addition to iron. He reports that his father sold the raw materials as well.[57] That this refers to the sale of ivory left over from the manufacturing process is likely. An inscription from the Acropolis at Athens records not only expenses for the materials used by Pheidias in fashioning the chryselephantine statue of Athena Parthenos but also the purchase of the ivory for the work and the sale of what was left over afterward.[58] Taken together, these models may go far in explaining why evidence for the carving of ivory is rare at manufacturing sites.

Evidence for the actual working of ivory is also scarce and, as we have noted in the case of softening, at best enigmatic. Given the fact that most authors' experiences of ivory as an artistic medium appear to have been with composite works of art such as furniture or, more distantly viewed, chryselephantine statuary, this is not surprising. Sawing, polishing, gluing, aligning, and gilding, for example, are the skills attributed by Lucian to great sculptors, including Pheidias.[59] In addition to gilding, both Greek and Roman authors refer to ivory that has been stained, and Pliny mentions the use of colored waxes or encaustic on ivories that were first engraved, and recommends polishing ivory with rough fish skin, pumice, or emery to remove traces of tool marks.[60] Pausanius reports that ivory and wood parts of statues were protected from desiccation by being placed over a well or underground cavern, or by being treated with oil (at Olympia) or water (at Athens).[61] The mention of drops of water on ivory statues, sometimes associated with tears, may reflect similar practices.[62] At Rome it was believed that Tibur air kept ivory from turning yellow.[63]

Perhaps following in the footsteps of the ancients, the modern approach to bone and ivory until recently has been remarkably similar. Perceptions of art versus craft, combined with the perceived disparity in the value of the two materials and the frequent failure to distinguish between them, have led scholars to isolate bone carving as an inferior craft, despite the existence of bone carving of high quality from the Greco-Roman world. Until recently, although bone objects were among the commonest classes of finds from Greek and Roman excavations, they were among the least studied. In many cases, small-scale or fragmentary artifacts and manufacturing waste were not separated from faunal remains, and either not registered as archaeological finds or discarded. In addition, skeletal materials were often confused in archaeological records; bone was frequently mistaken for ivory, especially when carved, and antler was often not distinguished from bone.

As an artistic medium, bone continues to be dismissed as a poor substitute for ivory, an intrusion into the domain of luxurious artifacts, called into service only when ivory was unavailable or too expensive, and associated with a low level of craftsmanship. Publication of large numbers of bone relief plaques from Roman Egypt has done little to dispel this notion.[64] Despite considerable variety in style and execution, they have continued to be characterized by the "coarseness" of execution and "vulgarization of Greek themes" of their lowest common denominators.[65]

In contrast to ivory carving, however, the elucidation of bone carving as craft and industry has been facilitated by the survival of significant amounts of carving debris. Recent studies of the material, finished objects, and manufacturing waste from the Roman period have done much to expand our knowledge, revealing a wide range of skills and production techniques. The analysis of concentrations of debris, including raw material and interim stages of manufacture, has confirmed the existence of production centers where craftsmen employed a variety of tools and materials to produce a wide range of artifacts, from the simplest to the most luxurious.[66] Our knowledge of bone carving in the West, especially in the Roman provinces and bordering areas, has been enhanced by the publication of extensive remains in several museum collections, and by detailed analyses of remains from archaeological excavations, especially of cemeteries and manufacturing waste.[67] Our understanding of bone in relation to ivory has expanded as well, especially as scholars have become more adept at distinguishing the two materials.[68] The remains at Palatine East and elsewhere point clearly to the working of ivory and bone within the same setting, and the publication of bone sculpture of high quality, especially from the Roman world, has begun to alter traditional notions of bone carving as an inferior craft practiced by artisans of limited skill.[69]

Recent scholarship has greatly expanded our knowledge of ivory carving as well. Analyses of the ancient and medieval literary sources have shed considerable light on the sources of trade in, and perception of, ivory in antiquity and the Middle Ages.[70] Publication of carving debris from Bronze Age sites and from fifth-century B.C. Olympia, along with close examination of finished objects, especially from the late antique and Byzantine periods, has allowed scholars to bring voice to those issues on which the ancients remained silent—namely, techniques of carving and so-called workshop practices.[71] In contrast to bone carving, which has been elucidated through the publication of significant amounts of carving debris, however, the study of ivory carving as craft and industry, especially in the Roman world, has been hindered by a lack of material remains directly associated with the manufacturing process.

3

MATERIAL REMAINS

THE GRECO-ROMAN WORLD

In contrast to the literary evidence, material remains from the Greco-Roman world provide valuable and abundant evidence of artisanal practices that embraced a wide variety of materials and range of skills. Bone and ivory were only two of several materials employed to make similar or identical objects. Bone and ivory artifacts can be paralleled in wood, metal, antler, glass, jet, or even clay, and small-scale sculpture was made in a similarly broad range of materials. Imperial portraits survive not only in precious materials, for example, but in bone and terra-cotta as well.[1] The choice of material depended on a variety of factors, including its mechanical properties, availability, price, the vagaries of fashion, and, in some cases, its symbolic significance.

Within some classes of objects, there appears to be no clear preference for one material over another, making it difficult to evaluate relationships, especially whether one material influenced the other. Wood, for example, was commonly used for objects ranging from simple artifacts to statuary, and it has been suggested that wood carving is the craft most closely related to ivory carving. According to Pausanius, both Dipoenus and Scyllis, whom he credits with first using ivory to represent human flesh, and Endoeus, who caved the ivory statue of Athena Alea at Tegea, also worked in wood.[2] Unfortunately, although scattered remains testify to the use of wood in most classes of objects, too few examples survive to allow us to analyze its relative importance.[3]

The relation between metal and bone and ivory remains unclear as well, although there are considerably more remains. Ivory statuettes from sixth-century B.C. Ephesus, for example, are directly paralleled by electrum examples from the same site.[4] In the case of implements and items of personal adornment, objects in bone and ivory are most frequently paralleled in metal, and it has been generally assumed that bone types imitate metal. In fact, the relationship between the two materials is unclear. The need for flexibility and elasticity recommended both materials, especially over ivory, and forms are in some cases identical. The discovery of clay molds with impressions made by associated bone pins at a number of Scottish sites from the Roman period, and another possible example from Italy, confirm that at least in some cases bone examples were used for preparing molds for bronze pins.[5] But in most cases the relationship is not straightforward. Metal pin shafts are often thinner in profile and without the distinct bulge or flare in the upper portion of the shaft that is common in bone and ivory examples, reflecting the difference in the nature of the materials. Bone and especially ivory were more prone to breakage when the shaft was subjected to pressure, a problem compensated for by thickening the shaft at its most vulnerable point. There are differences in head types as well. Whereas simple geometric head forms are common to both, figured or elaborately decorated heads are more popular in bone and ivory, undoubtedly because they could be more easily carved than cast.[6] Within other classes of objects the relationship is equally ambiguous. For example, Greek bone and ivory fibulae of the "spectacle" type, which take the form of two contiguous disks, are generally thought to imitate more desirable bronze examples, made of coils of wire.[7] In at least one case, however, the relationship is reversed. Among the numerous examples from geometric and archaic contexts at Sparta is a bronze example that carefully copies the disk form of its skeletal counterparts.[8]

Contrary to the popular picture of bone as a poor substitute for ivory, pressed into service only when the latter was unavailable, increased production of bone objects corresponds with those periods when ivory was both popular and readily available to those who could afford it. For example, the fashion for ivory among the Hellenistic and early Roman elite as a medium for furniture, small-scale sculpture, and artifacts appears to have stimulated a flourishing bone industry in the same classes of objects. At Corinth and Delos, the material remains, which are primarily artifacts, reveal a notable increase in the use of bone along with ivory in the late Hellenistic and early Roman periods, when both replace metal as the most popular material for such objects.[9] At a higher level of craftsmanship, namely furniture making, the situation is similar. Whereas ancient authors refer solely to ivory, there is extensive evidence for the use of bone, both in combination with ivory and by itself, to create furniture of high quality. These remains are vivid reminders that the material of the finished product may well have been distinguishable only to the practiced eye.

Late antique remains similarly suggest a dramatic increase in the manufacture of bone objects, ranging from the simplest artifacts to furniture mounts and statuary. The phenomenon is typically associated with economic decline and impoverishment, but once again the flourishing of the bone industry corresponds to a period when the fashion for ivory was at a peak, a readily available if expensive commodity and a highly visible symbol of official or elite status.[10] Late antique bone industries have been identified at several Mediterranean sites, as

well as in Rome, where, at Palatine East, bone and ivory carving coexisted. A
relationship between the two industries is confirmed by recent studies of cemeteries in the western provinces as well, where bone grave goods are associated not
with impoverished levels of society but with the well-to-do Romanized middle
and upper classes, whose graves contained a high percentage of Roman import
wares.[11] Whether imported or locally produced, it appears likely that the taste
for bone objects was stimulated by the current fashion for ivory. Bone thus
served as a frugal equivalent in areas where ivory was readily available and as an
acceptable substitute elsewhere.

Although it has been argued that ivory was reserved for sacred iconography
and bone was considered more suitable for secular imagery in Byzantium,[12] surviving sculpture and reliefs from the Greco-Roman world document their use for
both types of imagery, and there is little evidence that either bone or ivory was
endowed with symbolic or magical associations that would have influenced the
choice of either material. A possible exception occurs in burials in the late
Roman cemetery at Tác, in Pannonia, where bone bracelets were associated with
the left arm whereas bracelets of bronze or iron were associated with the right,
but whether the practice stems from symbolic, magical, or practical reasons is
unknown.[13] Similarly enigmatic is a custom noted at Sabratha, where bone
pins appear to have been intentionally buried at the entrances to houses, probably as propitiatory offerings.[14] The better-known practice of placing bone and
occasionally ivory objects in the cement that sealed loculi in the catacombs has
been interpreted as prophylactic as well, but the significance of the materials is
uncertain.[15]

The craft of carving bone and ivory is also better documented through examination of material remains, although evidence for bone carving far exceeds evidence
for ivory carving. Given the fragility of ivory under most conditions, this disparity is not surprising. The fact that ivory was a valuable commodity also discouraged waste, and, as at Athens, surplus ivory may have been sold. In this regard,
Pliny the Elder mentions ivory and gold as materials employed in the creation of
medicine, presumably in the form of filings or powder. According to Barnett,
ivory waste from workshops in the Great Bazaar at Istanbul continued to be collected and pulverized for this purpose as late as the 1950s.[16] In addition,
although the amount of highest-quality ivory within a given tusk was limited,
even the smallest leftover pieces could be utilized, for example, for dice or for pin
heads that could be mounted on bone or metal shafts. This is in contrast to bone
carving, where large amounts of material were discarded during the preliminary
carving process.

Despite this disparity, material remains provide overall a broader and more
complex, though still incomplete, picture of bone and ivory carving in antiquity.

Perhaps most significantly, they document the use of bone across a far wider spectrum than is suggested by the literature, from the most humble to the most exalted classes of objects, including furniture decoration and sculpture in the round. The notion of bone carving as an inferior medium distinct from the luxury art of ivory carving is contradicted again and again by the existence of bone carvings of high quality, often wrongly identified as ivory, and by evidence for bone carving in association with ivory carving throughout the Greco-Roman world. Ivory emerges in a different light as well. Material remains suggest that in many cases the two materials were used interchangeably, often in combination with one another, and that the same artists worked indifferently in both materials, probably together rather than in independent workshops.

ARCHAIC AND CLASSICAL GREECE

The relation between bone and ivory as materials and, more specifically, their artisanal association within a single class of objects can be best documented in archaic and classical Greece through the extensive remains associated with furniture. A significant percentage of these remains belongs to couches, many of which owe their preservation to their use as funerary beds in tombs. The practice of attaching relatively thin ivory or bone plaques to a wooden core or framework to create such furniture was well established in Greece by the sixth century, and scattered remains suggest its appearance much earlier. Bone furniture appliqués occur in association with ivory statuettes from an eighth-century B.C. tomb in the Kerameikos cemetery outside Athens's Dipylon Gate, for example.[17] Unfortunately, such furniture rarely survives intact, even in tombs. Either the wooden frameworks have disintegrated over time, leaving only fragmentary and broken veneers, or, in the case of cremation graves, the furniture was burned along with the deceased, leaving only charred fragments, mixed with human remains. Only rarely, as in the case of a couch decorated with bone, ivory, and amber from a late sixth-century undisturbed shaft grave in the Kerameikos cemetery, can such furniture be reconstructed.[18] This couch combined ivory veneers with decorative inlaid palmettes, consisting of alternating bone and amber leaves (Illus. 3.1). The combination suggests that the materials were worked together, and the couch provides early evidence of the Greek propensity for creating composite works of art, a trend culminating in the chryselephantine statues of the classical period and in the gold-, glass-, and ivory-veneered couches from the fourth-century B.C. tombs at Vergina.[19] Remains of funerary couches in Etruria and in Grafenbühl, near Asperg, which are dated around 600 B.C. and are closely related to the example from Athens, suggest that the fashion for such composite couches was widespread in elite circles from an early date, and that they, or at the least their

CARVING AS CRAFT

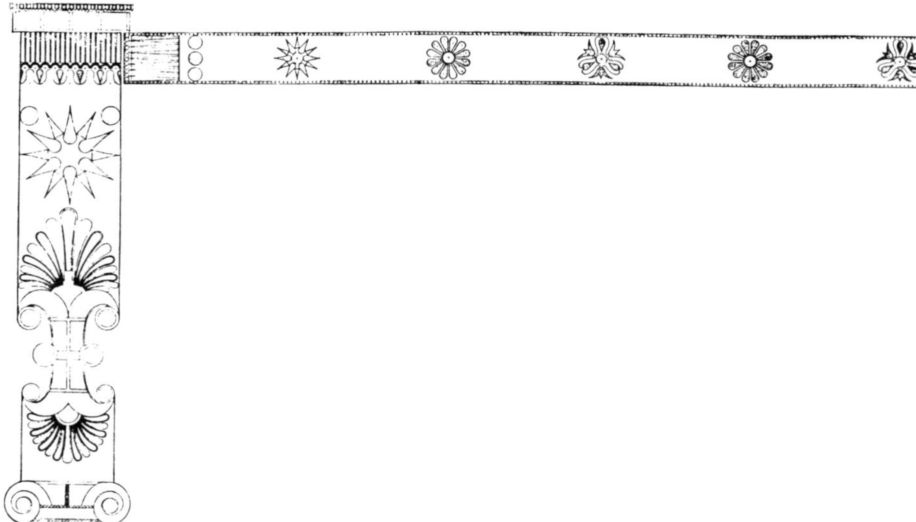

decorations, were exported either directly from workshops in Greece or from Magna Grecia.[20]

Sparta

Evidence for bone and ivory carving in an industrial setting is preserved from at least two Greek sanctuary sites. Sparta is renowned for yielding the largest group of ivory carvings found to date at a Greek site, and the extensive remains provide evidence for a carving industry that spanned at least two generations, from the late eighth or early seventh through the first quarter of the sixth century B.C.[21] At Ephesos the carving industry appears to have developed slightly later and was most active from the late seventh through the first half of the sixth century B.C.[22] Although both sites produced similar classes of objects, the greater range and number of objects from Sparta allows a better assessment of the bone- and ivory-carving industry. The remains include figures in the round, plaques and seals carved in relief and intaglio, as well as combs, fibulae, amulets, and pins. A single bone eye with incised pupil, possibly intended for a wooden figure, suggests that composite statues may have been manufactured as well.[23] These diverse classes of objects are connected by both stylistic traits and motifs, suggesting that carvers worked on various classes of objects within a single setting, rather than independently.[24] The presence of partially finished objects confirms that work was carried out locally, in association with the sanctuary.[25]

Bone is present in all classes of objects and is the predominant material overall. The use of bone as well as ivory, spans the entire period of production, and there is identity of style across the two mediums, indicating that the same artists

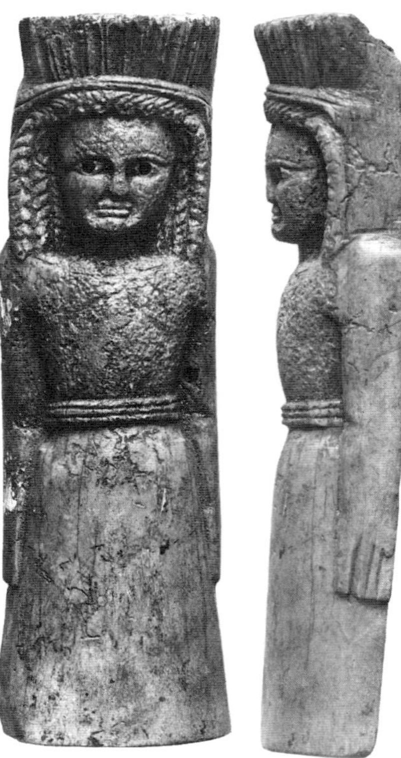

worked in both materials. In some classes, bone was clearly the material of choice. It appears to have been used exclusively for the series of forty female figures that are generally thought to bear some resemblance to the wooden cult image of Orthia that stood in the temple (Illus. 3.2).[26] The *polos*-crowned figures average 0.10 meter in height and are carved from complete or longitudinal half-sections of metapodials. They span almost the entire period of production, from the seventh to the first half of the sixth century B.C., and are representative of a type of votive figure that has a long history in the eastern Mediterranean, surviving well into late antiquity.[27] Another class of bone objects that may have been associated with the goddess is made up of strips 0.080–0.120 meter long, which are pierced at the bottom with holes for attachment and taper to pointed tops. Some are inscribed with dot and circle designs.[28] Hammond suggests that these strips may have been attached to a headband and constituted part of a *polos,* possibly a lasting dedication to the goddess in place of a real leaf crown.[29] Bone is used as well for twenty-one small seated figures 0.030–0.040 meter high, which may have served as amulets.[30]

Other types of objects, including disk and four-sided seals, spectacle fibulae, rings, combs, and beads, occur in bone and ivory. Bone is predominant, but the inherent fragility of ivory makes it impossible to draw conclusions concerning original percentages. In the case of combs, fibulae, and seals, the ivory examples tend to be among the largest within their group.[31] Surviving seals provide insights

CARVING AS CRAFT

into the use of the two materials.[32] Like the bone statuettes, the seals served as votaries, a type that continued to be popular for this purpose through the fourth century B.C.[33] The twenty-five four-sided examples range in length from 0.012 to 0.025 meter. Seven are ivory. All of the ivory seals are solid, as are the smaller bone examples. The larger bone seals, however, which are carved from horizontal sections of metapodials, required bone plugs at top and bottom to close the marrow cavity. Carvers overcame similar constraints with disk seals. A group of fourteen, of which twelve are bone, are carved with dedalic heads in relief on the obverse and intaglio birds and griffins on the reverse.[34] The seals range in diameter from 0.020 to 0.040 meter. The two ivory examples are among the largest at 0.040 and 0.036 meter, although paralleled by a 0.040-meter bone example.[35] As with the seals, the marrow cavities of the larger bone examples were plugged, typically below the neck and at the crown of the head (Illus. 3.3).[36]

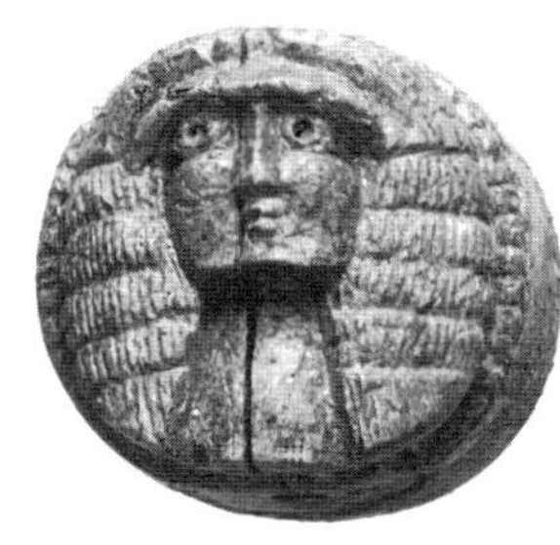

3.3.
Sparta, bone disk seal, sixth century B.C. (photo: Deutsches Archäologisches Institut, Athens)

Ivory is the predominant material in only two groups of objects. The first is a series of small couchant animals on rectangular or round bases, generally dated from the late eighth to the mid-seventh century, most of which are carved with intaglio designs on their bases and probably functioned as seals.[37] The second is a large series of plaques, both incised and in relief, which span the entire period of the excavation, and for which the site is most renowned.[38] Among the plaques, forty-four examples are ivory and thirty-six are bone. While the difference in numbers is small, this class of objects is distinctive in that the ivory examples are concentrated in the seventh century whereas bone becomes predominant in deposits beginning around 600 B.C., concomitant with the reconstruction of the sanctuary after the early temple was destroyed.[39] Whether the supply of ivory or the market for it disappeared at Sparta remains uncertain, but various reasons for the shift have been suggested, including the possible interruption of the ivory trade caused by the fall of Tyre, or an increase in the price of the raw material that placed it beyond the reach of most Lakonians who dedicated votives at the local sanctuary.[40] Carter suggests that the decline of ivory carving at Sparta was instead the result of more lucrative carving opportunities elsewhere,[41] but the remains clearly point to an industry that continued to flourish, even though ivory was less available. That Sparta exported artwork or artists, however, is a distinct possibility. Noting the similarity between plaques carved in Sparta and those associated with the funerary couches from Quinto Fiorentino and Grafenbühl, Mastrocinque proposed that either the plaques were exported from Sparta or that Spartan artists migrated to Taranto, the Spartan foundation in Magna Grecia, where they met the needs of the local elite.[42]

The predominance of ivory among the early Spartan plaques has contributed to their renown. The majority served as fibula plates, attached by means of two rivets to a bronze safety-pin-type fastener. One example, probably for a fibula, is unfinished, providing evidence that the carving was indeed carried out in the vicinity of the sanctuary.[43] As items of personal adornment that were dedicated as ex-votos, the material, workmanship, and size conveyed the wealth and status of the donor. Because in most cases the width of the plaques exceeds the width that was readily available in bone, ivory was a practical if more expensive choice as well.

Fibula plaques of this type are absent from the post-600 B.C. material, when bone becomes predominant. Surviving plaques appear to have served primarily as furniture mounts. They are carved in relief or incised, and some have the background cut away in a technique known as ajouré. These would have been mounted against a contrasting background.[44] One partially finished example provides valuable evidence of technique (Illus. 3.4). The ground has been sunk slightly, using a chisel, and pierced with round holes to admit a fret saw, by which the ground would have been cut away.[45] In response to the size limitations imposed by the metapodials from which they were cut, two or more pieces of bone often were joined together to create a wider plaque. In the case of one plaque depicting part of a four-horse chariot drawn by winged horses, it has been suggested that as many as five bone plaques were joined to create the final work (Illus. 3.5).[46] This plaque also illustrates the high quality of carving that characterizes some of the later work in bone from Sparta. It is by far the finest of three plaques carved with similar subject matter, the other two of which are ivory.[47] Clearly, despite the changes that took place around 600, skilled carvers remained at Sparta and continued to work in both materials.

Although it is difficult to draw conclusions concerning the relative values attached to the materials during the geometric and archaic periods, the fact that votive statuettes generally identified as Orthia are bone, even during periods when ivory was readily available, suggests that the association of images of the

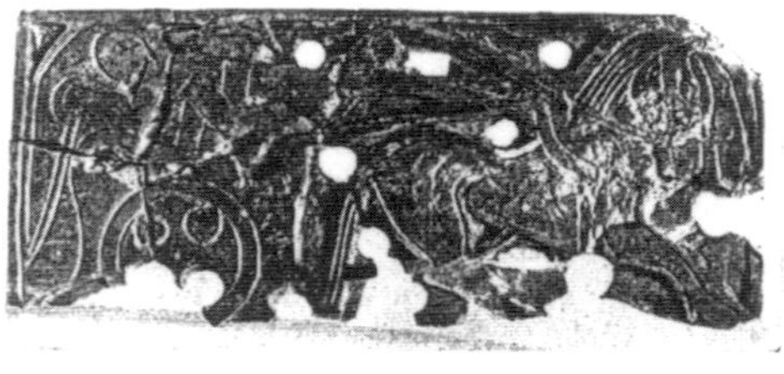

3.4.
Sparta, unfinished bone plaque, sixth century B.C. (Dawkins 1929, Pl. CXVI, 2)

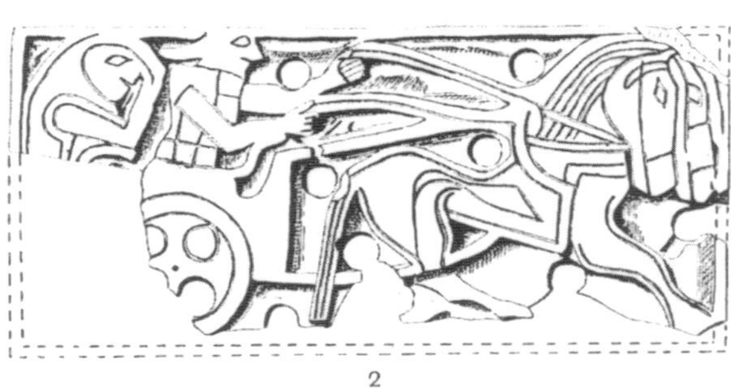

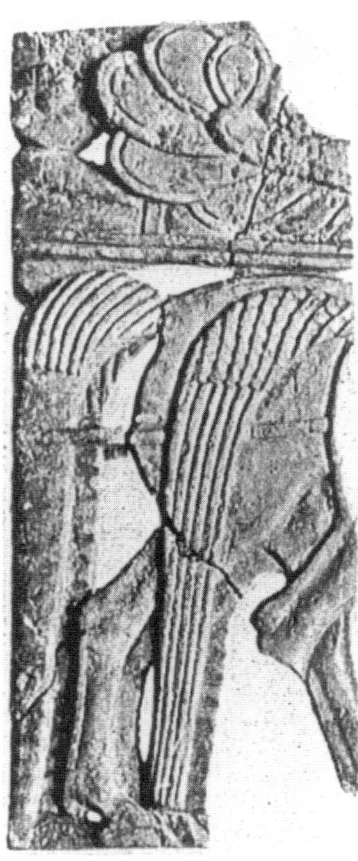

3.5.
Sparta, ajouré bone
plaque, sixth century
B.C. (Dawkins 1929,
Pl. CXVI, 3)

gods with precious materials was not yet a determining factor. After all, the cult image of Orthia, like other highly revered cult statues of the period, was itself wooden and of modest dimensions.[48] On the other hand, the seventh-century fibula plaques suggest that ivory was a favored material for items of personal adornment, conveying the status or wealth of the wearer or donor.

Remains from centers such as Sparta confirm the notion that carvers were concentrated at sanctuary sites and seem to contradict the equally common notion, suggested in Philostratus, of the ivory carver as an itinerant journeyman.[49] Although Philostratus's model was undoubtedly valid in some instances, Sparta offers a model of an established industry that carved bone and, when available, ivory over a period of at least two generations, and that may have exported its wares well beyond the sanctuary boundary. The remains leave no doubt that ivory and bone carvers worked together, carving a wide range of objects. It is also clear that ivory and bone carvers worked in alliance with metalworkers and woodworkers. Not only did bone and ivory spectacle fibulae imitate designs in metal, but they were also mounted either directly to the bronze fastener or to a complete flat-backed plate in iron.[50] Bosses of amber and silver were sometimes attached to bone and ivory plaques, while bone bosses decorated metal examples.[51] The majority of pins were composite as well, with bone or ivory heads mounted on metal shafts.[52]

Olympia

In addition to extensive remains in bone and ivory uncovered from sixth-century contexts at Ephesus, excavations at Delphi uncovered fragments of ivory ajouré furniture decoration that testify to the continuation of carving traditions observed at Sparta, as well as the remains of at least eleven composite figures, three of which were approximately life-size.[53] Faces and limbs were ivory, although the surviving whites of the eyes of the largest figure were bone.[54] Along with other scattered remains, they are a prelude to the renowned chryselephantine cult images of the fifth century B.C., which were a major artistic focus of the period, but which unfortunately have not survived, making it difficult to reconstruct accurately their appearance or the techniques used to create them.[55] The discovery of the so-called workshop of Pheidias at Olympia, however, associated with the great chryselephantine statue of Zeus, has dramatically advanced our knowledge of both the statue type and of the circumstances of creation, providing evidence not only of the materials and techniques used in the construction of the figure but of the physical setting in which, according to Pausanius, Pheidias worked the image piece by piece.[56] The building had the same alignment and basic measurements (32.18 by 14.5 meters) as the cella of the temple for which the image was intended and is thus a likely location for at least the assembly of the statue. Within were two forges for metalworking and a large bronze cauldron used as a water container, which was filled from a well sunk within the building. The building thus functioned in part as a foundry.[57] The variety and amount of other remains, which were found primarily in a series of dumps outside its walls, suggest that work on the statue was not confined to the limited space within the building but was carried out in associated, perhaps temporary, structures nearby or in the open.[58] In addition to significant amounts of ivory- and bone-carving debris, the remains include tools; terra-cotta piece molds for the shaping of glass drapery; fragments of glasswork that were apparently rejects from the casting process; pieces of rock crystal, quartz, obsidian, ebony, and amber; bronze dross and wasters; pieces of iron and lead; chalk, pumice, gypsum; and scrap metal that had been collected for melting down.[59] The bone-carving debris includes discarded articular ends of metapodials, primarily from cattle but occasionally from sheep and goat; sawn transverse and longitudinal sections of long bone; and partially worked scapulae, or shoulder blades (Illus. 3.6). Blanks include shafts from the preliminary stages of working and sawn longitudinal sections of bone roughly shaped with the chisel. Lathing debris is present as well (Illus. 3.7). Finished objects include a group of bone tools, each with one spatulate and one pointed end, in a variety of sizes. The smaller examples are paralleled in bronze.[60] The

   CARVING AS CRAFT

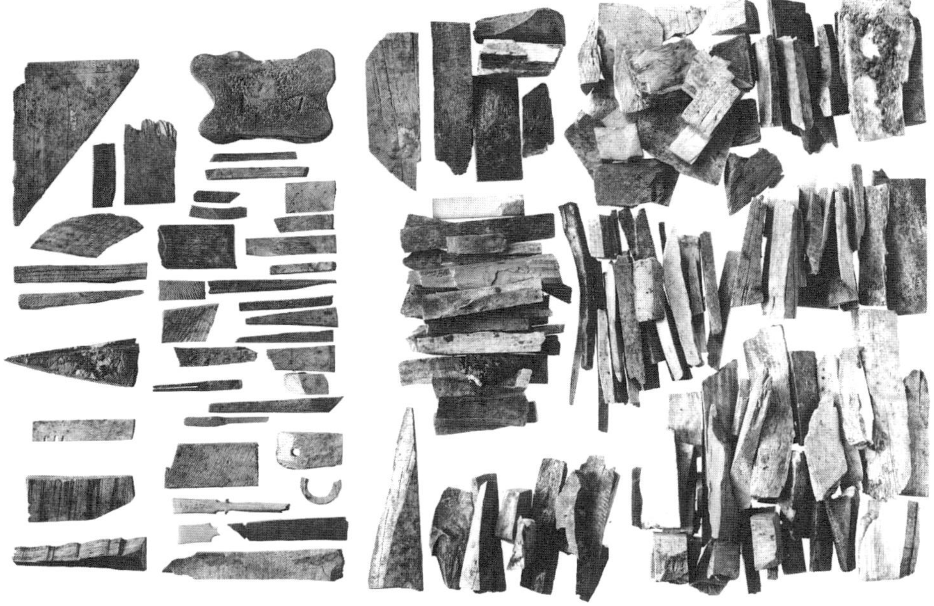

form is that of the stylus used for writing upon and smoothing the surface of wax tablets, but these examples were probably engraving and smoothing tools.[61] Three complete leaves and the fragment of a fourth, from the left half of an ornamental palmette (Illus. 3.8), indicate that bone also was used for decoration, probably on the throne associated with the figure, recalling the similar decoration on the sixth-century funerary couch from Athens (Illus. 3.1).[62] Other bone mounts, including a disk and fragmentary turned cylinders are probably associated with furniture as well (Illus. 3.7).[63]

Ivory remains are less numerous and, with few exceptions, are in the form of debris from the carving process; they include waste in the form of chips and splinters, as well as partially worked pieces that are for the most part fragmentary and may be discards (Illus. 3.6). The majority of debris is from longitudinal sections, with the grain flowing along the longer axis. In addition to saw and chisel marks from the preliminary stages of carving, a few examples are scored with incised lines in a grid pattern, a technique paralleled on plaques from the sixth-century B.C. Kerameikos funerary couch, and familiar from Mycenean and later ivory remains from Italy as well.[64] Scoring was used to roughen the back of plaques and veneers before gluing to a wooden core, and different patterns of scoring may have been used to indicate placement.[65] Fragments of thin, rectangular, ivory strips also survive.

With the exception of wood, which has not survived in sufficient quantity to be meaningful, the variety of material remains at Olympia corresponds with

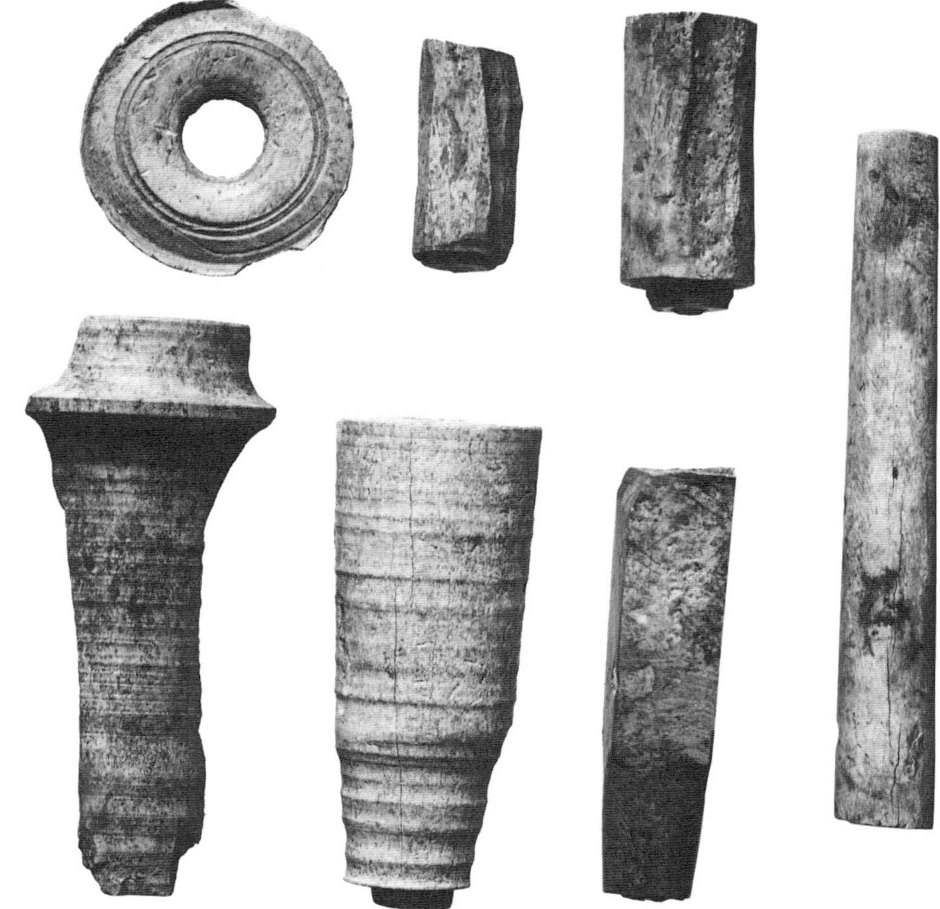

that associated with the remains of a life-size chryselephantine statue excavated in 1981 in Alexandria that was deliberately hacked into pieces and burned in the fifth century A.D.[66] Mixed with the ashes were significant pieces of burnt wood, along with pieces of ivory, glass in the form of appliqués and inlays of various shapes and colors, and gilded bronze and stucco. Although the date of the statue is unknown—objects associated with it date between the first and the fourth century A.D.—the remains point to a continuity of tradition and techniques that is readily recognizable within other classes of objects, such as furniture.

The precise method of construction is not known, but studies of the base of the Athena Parthenos suggest that composite figures were assembled over a wooden core, which was attached by means of struts to a central supporting member.[67] Unlike smaller figures, their monumental scale meant that limbs and faces could not be carved from solid tusks. Rather, as suggested by Pausanius's description of an unfinished chryselephantine statue at Megara, limbs and body were rendered in wood and then covered with ivory, gold, or other materials,

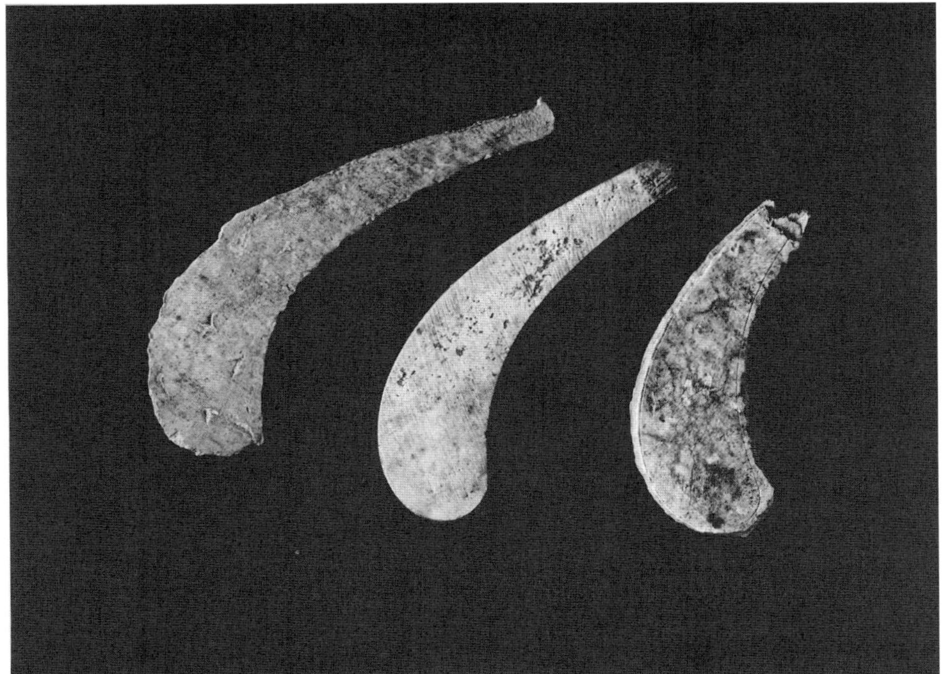

such as gilded glass.[68] The wooden core allowed for the easy attachment of metal
and ivory elements, as well as ornaments and accessories in other materials.

The manner in which the ivory flesh areas of such large-scale figures were
created is disputed. Lapatin has recently argued that a technique for
"unscrolling" elephant tusks developed in the nineteenth century was also known
in antiquity, enabling the creation of large thin plaques, which, in a second procedure, would have been softened and pressed into molds to obtain the desired
shapes.[69] As yet, however, material remains that would support this claim are
lacking. The size, shapes, and tool marks associated with the ivory debris from
Olympia, for example, point to more traditional and well-attested means of creating plaques or veneers from thinly sawn longitudinal sections, and although
molds for other parts of the statue, namely drapery, are present, none can be
associated with the shaping of ivory parts of the statue.

Given the evidence at hand, a more likely source of the technology that
allowed the creation of such figures, implied in the second-century account of
Lucian,[70] would appear to be the already well-established craft of furniture
veneering. Chryselephantine statuary, although on a larger scale, was essentially
an extension of the furniture maker's craft, in which ivory and other materials
were fitted to a wooden core, secured by means of glue or small pegs or dowels.[71]
The funerary couch from the sixth-century tomb in Athens (Illus. 3.1) provides
evidence of the use of identical materials (ivory, bone, and amber), motifs (decorative palmettes), and techniques (scoring) found in the debris at Olympia.[72]
There is no record of the use of glass, but the funerary couches discovered in the

fourth-century "royal" tombs at Vergina make extensive use of glass, in the form of palmette leaves and strip inlay, as well as of gilding, in combination with ivory, suggesting that at least at the highest levels, these materials were part of the furniture makers' vocabulary as well.[73]

It has been presumed, however, that this technique was not feasible for the flesh areas, composed primarily of curved surfaces. After all, the rectangular legs and bed frame of the Athens couch required only the application of veneers to flat surfaces. But furniture with turned legs is attested in vase painting from at least the sixth century and is represented in a variety of mediums in the fifth.[74] Fragments of two wooden examples, dated to the fifth century, and numerous bronze examples, primarily from the Hellenistic period, survive along with fragments of couches in ivory and more complete examples of funerary couches in bone.[75] With few exceptions the so-called bronze couches were constructed by attaching bronze fittings to a wooden framework or, in the case of turned legs, to a wooden core fitted around a central iron rod.[76] Ivory and bone examples employ the same technique. Separately turned pieces or thin veneers of ivory or bone were attached to the curved surface of the turned wooden core or, exceptionally, directly to the central iron core.

The best-preserved examples of this technique are the series of fragmentary couches with complex fulcra and turned legs dating from the second century B.C. to the first century A.D. (Illus. 3.9, 3.10).[77] The couches are a direct descendant of Hellenistic Greek types known from at least the third century B.C. and, in their use of bone or ivory in combination with glass inlay and amber, continue the older traditions of the Athens and Vergina couches.[78] Standard elements of the legs were bell-shaped and ribbed torus components, as well as drumlike components with concavo-convex tops and bottoms created by attaching thin plaques with glue to a turned wooden core (Illus. 3.10). The veneer consisted of thin rectangular plaques assembled in registers. Each register was made up of separate pieces carefully shaped to fit each other and the underlying core. In some cases the interior surface of one register was cut back to receive the next, assuring a seamless transition. The veneer was then smoothed, and carved with relief decoration where desired, a practice already noted at Sparta, where bone plaques were joined together before being carved in relief. Between these larger leg components, intermediate sections of smaller diameter were fitted with turned cylinders directly over the metal rod, sometimes secured with wood packing. When these areas were carved in relief—in the case of sculptural groups, for example—additional laminations were sometimes glued one on top of the other to provide the necessary depth for relief carvings, an ancient technique known to have been practiced in Egypt.[79]

While our knowledge of ancient veneering techniques is based largely on surviving furniture fragments, Pausanius's mention of the image of the goddess from Proconnesus, whose face was made from hippopotamus teeth, and Dioge-

    CARVING AS CRAFT

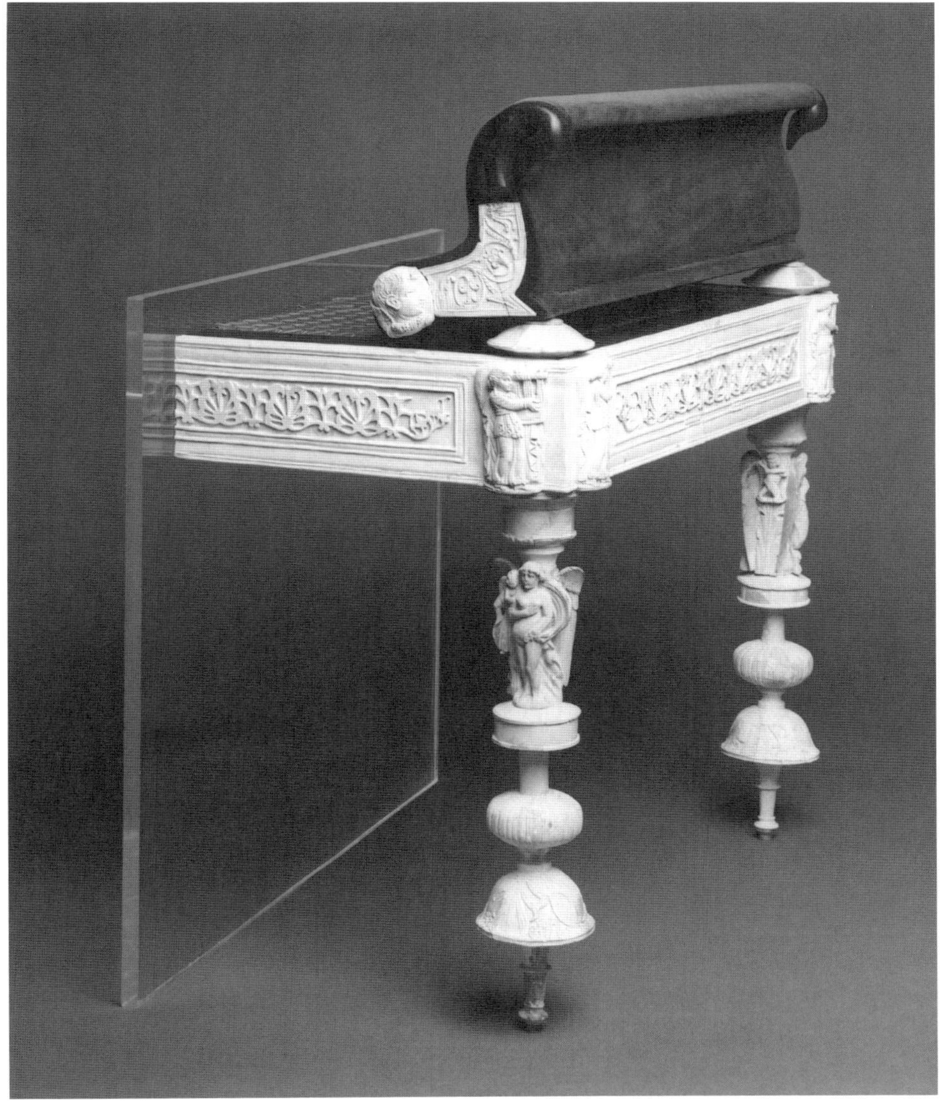

3.9.
Cambridge, funerary
couch, first century B.C–
first century A.D. (photo:
Fitzwilliam Museum,
University of Cambridge)

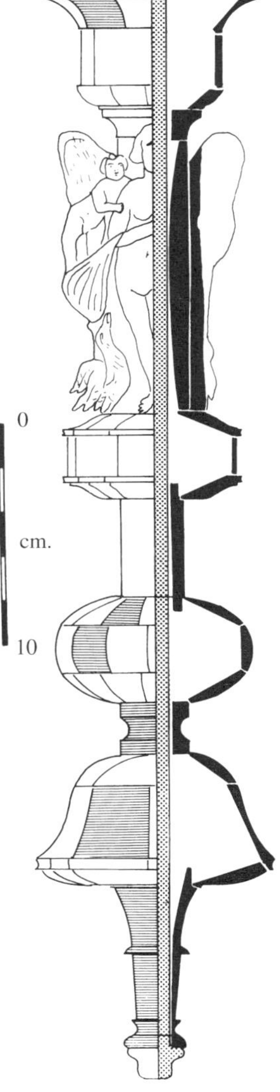

3.10.
Cambridge, profile of leg,
funerary couch, first
century B.C.–first century
A.D. (Béal 1986, Fig. 2)

nes Laertius's description of the ivory veneer of the shield dedicated by Menelaos
at the temple of Apollo at Didyma suggest that these techniques were adapted to
objects both larger in scale and for different purposes, probably within the same
setting.[80] Demosthenes' father, it should be recalled, used ivory in the manufacture of both furniture and weapons. These techniques could be easily adapted to
the curved flesh areas of chryselephantine statuary as well, and the ivory remains,
although limited to debris, suggest that this was the case. Fragments of strips
0.002–0.003 meter thick confirm that ivory was cut into thicknesses suitable for
veneer. Although many of the ivory fragments are broken, the length of the longitudinal fragments rarely exceeds 0.120 meter, making it likely that plaques
were cut to standard lengths. This consistency favors the theory that ivory was
worked in the form of thin plaques cut to regular lengths, carefully joined to cre-

ate a seamless fit, and, having been scored for better adhesion, glued and/or secured with pegs to a wooden core.[81] It seems likely that this technique, which was undoubtedly used for the oversized throne of the god, would have been used for other areas of the sculpture as well. As Lapatin has demonstrated, and ancient furniture attests, thin veneers could indeed be softened for attachment to curved surfaces if needed, and protruding areas could easily have been built up using laminations.[82] Carvers could also take advantage of the naturally curved surface of ivory to create or cover curved surfaces. After polishing and surface carving, the impression, as with the furniture celebrated by the ancients, was of solid ivory.

Pheidias's workshop confirms a continuing association of bone and ivory carving, as well as of related industries, with sanctuary sites. But there is no reason to assume a monopoly in this regard. Finds in tombs point clearly to the wider demand for ivory and bone objects, as well as for composite furniture throughout the Greek world and beyond. In Etruria, most of the ivory and bone remains, ranging from simple artifacts to elaborate furniture and boxes, were found in tombs, presumably the earthly possessions of the deceased. These finds suggest primarily a lively trade in sumptuary goods, but local manufacture is attested as well.[83] At Ashkelon, bone carving was a flourishing industry from at least the fifth century B.C., producing a similar variety of objects from the bones of cattle, camels, and donkeys, presumably for a wide audience.[84]

THE HELLENISTIC AND ROMAN WORLDS

The association of ivory, particularly ivory-veneered furniture, with royalty is suggested by the remains from Vergina and confirmed by finds of both tusks and finished objects from Hellenistic and early Roman sites. A cache of tusks was discovered in the ruins of the first-century B.C. palace of Queen Amanishakhete, called Candace by Roman writers, south of Meröe in the Sudan.[85] The treasury of the royal palace at Nysa, ruled by Mithradates I (173–137 B.C.), contained thirty-three furniture legs with ivory attached both directly to the metal legs and to turned wooden elements and a collection of ivory rhyta.[86] Excavators uncovered a far larger group of remains at Begram, summer capital of the Kushan kings and an important stop on the trade routes connecting Rome with the East; the hundreds of fragments of veneer from chairs, stools, and boxes, carved in a variety of techniques and combining Roman and Indian styles, provide striking testimony to the movement of models, and perhaps craftspeople as well, between Italy and India in the first and second centuries.[87] In many cases, letters in ink on their backs indicated the placement of panels. Especially relevant to this study is the fact that, although the cache is referred to as the "Begram ivories," the predominant material is bone, and those pieces that have been reconstructed clearly indicate a common craft tradition, with bone and ivory combined both on furniture and on boxes.

Complementing these well-documented "royal" remains are finds associated with a variety of nonroyal settings and scattered remains in museums, including turned legs, revetments, and small-scale sculpture, that confirm the existence of a flourishing industry in both materials and the preeminence of furniture making during the Hellenistic and early Roman periods.[88] Works of extraordinary quality in bone, such as the remains of furniture veneers from third- or second-century B.C. Corinth, testify to the high level of craftsmanship associated with the material.[89]

Many of the remains in both bone and ivory are associated with the particular type of veneered couch, with s-shaped fulcra and turned legs, discussed in relation to the remains from Olympia (Illus. 3.9, 3.10). With few exceptions, these couches owe their preservation to the fact that they served as funerary couches, surviving for the most part as charred remains from cinerary urns.[90] Letta's 1984 study catalogued the remains of at least 33 ivory and 153 bone examples dating from the third century B.C. to the first century A.D., and more recent publications have added to this corpus.[91] The finds are concentrated in central Italy, although remains have been found in other parts of Italy, Gaul, Germany, and elsewhere in the empire.[92] Examples veneered entirely in bone are attested beginning in the second century B.C. The remains from central Italy range in date from the first half of the second century B.C. to the middle of the first century A.D., with the majority dated to the first centuries B.C. and A.D. Provincial finds in Gaul continue until the end of the first century A.D. Letta distinguished two bone groups, the first with fulcra decorated in low relief in imitation of ivory models, and the second with fulcra decorated in high relief in imitation of bronze models. Both are decorated primarily with Dionysiac themes and are based on Hellenistic models that can be documented at least from the third century B.C. in Greece and Magna Grecia.[93] Their appearance in Italy corresponds to the introduction of Hellenistic luxury goods as a result of Roman military conquests, and to the fashion for such couches in the funerary processions of the elite, as recorded in contemporary literature. The abundance of remains and the fact that some of the bone examples imitate bronze models confirm the notion of a growing fashion for objects of bone and ivory at various levels of society, perhaps at the expense of metal, a trend already noted with artifacts.[94] Quality of execution varies, but the best bone examples rival the finest works in ivory of the period.

Scholars have generally avoided assigning the couches to specific production centers, given the lack of concrete evidence. Exceptions are Talamo and Bonacassa Carra, who suggested an Alexandrian origin for the example from the Esquiline Hill in Rome, based on its Dionysiac iconography and outstanding quality, and Letta, who proposed Ancona and Norcia as production centers for couches discovered in that area.[95] Letta and Nicholls suggested that examples found in the western provinces were probably imported from Italy.[96] In their studies of the Vindonissa (Germany) examples, Eckinger and, more recently, Holliger Wiesmann postulated that the more refined elements, especially figural, were imported from Italy, while the simple veneers and framing elements and frames may have been made locally.[97] Béal suggested a similar scenario for examples from Gaul, although he noted that the close association between both simple and complex elements on the couches from Aosta (Italy) and Cucuron (Gaul), as well as elsewhere, argues for a single atelier.[98] The discovery of the remains of a funerary couch of this type in the cargo of a shipwreck off the island of Ventotene (Pontine Islands, Italy) indicates that they were indeed articles of trade, most likely in finished form.[99]

The Palatine East remains, which provide clear evidence for the manufacture of furniture during this period in Rome, allow us to consider the capital as a likely center of production for such furniture. It is an obvious choice, given the literary evidence for their use in Rome, the distribution of the remains, and their dependence on both the fashions of the elite and on imported Hellenistic models, which would have been readily available there.[100] Like the scattered remains of chryselephantine and other Greek-inspired statuary on Roman soil, the funerary couches reflect not only the taste for Greek art, but a demand that could be met both by importation of Greek originals and by opportunistic workshops in Rome and perhaps elsewhere working in both materials.

Whether the prevalence of bone examples signals a shortage of ivory in Italy is arguable. Ivory, though in unknown amounts, was clearly available in Rome during this period, and a fragment of ivory furniture decoration from a second-century B.C. tomb on the Esquiline testifies to its use for furniture within a funerary context.[101] That so few ivory remains survive is undoubtedly in part a reflection of the fragility of the material. The disintegration and collapse of wooden frameworks was far more destructive to ivory veneers than bone, as was the practice of cremation. The large number of bone remains thus is a more likely indicator of a fashion that stimulated production in both materials. Caesar's funerary couch probably was, as reported by Suetonius, of ivory—although of ivory combined with bone and other materials if the past is a reliable guide—and, like its Hellenistic predecessors, a stimulus to imitation at various levels of society in both materials.

LATE ANTIQUITY

The apparent decline in production of elaborate funerary couches in Rome after the middle of the first century, and in the provinces at the end of the century, corresponds with the overall decline in the fashion for, and imitation of, Hellenistic models in Roman art. Scattered remains from throughout the Roman world testify to the continued use of both ivory and bone for furniture and a variety of other objects during this period, however, ranging from dolls—where the two materials largely replaced terra-cotta—to boxes, pins, and utensils.[102] Pausanius's admiration for chryselephantine statuary, Hadrian's commission of one for the temple of Zeus at Olympia, and the use of ivory funerary couches in second- and third-century apotheosis ceremonies point to a continuing appreciation both for the classical past and for the material, moreover, at least at the highest levels of society. The recent discovery that the glass inlay decorating the reconstructed first-century couch in the Metropolitan Museum, and presumably its bone veneers, came from the second-century villa of Lucius Verus on the Via Cassia suggests that not only ivory- but bone-veneered furniture was treasured as well, if indeed owners could tell the difference.[103]

It is not until the late third century that an increase in the number of material remains suggests a flourishing of ivory and bone industries in the Roman Empire comparable with that stimulated by the earlier fashion for Hellenistic models. Cutler has presented evidence for this late antique revival in a valuable series of studies, and abundant remains document the reemergence of ivory as a preeminent and highly visible luxury material widely associated with official status and with the elite of Roman society.[104] Consular diptychs, which advertised the status both of the patron and the material to a broad audience, are but the most visible evidence of this resurgence, which can be demonstrated across a wide range of both secular and religious objects.[105]

A concomitant flourishing of bone carving occurred in Rome and throughout the Mediterranean area as well. Like ivory, bone was used for carving sacred and secular subjects and even, on occasion, imperial portraiture.[106] Highly skilled artists worked in both materials, and similarities in compositions, figure styles, and carving techniques suggest a continuing association. A relief in the Benaki Museum that is paralleled on the ambo of Henry II, or another in the Walters Art Museum that is reflected on the ivory cathedra of Maximianus, for example, testify not only to a common vocabulary but to a common technique as well.[107]

Material remains point once more to a flourishing furniture industry. The cathedra of Maximianus, the Pola and Brescia caskets, and numerous ivory pyxides are among the most visible examples of a fashion for sumptuous furniture and boxes. Five-part plaques or diptychs, with individual pieces fitted onto a wooden framework, belong to the same craft tradition.[108] The large number of bone remains of this type, although for the most part fragmentary and scattered among museums, testify equally vividly to a demand for this class of objects by a wide public.[109] While the most frequently reconstructed objects that employ bone are boxes (Illus. 3.11), fragments discovered at Kenchreai, the port of Corinth, provide striking evidence of bone-veneered furniture on a larger scale.[110]

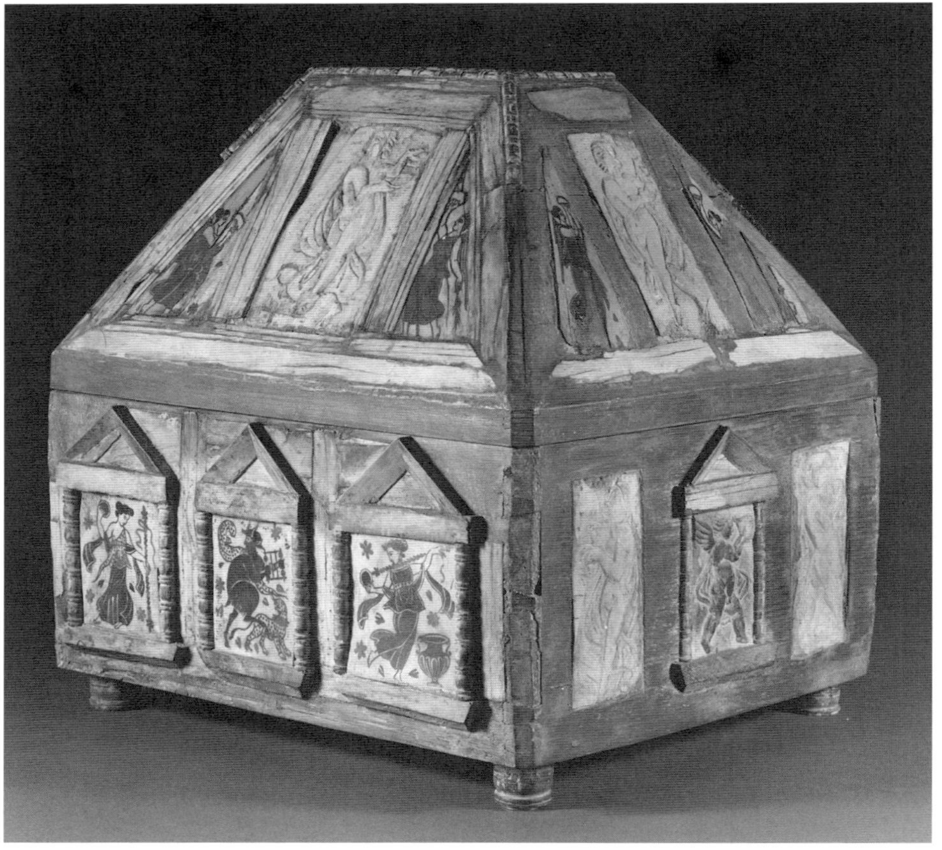

The significant numbers of surviving convex mounts, created from longitudinal
sections of metapodials and meant to be mounted vertically on a wooden or
metal support, were clearly intended for larger-scale furniture as well.[111] Like the
late antique fashion for bone adornment in the western provinces, the demand
for bone-veneered furniture and boxes was undoubtedly stimulated by the fashion for ivory among the elite and filled the needs of a less demanding or less
wealthy consumer.[112]

Alexandria

Although clearly a widespread phenomenon, the flourishing late antique bone-
carving industry has been best documented in Egypt. Marangou's 1976 publication of bone reliefs in the Benaki Museum remains a primary text for the late
antique efflorescence of bone carving, despite the fact that considerable variety in
style and execution and a lack of specific provenances for most of the material
makes the development of a chronology difficult.[113] A similarly large and more
varied collection in the Greco-Roman Museum of Alexandria includes relief
plaques in preliminary stages of execution, although again not securely dated or
localized.[114] A more revealing picture of bone carving as industry comes from

archaeological excavations, which document Egypt, and specifically Alexandria, as a bone-carving center in late antiquity, although not for the Ptolomaic or earlier Roman period. As early as 1947, excavations carried out by Wace at Kom el-Dikka, in the center of the ancient city of Alexandria, uncovered debris from late Roman period dumps that included large numbers of fragments belonging to furniture or boxes, as well as workshop debris that included sawn animal bones and partially worked pieces.[115]

Further evidence was uncovered beginning in 1960 by the Polish Center of Mediterranean Archaeology in Cairo, and by Shenouda in the 1970s, documenting the area as a production center from the fourth to the ninth century A.D.[116] In contrast to Sparta and Olympia, but in keeping with the secular and urban model suggested by Demosthenes, the carving industry in this area was associated with a quarter in the vicinity of an imperial bath and theater that combined habitations with artisans quarters.[117] Evidence of artisanal activity in bone, in the form of production debris and unfinished objects ranging from utensils to decorative plaques, occurred primarily in deposits linked topographically and chronologically to the buildings. One building, consisting of four separate units accessed independently, with a shared cistern but no sanitary facilities, was likely constructed with solely artisanal functions in mind.[118] Reminiscent of Pheidias's workshop, there is evidence for glassworking in the form of colored strips that were probably for inlay, as well as beads and slag, and for metalworking in the form of bronze foundry waste. In addition, the carving of agate and other semiprecious stones and the working of coral occurred at the site.[119] Bone, and less frequently ivory, remains include a wide range of finished objects, from utensils and gaming pieces to furniture and box mounts carved in relief with simple geometric or floral, and occasionally figural, designs.[120] Surprisingly, intaglio plaques, in which outlines or larger hollowed-out fields were filled with colored paste, and which are routinely associated with Egypt, are absent.[121] Noting the similarity of the technique to glass incrustation opus sectile, Rodziewicz suggested that this art might have been practiced separately and centered elsewhere, perhaps at Saqqara, where numerous examples along with possible "trial pieces" were excavated, or at centers such as Bawit and the Kharga Oasis.[122] The fact that intaglio and relief plaques appear to have been used side by side on boxes, however, argues for common places of manufacture. The greater fragility of such plaques, on which much of the already thin compact layer of bone is carved away to receive colored paste, may be one factor that accounts for their greater rarity at, although not their absence from, archaeological contexts.

Despite the presence of ivory objects, no debris from ivory carving has been discovered at Kom el-Dikka, leaving open the question of local production, at least in this area. Convincing arguments for ivory-carving centers in Egypt continue to be made on stylistic grounds, however. Ivory remains discovered along with bone remains in seventh- and eighth-century A.D. deposits at Abu Mena, for example, have been attributed to the area primarily on stylistic grounds by Engemann, who argues that the source of these objects was probably Alexandria, only sixty kilometers away.[123]

The model provided by Kom el-Dikka of an urban setting that included artisanal and domestic spaces finds its counterparts in the late antique insulae of Rome and Ostia and today in urban centers throughout the Mediterranean world. But equally striking is the continuity with the past. The materials worked in close association with each other, for example, including bone, metal, glass, and semiprecious stones, are the same materials associated with bone and ivory industries at Sparta and Olympia. Whereas these industries were centered at sanctuaries, however, Kom el-Dikka provides valuable evidence of the concentration of artisanal activity, particularly bone working, on an industrial scale within an urban center, a model confirmed in Rome on the northeast slope of the Palatine. In the case of Palatine East, however, there is evidence for the carving of ivory as well, thus identifying Rome as a center for the carving of both materials in late antiquity.

Unlike the ivory-carving industry, bone-carving industries that produced furniture as well as more utilitarian objects probably flourished in centers throughout the empire in late antiquity, because the demand for bone objects could be met wherever a supply of bone and the requisite level of craftsmanship existed. The reevaluation of remains and recent discoveries of bone-working evidence confirm the existence of regional centers employing a common Mediterranean artistic vocabulary and technique, at various levels of craftsmanship. Ashkelon, for example, appears to have experienced a second flourishing of its bone-carving industry in late antiquity.[124] Bone and ivory fragments from furniture and boxes, including strips, plaques, and concave mounts carved primarily with geometric and floral decoration, survive from Corinth, although published evidence for a carving industry in bone is limited to sawn bones from several sites and blanks for utensils.[125] Bone manufacturing waste from Knossos, Carthage, and Sagalassos suggests furniture-making activity, although not on the scale or artistic level suggested by the Egyptian remains.[126] Local production also has been posited for various centers in Egypt, as well as in Palestine and at Leptis Magna, although often without direct evidence of manufacture.[127] Remains from other likely centers of bone as well as ivory carving—including Constantinople, for example—so far confirm only a demand for a wide range of bone and ivory objects.[128]

In western Europe, flourishing bone industries met the demands of local populations as well, not only for essentials but also for luxury items such as jewelry and furniture, stimulated by the fashion for these items in ivory among the elite. The scattered remains suggest the increased popularity of veneered furniture and boxes during this period as well, perhaps stimulated by ivory imports.[129] Over seventeen hundred bone fragments were excavated from a fourth- or fifth-century context at the Market Hall, Gloucester, consisting primarily of simple rectangular or mitered bone framing bands, sometimes formed from split bovine ribs.[130] Ajouré mounts are present as well, along with squares, trapezoids, and lozenges. Many are pierced by attachment holes, and some preserve bone or metal rivets. For the most part decoration is limited to incised linear or geometric designs. Evidence for on-site manufacture of furniture and utensils comes from a fourth-century deposit at Colchester containing twenty-one rough-cut and unfinished plaques in various foliate and bird shapes, in addition to mitered framing bands and convex or tubular mounts.[131] Debris from preliminary stages of carving was absent, leading Crummy to speculate that the site was not a bone carver's workshop but a joiner's, where veneered furniture and boxes were finished and assembled on their wooden frameworks.[132]

In contrast to bone-carving sites, centers of late antique ivory carving that can be identified on the basis of manufacturing debris are rare. Nonetheless, numerous claims have been made for diverse "schools" of late antique ivory carving based primarily on findspots and stylistic groupings.[133] Some of these claims—Constantinople and Alexandria, for example—have obvious merit. But without direct evidence of manufacture, arguments for widespread carving of ivory, especially in the provinces, is less convincing. The widely scattered remains of objects in both materials suggest that, along with other sumptuary and essential goods, they were widely traded throughout the Greco-Roman world. The discovery of glass opus-sectile panels still in their shipping crates at Kenchreai, the port of Corinth, for example, where they apparently had been shipped from Egypt, confirms Philostratus's story of a lively Mediterranean trade.[134] As Melucco Vaccaro has suggested, it is far more likely that this lively trade in sumptuary goods, as well as a highly mobile aristocracy, accounts for the broad distribution of certain types of late antique ivories in the West, rather than local workshops.[135] The remains from Palatine East, moreover, provide a cautionary tale for those who argue for such centers on the assumption that direct evidence of manufacture in ivory could not have survived. Material remains and common sense suggest so far that ivory was carved close to the source as well as in urban centers like Rome that boasted a long tradition of craftsmanship, a clientele that appreciated and could pay for its special qualities, access to trade routes that supplied the raw material, and a wider audience for the finished products.

4

MATERIAL REMAINS

PALATINE EAST

The bone and ivory objects excavated to date from the northeast slope of the Palatine Hill (Illus. 4.1, 4.2) number over fifteen hundred objects and span the period from the first through the fifth century, with scattered remains in disturbed medieval (Sector C) and later contexts. The heaviest concentrations of material are in two series of contexts. The first consists of first- and early second-century A.D. layers of mixed debris that were deposited as fill over and around second- and first-century B.C. constructions to the north and east of the fountain complex (Sector D) and in the areas to the south of the apsidal hall (Sector A).[1] The second and larger series is associated with the mid-third through the fifth century, with the heaviest concentrations in layers of mixed debris that were deposited as fill to the south of the apsidal hall and, beginning probably around A.D. 300, into the barrel-vaulted chambers beneath it (Sector B). The relative scarcity of architectural and stratigraphic evidence from the mid- to late second century at the site may be the result of the removal of material during later leveling or building activities.

The bone and ivory finds from these deposits provide valuable evidence for artisanal activity in the city and point to Rome as a carving center that, like Sparta, functioned over several centuries and embraced both materials. It should be emphasized, however, that the picture they present is not complete. The area to the south of the apsidal hall that is associated with the heaviest concentration of bone and ivory remains (Sector A), for example, contains a sequence of unexcavated fills over three meters in depth, which appear to date to between ca. A.D. 50–100, if not earlier, and the early second century A.D. The barrel-vaulted chambers beneath the apsidal hall (Sector B), which are associated with heavy concentrations of late antique material, also were not completely excavated.[2] Finally, the geographical area explored represents only a small part of a far larger unexcavated area with associated structures that extend in all directions from the *domus* over an area of approximately four thousand square meters. In fact, much

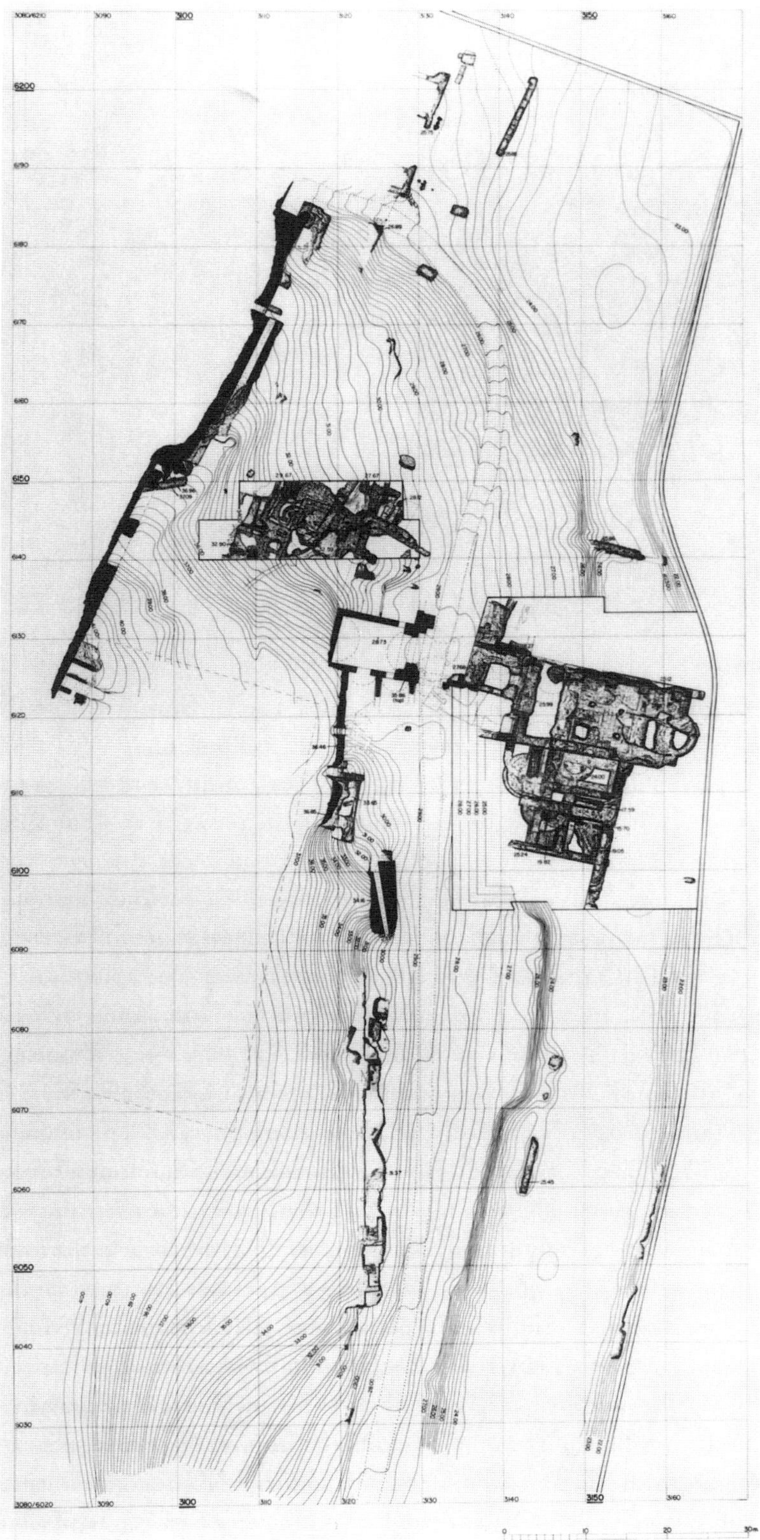

4.1.
Rome, topographical plan of the northeast slope of the Palatine Hill (Palatine East Excavation)

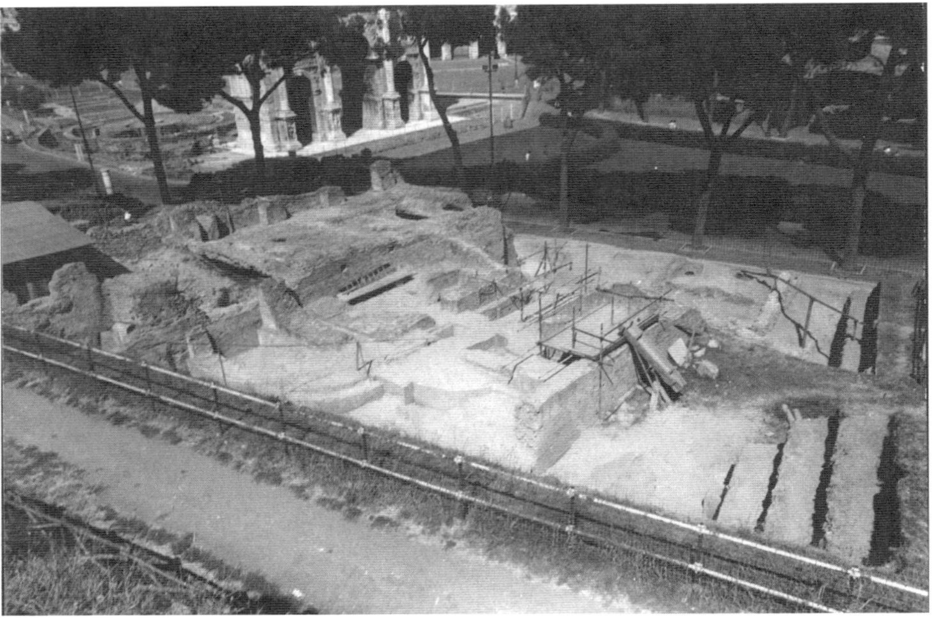

of the eastern slope of the Palatine has never been systematically explored and remains from an archaeological viewpoint largely unknown.

Both the first- and second-century and the late antique contexts contained significant amounts of carving debris, indicating the presence of a bone- and ivory-carving industry that appears to have functioned in the area over a considerable period of time. This evidence includes partially finished and rough-cut objects, blanks, and discards (objects broken or damaged during the carving process), as well as debris from earlier stages of manufacture. The amount of debris and finished objects from ivory working is far less than from bone, accounting for less than one-tenth of the material recovered. As we have noted, however, given the inherent fragility of ivory and the fact that tusks could be more fully exploited, this tells us little about the relative amounts carved. The remains associated with Pheidias's workshop, where bone remains also outnumber ivory, provide an apt comparison. The setting in which the Palatine East remains were unearthed, however, corresponds not to Olympia or Sparta but to the urban model encountered in Demosthenes' account of his father's factory and documented in the Roman world by sites such as Kom el-Dikka at Alexandria, where habitations and artisans quarters also coexisted in the vicinity of an imperial bath and theater.[3] Excavations at Palatine East, as well as in the area of the Meta Sudans to the northeast and in the Vigna Barberini upslope, reveal a lively mix of monumental and smaller-scale domestic and commercial structures during the late republican and early imperial periods, with the area between the Palatine and the Velian especially rich in tabernae.[4] Although interrupted by the fire of A.D. 64 and the subsequent short-lived transformation of some of the area under Nero, this model of mixed use, with domestic, monumental public, and commercial buildings side by side, remained the norm in the area during the empire.[5]

Although excavators have not identified an actual workshop, if we define the word as a shop or building where work is done, several factors combine to indicate a level of professionalism beyond that of the individual who may have carved objects to fill his personal needs.[6] First, the total number of objects is large, and the range of types, as well as the techniques used to create them, is wide. It includes most classes of object that we know to have been carved in both materials during these periods, from practical items such as simple pins to luxury items such as jewelry and decorative mounts, worked in intaglio, in high and low relief, and in the round. Second, and equally important, is the evidence for the exploitation of elephant ivory, both in the form of finished objects and of blanks and working debris that provide direct evidence that ivory was worked in Rome. Finally, the Palatine East remains suggest the ownership of somewhat specialized tools, including lathes, chisels, gouges, fine saws, drills, and a variety of knives, suggesting a level of professionalism beyond that encountered at sites where small-scale evidence of bone working, presumably by individuals, has been documented.[7]

The location where these materials were initially worked was likely nearby. The late antique layers with bone and ivory in stratigraphic sequence that were dumped to the south of the apsidal hall and in the barrel vaults below it represent primarily materials used and discarded over a short period of time, perhaps no more than a few decades each.[8] That such material was repeatedly brought from some distance for landfill is possible, but unlikely, especially in light of the presence of considerable working debris in first- and early second-century contexts upslope and to the south of the apsidal hall. These deposits point to a long history of ivory and bone working in the area. Once again, the remains associated with Pheidias's workshop at Olympia, which came not from within the building but from a series of dumps outside its walls, provide a comparison.[9]

THE FIRST- AND SECOND-CENTURY A.D. CONTEXTS

Both the first- and early second-century and the late antique contexts contained finished objects as well as manufacturing debris but reveal significant differences. Within the early contexts, remains associated with furniture manufacture predominate, especially the type represented by veneered couches that survive in funerary contexts in Italy and the western provinces.[10] They include framing strips; thin plaques for veneer; thicker decorated mounts; and cylindrical and columnar fittings primarily in bone but also in ivory. In no case can the furniture parts be reconstructed as a finished object whose wooden framework had perhaps disintegrated. Rather, their combination with unfinished pieces and considerable amounts of carving debris point to the area as a place of manufacture. Thin bone strips and wider veneers, for example, represent various stages of production, from blanks to finished pieces that are both plain and decorated (nos. 104–122, 169–170). Strip molding is commonly used as a framing device for recessed veneers, appearing on the first-century B.C.–first-century A.D. funerary couch from the Esquiline and on the reconstructed couch in Cambridge, for example (Illus. 3.9).[11] On the latter, the inner edges abutting the veneers are beveled, a feature shared by Palatine East examples (nos. 109, 111, 121). Strips with one or both ends mitered at a 45-degree angle for attachment at a corner are common as well (nos. 105, 110, 112; Fig. 9a,b; Pl. 14a,c). More elaborate mounts include a fragment decorated with an ovolo molding (no. 186; Fig. 12c; Pl. 20b), and another decorated with an incised cross pattern (no. 214; Fig. 14a), both of which are paralleled on the first-century B.C.–first-century A.D. funerary couch from Cucuron (Vaucluse) in Gaul, which Béal suggested was imported from Italy.[12] A thicker rectangular plaque is decorated with a foliate pattern (no. 215; Fig. 14b; Pl. 20a).[13] Similar plaques are associated with several surviving couches in Italy, and one in Cologne, although once again the Palatine East example is most closely paralleled on the example from Cucuron.[14] The thickness of the plaque suggests that it was probably associated with the legs or feet. Debris from veneers cut from scapulae illustrates various stages of the manufacturing process (nos. 23, 28, 29; Fig. 5a; Pl. 4c,d). The scapula was especially valued as the source for large one-piece veneers that could be used to cover the sides of fulcra or the frames of couches.[15]

Fragmentary cylindrical mounts in various stages of manufacture find parallels on first-century B.C.–first-century A.D. funerary couches from Italy and Gaul as well (nos. 159–161, Fig. 16a–c; Pl. 26d).[16] Surviving evidence documents their use primarily on furniture legs, which were assembled around an iron rod. Rings turned on the lathe from a single length of hollowed bone, often with cylindrical tenons at one or both ends, separated the more voluminous components. They were fitted directly over the rod or, if too broad, were packed with wood and then drilled through to receive the rod. They vary considerably in size and elaborateness of decoration depending upon their location. One Palatine East example (no. 160; Fig. 16b) is identical to a mount associated with the legs of a funerary couch from the necropolis of Saint-Lambert (Gaul).[17] A cylindrical bone relief fragment from a context dated to the second half of the first century (no. 227; Fig. 17a; Pl. 28) is probably from a pyxis, although the form and subject are common to surviving funerary couch mounts as well.[18] Such objects, whose manufacture required similar technical skills, were probably made in the same workshops and used in the same contexts. Bone pyxides were found in association with the Aielli and Cambridge funerary couches, for example.[19]

Leg components of larger diameter were assembled over a wooden core, with

CARVING AS CRAFT

pieces of bone or ivory cut to fit and glued directly to them.[20] The mount with a concavo-convex profile (no. 216; Fig. 14c) is an example of this type, which was assembled in registers over the core. The back surface is cut back to receive the next register or to fit the core. Similar mounts form the top register of drumlike members on the reconstructed first-century B.C.–first-century A.D. funerary couch in Cambridge (Illus. 3.10), and numerous similar plaques are associated with couches in Italy and Gaul.[21]

An ivory disk-shaped mount with lathe-turned decoration, pierced by a central hole (no. 238; Fig. 18a; Pl. 27b), belongs to a type associated with furniture manufacture as well. Disk-shaped mounts were typically used on fulcra, as corner bosses set on top of the frame, and as crowning elements of cylindrical leg members.[22] They also served as lids or bases for pyxides and to close the ends of hinges.[23] Stray finds with a central hole are routinely catalogued as spindle whorls or spindle weights, and occasionally as buttons and gaming pieces as well, but their well-documented appearance in a variety of shapes and sizes in direct association with furniture and pyxides suggests that in many cases their function should be reevaluated.[24] The fact that no spindles were found among the Palatine East remains supports their identification in both the early and late contexts as furniture and box components for the most part, although it is impossible to be specific concerning their function, given the standard form and decoration.

The associated manufacturing debris includes large numbers of offcuts for circular mounts (nos. 78–86; Figs. 7a–c; Pl. 11). They take the form of longitudinal slices of bone from which disks have been cut by turning on a lathe. The diameters of the disks cut from these blanks range from 0.045 to 0.090 meter, but the majority fall between 0.060 and 0.080 meter, a size more typical for mounts than counters or gaming pieces. The gaming pieces discovered in these early contexts, moreover (nos. 578–581), are of a flat-topped type that was differently manufactured.

A bone cylinder, which formed part of a hinge, also may have been associated with furniture production (no. 246; Fig. 16g). Cylinders formed from turned hollowed sections of long bones were combined in series to provide hinges for chests and boxes of various sizes. The interiors of the cylinders were filled with wooden plugs, and holes in the lateral walls, which were frequently sited in the natural longitudinal groove formed by the fusion of two digits, were fitted with dowels that projected at right angles and attached alternately to the lid and framework of the box or chest.[25]

Other possibly related materials from these contexts include glass tesserae and a large number of iron nails.[26] As we have seen, glass inlay was frequently combined with bone and ivory on surviving funerary couches, while nails were essential for the assembly of the wooden frame.[27] There is as yet no evidence for manufacture of either, however.

It is unlikely that the bone- and ivory-carving industry revealed in these early contexts was limited to one or two classes of object, but in the contexts excavated so far there is little evidence for the variety that characterizes the late antique contexts. In addition to flat-topped bone counters or gaming pieces, there are small numbers of dice in bone and ivory (nos. 597–600, 609–610). Bone handles (nos. 523, 524), needles (nos. 476, 477, 485–490, 493), ligulae (nos. 498–503), and spatulae (nos. 508–513) are also present. The small number of pins, especially in comparison with the late antique contexts, is striking. Those recovered are bone, and predominantly small and undecorated types that are rarely catalogued (nos. 248–254). Larger pins of the type usually called "hair pins," which are a major component of the late antique contexts, are rare, suggesting that the fashion for this type of pin, as well as the preference for bone and ivory over metal pins, is a later phenomenon in Rome. The absence of rings and bracelets in bone and ivory may reflect a similar preference for other materials.

THE LATE ANTIQUE CONTEXTS

While the late antique contexts include some residual material that may be associated with the first- or second-century remains, for the most part similarities between the two series of deposits point to the continuity of carving traditions over a long period in the area.[28] At the same time, the late antique contexts provide evidence for the use and manufacture of a wider variety of objects in both bone and ivory, in keeping with what we know about the flourishing bone- and ivory-carving industry elsewhere. As in the earlier contexts, bone is by far the predominant material, but ivory is present in greater abundance than in the earlier contexts, both in the form of finished objects and manufacturing debris, perhaps an indication of its more ready availability.

As in the earlier contexts, a large amount of debris is associated with furniture and box manufacture. Thin bone framing strips in various stages of manufacture are common, along with triangular and diamond-shaped inlays (nos. 150–154; Fig. 10g,h; Pl. 16e,f). The commonest decoration consists of two or three convex horizontal bands separated by V-shaped grooves. Several examples retain traces of red stain (nos. 140, 149, 174, 177; Figs. 10b, 11c; Pls. 15c, 18e). Such strips are familiar components of furniture and of simple boxes that survive as grave goods from Rome and elsewhere, as well as more elaborate boxes that survive from sites throughout the empire but are associated primarily with late antique Egypt (Illus. 3.11).[29] Numerous identical strips that are presumed to have decorated boxes are preserved in the nearby Antiquarium Comunale at Rome.[30] Strip mounts and thin undecorated veneers continued to be used on larger-scale furniture as well, however, as the fourth-century remains from Kencherai, the port of Corinth, indicate.[31] Because such furniture was no longer associated with funerary contexts, however, it rarely survives.

   CARVING AS CRAFT

Fragments of square or rectangular plaques with hand-carved or lathe-turned decoration, which would have been attached to wooden frameworks, are present as well. Only broken or unfinished plaques would normally be found among workshop debris, and the few Palatine East examples are likely discards. The simple turned designs (nos. 223, 225; Fig. 14h,i; Pl. 21b) are impossible to date accurately, and some examples may be residual, but the fragmentary female figure carved in high relief (no. 221; Fig. 15a; Pl. 23), perhaps a maenad, finds numerous parallels on late antique plaques that have been found throughout the empire in bone and in other mediums.[32]

Strips and plaques carved in intaglio, with areas cut back to create recessed fields for wax inlay, are hallmarks of the late antique contexts. Traditionally associated with Egyptian manufacture, although it is missing from Kom el-Dikka,[33] the type is best represented at Palatine East by the square plaque carved with a beribboned horse (no. 224; Fig. 15c; Pl. 21a). The scene is closely related to late antique representations of horses associated with the chariot races in other mediums,[34] while the technique finds parallels elsewhere in Rome, for example, on a series of mounts that decorated boxes or furniture from a bath complex in the urban quarter near the Termini station.[35] Although attributed by Albertoni to Egypt based on technique, both the style and iconography of these plaques find parallels on objects associated with Rome,[36] and the Palatine East evidence, which includes carving debris, indicates that the technique was indeed practiced there. Another form of intaglio, in which the linear incisions rather than recessed fields were filled with colored paste, is represented by a fragmentary plaque with a female figure (no. 222; Fig. 15b; Pl. 22), perhaps a victory. A chronology of this form has not been established, but it was popular in late antique Rome, as seen, for example, on a plaque depicting Peter from the Roman catacombs.[37]

Strips and plaques with linear designs in combination with ring and dot motifs are another distinctive feature of the late antique and disturbed contexts containing significant amounts of medieval and earlier residual material (nos. 200–204; Fig. 12i–l; Pls. 19b,c, 20e). In addition to furniture mounts, side plates for composite combs and comb cases and bone strip bracelets, especially in the western provinces, feature ring and dot motifs.[38] Although these functions can be hard to distinguish, the presence on many Palatine East examples of mitered ends and one beveled edge, both associated with furniture manufacture, and the lack of other evidence for the manufacture of combs or bracelets of this type at the site suggest that the Palatine East examples were primarily furniture mounts.

Other objects associated with furniture include cylindrical (nos. 162–164, 230–234), columnar (nos. 208–213), and disk-shaped mounts (nos. 239–242) that can be paralleled on late antique furniture, although the types frequently span the entire Greco-Roman period and hence are difficult to date accurately. The cylindrical mounts and other fittings associated with elaborate turned legs that were present in the early contexts are significantly absent in these contexts, however, reflecting a late antique preference for furniture without the complex legs typical of earlier periods.[39] The number of offcuts for disk-shaped objects is smaller as well, although these contexts are distinguished by the presence of examples in ivory apparently associated with mounts (nos. 89, 92; Fig. 7e,f; Pls. 6c, 7e). The single large example of an undecorated cylindrical bone mount with tenons at both ends (no. 163, Fig. 16h; Pl. 25a) is of a type also associated with furniture legs of first-century B.C.–first-century A.D. funerary couches, and may or may not be residual.[40] A partially lathe-turned fragment of a cylinder (no.164; Fig. 16i; Pl. 25c) that is closely paralleled in the debris from Olympia (Illus. 3.7) is a striking reminder of the continuity of the craft tradition over centuries.[41]

Several mounts in the form of half columns and plaques have spiral decoration and reflect the popularity of this type in late antiquity, although the form is an ancient one (nos. 209–210, 219; Figs. 13b,e, 14f; Pls. 24a,b, 25b). Spiral columns and half columns, often with similarly irregular designs, appear frequently on late antique diptychs, furniture, and boxes.[42] One example has a cubical capital that may be unfinished (no. 210; Fig. 13c; Pl. 25b).

Lathe-turned, disk-shaped mounts, sometimes pierced at their centers, are especially difficult to date—identical designs appear in the debris from Olympia—or to attribute to a specific use.[43] As in the earlier contexts, they may have served as furniture bosses, pyxis lids or bases, or to close the ends of hinges (nos. 239–242; Fig. 18e–h; Pl. 27a,e). The increase in the number and variety of gaming pieces and counters in these late antique contexts suggests that some may have served that purpose as well.

Dice and disk-shaped counters, as well as more elaborate gaming pieces, are present in bone and ivory. Dice are indistinguishable from their counterparts in earlier contexts, but there is a wider variety of disk-shaped counters or gaming pieces. They cannot be associated with particular games, and it is likely that identical counters were used in a variety of games, as well as in commerce and as gambling tokens. The simple flat-topped counters found in the first- and second-century contexts, however, are absent from the late antique contexts, replaced by counters that are plano-convex in section (nos. 584–587; Pl. 54). Although it is difficult to draw chronological distinctions between types, counters with a plano-convex section are commoner in late Roman periods, and have been frequently documented in funerary contexts.[44] Small disks with lathe-turned concentric rings on the obverse, producing varying profiles, may be counters as well.[45]

Two flat-topped ivory disks of exceptional size survive from fifth-century contexts (nos. 582, 583; Fig. 44a,c; Pl. 53a,b). Decorated with incised concentric circles, in one case combined with a ring and dot motif, they probably served as gaming pieces. In both size and decoration they are similar to pieces that have been recovered from later medieval contexts in western Europe in materials rang-

CARVING AS CRAFT

ing from bone to antler and walrus ivory.[46] Their function in late antiquity is uncertain, but the use of large diskoid counters has been associated with the game, or series of games, of tables, attested in the eleventh century.[47]

The most elaborate gaming pieces are formed from horizontal sections of long bone that have been closed at both ends by bone plugs before being turned on the lathe to create a domed shape (nos. 592–595; Fig. 45; Pls. 55, 56). Three Palatine East examples have retained plugs at their summits, and one has two plugs in place, an arrangement that was probably typical. These gaming pieces are paralleled by examples from Carthage, one of which is from a sixth-century context, and the type occurs in disturbed contexts from Sarachane in Istanbul.[48] Elaborate pieces of this type were undoubtedly hoarded, however, and may be much older.

The number of needles, spatulae, and ligulae is smaller than in the first- and second-century contexts. Handles in both ivory and bone, continue to be present in these contexts, as well as in disturbed contexts containing significant amounts of medieval and earlier residual material (nos. 525–532). Most striking, however, is the dramatic increase in the number and types of bone and ivory pins, a phenomenon that has been documented elsewhere, and which reflects the fashion for ivory, along with its cheaper counterpart, that is a hallmark of late antiquity. In contrast to the early contexts, most are of the size and shapes best documented as hairpins, although they undoubtedly could serve a variety of purposes. Hairpins were prominent adjuncts of fashionably jeweled and coifed women from at least the second half of the second century. On the fourth-century Projecta casket, both Projecta and Venus hold hairpins as essential elements associated with the privileged woman's toilet, for example,[49] and on painted and plaster portraits from Roman Egypt, pins of ivory or bone, sometimes with a gilded head, project frequently as components of fashionable hairstyles.[50] In late antique Roman inhumation tombs in Gaul, bone pins are often found placed close to or around the head.[51]

Pins of this type rarely exceed 0.100 meter in length. A notable exception, which comes from a disturbed context and cannot be specifically dated, is the highly polished bone example that measures 0.118 meter in length (no. 473; Fig. 32h; Pl. 36a). Bone examples range from summarily carved to highly finished and are both hand-carved and lathe-turned. Decoration is primarily nonfigural, an exception being a pin carved with a pinecone head (no. 473; Fig. 32g; Pl. 39a). The small bone figure of Aphrodite Anadyomene that is broken at its base was probably a pinhead as well (no. 475; Fig. 32k; Pl. 40).[52] Ivory pins are fewer and generally have decorated heads. In several cases the pinheads were made separately and attached to a shaft (nos. 451, 455; Fig. 31b,f; Pl. 36e,f). Davidson associates this practice with earlier periods at Corinth,[53] but several shafts designed to receive separate heads survive from these contexts as well, suggesting that the practice may have continued in late antiquity.

In addition to blanks and unfinished examples, a large number of pins appears to be finished, and some show staining on the tips or elsewhere that may or may not be associated with use.[54] Such items were undoubtedly manufactured in significant numbers for sale to the public, and the large number from Palatine East may represent, at least in part, such an inventory. Most of the undecorated types are common throughout the Roman world,[55] but decorated pins are less common and, because they are prized by collectors, frequently lack a secure archaeological context, although a wide range has been published from Corinth.[56]

Bracelets and rings formed from horizontal sections of bone or ivory constitute another distinctive feature of the late antique contexts (nos. 533–548). Most appear to have been originally unbroken circles, but two ivory examples provide evidence for a second type in which segments, or two semicircles, were joined by sleeves of metal held in place by rivets, sometimes linked by a joint and pin fastener (nos. 536, 547; Fig. 41i; Pl. 50e,f). This form was common when other materials were used, such as jet.[57] Although most are undecorated, five ivory examples have simple bands or incised patterns (nos. 544–548; Fig. 41h–k; Pl. 50c,e). The wide range of sizes suggests that, in addition to bracelets, such rings served varied functions, ranging from jewelry for humans, statuettes, and dolls to possibly more prosaic uses such as pulls for furniture and boxes.[58] A third type of bone bracelet, which was formed from thin longitudinal strips bent into a circle and closed by rivets or sleeves, is absent from Palatine East. This type is predominant in the western provinces during late antiquity, where it is among the commonest grave finds in late Roman cemeteries.[59] The fashion does not appear to have been widely adopted in Rome, however.

The fact that bracelets and rings are associated exclusively with these late antique contexts is consistent with what we know about the growing fashion for ivory and bone objects of this type in Rome and elsewhere.[60] Rings of bone and occasionally of ivory are frequently associated with burials in the catacombs, where along with other objects they were pressed into the cement that sealed the graves.[61] They vary in size, but most are of small diameter and simply decorated or plain. Their small size has led to the assumption that they were for infants or children, but many are found in association with adult burials.[62]

Other specifically late antique objects manufactured on site are articulated dolls of a type that also survives primarily in association with late third- and fourth-century burials in the Roman catacombs (nos. 550–577).[63] In Italy, ivory and bone had largely replaced terra-cotta as the preferred material for articulated dolls by the second century. Surviving examples fall roughly into two groups. The first consists of examples associated with burials dated to the second and early third centuries, many of which are of high quality, with carefully formed bodies and limbs and individualized features.[64] A second group, to which the Palatine East examples belong, is usually dated to the late third and fourth centuries and consists of more highly stylized dolls, primarily in bone, with summary modeling of the anatomy.[65] Limbs were attached to bodies with pins through the shoulders and through a flange at the base of the body (Pl. 51). Bodies are crudely shaped, with details of anatomy suggested by incised lines and circular indentations (nos. 550–557; Fig. 42a,b,e–g; Pl. 52a–c).[66]

The Palatine East remains are from contexts dated from the second through the fifth century, with scattered, possibly residual, remains in later contexts, although Ricci has postulated the continued manufacture of this type based on the presence of a single torso from a seventh-century context in the exedra of the Crypta Balbi.[67] Although for the most part fragmentary and crudely executed or unfinished, legs and arms can be distinguished by their forms. Arms are pierced for attachment through the shoulder and are usually more rectangular in section, with wrists indicated by notches or occasionally bands or incisions suggesting bracelets. Fingers are sometimes suggested by V-shaped incisions (nos. 567–577; Fig. 43f–k; Pl. 52d–f). Legs are inset at the top and pierced to receive the flange for attachment. They are for the most part oval or circular in section with a pronounced taper ending in a banded "ankle" and pointed "foot" (nos. 558–566; Figs. 42c,d, 43a–e; Pl. 52g–i). All of the bodies uncovered in these contexts are broken at the neck. However, no heads, which in preserved examples are of one piece with the body, have been found. It is possible that heads were intentionally broken off for some unknown purpose, but it seems more likely that the Palatine East examples are rejects, unintentionally broken during manufacture at their thinnest and most vulnerable point—the neck—and discarded.

Several letters of the alphabet in bone survive from the late antique contexts (nos. 645–647; Fig. 47a–c; Pl. 58a–c). Bone letters have been found in fourth-century A.D. contexts at Carthage as well, where they were identified as inlay.[68] Both Quintilian and Jerome mention letters of boxwood or ivory that were given to children in the guise of toys, as an aid to learning, suggesting another possible function.[69] Here, as in so many cases throughout the Greco-Roman world, bone proved the more practical alternative to ivory. One example, probably intended as separate letters, appears to be unfinished and gives insight into the manufacturing process (no. 645; Fig. 47b; Pl. 58a).

MANUFACTURING EVIDENCE

The finished object traditionally attracts the viewer; however, any attempt to define the setting for bone and ivory carving, specifically the existence and location of workshops and the techniques and tools of the trade, is likely to profit more from the examination of manufacturing evidence in the form of waste or unfinished objects. The Palatine East remains provide valuable evidence not only for the types of objects that were manufactured there but for the use of tools and of working procedures as well. Unless broken or rendered unusable, tools are unlikely to be found in association with carving debris, and they rarely can be associated with a particular purpose. As a result, evidence for carving techniques and for the tools employed has relied on somewhat fanciful medieval miniatures,[70] or on examination of the finished object, from which tool marks often have been intentionally obliterated by final polishing.[71] At Palatine East, handles of bone and ivory and remains of metal implements, notably chisels and knives, were excavated from contexts containing significant amounts of carving debris.[72] Nonetheless, analysis of the carving debris itself provides more direct evidence of tools and working methods.

Evidence for the preliminary stages of bone working at Palatine East is primarily in the form of discarded epiphyses and rings. Epiphyses were usually removed before the long bone was carved (nos. 1–5; Fig. 1; Pl. 1). Whether they were removed as part of the butchering process or by the craftsperson at a later date appears to have varied. Tanners may have played a role as suppliers as well, because long bones were often removed from the carcass with the skin, which was separated from them at a later stage.[73] At Palatine East the relatively small number of sawn examples (approximately twenty, of which only one was recovered from the first- and early second-century A.D. contexts) suggests that for the most part they may have been removed elsewhere. Epiphyses were sometimes put to use at this location, however. Two examples from disturbed contexts are decorated with crosses, and one is pierced by a hole, suggesting that it may have been worn as an amulet (nos. 102, 103; Fig. 8k; Pl. 13a,b). They are impossible to date with assurance, however, and may be medieval or later. Examples inscribed with various designs are documented in western Europe in the early Middle Ages, primarily as gaming pieces.[74] Epiphyses that are debris exhibit both careful sawing at a right angle to the bone (no. 2; Fig. 1b) and less precise oblique sawing in combination with percussion (no. 4; Fig. 1a).[75] Those from metapodials, which were the most prized bones for carving, were most often carefully sawn at right angles, so that little material was wasted.

Transverse slices of long bones in the form of rings, which are also primarily discards, are among the most common manufacturing debris from both the early and late antique contexts at Palatine East (nos. 6–20; Fig. 2a,c; Pl. 2). Over fifty complete examples survive, along with more numerous fragments. Most are between 0.010 and 0.020 meter long and were produced when the craftsperson cut the bone to size after removal of the epiphysis. In many cases the end with the larger diameter exhibits the combination of partial sawing with percussion that is associated with removal of the epiphysis, whereas the other end is sawn cleanly at a right angle to the long axis in order to produce a matrix with a straight edge (no. 13; Fig. 2a). Thicker rings may have been intended as blanks for cylindrical or square objects, such as dice.[76]

Both forms of debris provide valuable evidence of sawing techniques. The series of parallel striations on the sawn surface can reveal the carvers' methods.

Sawing begins at an oblique angle—approximately 20 degrees—to the surface. As sawing progresses, changes in the angle of the saw blade—either as a product of rotation of the matrix or change in the position of the saw—and in the amount of pressure exerted are expressed in the changing alignment, spacing, and overlapping of striations (nos. 4, 18, 20; Figs. 1a, 2c; Pl. 2d).[77] There is no evidence at Palatine East to support Plutarch's statement that bone or ivory could be softened and cut with a thread.

In addition to debris from the preliminary preparation of bones for carving, Palatine East remains include rectangular, square, cylindrical, and wedge-shaped blanks and debris that were created from sawn longitudinal or horizontal sections of long bones or elephant tusks, as well as from scapulae and ribs. Blanks cut from long bones and from tusks often retain the curved profile of the raw material (nos. 32, 50, 64, 87, 89; Figs. 4a,g, 7e,g; Pls. 6b,d, 7a,b,e). In some cases, the remains can be identified as blanks for specific types of objects such as pins, dice, or furniture mounts, but most of the remains are debris. The numerous short, thin strips that are associated with furniture decoration, for example, are for the most part scraps left over after mounts were either cut to size or mitered for attachment at a corner. Many are decorated and have one beveled edge. In some cases the decoration is interrupted or bisected by the cut, indicating that the strips were decorated before being cut to size and set in place (no. 197; Fig. 12d; Pl. 19d).[78] In others the decoration does not extend the entire length of the strip. The undecorated end would have been removed when the strip was cut to size (no. 180; Pl. 17b).

Preliminary shaping of blanks was achieved using primarily the saw and chisel. When working perpendicular or at an angle to the grain, sawing remained the preferred method, although chisels were used to divide thin blanks. In the case of very thin strips, one or both ends often were scored with a knife or chisel and then broken by percussion (nos. 186, 197; Fig. 12c,d; Pls. 19d, 20b). When working parallel to the grain, there is a preference for the chisel over the saw for preliminary shaping. Evidence for the use of straight-edged chisels along longitudinal surfaces, often with the "stop and go" marks in the form of ridges that indicate use in combination with a mallet or hammer, is provided by numerous blanks and unfinished objects (nos. 62, 99, 101; Figs. 6d, 8f,g; Pls. 9e, 12d,f).[79] Longer facets, visible on surfaces that have been prepared for turning on a lathe or on blanks for circular objects such as pins, were probably made with a knife (nos. 40, 97; Fig. 6h, 8d; Pl. 10c). Chisels were also used to remove surface material for intaglio and to create decorative patterns (nos. 170, 224; Figs.12 m, 15c; Pl. 21a).[80] Claw or toothed chisels also were applied parallel to the grain. They were used to roughen the back surfaces of plaques for better adhesion as well as to remove material and appear to have been pushed across the surface (nos. 22–24, 58; Fig. 2e, 6a,b; Pl. 5b,c,d). Rasps, which produce thinner toothed striations, also served to roughen back surfaces for adhesion. Evidence for the use of chisels with a curved blade and of gouges with a u-shaped blade for decoration is present as well (no. 206; Fig. 12g). Both leave a channel with a rounded profile. The gouge's primary purpose was to remove cancellous tissue from the medullar cavity of long bones, a preliminary step in the creation of pyxides, for example.

Both saws and knives were used for incised decoration. In the case of simple linear incisions, the v-shaped incision left by the knife distinguishes it from the straight-walled channel left by a saw (nos. 33, 215; Figs. 3c, 14b; Pls. 5a, 20a). A saw blade measuring 0.001 meter in thickness was used to create incised decoration on a mount fragment for example (no. 196; Fig. 12a; Pl. 24d). Knives with similarly thin blades are attested on objects ranging from simplest strip mounts to the most intricate pinheads and plaques carved in relief.

Both knife blades and chisels were recovered from Palatine East, along with bone and ivory handles in a variety of sizes (nos. 523–530; Figs. 39, 40; Pls. 47–49). The small knife blades recovered from both the first- and second-century contexts and late antique contexts are fragmentary and moderately or heavily corroded. In two cases they appear to fit bone handles that were discovered in the same contexts.[81] Because knives served a variety of purposes, however, they cannot definitely be associated with the carving industry. Of the fifteen straight-edged chisels uncovered, seven were concentrated in a single large late antique context with quantities of worked bone and ivory, and their diminutive size, with blades ranging from 0.008 to 0.023 meter in width, suggests that they may be part of the workshop assemblage.[82]

Drill holes, probably made using a bow drill, testify to the use of both center bits, in which the cutting element describes an arc around a point leaving a characteristic cylindrical hole with a central indentation (no. 101; Fig. 8f; Pl. 12f), and twist or auger bits, which leave a hole that is ogival or conical in form (no. 99; Fig. 8g; Pl. 12d). Although Roman compasses with variable radii are known, implements of the center bit type, with fixed radius scribing points, appear to have been preferred for the small ring and dot motifs that are both common decorative motifs and mark the values on dice.[83] Double ring and dot motifs may have been created using a tool with two or more scribing points or by using two tools with scribing points of varying radii.[84] Pressure from the center bit sometimes deforms thin strips, leaving protrusions on the back surface (no. 201; Fig. 12i; Pl. 19c).

Palatine East is especially rich in lathe-turning evidence. Not only do finished objects display the remarkable skill of the artisan working on a very small scale— the decoration of pin heads, for example—but unfinished pieces and debris in bone and ivory testify to the use of the lathe for a variety of objects. The small lathes used for these purposes were most likely reciprocating bow-driven models, although evidence from turned metal vessels suggests that continuous-rotation lathes may have been available as well.[85] Finished and unfinished objects frequently retain the characteristic indentation where the matrix was attached to the lathe stock, as well as chatter marks associated with turning (no. 587; Fig. 44f; Pl. 54a).[86] Unfinished pieces allow us to follow the progression from preliminary shaping of the matrix with a chisel or knife, to attachment to the lathe stock, through the turning process (nos. 95, 96; Fig. 8b,c; Pl. 12a,b). In the case of small cylindrical objects, the roughly shaped blank was fitted between two non-rotating, pointed or conical centers (the head and tail stocks), and rotated against a cutting tool by means of a cord wrapped around one end of the blank and pulled back and forth. Hollow cylindrical matrices—used for hinges, for example (nos. 246, 247; Fig. 16g)—were attached to the centers by means of wooden plugs passed through the bone or inserted at both ends. Debris from the turning of flat or concave surfaces is especially prevalent in the first- and early second-century A.D. layers.[87] It takes the form of segments of roughly square (in the case of bone) or circular (in the case of ivory) offcuts that are the debris remaining after the disk had been shaped using the lathe and freed from the blank (nos. 78–92). On some examples, a jagged bottom edge indicates that the disk was not cut completely through on the lathe (no. 86; Fig. 7b; Pl. 11c). Many offcuts have one or two oblique chisel cuts, by which the blank was broken apart to free the disk after turning (no. 88; Fig. 7a). Given the thinness of the offcuts, it is likely that they were mounted on a faceplate by means of nails or glue before being turned on an axis perpendicular to the center, or headstock. The presence of considerable lathing debris of this sort distinguishes the Palatine East material from that of Pheidias's workshop, where the ivory debris is primarily in the form of blanks or debris cut from longitudinal sections.[88]

Viewed together, the finished and unfinished objects and the considerable amounts of manufacturing debris provide a picture of a flourishing urban industry. The remains chart not only the changing fashions and patterns of consumption of its clientele over several centuries but expand our knowledge of the relation of the materials to one another at the artisanal level, especially bone to ivory, beyond what can be gleaned from ancient literary sources.

Whether the site functioned at a higher level as well in late antiquity—that is, as a center for ivory carving of the sort preserved on ceremonial diptychs and on relief plaques for furniture—remains an open question. Valuable remains of this type are not likely to be preserved among the debris associated with manufacturing sites. Larger objects, such as plaques that were broken or damaged during the carving process, could be recycled as more mundane objects—dice, gaming pieces, or even pin heads, for example—or resold for other uses, leaving little if any evidence of the range of objects that may have been created. As at Sparta and elsewhere, however, it is likely that carvers at Palatine East worked at various levels and on a variety of objects in both materials. Ivory caskets and diptychs were extensions of the furniture makers' craft, which was practiced at Palatine

East in both the early and late antique periods, and the exceptional presence of ivory debris suggests that, at least in late antiquity, the more expensive material was readily available there and exploited not merely for utensils but as part of the furniture makers' art. Further excavation of the area would be an important step in attempting to clarify this and other issues and in better documenting Rome as a center for the continuation and dissemination of a revered craft tradition in late antiquity.

Whether the industry continued beyond the fifth century, when the series of deposits ends at this location, is also open to question. Archaeological evidence demonstrates that the Palatine, like many other sectors of the city, had begun to undergo substantial transformation already at the beginning of the fifth century, with some areas subject to abandonment and despoliation, while others were maintained and remained in use. At Palatine East, for example, parts of the domus were abandoned and filled with rubble during the course of the forth and fifth centuries and the fountain complex was abandoned sometime after A.D. 425–455.[89] Despoliation and dumping in the Vigna Barberini above Palatine East point clearly to the gradual abandonment of buildings in that area as well, with many buildings falling into disuse by the beginning of the fifth century, before the sack of Genseric in A.D. 455, even though the imperial palace continued to function as a seat of power well beyond this date.[90] Burials, both sporadic and in the form of small cemeteries, beginning in the sixth or perhaps late fifth century, further testify to the transformation of the area in the early medieval period.[91] Whether these disruptions had a significant impact on the trade in ivory or on the carving industry in late fifth- and sixth-century Rome cannot be known for certain. Given the dearth of manufacturing evidence, however, it is interesting to note the corresponding lack of ivory carvings assigned on the basis of style or iconography to the western Mediterranean area during this period. For example, only one sixth-century consular diptych has been assigned to Rome.[92]

Recent studies, however, have painted a less bleak picture of the changing fabric of the city than such transformations suggest.[93] Although depopulated, Rome remained a significant economic and religious center, with many functioning and well-maintained areas.[94] Even in areas of despoliation and depopulation, spaces were often only partially abandoned, as in the case of the Palatine East domus, or reutilized. On the nearby Celian, for example, abandoned spaces in the northern sector of the mid-second-century Basilica Hilariana were reoccupied by artisans workshops.[95] Recent excavations in the exedra of the Crypta Balbi at the southern edge of the Campus Martius, moreover, suggest that at least by the second half of the seventh century Rome was again a center for the carving of both bone and ivory.[96] Located in an area of the city that was continuously inhabited, even when the city shrank during late antiquity and the Middle Ages, the deposit included tools and objects and manufacturing debris in metal, glass, bone, and ivory, which documents the area as a center of artisanal activity during this period. Comparison with objects of the same kind found in Lombard tombs in Italy and elsewhere suggests that the output was at least partially exported.[97] The excavators have speculated that the workshop was located in the nearby monastery of San Lorenzo in Pallacinis.[98] The remains of an ecclesiastical throne veneered in bone from a tenth-century context at the same site are dated by the excavators to the second half of the eighth century.[99] The throne, which features ajouré bone plaques with incised decoration, not unlike their distant ancestors from Sparta, was probably locally made as well. Such remains bring us full circle, from artisanal centers associated with Greek sanctuaries to those working in proximity to, and frequently in the service of, the church in the Middle Ages and beyond. Together with Palatine East, they point to the need to reevaluate Rome's role as an artistic center, with artisans carrying on a respected and long-standing tradition of carving ivory and bone within the same setting for a variety of clients.

CATALOGUE

The bone and ivory assemblage presented here represents a selection from over fifteen hundred objects in bone and ivory recovered from the northeast slope of the Palatine Hill. It includes both a wide variety of artifacts and considerable amounts of manufacturing debris, with emphasis on material that provides evidence for a bone- and ivory-working industry that appears to have functioned over several centuries. All significant artifacts are included. In the cases of manufacturing evidence in the form of debris and of artifact types with nondiagnostic character, a representative sample of material has been selected, with the goal of elucidating the nature of a production center. The organization of the catalogue reflects this emphasis as well, beginning with manufacturing evidence of a general nature, followed by classes of material—notably furniture and pins—for which significant amounts of identifiable manufacturing debris survive, suggesting specialization at an industrial level. The remaining classes of material, including jewelry, dolls, and gaming pieces, survive in smaller numbers but also in association with identifiable manufacturing debris, providing evidence of the diverse production associated with the site. In many cases, given the continuity of carving traditions and types of artifacts over long periods, precise dating of objects is difficult or impossible.[1]

Unless comparison to securely dated material allows greater precision, entries are grouped by period (I–XII) and by stratigraphic context. The context date represents an estimate of when the deposit was closed, based usually on analysis of pottery and/or coins, and provides only a terminus ante quem for the bone and ivory contained within the context. Moderate amounts of residual, or earlier, material are present in many of the late antique contexts, and in some cases objects may considerably predate the time when they became part of the Palatine East stratigraphic sequence. The "heirloom" factor also must be taken into account. Prized objects in ivory, as well as bone, were undoubtedly hoarded, surfacing in deposits that considerably postdate their manufacture. Significant remains that appear to belong to this assemblage from disturbed medieval (Sector C) and later contexts containing large amounts of residual material have been included in the catalogue as well.[2]

In keeping with the focus of this study, a large proportion of the material has been drawn, with the aim of providing multiple views and details of manufacture, such as tool marks, that are not visible in photographs.

A	Sector A
B	Sector B
C	Sector C
D	Sector D
SF	Surface find
L.	Length
W.	Width
H.	Height
Th.	Thickness
DH.	Diameter of head
DN.	Diameter of neck
DS.	Diameter of shaft
HH.	Height of head

Periods

I	Fourth–third centuries B.C.
II	Second–first centuries B.C.
III	Ca. A.D. 1–50
IV	Ca. A.D. 50–100
V	Second century A.D.
VI	Ca. first half of the third century A.D.
VII	Ca. mid- to late third century A.D.
VIII	Ca. late third or early fourth century A.D. through ca. A.D. 500
IX	Ca. A.D. 500–1000
X	Ca. A.D. 1000–1400
XI	Ca. A.D. 1400–1900
XII	Twentieth–twenty-first centuries

Within the catalogue, excavated material is identified, for example, as "5. Ring. D105:IV/1883"; the entry represents:

Catalogue number = 1–648

Catalogue object = ring, etc.

Excavation sector = A–D

Context number = arabic numeral

Period = roman numeral

Accession number = arabic numeral

Material is bone, unless indicated as "ivory." All measurements are in meters.

Remains from both the first and second centuries and from late antique contexts allow us to follow the manufacturing process from the initial preparation of blanks to the finished object. In addition, they provide insights into the materials, tools, and techniques used to create a variety of objects. Most of the material is debris. The large amount from bone carving includes epiphyses and rings that were discarded when the bone was cut to size, as well as blanks and debris from more advanced stages of carving. Ivory debris is in the form of offcuts, blanks, and small pieces that are discards. In some cases the remains can be identified as blanks for specific types of objects, such as pins, dice, or mounts, but in many cases the preliminary shape is generic and could serve for a variety of objects. In addition, it is sometimes difficult to distinguish blanks from material discarded after the matrix was cut to size. In the catalogue, objects identified as blanks have defined shapes for the most part, such as wedges or rectangles, and two or more sawn edges.

Evidence for the use of drills with center and auger bits, scribing tools, and lathes is present in the form of debris and unfinished objects. They testify to the industrial level of activity at Palatine East. Lathing debris includes offcuts in bone and ivory from the turning of flat or convex surfaces as well as debris from the turning of roughly cylindrical blanks, preliminarily shaped with a chisel or knife, to create objects ranging from pins to furniture mounts and hinges.

I. Preliminary Cutting and Shaping
A. Epiphyses
The small number of sawn epiphyses (approximately twenty, of which a representative sample is catalogued), especially in relation to the number of rings and other working debris, suggests that for the most part they were removed elsewhere at the time of slaughter. The metapodials were then cut

to size by the craftsperson. Epiphyses from Palatine East exhibit both careful sawing at a right angle to the bone and oblique sawing in combination with percussion.

SECOND CENTURY

1. Epiphysis. D82:V/3256 (Pl. 1c)

   L.0.047; W.0.046. Sawn cattle metacarpus, distal.

MID- TO LATE THIRD CENTURY

2. Epiphysis. A135:VII /2403 (Fig. 1b)

   L.0.070; W.0.060. Sawn cattle metacarpus, distal.

EARLY FOURTH CENTURY

3. Epiphysis. A38:VIII/1689 (Pl. 1d)

   L.0.057; W.0.079. Sawn cattle metacarpus, distal.

SECOND HALF OF THE FIFTH CENTURY

4. Epiphysis. B180:VIII/2445 (Fig. 1a; Pl. 1b)

   L.0.045; W.0.048. Partially sawn cattle metatarsus, proximal. Separated from matrix by percussion.

5. Epiphysis. B270:VIII/3143 (Pl. 1a)

   L.0.039; W.0.070. Sawn cattle metacarpus, proximal. Preliminary cut from saw blade at upper edge.

B. Rings

More than fifty complete examples of sawn horizontal sections from long bones survive along with more numerous fragments. Most are between one- and two-centimeters long and are debris produced when the craftsperson cut the bone matrix to size after removal of the epiphysis. One end frequently exhibits a combination of sawing at an oblique angle and percussion, a procedure commonly associated with removal of the epiphysis. The other end is usually cleanly sawn at a right angle to the bone. In cases where both ends are cleanly sawn, the rings may have been intended as blanks. Frequently, the medullary cavity has been scraped to remove cancellous tissue, a step preliminary to mounting

the bone on a lathe or to the creation of hollow objects such as pyxides.

FIRST CENTURY

6. Ring. A194:III–IV/3990 (Pl. 2c)

   L.0.025; D.0.032. Both ends and one side cleanly sawn.

7. Ring. D105:IV/1883

   L.0.033; D.0.043. Both ends cleanly sawn. Interior smoothed. Probable blank.

LATE FIRST TO SECOND CENTURY

8. Ring. D83:IV–V/3446

   L.0.033; D.0.044. Both ends cleanly sawn. Interior partially smoothed.

9. Ring. D83:IV–V/3471 (Pl. 2e)

   L.0.010; D.0.042. Oblique sawing with percussion on one end. Interior smoothed.

10. Ring. D85:V/3359

    L.0.010; D.0.047. Oblique sawing on one end. Interior smoothed.

EARLY FOURTH CENTURY

11. Ring. A36:VIII/711

    L.0.022; D.0.045. Oblique sawing with percussion on one end.

    St. Clair in Hostetter et al. 1994, 170, Fig. 52.

12. Ring. A36:VIII/704

    L.0.025; D.0.044. Oblique sawing with percussion on one end.

    St. Clair in Hostetter et al. 1994, 170, Fig. 52.

13. Ring. A67:VIII/1729 (Fig. 2a)

    L.0.012; D.0.040. Oblique sawing with percussion on one end. Interior smoothed.

14. Ring. A33:VIII/1710

    L.0.020; D.0.049. Oblique sawing with percussion on one end.

MID-FOURTH TO FIFTH CENTURY

15. Ring. A20:VIII/1706

    L.0.014; D.0.047. Oblique sawing with percussion on one end.

16. Ring. B180:VIII/2440 (Pl. 2d)

    L.0.015; D.0.045. Oblique sawing on one end. Saw marks indicate rotation of matrix. Interior smoothed.

17. Ring. B270:VIII/3638 (Pl. 2b)

    L.0.012; D.0.033. Both ends cleanly sawn.

MEDIEVAL TO MODERN

18. Ring. B255:X/2535 (Pl. 2a)

    L.0.010; D.0.032. Oblique sawing with percussion on one end.

19. Ring. B263:X/2476

    L.0.015; D.0.055 Oblique sawing with percussion on one end. Saw marks indicate rotation of matrix. Interior smoothed.

20. Ring segment. B258:X/2558 (Fig. 2c)

    L.0.007; W.0.041. Half ring. Oblique sawing on one end. Saw marks indicate rotation of matrix. Interior partially smoothed.

C. Blanks and Debris

Rectangular, square, cylindrical, and wedge-shaped blanks were created from sawn longitudinal sections of elephant tusks and long bones. Scapulae and ribs were used to create thin blanks. In the case of bone, cancellous material is frequently visible on one or more surfaces. Blanks for specific types of objects such as dice or pins can sometimes be identified, but most of the remains are debris discarded after the matrix was cut to size. In addition to sawing, many examples provide evidence for the use of straight-edged and claw chisels, as well as rasps. Thin strips or plaques frequently have one edge sawn obliquely, or mitered. In most cases they are debris or blanks for furniture or box molding strips, which were cut at 45-degree angles to make 90 degree square corners.

SECOND HALF OF THE FIRST CENTURY

21. Blank or debris. A189:IV/3985 (Pl. 9a)

    L.0.059; W.0.010; Th.0.013. Rectangular piece sawn on three sides. Fourth side concave with traces of cancellous tissue.

22. Blank or debris. D219:IV/4764 (Fig. 6b; Pl. 5d)

    L.0.091; W.0.026; Th.0.002. Broken on one side. Thin subrectangular blank sawn obliquely at one end. One convex surface. Claw chisel marks on both surfaces.

23. Debris. D219:IV/4775 (Fig. 6a; Pl. 5c)

    L.0.049; W.0.047; Th.0.003. Broken on one side and at one angle. Thin triangular fragment probably from scapula. Claw chisel marks on both surfaces.

24. Blank or debris. D219:IV/4763 (Fig. 2e)

    L.0.107; W.0.026; Th.0.004. Broken at one end. Subrectangular fragment. One convex surface with claw chisel marks.

    St. Clair 1996, 373–374, Fig. 16.

25. Blank or debris. D98:IV/3717

    L.0.031; D.0.004. Ivory. Broken at both ends. Fragment of cylinder, slightly curved at one end.

LATE FIRST TO SECOND CENTURY

26. Blank. D83:IV–V/3585 (Fig. 3a; Pl. 4b)

    L.0.092; W.0.050; Th.0.010. Broken at one end. Roughly wedge-shaped blank with one convex surface and polygonal rod-shaped protrusion, created by chisel, at one end. Traces of cancellous tissue on edges and back of blank.

27. Blank or debris. D83:IV–V/2820 (Pl. 4a)

    L.0.071; W.0.029; Th.0.008. Roughly rectangular piece sawn on three sides. Convex in section at top.

28. Blank or debris. D83:IV–V/342 (Pl. 4c)

    L.0.111; W.0.047; Th.0.002. Broken on two edges. Thin subrectangular piece from scapula. Cancellous tissue on one surface.

29. Blank or debris. D83:IV–V/3580 (Fig. 5a; Pl. 4d)

    L.0.111; W.0.067; Th.0.003. Partially broken along two edges. Thin triangular piece from scapula. Slightly convex in section.

30. Blank. D83:IV–V/3601 (Fig. 5b)

L.0.085; W.0.23; Th.0.004. Broken at both ends with remnant of sawn edge at one end. Probably from rib. Diminishing thickness of compact tissue visible in horizontal section. Cancellous tissue on back.

31. Blank. D193:IV–V/4585 (Fig. 5e)

L.0.068; W.0.030; Th.0.004. Broken at one end. Wedge-shaped section of long bone, sawn on both sides and preserved edge. Cancellous tissue on back.

SECOND CENTURY

32. Debris. A194:V/4555 (Pl. 7b)

L.0.057; W.0.008; Th.0.003. Ivory. Sawn on one end. Partially delaminated sliver from longitudinal section of tusk.

33. Debris. D122:V/4201 (Fig. 3c; Pl. 5a)

L.0.046; W.0.026; Th.0.008. Roughly wedge-shaped piece sawn at top. Convex in section. Sawn incision 0.028 in length perpendicular to sawn edge.

34. Debris. D131:V/4901 (Pl. 9c)

L.0.035; D.0.015; Th.0.010. Ivory. Broken at one end, chipped on one side. Fragment of rod shaped by chisel. Polygonal to oval in section.

LATE SECOND TO THIRD CENTURY

35. Blank. A123:V–VI/2363 (Pl. 10e)

L.0.072; W.0.007; Th.0.004. Wedge-shaped piece. Roughly rectangular in section with one slightly concave side. Probable pin blank.
St. Clair 1996, 373–374, Fig. 11.

36. Debris. A123:V–VI/ 2378 (Fig. 5c)

L.0.036; W.0.011; Th.0.010. Broken at one end. Rectangular fragment tapering slightly in profile. Roughly rectangular in section with cancellous tissue on one surface.
St. Clair 1996, 373–374, Fig. 11.

37. Blank or debris. A123:V–VI/2355

L.0.082; W.0.010; Th.0.005. Wedge-shaped piece. Roughly rectangular in section with one concave surface.
St. Clair 1996, 373–374, Fig. 11.

LATE THIRD CENTURY

38. debris. A148:VII/2930 (Fig. 4b; Pl. 7d)

L.0.033; W.0.020; Th.0.003. Ivory. Broken at one end and on one side. Delaminated. Roughly rectangular fragment.

EARLY FOURTH CENTURY

39. Debris. B353:VIII/4374

L.0.051; W.0.008; Th.0.004. Broken at one end. Rectangular fragment with two obliquely sawn edges.

40. Blank. B357:VIII/4369 (Fig. 6h; Pl. 10c)

L.0.064; D.0.008. Polygonal blank shaped with a knife or chisel, tapering from pyramidal head to tip. Probable blank for pin.
St. Clair 1996, 373–374, Fig. 11.

41. Debris. A36:VIII/1685

L.0.027; W.0.010; Th.0.006. Ivory. Broken at one end and on one side. Rectangular fragment with oblique chisel cut on one surface. Rectangular in section.

42. Debris. A36:VIII/691

L.0.042; W.0.015; Th.0.006. Ivory. Broken at top and bottom. Wedge-shaped fragment sawn on four sides. Polygonal in section, with one concave surface.

43. Blank. A16:VIII/431 (Fig. 6g)

L.0.060; D.0.010. Tip missing. Cylindrical piece tapering from flat summit to tip. Upper portion ovoid, lower circular in section. Probable blank for pin.
St. Clair in Hostetter et al. 1994, 168, Fig. 50.

44. Blank. A67:VIII/1757 (Pl. 3a)

L.0.111; W.0.023; Th.0.028. Radius with attached ulna. Sawn on four sides.

45. Blank. A67:VIII/1841 (Fig. 3b)

L.0.099; W.0.026; Th.0.008. Radius with attached ulna. Sawn on three sides.

46. Blank or debris. A22:VIII/1765 (Pl. 3d)

L.0.094; W.0.049; Th.0.017. Broken at one end. Metapodial sawn longitudinally.

47. Blank or debris. A33:VIII/1700 (Pl. 10a)

L.0.095; W.0.022; Th.0.008. Wedge-shaped piece
sawn on three sides. Polygonal in section. One
concave surface with cancellous tissue.

St. Clair 1996, 373–374, Fig. 11.

48. Blank. A34:VIII/746

L.0.053; W.0.010; Th.0.005. Broken at top and
bottom. Wedge-shaped blank sawn on four sides.
Cancellous tissue on two sides. Rectangular in
section.

49. Blank or debris. A12:VIII/1736 (Pl. 3c)

L.0.100; W.0.044; Th.0.023. Broken at one end.
Sawn longitudinal section of metapodial.

50. Debris. A20:VIII/771 (Fig. 4a; Pl. 6b)

L.0.042; W.0.018; Th.0.004. Ivory. Chipped and
delaminated. Oval fragment with one sawn surface.

St. Clair in Hostetter et al. 1994, 170, Fig. 52.

51. Debris. A67:VIII/1816 (Fig. 6c)

L.0.033; W.0.0012; Th.0.005. Half-cylindrical
piece tapering at one end. Pierced at wide end.
Chisel marks on outer surface. Saw marks on back.
Possible debris from half-columnar mount.

MID-FOURTH TO FIFTH CENTURY

52. Blank or debris. A20:VIII/772 (Pl. 8a)

L.0.052; W.0.007; Th.0.006. Ivory. Broken at one
end. Rod, shaped with chisel. Roughly rectangular
in section.

St. Clair in Hostetter et al. 1994, 168, Fig. 50.

53. Blank. A20:VIII/177 (Pl. 10b)

L.0.070; D.0.007. Chipped at summit. Cylindrical
piece tapering from flat summit to tip. Upper portion ovoid, lower portion circular in section. Rasp
marks on surface.

St. Clair in Hostetter et al. 1994, 168, Fig. 50.

54. Blank or debris. A12:VIII/402 (Fig. 6f)

L.0.088; W.0.012; Th.0.005. Wedge-shaped
piece. Polygonal in section. Cancellous tissue on
one surface.

55. Debris. A12:VIII/1724 (Fig. 4f)

L.0.024; W.0.007; Th.0.006. Ivory. Numerous
cracks. Irregular wedge-shaped splinter.

56. Blank or debris. B342:VIII/4751 (Pl. 9d)

L.0.045; W.0.010; Th.0.011. Rectangular piece
sawn on both ends. Oval in section at top, convex
at bottom, with cancellous tissue on concave
surface.

St. Clair 1996, 373–374, Fig. 12; St. Clair in
Hostetter et al. 1994, 168, Fig. 49.

57. Debris. B327:VIII/4378 (Fig. 4d)

L.0.028; W.0.010; Th.0.005. Ivory. Broken at one
end and on one side. Rectangular fragment with
oblique chisel cut on one surface. Rectangular in
section.

58. Debris. B276:VIII/2928 (Pl. 5b)

L.0.050; W.0.010; Th.0.003. Ivory. Broken one
end and one side. Rectangular fragment with claw
chisel marks on one surface.

59. Blank or debris. B295:VIII/3967

L.0.045; W.0.030; Th.0.002. Thin rectangular
piece from scapula or rib. Cancellous tissue on one
surface.

60. Blank. B270:VIII/3672 (Pl. 3b)

L.0.111; W.0.021; Th.0.012. Radius with
attached ulna. Sawn on four sides.

61. Blank or debris. B264:VIII/2683 (Fig. 5d;
Pl. 9b)

L.0.051; W.0.020; Th.0.009. Broken at both
ends. Wedge-shaped piece. Polygonal in section
with one convex and one concave side.

62. Blank or debris. B295:VIII/3737 (Fig. 6d;
Pl. 9e)

L.0.032; W.0.011; Th.0.008. Rod sawn on both
ends and shaped with a chisel. Polygonal in section. One concave side with cancellous tissue.

63. Debris. B294:VIII/3405 (Pl. 9f)

L.0.012; W.0.008; Th.0.006. Fragment of rod,
shaped with a chisel or knife. Polygonal in section.
See no. 62. A third similar piece (L.0.010) survives
from the same context.

64. Blank. B310:VIII/4149 (Fig. 4g; Pl. 6d)

L.0.059; W.0.037; Th.0.013. Ivory. Thick,
roughly rectangular piece sawn on four sides. Possible shadow of pulp cavity on concave surface.

St. Clair 1996, 373–374, Fig. 12.

65. Blank or debris. B340:VIII/ 4135 (Fig. 6i; Pl. 7c)

L.0.070; W.0.008; Th.0.005. Ivory. Rectangular piece with incised knife-cut design at one end. Rectangular in section.

66. Blank or debris. B270:VIII/ 3649 (Fig. 4c; Pl. 8d)

L.0.049; D.0.011. Ivory. Chipped. Thick rod, shaped by chisel. Roughly circular in section.

67. Blank or debris. B270:VIII/3666 (Pl. 8b)

L.0.084; W.0.006; Th.0.005. Ivory. One end broken. Wedge-shaped piece. Rectangular in section at top, triangular at bottom.

68. Debris. A9:VIII/1779 (Fig. 4e)

L.0.038; W.0.006; Th.0.007. Ivory. Broken at both ends and one side. Cracked. Rod fragment. Approximately square in section.

69. Blank. B270:VIII/4137

L.0.044; W.0.010; Th.0.009. Roughly rectangular piece with tapering profile. Square in section at larger end, rectangular at smaller.

70. Blank. B309:VIII/4013 (Fig. 5f)

L.0.030; W.0.009; Th.0.010. Rectangular piece tapering slightly in profile. All sides sawn. Square in section. Probable dice blank.

71. Blank. B310:VIII/4248

L.0.040; W.0.011; Th.0.008. Rectangular piece tapering slightly in profile. Approximately square in section. Possible blank for dice.

72. Blank or debris. B294:VIII/3341 (Pl. 10d)

L.0.080; D.0.008. Broken at tip. Roughly cylindrical fragment tapering from flat summit to tip. Ovoid in section at top, polygonal at bottom. Chisel and rasp marks on surface.

73. Blank. B340:VIII/4134 (Fig. 2b)

L.0.050; W.0.014; Th.0.008-0.005. Rectangular piece, roughly square in section. Sawn at both ends. Cancellous tissue on one side.

74. Blank or debris. B102:IX–X/1653

L:051; W:037. Rectangular piece sawn from diaphysis. Convex in section. Cancellous tissue on interior surface. Convex surface has chisel marks from preliminary shaping.

75. Debris. D16:X/2441

L.0.044; W.0.010; Th.0.010. Broken both ends. One surface chipped. Subrectangular fragment with slightly tapering profile. Sawn on four sides. Roughly rectangular in section.

76. Blank or debris. D12:XI–XII/3624

L.0.044; W.0.013; Th.0.009. Rectangular piece. Convex in section. Cancellous tissue on interior surface.

77. Blank. B31:XII/114

L.0.092; D.0.006. Tip missing. Cylindrical piece tapering from flat summit to tip. Saw and rasp marks from preliminary working. Upper shaft oval, lower circular in section. Probable blank for needle or other utensil.

II. Turning

A. *Offcuts*

Debris from the turning of flat or convex bone blanks to create disks of varying dimensions is the dominant form of lathing evidence in the early contexts, although it occurs in the late antique contexts as well, along with ivory debris from the turning of more complex objects.[3] A jagged bottom edge indicates that the object was not cut completely through on the lathe. Many examples have one or two oblique chisel cuts, by which the blank was broken apart to free the disk after turning.

78. Offcut. D97:III–IV/3648

D.0.080; L.0.04; W.0.035; Th. (max.) 0.007. Broken at one end. Fragment of long bone from which disk was cut. Oblique chisel cut at one end.

79. Offcut. D98:IV/3683

D.0.050; L.0.025; W.0.025; Th.0.010. Broken at both ends. Fragment of long bone from which disk was cut. Bottom edge incompletely turned.

80. Offcut. D98:IV/3687 (Pl. 11b)

D.0.050; L.0.037; W.0.035; Th.0.004. Broken at both ends. Fragment of long bone from which disk was cut. Bottom edge incompletely turned.

St. Clair 1996, 371, Fig. 14.

LATE FIRST TO EARLY SECOND CENTURY

81. Offcut. D64:IV–V/3193

D.0.080; L.0.051; W.0.034; Th. (max.) 0.008. Broken at one end. Fragment of long bone from which disk was cut. Oblique chisel cut at one end. Bottom edge incompletely turned.

82. Offcut. D72:IV–V/3125 (Pl. 11a)

D.0.065; L.0.071; W.0.025; Th.0.006. Broken at one end. Fragment of long bone from which disk was cut. Cancellous tissue on top surface. Oblique chisel cut at one end.

St. Clair 1996, 371, Fig. 14.

83. Offcut. D83:IV–V/3296 (Pl. 11d)

D.0.065; L.0.039; W.0.043; Th.0.005. Broken at both ends. Fragment of long bone from which disk was cut. Cancellous material on back.

St. Clair 1996, 371, Fig. 14.

84. Offcut. D83:IV–V/3321

D.0.080; L.0.035; W.0.033; Th.0.004. Broken at both ends. Fragment of long bone from which disk was cut. Cancellous material on back. Encrusted and uniformly gray from burning.

85. Offcut. D83:IV–V/3452 (Fig. 7c; Pl. 11e)

D.0.065; L. (max.) 0.038; W.0.063; Th.0.007. Broken at both ends. Fragment of long bone from which disk was cut. Cancellous material on back.

St. Clair 1996, 371, Fig. 14.

86. Offcut. D83:IV–V/3453 (Fig. 7b; Pl. 11c)

D.0.050; L.0.038; W.0.035; Th.0.005. Broken at one end. Fragment of long bone from which disk was cut. Oblique chisel cut at one end. Bottom edge incompletely turned.

St. Clair 1996, 371, Fig. 14.

EARLY FOURTH CENTURY

87. Offcut? A33:VIII/1718 (Fig. 7g; Pl. 7a)

D.0.210; L.0.050; W.0.007; Th.0.008. Ivory. Broken at both ends. Fragment of tusk with evidence of turning on concave surface. Oblique chisel cut on outer convex surface. Top surface partially pierced by small hole.

88. Offcut. A38:VIII/890 (Fig. 7a)

D.0.050; L.0.036; Th.0.007. Broken at one end. Fragment of long bone from which disk was cut. Oblique chisel cut at one end.

St. Clair in Hostetter et al. 1994, 170, Fig. 52.

89. Offcut or debris. A67:VIII/1747 (Fig. 7e; Pl. 7e)

D.0.111; W.0.012; Th.0.010. Ivory. Cracked and delaminated. Restored from several pieces. Fragment of tusk with evidence of turning on concave surface. Both ends cut at oblique angle to surface.

90. Offcut or debris. A37:VIII/652 (Fig. 8h)

D.0.075 (ext.), 0.035 (int.); L.0.020; Th.0.003. Broken at one end and on both sides. Thin fragment turned with series of concentric grooves on one surface.

91. Offcut or debris. A67:VIII/1835 (Fig. 7d)

L.0.034; W.0.006. Ivory. Sliver with evidence of turning on concave side.

MID-FOURTH TO FIFTH CENTURY

92. Offcut. A12:VIII/1812 (Fig. 7f; Pl. 6c)

D.0.070; W.0.007; Th.0.011. Ivory. Broken at both ends. Cracked and delaminated. Fragment of tusk from which ring was cut. Bottom interior and exterior edges incompletely turned.

St. Clair 1996, 373–374, Fig. 12.

B. Other Turned Blanks and Debris

Debris from the turning of cylindrical objects is frequently in the form of partially turned blanks that preserve evidence of preliminary shaping with a chisel or knife, the indentation from attachment to the lathe stock, and the turning that created the final form.[4]

93. Debris. D58:V/3009 (Fig. 8a; Pl. 12c)

D.0.008; L.0.006. Broken at one end. Fragment of turned cylinder. Lathe stock center mark on turned end.

St. Clair 1996, 373–374, Fig. 13.

EARLY FOURTH CENTURY

94. Blank. A34:VIII/745 (Fig. 8e; Pl. 8c)

L.0.035; W.0.014. Ivory. Broken at turned end. Rod, with traces of turning on one end. Triangular in section,

St. Clair in Hostetter et al. 1994, 170, Fig. 52.

MID-FOURTH TO FIFTH CENTURY

95. Blank. A20:VIII/244 (Fig. 8b; Pl. 12a)

L.0.040; D.0.008. Partially turned cylindrical blank shaped with knife or chisel. Turned end has series of raised rings. Lathe stock center mark on turned end.

St. Clair 1996, 373–374, Figs. 13, 21; St. Clair in Hostetter et al. 1994, 168, Fig. 50.

96. Blank. A20:VIII/462.(Fig. 8c; Pl. 12b)

L.0.037; D.0.006. Partially turned cylindrical blank shaped with knife or chisel. Turned end has series of raised rings. Lathe stock center mark on turned end.

St. Clair 1996, 373–374, Fig. 13; St. Clair in Hostetter et al. 1994, 168, Fig. 50.

97. Blank. B309:VIII/3877 (Fig. 8d)

L.0.022; D.0.016; Th.0.009 (turned end). Broken at turned end. Cylindrical blank shaped with knife or chisel. Roughly oval in section. Remains of turned shaft on one end.

III. Drilling and Scribing

Drill holes, probably made using a bow drill, testify to the use of twist or auger bits, which leave holes that are ogival or conical in form, and center bits, in which the cutting element describes an arc around a point leaving a characteristic cylindrical hole with a central indentation.[5] Both types were used for a variety of purposes. It is speculated that tools of the center-bit type with fixed radius scribing points were used for ring and dot motifs rather than compasses, although Roman compasses with variable radii are known.[6] Double ring and dot motifs may have been created by a tool with two or more scribing points or by two or more tools with scribing points of varying radii. Two epiphyses from disturbed contexts drilled with cross patterns provide evidence of these techniques (nos. 102, 103). They may be practice pieces or debris, or they may have functioned as amulets or even gaming pieces.

FOURTH TO FIFTH CENTURY

98. Debris. D111:VIII/3883 (Fig. 8i; Pl. 12e)

L.0.032; W.0.015; Th.0.005. Broken on all sides. Probable compass-scribed fragment with incised concentric circles around a point. Saw marks on front and back. Possible practice piece.

St. Clair 1996, 373–374, Figs. 13, 20.

SECOND HALF OF THE FIFTH CENTURY

99. Debris. B296:VIII/4754 (Fig. 8g; Pl. 12d)

L.0.017; D.0.012. Broken in half longitudinally. Cylindrical piece shaped with knife or chisel. Sawn at both ends. One end pierced by hole 0.008 deep, 0.045 wide from auger bit.

St. Clair 1996, 373–374, Fig. 13.

MEDIEVAL TO MODERN

100. Debris. C59:IX–XII/2291 (Fig. 8j)

L.0.075; W.0.35; Th.0.013. Broken at one end. Long bone pierced by hole 0.004 deep, 0.007 wide from auger bit.

101. Debris. C153:IX–XII/3437 (Fig. 8f; Pl. 12f)

L.0.018; D.0.011. Broken in half longitudinally. Cylindrical piece shaped with knife or chisel. Sawn at both ends. One end pierced by hole 0.005 deep, 0.004 wide from center bit.

St. Clair 1996, 373–374, Figs. 13, 19.

102. Epiphysis with cross. B57:XI/665 (Fig. 8k;
     Pl. 13b)
     L.0.062; W.0.053; Th.0.035. Broken on one end.
     Decorated with ring and dot motifs in form of a
     cross, four vertical (the topmost is only partially
     preserved), and two indicating the arms.
103. Epiphysis with cross. B178:XI/5215 (Pl. 13a)
     L.0.076; W.0.043; Th.0.035. Broken on one side.
     Epiphysis drilled with five circular indentations in
     form of cross. The bottom hole is a nutrient
     foramen. Above the cross, the bone is pierced by a
     hole 0.004 in diameter, suggesting the possibility
     that this may have been worn as an amulet.

FURNITURE AND BOXES

Remains from the decoration of furniture and
boxes are present in both the early and late contexts. They are by far the predominant remains in
the first- and second-century contexts. They
include bands or strips that were used as framing
elements and as veneer; inlays; plaques; cylindrical
and circular mounts; and box parts. Several hinge
parts, perhaps associated with box lids, were uncovered. Decoration is executed in relief, incised lines,
and intaglio. Traces of red or brown stain are present on a few examples. For the most part, the
remains are debris associated with the manufacturing process. They include unfinished pieces and
pieces that were most likely broken during manufacture. There is considerable debris from bands
and framing strips that were cut to size before
being mounted on wooden frameworks.[7]

Remains from first- and second-century contexts find parallels among first-century B.C.–
first-century A.D. funerary couch remains from
tombs in Italy and Gaul, and point to Rome as a
likely center of manufacture for furniture of this
general type. The third through fifth century contexts contain some residual material that appears to
be associated with the first and second centuries

(nos. 218, 230, 237, 239), but for the most part
the remains find parallels among late antique
objects that are widespread throughout the empire
but often attributed to Egypt.[8] The Palatine East
remains point clearly to Rome as a carving center
in its own right, employing a common Mediterranean vocabulary to satisfy the fashion for bone and
ivory artworks and artifacts during this period.

I. Undecorated Mounts and Boxes
A. Strips, Veneers, and Inlay
Strips or bands that were used as framing elements
on furniture and boxes, as well as fragments of thin
veneer, appear in both the early and late contexts.
Veneer and inlays were applied to both flat and
turned surfaces. They were held in place by glue or
attached with dowels. Framing strips protected the
slightly recessed veneers in addition to forming the
borders at the edges of wooden frameworks. Finished examples rarely exceed 0.003 in thickness;
unfinished examples may be considerably thicker.
Most of the Palatine East examples appear to be
debris left over after the strips were cut to size, or
from preliminary stages of carving. Thicker examples were cut to size using a saw, but thin strips
often were scored with a knife or chisel and broken
by percussion. Many framing strips are mitered.
Some have one or two beveled long edges.

FIRST CENTURY
104. Strip fragment. D140:III–IV/4326
     L.0.030; W.0.013; Th.0.001. Broken at one end.
     Smoothed on both sides.
105. Veneer fragment. D98:IV/3813 (Fig. 9a;
     Pl. 14c)
     L.0.052; W.0.033; Th.0.001. Broken at one end
     and along one edge. Warped. Mitered at one end.
     Claw chisel marks on both sides. From scapula.
106. Veneer fragment. D98:IV/3816 (Pl. 14b)
     L.0.050; W.0.026; Th.0.001. Broken at one end.
     Other broken by scoring and percussion. Warped.
     Claw chisel marks on one side.

107. Strip fragment. D79:IV/3339

L.0.012; W.0.022.; Th.0.001. Broken at one end. Chisel marks on back.

108. Strip fragment. D103:IV/3801

L.0.041; W.0.023; Th.0.002. Broken at one end and along one edge. Other broken by percussion. Chisel marks on back.

109. Strip fragment. D103:IV/3817

L.0.042; W.0.019; Th.0.003. Broken at one end and along both edges. One beveled edge. Chisel marks on both sides.

110. Strip. D89:IV/3632 (Fig. 9b)

L.0.030; W.0.026; Th.0.001. Two mitered edges. Claw chisel marks on both sides. Probable debris from cutting to size.

111. Strip fragment. D89:IV/3667

L.0.044; W.0.027; Th.0.002. Broken along both edges. One beveled edge. Claw chisel marks on both sides.

112. Veneer fragment. D89:IV/3669 (Pl. 14a)

L.0.043; W.0.027; Th.0.001. Broken on both sides. Encrusted. Mitered at one end. Fragment of metal pinhead approximately 0.0025 in diameter preserved at one end. Claw chisel marks on both sides.

113. Strip or veneer fragment. D72:IV–V/3124

L.0.060; W.0.014; Th.0.002. Broken at both ends and along one side. Rasp marks on one side.

114. Veneer fragment. D83:IV–V/3365

L.0.080; W.0.039; Th.0.002. Broken at both ends. Rasp marks on both sides.

115. Veneer fragment. D83:IV–V/3465 (Fig. 9c; Pl. 14g)

L.0.131; W.0.20; Th.0.002. Broken at one end and along one side. Warped. Claw chisel marks on both sides.

116. Strip. D83:IV–V/3363 (Fig. 9d; Pl. 14d)

L.0.051; W.0.017; Th.0.001. Rectangular with inset at one end, perhaps for rabbeted joint.

117. Strip fragment. D83:IV–V3398 (Pl. 14e)

L.0.060; W.0.042; Th.0.001. Broken at one end. Thin rectangular fragment. Claw chisel marks on one surface.

118. Veneer fragment. D131:V/4133 (Pl. 14f)

L.0.035; W.0.021; Th.0.001. Broken at one end and along one side. Oblique tear at one end, 0.008 long, perhaps from nail. Green stain from contact with metal.

119. Strip fragment. D82:V/3298

L.0.45; W.0.018; Th.0.003. Broken at one end. Other end mitered.

120. Strip fragment. A194:V/4231

L.0.025; W.0.023; Th.0.001. Broken along one end and one edge. Thin square piece with both sides smoothed.

121. Strip fragment. D122:V/4244

L.0.050; W.0.014; Th.0.002. Broken at one end and along one side. Warped. Beveled at one end.

122. Strip fragment. D104:V/3804

L.0.047; W.0.018; Th.0.004. Broken at one end. Stained brown.

123. Strip fragment. A162:VII/3475 (Fig. 9e)

L.0.036; W.0.007; Th.0.002. One end broken by percussion. Other end mitered. Pierced by heavily corroded bronze nail. Claw chisel marks on one side.

124. Strip fragment. A97:VIII/2292

L.0.030; W.0.020; Th.0.002. Broken at one end. Claw chisel marks on back.

125. Strip fragment. A135:VIII/2434

L.0.027; W.0.024; Th.0.002. Broken at one end and along one edge. Claw chisel marks on back.

126. Strip fragment. A140:VIII/2418

L.0.031; W.0.008; Th.0.001. Broken at both ends. Narrow strip smoothed on both sides.

127. Strip fragment or debris. A148:VIII/2930
L.0.034; W.0.020; Th.0.003. Ivory. Broken at
both ends and along one side.

128. Strip fragment. A105:VIII/1959 (Fig. 9f;
Pl. 6a)
L.0.064; W.0.015; Th.0.004. Ivory. Restored from
numerous slivers. Broken one end. Roughly rectangular in section with one slightly convex surface
and one raised edge.
St. Clair 1996, 373–374, Fig. 12.

129. Strip. A38:VIII/880
L.0.080; W.0.020; Th.0.002. Broken along one
edge and at one end.
St. Clair in Hostetter et al. 1994, 170, Fig. 52.

130. Strip. A36:VIII/1688 (Fig. 9g; Pl. 18i)
L.0.063; W.0.017; Th.0.002. Slight taper in
width. Mitered at one end. Broken by percussion at other. Rasp marks on back. Stained
brown.

MID-FOURTH TO FIFTH CENTURY

131. Strip. A20:VIII/773
L.0.056; W.0.019; Th.0.001. Broken along one
side and on one end.
St. Clair in Hostetter et al. 1994, 170, Fig. 52.

132. Strip fragment. A67:VIII/2260
L.0.070; W.0.005; Th.0.002. Ivory. Broken at
both ends. Two beveled edges.

133. Strip fragment. B206:VIII/2262
L.0.032; W.0.006; Th.0.001. Broken at both ends
and along one edge. One inset edge.

134. Strip fragment. B209:VIII/2293
L.0.035; W.0.005; Th.0.002. Broken at one end.
Smooth on both sides.

135. Strip fragment. B270:VIII/3132
L.0.055; W.0.015; Th.0.001. Broken at both
ends. Warped. Chisel marks on one side.

136. Strip. B270:VIII/4575 (Fig. 10a)
L.0.122; W.0.024; Th.0.001. Broken at both ends
and on one side. Warped. Thin subrectangular
strip fragment with traces of cancellous tissue on
one surface.

137. Strip. B270:VIII/3662 (Fig. 9h)
L.0.039; W.0.010; Th.0.003. Mitered at both
ends. Cancellous tissue on back.

138. Strip fragment. B270:VIII/4573
L.0.087; W.0.017; Th.0.001. Broken at both
ends. Warped. Smoothed on both sides.

139. Strip fragment. B270:VIII/4575
L.0.128; W.0.026; Th.0.001. Broken at both ends
and along one edge. Traces of cancellous tissue on
back.

140. Strip. B276:VIII/2695 (Fig. 10b; Pl. 16e)
L.0.065; W.0.008; Th.0.002. Hole 0.001 in diameter for attachment at each end. Chisel marks
along one side. Traces of red stain.
St. Clair 1996, 370, Fig. 5.

141. Strip. B276:VIII/2928
L.0.048; W.0.009; Th.0.003. Ivory. One end partially sawn and broken by percussion. Other end
beveled. Claw chisel marks on one side.

142. Strip. B294:VIII/3393 (Fig. 9i)
L.0.038; W.0.018; Th.0.001. One mitered end.
Other end broken by percussion. Slightly convex
in profile, following natural curve at edge of bone.
One side scored with chisel. Saw marks on back.
Traces of white paint.

143. Strip. B295:VIII/3967
L.0.045; W.0.020; Th.0.002. Broken at both
ends. Cancellous tissue preserved on back. Probably from scapula.

144. Strip fragment. B209:VIII/2259 (Fig. 10e;
Pl. 15a)
L.0.056; W.0.015; Th.0.002. Broken at both
ends. Warped. Hole 0.002 in diameter for attachment near one edge. Cancellous tissue on back.

145. Strip fragment. B222:VIII/ 2265 (Pl. 15e)
L.0.041; W.0.005; Th.0.001. Broken at one. One
mitered end. One beveled edge.

146. Strip fragment. B222:VIII/ 2289
L.0.059; W.0.008; Th.0.002. Broken at both
ends and along both edges. Warped. Remains of
hole 0.002 in diameter for attachment at one
end.

147. Strip fragment. B222:VIII/2268 (Fig. 10d;
   Pl. 15d)
   L.0.048; W.0.007; Th.0.002. Broken at both
   ends. Warped. One beveled edge. Remains of
   hole 0.002 in diameter for attachment at one
   end.

148. Strip fragment. B310:VIII/3760 (Pl. 15b)
   L.0.040; W.0.010; Th.0.002. Broken one end.
   Traces of cancellous tissue on back.

149. Strip or veneer fragment. B270:VIII/2614
   L.0.060; W.0.033; Th.0.001. Broken at both ends
   and along one edge. One side preserves saw marks
   partially overlain by chisel marks over traces of
   cancellous tissue. Other side has chisel marks and
   traces of red stain.

SECOND HALF OF THE FIFTH CENTURY

150. Inlay. B209:VIII/2254 (Fig. 10g; Pl. 16f)
   L.0.038; W.0.021; Th.0.002. Ivory. Dia-
   mond-shaped. Rasp marks on back.
   St. Clair 1996, 370, Fig. 5.

151. Inlay. B296:VIII/3263 (Fig. 10h; Pl. 16e)
   L.0.025; W.0.021; Th.0.001. Triangular shape.
   Rasp marks on back.
   St. Clair 1996, 370, Fig. 5.

MEDIEVAL TO MODERN

152. Inlay. C9:IX–XII/964
   L.0.021; W.0.019; Th.0.002. Triangle with hole
   0.003 in diameter in center for attachment. This
   and no.153 are a type found throughout the
   Roman period.[9]

153. Inlay. C139:IX–XII/3116
   L.0.015; W.0.016; Th.0.002. Triangle with hole
   0.002 in diameter in center for attachment.

154. Inlay or debris. C74:IX–XII/1469
   L.0.019; W.0.009; Th.0.005. Ivory. Irregular diamond shaped with chisel marks on back.

155. Strip. B179:X?/2560 (Fig. 10c; Pl. 16a)
   L.0.090; W.0.019; Th.0.001. Broken at both ends
   and along one edge. Warped. Surface cracked and
   chipped. Hole 0.002 in diameter for attachment at

one end. Rasp marks and remains of cancellous
tissue on back.
St. Clair 1996, 370, Fig. 5.

156. Strip. B51:XI/1797 (Pl. 16c)
   L.0.034; W.0.014; Th.0.001. Broken at one end.
   Highly polished. Strip ending in circle with hole
   0.003 in diameter for attachment. This type is paralleled in metal on pyxides, where such strips
   served to secure the bottom of the box to the sides.
   Flexible bone examples may have been used for
   this purpose as well. On some pyxides, areas of
   this shape were left blank or recessed for attachment of the band to secure the bottom.[10]
   St. Clair 1996, 370, Fig. 5.

157. Strip. B51:XI/1798 (Pl. 16d)
   L.0.041; W.0.010; Th.0.001. Highly polished.
   Tapering in width. One rounded end. Like
   no.156, such strips may have been used to hold
   box parts together.
   St. Clair 1996, 370, Fig. 5.

158. Strip. B51:XI/1032 (Pl. 16b)
   L.0.086; W.0.009; Th.0.001. Broken at both ends.
   Warped. Highly polished. Undulating profile
   ending in circle pierced by a hole for attachment. A
   similar example dated to the second or third century comes from Knossos.[11] Like nos.156 and157,
   such strips may have been used to hold box parts
   together.
   St. Clair 1996, 370, Fig. 5.

B. Cylindrical and Ring-Shaped Mounts

Surviving evidence documents the use of cylindrical
and ring-shaped mounts primarily on furniture
legs, which were assembled around an iron rod.
Cylindrical members turned from a single length of
hollowed bone, often with cylindrical tenons at one
or both ends, were fitted directly over the rod, or
packed with wood and then drilled through to
receive the rod. They vary considerably in size and
are both undecorated and decorated. Cylindrical
mounts survive from Pheidias's workshop at Olympia (Illus. 3.7) and they are common among the
remains of funerary couches from the first century

B.C.–first century A.D.[12] One example (no.164) is unfinished and provides a good example of the preliminary stages of lathe turning.

159. Ring-shaped mount fragment. D89:IV/3652
(Fig. 16a)

L.0.011; Th.0.007; D.0.025. Approximately one-half of diameter missing. Highly polished ring, convex in profile. Interior surface roughly shaped with chisel. Identical mounts are associated with the remains of the legs of a first-century B.C.–first-century A.D. funerary couch from the necropolis of Saint-Lambert (Gaul).[13] Rings of this sort separated the more voluminous components.

160. Ring-shaped mount fragment. D89:IV/3594
(Fig. 16b)

L.0.009; Th.0.005; D.0.030. Less than half of the diameter survives. Surface chipped. Convex outer profile. Interior surface roughly shaped with chisel. Like no. 159 the mount is paralleled in the remains of a first-century B.C.–first-century A.D. funerary couch from the necropolis of Saint-Lambert (Gaul).[14]

161. Cylindrical mount fragment. D83:IV–V/3353
(Fig. 16c; Pl. 26d)

L.0.017; Th.0.005; projected D.0.025. Approximately two-thirds of diameter missing. Burned. Fragment of turned cylinder with slightly concave profile, projecting rims, and tenon at one end. Uniform dark gray in color with whitish encrustation on interior wall. These "bobbin"-shaped mounts are commonly found with remains of legs of funerary couches from the first century B.C. and A.D. where they separated the more voluminous cylindrical components. The tenon allowed the pieces to fit together tightly.[15]

162. Cylindrical mount. D100:VIII/4130
(Fig. 16d)

L.0.007; Th.0.001; projected D.0.010. Broken in three pieces (modern) and at bottom. Raised polished band 0.003 in height above slightly inset tapering sleeve.

163. Cylindrical mount fragment. A20:VIII/481
(Fig. 16h; Pl. 25a)

L.0.106; W.0.040; Th.0.008; D.0.004. Approximately one-half of diameter remains. Top and bottom edges chipped. Tenon at both ends. Interior walls roughly scraped leaving some cancellous tissue. Nutrient foramina runs obliquely through bone wall. Plain cylindrical members turned from a single piece of bone with tenons at each end are associated with furniture legs of first-century B.C.–first-century A.D. funerary couches.[16]

164. Cylindrical mount fragment. B281:VIII/2802
(Fig. 16i; Pl. 25c)

L.0.065; W.0.026; Th.0.003; D.0.030. Broken along both sides. Unfinished. Surface turned with series of bands of unequal width. Interior scraped to remove cancellous tissue. This piece, presumably a discard, exhibits a preliminary stage of turning. A similar unfinished mount survives from Pheidias's workshop at Olympia (Illus. 3.7) and was probably similarly associated with furniture components.

C. Plaques

Three undecorated plaques that illustrate joinery techniques survive from late antique contexts. The joining of small plaques to produce almost seamless joints was practiced on turned furniture components, where plaques were joined in registers over members with curved surfaces, and strips were joined in series on both furniture and boxes. Plaques were joined by means of dovetails to form the walls of boxes. A fourth example, a rod with a cross-grain groove, is probably a box or furniture part as well.

165. Furniture or box part? D131:V/4150

L.0.031; Th.0.006. Groove: W.0.004. Rod

approximately square in section with rabbeted edge at one end and rectangular cross-grain groove for tongue and groove joint.

166. Plaque fragment. A33:VIII/1717

L.0.032; W.0.018; Th.0.003. Broken on both ends and along one side. Preserved edge has a rectangular groove, presumably to receive a second piece, forming a rabbeted tongue and groove joint.

167. Plaque. A33:VIII/553 (Fig. 10i)

L.0.082; W.0.034; Th.0.003. Broken into three pieces. Rectangular piece at center missing. Sawn on three sides. Fourth is dovetailed for joining to an intersecting plaque at a right angle. Dovetails have beveled edges. Cancellous tissue on back.

St. Clair in Hostetter et al. 1994, 170, Fig. 52.

MODERN

168. Plaque fragment. A14:XII/1245 (Fig. 10f; Pl. 18f)

L.0.028; W.0.027 Th.0.003. Broken one end and one side. Fragment of plaque with V-shaped groove creating narrow border. Back has single wedge-shaped incision along edge to receive a second plaque at a right angle, forming a stopped, or invisible, dovetail joint.

II. Decorated Mounts and Boxes

A. Moldings and Strip Mounts

Decorated framing bands or moldings, mostly in the form of debris, are the commonest mount type at Palatine East. Most are carved with simple designs in imitation of architectural moldings. The range of types is wide, from simple division into two or more bands, to more elaborate imitations of architectural moldings, all of which may appear on a single piece of furniture.[17] Some examples retain holes for attachment, and in a few cases the nail is partially preserved. In most cases the back is scored with chisel or rasp marks. Strips decorated with three convex bands of approximately equal width

separated by V-shaped grooves are the most common. Edges are frequently beveled. This type of molding occurs as a framing device for recessed veneers on funerary couches from the Esquiline and in Cambridge, for example, and on numerous Roman boxes.[18] The inner edges, abutting the veneers, often are beveled. Thicker mounts, often with one convex surface and with more elaborate architectural or vegetal decoration, survive as well, concentrated in the early contexts. Incised linear designs that are not architectural in nature and ring and dot motifs appear primarily on strips from late antique and later contexts. The presence of mitered edges and one beveled long edge on many examples, both associated with framing, suggests that these served primarily as furniture mounts as well. Strips with intaglio designs also appear in late antique contexts. Some find parallels among strips preserved along with plaques in the Antiquarium Communale in Rome.[19]

FIRST CENTURY

169. Molding. D27:III–IV/2931

L.0.016; D.0.020; Th.0.002. Chipped. Mitered at both ends. Six narrow bands of unequal width. Sawn obliquely along two edges. Probable debris from mitering.

SECOND CENTURY

170. Strip fragment. D131:V/ 4381 (Fig. 12m)

L.0.025; W.0.019; Th.0.009. Broken at one end, other sawn. Border and surface decorated with series of oblique chisel cuts.

LATE THIRD CENTURY

171. Molding fragment. A93:VII /2288 (Fig. 11d)

L.0.031; W.0.008; Th.0.002. Broken at both ends. Concavo-convex molding topped by flat framing band.

172. Molding fragment. A93:VII/1820 (Fig. 11g; Pl. 18a)

L.0.097; W.0.008; Th.0.002. Broken at one end and along one edge. Mitered at one end. One bev-

eled edge. Two convex and one flat band of
unequal widths. Chisel marks on back.

173. Molding fragment. A97:VII/2175 (Fig. 11j;
Pl. 18d)

L.0.076; W.0.014; Th.0.001. Broken at one end.
One side chipped. One beveled edge. Four convex
bands of unequal width.

174. Molding fragment. A22:VIII/1777 (Fig. 11c;
Pl. 18e)

L.0.035; W.0.010; Th.0.002. Broken at both
ends. Convex band with narrow convex border.
Chisel marks on back. Traces of red stain.

175. Strip fragment. A105:VIII/2257

L.0.050; W.0.010; Th.0.003. Ivory. Broken at one
end. Other end mitered. Convex band with
narrow convex border that widens toward broken
end.

176. Molding fragment. A33:VIII/1716 (Pl. 18h)

L.0.040; W.0.014; Th.0.001. Both ends broken.
One beveled edge. Convex band with narrow
convex border. Rasp marks on back.

177. Molding fragment. A36:VIII/3192

L.0.050; W.0.025; Th.0.004. One straight end
broken by scoring and percussion. Other end
mitered. Two flat bands. One edge recessed. Saw
and rasp marks on both surfaces. Traces of red
stain. Possibly unfinished.

178. Molding fragment. D100:VIII/3869
(Fig. 11f)

L.0.060; W.0.020; Th.0.001. Broken at both ends
and along one side. Partially preserved hole for
attachment at one end. Three flat bands. Rasp
marks on front and back.

179. Mount fragment. A36:VIII/1686

L.0.040; W.0.015; Th.0.003. Broken at both ends
and along one side. Three convex bands of equal
width.

180. Molding fragment. A36:VIII/1405 (Pl. 17a,b)

L.0.058; W.0.029; Th.0.002. In two pieces.
Broken at one end. Other end mitered. Central
convex band framed by narrow raised convex

bands. Carving extends two-thirds of the strip's
length. One beveled and one recessed edge. Probable debris from cutting to size.

181. Molding fragment. A42:VIII/1831 (Fig. 11h;
Pl. 17c)

L.0.080; W.0.011; Th.0.003. Broken at both
ends. Warped. One beveled edge. Three convex
bands. Chisel marks on back.

182. Molding fragment. A67:VIII/1727 (Fig. 11e;
Pl. 17f,g)

L.0.028; W.0.022; Th.0.003. Ivory. In two pieces.
Broken at both ends, and longitudinally along
grain. Chipped along one edge. One recessed edge.
Convex central band framed by flat and pyramidal
bands. Rasp marks on back.[20]

183. Molding. 67:VIII/1836

L.0.062; W.0.015; Th.0.002. Broken in two
pieces (modern). Three convex bands. Chisel
marks on back.

184. Molding fragment. A105:VIII/2256
(Pl. 18g)

L.0.134; W.0.023; Th.0.004. Broken along one
side. Both ends mitered. Two convex and one flat
band. One rounded edge. Chisel marks on back.

185. Molding fragment. D40:VIII/2927
(Fig. 11b)

L.0.030; W.0.019; Th.0.002. Broken at both
ends. One side chipped. One beveled edge.
Three convex bands of unequal width.

186. Molding fragment. A36:VIII/750 (Fig. 12c;
Pl. 20b)

L.0.036; W.0.022; Th.0.002. Ivory. Broken at one
end. Other end mitered by scoring with a chisel
and percussion. Surface cracked and flaked. Ovolo
design with raised flat border. Miter cuts through
decoration, indicating that the strip was decorated
before being cut to size. Chisel marks on back.
Moldings of this type are common elements of
first-century B.C.–first-century A.D. funerary
couches, as well as of later furniture and boxes,
appearing as a framing element on depictions of
thrones on consular diptychs, for example, and on
ivory pyxides.[21]

187. Molding fragment. A20:VIII/339

L.0.046; W.0.020; Th.0.003. Ivory. Both ends broken. One beveled edge. Flat band with narrow raised convex border.

188. Molding fragment. B276:VIII/2932

L.0.041; W.0.017; Th.0.002. Ivory. Broken along one edge. Flaked on front surface. Both ends mitered. Band with narrow raised convex border. Probable debris from mitering.

189. Molding fragment. A105:VIII/2252

L.0.035; W.0.008; Th.0.002. Broken at both ends and along one side. Convex band with raised irregular convex border. Claw chisel marks on back.

190. Molding fragment. B209:VIII/2261

L.0.060; W.0.015; Th.0.003. Broken at one end. Other end sawn. Stained brown. Three slightly convex bands. Back has longitudinal v-shaped groove.

191. Molding fragment. B223:VIII/2989 (Fig. 11a)

L.0.035; W.0.014; Th.0.001. Chipped. Broken at one end. Other end mitered. Two flat bands with narrow raised convex border.

192. Molding. B270:VIII/3628 (Pl. 17d)

L.0.129; W.0.020; Th.0.001. Broken at one end and along one edge. Other end mitered. Warped. Three bands separated by crudely carved v-shaped incisions. Possibly unfinished.

193. Mount fragment. B276:VIII/2933 (Fig. 11i; Pl. 17e)

L.0.044; W.0.018; Th.0.002. One side and corner chipped. Three convex bands of approximately equal width. Stained brown. Chisel marks on back.

194. Molding fragment. B264:VIII/3987

L.0.082; W.0.017; Th.0.002. Broken at one end. One beveled edge Three bands separated by rough-cut incisions. Cancellous tissue on back. Probably unfinished.

195. Strip fragment. B209:VIII/2224 (Fig. 12b; Pl. 24c)

L.0.063; W.0.013; Th.0.004. Broken along one edge. Undulating concavo-convex profile created by series of oblique chisel-cut gouges. Cancellous tissue and saw marks on back. A second strip fragment with identical decoration was found nearby.[22]

196. Strip fragment. B270:VIII/2985 (Fig. 12a; Pl. 24d)

L.0.043; W.0.007; Th.0.004. Broken at one end. Undulating concavo-convex profile created by series of oblique chisel-cut gouges. Sawn diagonal incisions. The technique is the same as that used to create columnar mounts with spiral decoration. The surface perforation is a natural nutrient foramen running obliquely through the strip.

197. Strip fragment. B270:VIII/3020 (Fig. 12d; Pl. 19d)

L.0.041; W.0.020; Th.0.002. Broken along one edge and at one end. Other end mitered by scoring with a chisel and percussion. Two squares framed by narrow borders enclosing incised Xs and four dots. Miter cuts through design, indicating that the strip was decorated before being cut to size. Traces of cancellous tissue and saw marks on back. The design is paralleled on consular diptychs of Areobindus.[23]

198. Strip fragment. B296:VIII/4138 (Fig. 12f; Pl. 19e)

L.0.035; W.0.017; Th.0.001. Intaglio. Broken on three sides. Flat band with border of triangles on recessed field. Chisel marks on back. Another piece with the same pattern survives from this. This design is paralleled on late antique mounts from Egypt.[24]

199. Strip fragment. B296:VIII/3340 (Fig. 12e; Pl. 20d)

L.0.035; W.0.012; Th.0.001. Intaglio. Broken at both ends and along both edges. Series of four-petal flowers on recessed field. Saw marks on back. The design is paralleled on strip mounts in the Antiquarium Comunale at Rome, and on a late antique casket from Saqqara, now in the Coptic Museum, Cairo. However, the four-petal motif is common and widespread, appearing on the consular diptychs of Areobindus and Anastasius, for example.[25]

200. Strip fragment. B296:VIII/3986 (Pl. 20e)

L.0.038; W.0.010; Th.0.001. Intaglio. Broken on three sides. Ring and dot motif set within recessed field. Upper rings cut into border, while upper right ring is cut by larger partially superimposed ring. Narrow recessed border.

201. Strip fragment. B270:VIII/3659 (Fig. 12i; Pl. 19c)

L.0.040; W.0.010; Th.0.001. Broken at both ends. Warped. Strip decorated with series of ring and dot motifs. Narrow border. Circular protrusions on back surface from pressure exerted by center bit used to make decoration. Similar ring and dot designs appear on bracelets from the Roman period, but examples with mitered ends indicate that they served as framing strips as well.[26]

MEDIEVAL TO MODERN

202. Strip fragment. C59:IX–XII/968 (Fig. 12k)

L.0.045; W.0.012; Th.0.003. Broken at both ends and along one side. Chipped. Ring and dot motifs separated by diagonal knife-cut incisions. One beveled edge. Chisel marks and cancellous tissue on back. This design was widely popular. A similar strip mount survives from Saraçhane in Constantinople.[27] Strips with similar decoration have been identified as bracelets and comb plates.[28] This example is too thick to have served as a bracelet.

203. Strip or comb side plate fragment. C145:IX–XII/3476 (Fig. 12l)

L.0.034; W.0.013; Th.0.002. Broken at both ends and along one side. Remaining side chipped. One beveled edge. Alternating ring and dot motifs and diagonal knife-cut incisions in a checkmark pattern. Hole 0.003 in diameter for attachment. Remains of a second hole at one end. Possibly a side plate for a comb. [29]

204. Strip. C155:IX–XII /3655 (Fig. 12j; Pl. 19b)

L.0.047; W.0.014; Th.0.002. One mitered end. One beveled edge. Irregular line of ring and dot motifs with center holes 0.003 in diameter made by center bit drill. Strips of this type were mounted against contrasting or metallic backing on late antique and medieval caskets and combs.[30] Probable mitering debris.

205. Molding fragment. D73:XI–XII/3142 (Fig. 11k)

L.0.078; W.0.016; Th.0.002. One end broken. Other end partially scored and mitered. One beveled edge. Two convex bands with narrow recessed convex border.

206. Strip fragment. D96:XI–XII/3668 (Fig. 12g)

L.0.044; W.0.016; Th.0.001. Broken at one end and one side. Warped. Shallow u-shaped gouges alternating with knife-cut incisions. Raised flat border with beveled edge. The type of frieze is closely paralleled on remains of funerary couches from the first century B.C.–first century A.D., including the example from the Mausoleum at Cucuron (Gaul), thought to be an import from Italy.[31]

207. Strip fragment. B51:XI/1796/1829 (Fig. 12h; Pl. 19a)

L.0.093; W.0.010-0.015; Th.0.001. One end broken. Tapering in width with series of paired diagonal parallel incisions. Back scored with chisel. Similar incised designs occur on strips from late antique comb cases.[32]

B. Columnar Mounts

Decorated columnar and half-columnar mounts survive from the late antique contexts and probably served as framing elements on boxes or furniture. Many take the form of spiral half columns, a type that was common throughout the Greco-Roman world and popular in late antiquity. Spiral columns and half columns, often with similarly irregular designs, appear frequently on late antique diptychs, furniture, and caskets.[33]

MID- TO LATE THIRD CENTURY

208. Columnar mount fragment. A157:VII/2948 (Fig. 13a; Pl. 26b)

L.0.050; W.0.023; Th.0.010. Broken along sides and at top. Surface chipped and cracked. Bottom edge preserved. Flaring shaft topped by a ball with

an incised horizontal line. Right longitudinal edge
preserves traces of sawing. Bottom edge has inset
channel on interior, probably to receive a second
element, a joining system common for components of furniture legs, for example.[34] A cylindrical
mount from Corinth, described as "probably
Roman," has a similar form.[35]

EARLY FOURTH CENTURY

209. Columnar mount fragment. A38:VIII/1404
   (Fig. 13e; Pl. 24b)

   L.0.55; W.0.020; Th.0.007. Broken at one end.
   One edge and one corner chipped. Shaft with
   series of diagonal irregularly spaced U-shaped
   grooves. Incised horizontal line at one end. Saw
   and chisel marks on back, with medullary cavity
   visible at one end. A mount with similarly irregular spiral decoration is associated with the
   first-century B.C.–first-century A.D. funerary couch
   from Vindonissa.[36] Similar irregular designs appear
   frequently on late antique diptychs, furniture, and
   caskets as well.[37] A similar fragment from a late
   medieval deposit at the Crypta Balbi is identified
   as a handle.[38]

210. Columnar mount. A66:VIII/698 (Fig. 13c;
   Pl. 25b)

   L.0.091; W.0.020; Th.0.009. Sawn on four sides.
   Shaft with spiral decoration of diagonal bands separated by V-shaped incisions topped by roughly
   cubical capital on a neck that is concave in profile.
   Shaft sawn at oblique angle after decoration. Interior scraped. Cancellous tissue visible on left front
   surface. Similar spiral columns with bands separated by incisions are depicted on late antique
   diptychs, furniture, and caskets, although with
   more elaborate capitals.[39] The cubical capital on
   this example may be unfinished.

211. Columnar mount fragment. A102:VIII/1825
   (Fig. 13b; Pl. 25d)

   L.065; W.0.016; Th.0.003. Broken at one end.
   Both longitudinal edges sawn. Stained brown.
   Convex surface decorated with flat bands at top
   and bottom framing series of wide convex bands
   alternating with pairs of narrow bands.

SECOND HALF OF THE FIFTH CENTURY

212. Columnar mount fragment? B270:VIII/3656

   H.0.011; W.0.023; Th.0.009. Broken at bottom.
   Perhaps a concavo-convex capital or base.

213. Columnar mount fragment? B186:VIII/2816
   (Fig. 13d; Pl. 26c)

   H.0.019; W.0.030; Th.0.007. Ivory. Broken on
   both sides. Surface cracked. Interior surface flaked.
   Perhaps a concavo-convex capital or base.

C. Plaques

A small number of decorated square or rectangular
plaques were uncovered, which would have been
attached to wooden frameworks. They are all fragmentary and, given their association with other
debris, may be discards from the manufacturing
process. They are decorated with geometric and
figural designs in relief and in intaglio. Present as
well are plaques decorated with simple moldings
that were components of turned furniture members. They were joined horizontally in series, and
often vertically in registers, over a turned wooden
core (Fig. 3.10). The remains associated with the
first- and second-century contexts are closely paralleled among the remains of first-century B.C.–
first-century A.D. funerary couches from Italy and
Gaul.[40] The third through fifth century and, to a
lesser degree, the medieval and modern contexts
with large amounts of residual material contain
plaques such as the intaglio horse (no. 224) that are
impressive examples of late antique craftsmanship.
Although material of this type, wherever found, is
generally assumed to be of Egyptian manufacture,
the Palatine East remains point to the likelihood of
local workshops employing a common vocabulary.

LATE FIRST TO EARLY SECOND CENTURY

214. Plaque fragment. D83:IV–V/4217 (Fig. 14a)

   L.0.028; W.0.13; Th.0.0.004. Broken at both
   ends. Incised decoration in form of an X, one arm
   of which extends beyond two horizontal parallel
   lines. The shape and decoration are similar to

mounts from the first-century B.C.–first-century
A.D. funerary couch from the Mausoleum at
Cucuron (Gaul), thought to be an import from
Italy, and tentatively associated with legs.[41]

215. Plaque. D72:IV–V/3394 (Fig. 14b; Pl. 20a)
L.0.046; W.0.027; Th.0.007. Leaf pattern formed
by knife cut, V-shaped incisions. Saw marks and
cancellous tissue on back. Possibly unfinished.
Another plaque of this type was excavated from a
first-century context nearby in the area of the
Meta Sudans.[42] Similar plaques are associated with
the funerary couch from the mausoleum at
Cucuron (Gaul), dated to the first century B.C. or
A.D. and thought to be an import from Italy.[43]

216. Plaque fragment. A186:IV–V/3782 (Fig. 14c)
L.0.026; W.0.015; Th.0.004. Broken on two
sides. Concavo-convex molding formed by a central concave band, flanked by thin raised bands
and convex framing bands of unequal width. Back
surface is inset on one end and beveled at other.
Mounts with this general shape are common components of cylindrical members that decorated
furniture legs. They were assembled in registers
over a turned wooden core. As here, the back surface is frequently cut back to receive the next
register or to fit the wooden core.[44] Similar
mounts with concavo-convex profiles form the top
register of drumlike members of furniture legs on
the first-century B.C.–first-century A.D. funerary
couch in Cambridge.[45]

217. Plaque fragments. A105:VIII/2258 /1887
(Fig. 14d; Pl. 18b,c)
L.0.036; W.0.011; Th.0.004 (a). L.0.039;
W.0.010; Th.0.004 (b). Ivory. Both broken along
one edge and at one end where they possibly join.
Decorated with vegetal drapery or motifs in relief.

218. Plaque fragment. A20:VIII/389 (Fig. 14e)
L.0.031; W.0.024; Th.0.003. Broken along three
edges. Back inset at one end. Two flat bands sepa-

rated by a raised thin band and bordered by a
convex molding with rounded edge. Traces of
cancellous tissue and brown stain on back surface.
Like no. 216, this was a component for assembly
over the wooden core of a cylindrical member of
furniture, probably the leg. The back is inset to
receive a joining member or to fit the wooden
core. Numerous mounts of this type survive
among the remains of first-century B.C.–first-century A.D. funerary couches from Italy and Gaul, as
well as from a couch from Corinth dated by
Vermeule to the third century B.C.[46]

219. Plaque. A20:VIII/ 479 (Fig. 14f; Pl. 24a)
L.0.055; W.0.023; Th.0.009. Series of diagonal
concave bands separated by narrow convex bands
with linear V-shaped incisions. Raised V-shaped
design at upper corner, horizontal incision at lower
corner. Curved shape suggests attachment to the
curved edge of a furniture member. Spiral decoration of this type, with incised lines separating the
concave bands appear on no. 210 and on columns
that are framing elements on the silver Projecta
casket and on late antique furniture, diptychs, and
boxes.[47]

220. Plaque fragment. A12:VIII/116 (Fig. 14g;
Pl. 20c)
L.0.060; W.0.011; Th.0.004. Intaglio? Broken
along one edge. One end partially sawn and
broken by percussion. Convex border with
rounded edge above convex band with incised
floral-vine design. Two heart-shaped leaves at
center. Saw and chisel marks on back. Engemann
noted the presence of heart-shaped leaves in
sixth-century frescoes at Abu Mena in Egypt, and
of stylized heart shapes within an opus sectile
design at Hagia Sophia in Constantinople.[48] The
ivory passion plaque from Milan, dated around
400, similarly combines heart-shaped leaves and an
undulating vine.[49]

221. Plaque fragment. B294:VIII/4770 (Fig. 15a;
Pl. 23)
L.0.042; W.0.023; Th.0.006. Broken on three

sides. Surface chipped and flaked. Female head, with hair held in place by a band, before a segment of an arch that is probably drapery. Top edge of border sawn at an oblique angle for setting in frame. General parallels for such figures, a standing or reclining nude (nereid) or clothed female (maenad) with head in profile against a background of arching drapery, can be found in a variety of mediums throughout the Roman and late antique periods.[50]

222. Plaque fragment. B270:VIII/3741 (Fig. 15b; Pl. 22)

L.0.053; W.0.065; Th.0.002. Intaglio. Broken on three sides and in three pieces. Preserved edge is rough from partial sawing. Flat, slightly recessed border scored with oblique shallow incisions to receive framing strip.[51] Incised female figure with left arm extended to globe or disk with ring and dot motif in four quadrants. Back of head visible above shoulder at left. Drapery wraps around arm above elbow and flows behind arm toward head, then down and outward toward globe. Additional drapery flows downward at lower left. In contrast to the other pieces worked in intaglio, this plaque is characterized by a fine linear technique and the absence of broad recessed fields.[52] The incisions would have been filled with colored paste to highlight the design. A chronology for this type has not been established. A plaque depicting Peter, from the Roman catacombs, is technically similar.[53] Like no. 221, this type of figure, often identified as a maenad, is popular in a wide variety of mediums over a long period, although the placement of the hand atop the globe is reminiscent of victory figures.[54] Globes divided into quadrants appear on late antique plaques.[55]

MEDIEVAL TO MODERN

223. Plaque fragment. C111:IX–XII/1977 (Fig. 14h ; Pl. 21b)

L.0.052; W.0.035; Th.0.004. Broken on one side. Square with lathe-turned decoration consisting of a wide convex band bordered by a single ring and separated from raised central circle by a double ring. Center depression from lathe stock. Two corner holes 0.002 in diameter for attachment. Rasp marks on back. Parallels from Saraçhane and Kenchreai suggest a late antique date.[56]

224. Plaque fragment. B179:X?/2480 (Fig. 15c; Pl. 21a)

H.0.046; W.0.044; Th.0.003. Intaglio. Missing upper left corner. Lower left corner chipped. Bridled horse with decorative headpiece extending to right, braided and tied tail, wrapped lower legs. Body recessed to receive colored paste. Cancellous tissue on back. The depth of cancellous tissue on the left side of the plaque, and the resulting lack of compact, carvable bone in the area of the head suggest that the plaque may have broken during manufacture. Similarly caparisoned horses are depicted in late antique circus and chariot racing contexts—for example, in the fourth-century mosaics of the Piazza Armerina in Sicily—and on sixth-century consular diptychs.[57]

225. Plaque fragment. B146:XI/1961 (Fig. 14i)

L.0.042; W.0.023; Th.0.002. Two edges partially preserved. Square with decoration of lathe-turned concentric circles consisting of six V-shaped grooves. Corner has double ring and dot motif. Cancellous tissue on back. The plaque is of the same general type as no. 223.

D. Cylindrical Mounts and Boxes

Like their undecorated counterparts, decorated hollow cylindrical mounts are associated primarily with furniture legs that were assembled around an iron rod. Cylinders of bone and ivory were used to form boxes, or pyxides, as well. Smaller-scale solid cylindrical blanks were turned on the lathe to create decorative mounts, handles and finials on pyxis lids, and the ends of hinges.[58] Cylindrical mounts survive from Pheidias's workshop at Olympia (Illus. 3.7), and they are common among the remains of funerary couches from the first century B.C. or A.D.[59] They occur in both early and late contexts at Palatine East.

226. Cylindrical mount fragment. D137:IV/4506 (Fig. 16f)

L.0.009; D.0.040; Th.0.003. Ivory. Approximately one-third of diameter survives. Base with lathe-turned moldings surmounted by inset shaft or tenon. Interior roughly shaped with chisel. Probable furniture leg component. Similar mounts survive from first-century B.C.–first-century A.D. funerary couches.[60]

227. Pyxis fragment. A215:IV/4407 (Fig. 17a; Pl. 28)

H.0.053; D.0.035; Th.0.004. Broken at top and sides. Part of base missing. Top preserves trace of inset edge. Relief of winged putto running left, carrying wreath or crown in raised right hand. Cape falls behind body. Interior wall smoothed with chisel. Putti are among the most popular subjects on Roman bone pyxides, which were produced primarily in the first century. A crown-carrying putto appears on a pyxis dated to the first century in the Walters Art Museum.[61] Both the shape and decoration of this example are most closely paralleled on a pyxis with a wreath-carrying putto in the Musée Archeologique de Nimes, thought by Béal to be an import.[62]

228. Cylindrical mount. D81:IV–V/3319 (Fig. 17g)

L.0.015; D.0.007. Chipped at top and bottom. Solid shaft topped by projecting knob, convex in profile. Indentations from lathe stock at both ends. Probable handle for a lid. Small turned handles or finials are associated with pyxis lids, as well as with elements that closed the ends of hinges.[63]

229. Cylindrical mount fragment? D83:IV–V/3345 (Fig. 17e)

L.0.053; D.0.003. Top missing. Solid cylindrical shaft tapering to inset foot decorated with four narrow concave bands. The form suggests a furniture leg, perhaps of a miniature object. One slightly flattened side suggests the possibility of a mount, however.

230. Cylindrical mount fragment. A140:VII/2412 (Fig. 16e; Pl. 26e)

L.0.024; Th.0.006; projected D.0.044. Approximately one-third of diameter survives. Chipped. Highly polished. Hollow mount decorated with two central bands framed by rings. Convex profile. Inset cylindrical tenons at both ends. Interior surface roughly shaped with chisel. Probable fitting for furniture leg. Similar fittings survive from first-century B.C.–first-century A.D. funerary couches.[64]

231. Cylindrical mount fragment? A38:VIII/1385 (Fig. 17f)

L.0.035; D.0.007. Broken at both ends. Solid cylinder decorated with central crosshatched band framed by rings.

232. Cylindrical mount or box wall fragment? A72:VIII/1677 (Fig. 17c)

L.0.030; W.0.017; Th.0.002. Convex fragment decorated with a central quatrefoil of ring and dot motifs framed by ring and dot motifs. Series of parallel incisions at upper edge.[65]

233. Cylindrical knob or boss. A33:VIII/657 (Fig. 17j)

H.0.005; D.0.010. Solid knob, pyramidal in section incised lathe-turned incision. Circular indentation from lathe stock at top and inverted V-shaped indentation on bottom. Probably a corner boss for a box or furniture.

234. Cylindrical mount fragment. B180:VIII/2617 (Fig. 17b)

L.0.061; W.0.033; D.0.040; Th.0.006. Two pieces. Broken at bottom and on sides. Inset wall or tenon at one end. Surface chipped and cracked. Heavy dark brown incrustation on interior wall. Lighter incrustation on outer surface. Hollow mount decorated with horizontal lathe-turned incisions. Simple lathe-turned cylinders are common in the Greco-Roman period.[66]

235. Pyxis fragment. B184:X/2154 (Fig. 17d;
     Pl. 26a)

L.0.054; W.0.021; Th.0.004; projected D.0.030.
Less than one-half of diameter remains. Top edge
chipped. Surface highly polished. Decorated with a
wide slightly convex central band framed by five
narrow convex bands at each end. Interior wall
scraped with a chisel and inset at one end, possibly
for base or lid. Bíró identifies similar objects from
the Roman period in the Hungarian National
Museum as dice boxes.[67]

236. Lid handle. B184:X/2153 (Fig. 17h)

L.0.028; D.0.006. Broken at one end.
Lathe-turned handle with concavo-convex profile
topped by a ring. Pierced horizontally by hole
0.002 in diameter. Small turned handles, or finials,
are associated with pyxis lids, as well as with elements that closed the ends of hinges. This example
was probably part of a pyxis lid.[68]

237. Cylindrical mount. D96:XI–XII/3711
     (Fig. 17i)

L.0.050; D.0.006. One end chipped. Solid slightly
tapering shaft with turned moldings at both ends.
Top has projecting tenon above convex rings;
bottom has mortise and concavo-convex molding
consisting of a band framed by rings. Similar small
lathe-turned pieces with tenons are associated with
Greco-Roman remains from Delos and Ashkelon,
and with first-century B.C.–first-century A.D.
funerary couch fragments from Cologne.[69]

E. Circular Mounts

Circular, or disk-shaped, mounts, often with
lathe-turned decoration, are common archaeological finds, and unless they are found in association
with specific types of objects, it is difficult to ascer-
tain their function. They are well documented in a
variety of shapes and sizes in direct association with
furniture, where they were used on fulcra, as corner
bosses, and as crowning elements of cylindrical leg
members.[70] Circular mounts survive from Pheidias's workshop at Olympia (Illus. 3.7), and they

are common among the remains of funerary
couches from the first century B.C.–first century
A.D.[71] They also served as lids and bases for pyxides,
and to close the ends of hinges.[72] Gaming pieces
take this form as well. The Palatine East remains
are probably associated with furniture manufacture
for the most part.

LATE FIRST TO EARLY SECOND CENTURY

238. Circular mount. D83:IV–V/3264 (Fig. 18a;
     Pl. 27b)

D.0.015; Th.0.004. Ivory. Edges chipped.
Lathe-turned decoration of one wide and one
narrow band central hole 0.004 in diameter.
Narrow convex border. Similar mounts are associated with furniture legs and with corner bosses on
funerary couches from the first century B.C.–first
century A.D.[73]

EARLY FOURTH CENTURY

239. Circular mount fragment. A22:VIII/304
     (Fig. 18f)

D.0.055; Th.0.025. Approximately two-thirds of
diameter missing. Broken on three sides. Series of
lathe-turned concentric bands. Innermost raised
band is flat in profile and frames recessed central
area. A similar profile appears on pierced circular
mounts associated with first-century B.C.–first-century A.D. remains of funerary couches in Frejus
(Gaul) and Italy.[74]

240. Circular mount fragment. A33:VIII/630
     (Fig. 18h)

D.0.051; Th.0.003. Approximately two-thirds of
diameter missing. Bottom chipped and scored
with irregular scratches, perhaps to roughen surface. Outer edge has vertical chatter marks. Raised
concentric bands framing a recessed flat central
band.

241. Circular mount or lid. A16:VIII/445
     (Fig. 18g; Pl. 27e)

D.0.035; Th.0.006. Bottom surface and sides
chipped and pitted. Six lathe-turned concentric
bands rising to central hole 0.004 in diameter.

Innermost band is flat in profile. Bíró identifies a similar piece as a lid for a hinge.[75] It may also have served as a furniture mount.

242. Circular mount fragment. B270:VIII/3722 (Fig. 18e; Pl. 27a)

D.0.039; Th.0.005. One half of diameter missing. Edge worn. Broad convex band with irregular, narrow, convex border. Central hole 0.007 in diameter. Cancellous tissue on back surface and along interior edge of border. A similar piece is restored as the top of a corner boss on the first-century B.C.–first-century A.D. Cambridge funerary couch, and the type is common in later Roman contexts as well.[76]

243. Circular mount. C160:IX–XII/4398 (Fig. 18d; Pl. 27d)

D.0.032; Th.0.004. Edges and top surface chipped. Saw marks and traces of cancellous tissue on back. Series of lathe-turned flat and convex bands. Central hole 0.004 in diameter. Nutrient foramen visible at one edge and on back.[77]

244. Circular mount fragment. B263:X/2562 (Fig. 18b; Pl. 27c)

D.0.020; Th.0.004. Ivory. Broken on one side. Three lathe-turned concentric bands rising to central hole 0.007 in diameter. Innermost band is flat in profile. Back is recessed for mounting.[78] Probable boss.

245. Circular mount or lid. B18:XII/1696 (Fig. 18c)

D.0.023; Th.0.002. Chipped. Series of four concentric bands, concavo-convex profile. Central indentation from lathe stock. Cancellous tissue on back. This type is paralleled among remains of first-century B.C.–first-century A.D. funerary couches from Italy and Gaul, and similar pieces, although cruder in execution, have been identified as counters and gaming pieces.[79]

III. Hinges

Bone cylinders with lateral perforations were combined in series to provide hinges for doors, chests, and boxes of various sizes. They were fitted with dowels that projected at right angles and attached alternately to the lid and framework of the box or chest. Individual cylinders are common finds in Roman excavations. Decoration is generally confined to incised lines, which were sometimes filled with black pigment.[80]

246. Hinge fragment. D27:IV/2615 (Fig. 16g)

L.0.020; D.0.050; Th.0.005. Approximately one-third of diameter remains. Both sides broken. Segment with two finished edges, top and bottom. Pierced by hole 0.005 in diameter 0.005 from edge at level of three lateral V-shaped incisions. Interior smoothed.[81]

247. Hinge fragment? C122/2684

L.0.047; W.0.017; Th.0.003-0.008; projected D.0.027. Less than one-third of diameter remains. Two sawn ends. Both sides broken. Surface cracked. Pierced by hole 0.008 in diameter.[82]

PINS

Bone and ivory pins occur in a wide variety of sizes and types, including small examples that are seldom catalogued, and which are concentrated in the early contexts. The third-through-fifth century contexts show a dramatic increase in the number and types of pins, a phenomenon that has been documented elsewhere, reflecting the fashion for ivory as well as its cheaper counterpart that is a hallmark of late antiquity.[83] Manufacturing debris includes blanks, partially finished examples, and discards. The undecorated pins include a wide variety of types, ranging from simple shafts with flat summits to pins with round, oval, and ogival heads. Both hand-carved and lathe-turned examples are represented, and there is a wide range of finish. For the most part the types correspond to examples that can be found in bone and ivory, and sometimes in metal, at a wide variety of sites throughout the Greco-Roman world. With few exceptions it is difficult to devise a chronology based on types. Some of the types from Palatine East correspond to types preserved in Lyon and Nîmes, which have been catalogued by Béal with extensive references to comparative material.[84] In these cases, references to comparative material include only a selection of sites to suggest the range of the type, with emphasis upon relevant material from Italy and more recent publications.

Ivory pins and pins with decorated heads are concentrated in fourth- and fifth-century contexts. They are both hand-carved and lathe-turned, and in several cases, the heads were carved separately and then fitted to a shaft. Decorated pins are less common generally than undecorated examples. Because they were prized in antiquity as well as in modern times, they are difficult to date, even when found in a secure archaeological context.

I. Pins with Undecorated Heads

A. Pins with shafts that are circular or polygonal in section with a diameter of 0.002 or less and flat or pyramidal summits (nineteen examples). Perhaps because of their simplicity and small size, pins of this type are rarely reported, although presumably common. Examples occur in contexts from the first half of the first century through the first or second decade of the fourth century, but they are concentrated in the first- and second-century contexts.

Similar examples are cited from Lyon from the first century A.D.[85]

FIRST CENTURY

248. Pin. D209:IV/4510 (Fig. 19a; Pl. 29d)
L.0.051; DS.0.001. Tip missing. Pyramidal summit. Shaft polygonal in section.

249. Pin fragment. A196:IV/3984
L.0.028; DS.0.002. Lower portion of shaft missing. Irregular pyramidal summit. Shaft circular in section.

250. Pin fragment. A201:IV/4207
L.0.011; DS.0.002. Lower portion of shaft missing. Pyramidal summit. Shaft circular in section.

LATE FIRST TO SECOND CENTURY

251. Pin. A182:IV–V/3857 (Fig. 19b; Pl. 29b)
L.0.080; DS.0.003. Pyramidal summit. Upper shaft rectangular in section.

252. Pin. A186:IV–V/4210
L.0.027; DS.0.002. Shaft stained. Flat summit. Shaft circular in section.

253. Pin fragment. D122:V/3982 (Fig. 19d)
L.0.034; DS.0.002. Lower portion of shaft missing. Pyramidal summit. Shaft polygonal in section.

254. Pin fragment. D122:V/3983
L.0.047; DS.0.002. Encrusted. Lower portion of shaft missing. Pyramidal summit. Shaft circular in section.

SECOND HALF OF THE SECOND TO THIRD CENTURY

255. Pin. A166:V–VI/3174 (Fig. 19e; Pl. 29c)
L.0.057; DS.0.002. Flat summit. Shaft circular in section.

256. Pin. A168:V–VI/3171 (Fig. 19f)
L.0.052; DS.0.002. Tip missing. Pyramidal summit. Shaft circular in section and curves slightly in profile.

257. Pin. A171:V–VI/3242 (Fig. 19g; Pl. 29a)

L.0.117; DS.0.002. Pyramidal summit. Shaft circular in section.

258. Pin fragment. A135:VII/2395

L.0.025; DS.0.002. Lower portion of shaft missing. Flat summit. Shaft circular in section.

259. Pin fragment. A144:VII/2506

L.0.005; DS.0.002. Only flat summit and upper portion of shaft preserved. Shaft polygonal in section.

260. Pin fragment. A20:VIII/478

L.0.028; DS.0.002. Lower portion of shaft missing. Flat summit. Shaft circular in section.

261. Pin. A36:VIII/769

L.0.041; DS.0.002. Pyramidal summit. Shaft circular in section.

262. Pin. A36:VIII/1388

L.0.041; DS.0.002. Tip missing. Flat summit. Shaft changes in section from circular to oval in lower portion and curves slightly in profile.

263. Pin. A38:VIII/1463

L.0.024; DS.0.002. Flat summit. Shaft polygonal in section.

264. Pin fragment. A33:VIII/530 (Fig. 19c)

L.0.038; DS.0.002. Lower portion of shaft missing. Flat summit. Shaft circular in section and curves slightly in profile.

MEDIEVAL TO MODERN

265. Pin fragment. B147:XI/1762

L.0.039; DS.0.002. Lower portion of shaft missing. Summit slightly rounded. Shaft circular in section.

266. Pin. C111:IX–XII/1998

L.0.052; DS.0.002. Summit flat. Shaft circular in section.

B. Pins with thin shafts that have one or more flat surfaces in section (sometimes changing to a circu-

lar section at the tip) and flat summits (six examples). Perhaps because of their shape, these pins frequently have a slightly curved profile. Examples occur in contexts from the first half of the second century through the first or second decade of the fourth century. This type is seldom catalogued, although presumably common.[86]

SECOND CENTURY

267. Pin. A180:V/3369 (Fig. 20a)

L.0.049; DS.0.002. Shaft curves in profile.

THIRD CENTURY

268. Pin fragment. A139:VII/2417

L.0.040; DS.0.003. Lower portion of shaft missing.

St. Clair in Hostetter et al. 1993, Fig. 43.

EARLY FOURTH CENTURY

269. Pin. A36:VIII/641 (Fig. 20b; Pl. 29f)

L.0.051; DS.0.002. Shaft curves in profile.

St. Clair in Hostetter et al. 1994, 162, Fig. 43.

270. Pin. A36:VIII/766 (Fig. 20c)

L.0.044; DS.0.002. Tip missing. Shaft curves in profile.

271. Pin. A38:VIII/790 (Fig. 20d)

L.0.031; DS.0.002. Tip worn. Shaft curves in profile.

272. Pin. A33:VIII/552 (Fig. 20e; Pl. 29e)

L.0.060; DS.0.002. Tip missing.

St. Clair in Hostetter et al. 1994, 162, 165, Figs. 43, 46.

C. Pins with shafts that are circular or polygonal in section and rounded summits (fifteen examples). Because of their simplicity, larger examples sometimes have been classified as tools or styli. The Palatine East examples are concentrated in third- and early fourth-century contexts, although one example survives from a late first- or early second-century context. This type survives from a wide variety of Roman sites.[87]

SECOND HALF OF THE FIRST CENTURY

273. Pin fragment. A179:IV/3373

L.0.020; DS.0.004. Only summit and upper portion of shaft survive. Shaft circular in section.

THIRD CENTURY

274. Pin. A160:VII/2992 (Fig. 21a)

L.0.099; DS.0.004. Upper shaft ovoid in section.

275. Pin fragment. A157:VII/3131

L.0.040; DS.0.003. Lower portion of shaft missing. Shaft polygonal in section.

St. Clair in Hostetter et al. 1994, 165, Fig. 46.

276. Pin. A152:VII/2682 (Fig. 21b; Pl. 30c)

L.0.070; DS.0.004. Tip missing. Shaft circular in section.

277. Pin fragment. A135:VII/2390

L.0.051; DS.0.003. Lower portion of shaft missing. Shaft circular in section.

278. Pin fragment. A135:VII/2389

L.0.045; DS.0.003. Lower portion of shaft missing. Shaft polygonal in section and slightly curved in profile.

279. Pin. A104:VII/2376 (Fig. 21c)

L.0.045; DS.0.003. Shaft polygonal in section and slightly curved in profile. Possibly unfinished.

EARLY FOURTH CENTURY

280. Pin fragment. A113:VIII/1898 (Fig. 21d)

L.0.043; DS.0.004. Lower portion of shaft missing. Shaft circular in section.

281. Pin fragment. A96:VIII/1860 (Fig. 21e)

L.0.031; DS.0.004. Lower portion of shaft missing. Shaft circular in section.

282. Pin fragment. A38:VIII/950

L.0.036; DS.0.003. Lower portion of shaft missing. Shaft circular in section.

St. Clair in Hostetter et al. 1994, 162, 165, Figs. 43, 46.

283. Pin fragment. A42:VIII/1870 (Fig. 21f)

L.0.055; DS.0.005. Lower portion of shaft missing. Top of shaft polygonal in section.

284. Pin fragment. A22:VIII/436 (Fig. 21g)

L.0.060; DS.0.004. Tip missing. Shaft circular in section.

MEDIEVAL TO MODERN

285. Pin fragment. A3:XII/120

L.0.047; DS.0.004. Longitudinal break. Lower portion of shaft missing. Head chipped. Shaft circular in section.

286. Pin fragment. C108:IX–XII/1974

L.0.026; DS.0.003. Lower portion of shaft missing. Shaft circular in section.

287. Pin. C111:IX–XII/1998

L.0.055; DS.0.003. Shaft circular in section.

D. Pins with shafts 0.003 or greater in diameter and circular in section with conical or pyramidal summits (eighteen examples). This type is widespread throughout the Roman Empire from the first through the fourth century and beyond.[88] Palatine East examples come from contexts dated from the second half of the first century through the mid-fifth century and beyond.

SECOND HALF OF THE FIRST TO SECOND CENTURY

288. Pin. D219:IV/4774 (Fig. 22e; Pl. 30b)

L.0.081; DS.0.005. Tip missing. Conical summit.

289. Pin fragment. D83:IV–V/3578

L.0.026; DS.0.005. Lower portion of shaft missing. Shaft ovoid in section. Flattened conical summit.

290. Pin fragment. D87:V/3596 (Fig. 22c)

L.0.031; DS.0.005. Lower portion of shaft missing. Pyramidal summit.

291. Pin. D216:V/4588 (Pl. 30a)

L.0.090; DS.0.005. Tip missing. Conical summit.

292. Pin. D131:V/4202 (Fig. 22d; Pl. 30d)

L.0.068; DS.0.006. Conical summit.

293. Pin fragment. A104:VII/1991 (Fig. 22f)

L.0.076; DS.0.008. Lower portion of shaft missing. Conical summit.

294. Pin. A135:VII/2375 (Fig. 22a)

L.0.052; DS.0.004. Tip missing. Conical summit. Cancellous bone on upper shaft.

295. Pin fragment. A96:VIII/1805

L.0.051; DS.0.005. Horizontal break (modern). Lower portion of shaft missing. Conical summit.

296. Pin fragment. A96:VIII/1864

L.0.034; DS.0.004. Lower portion of shaft missing. Conical summit

297. Pin fragment. A38:VIII/764 (Fig. 22b)

L.0.065; DS.0.004. Lower portion of shaft missing. Conical summit. Cancellous tissue on upper shaft.

298. Pin fragment. A36:VIII/767

L.0.041; DS.0.006. Lower portion of shaft missing. Conical summit.

299. Pin fragment. A20:VIII/257

L.0.043; DS.0.004. Lower portion of shaft missing. Pyramidal summit. Upper shaft polygonal in section.

300. Pin fragment. A18:XI?/152

L.0.063; DS.0.005. Lower portion of shaft missing. Conical summit.

St. Clair in Hostetter et al. 1994, 165, Fig. 46.

301. Pin. A18:XI/423

L.0.090; DS.0.005. Tip missing. Conical summit.

302. Pin fragment. C74:IX–XII/1470

L.0.031; DS.0.03. Lower portion of shaft missing. Pyramidal summit.

St. Clair in Hostetter et al., 162, 165, Figs. 43, 46.

303. Pin fragment. C77:IX–XII/1375

L.0.031; DS.0.05. Lower shaft missing. Conical summit.

304. Pin. C111:IX–XII/1992

L.0.060; DS.0.004. Tip missing. Conical summit.

305. Pin. DSF:XII/4440

L.0.065; DS.0.005. Tip missing. Conical summit. Lower shaft oval in section.

E. Pins with disk-shaped heads. Shafts are slightly flaring and circular or polygonal in section with a diameter of 0.003 or less (four examples). Perhaps because of their small size, pins of this type are rarely recorded.[89] The Palatine East examples are concentrated in late first- and second-century contexts.

306. Pin. A185:IV–V/3744 (Fig. 23d; Pl. 31d)

L.0.041; DN.0.001; DS.0.002; HH.0.001; DH.0.002. Pin curves in profile at neck. Shaft polygonal in section.

307. Pin. A176:V/3288 (Fig. 23c; Pl. 31c)

L.0.041; DN.0.002; DS.0.003; HH.0.002; DH.0.003. Head has projecting nipple at summit. Shaft polygonal in section. Probably unfinished.

308. Pin. A176:V/3308 (Fig. 23a)

L.0.028; DN.0.001; DS.0.002; HH.0.001; DH.0.002. Tip missing. Shaft polygonal in section.

309. Pin fragment. D31:XI–XII/2687 (Fig. 23b)

L.0.025; DN.0.001; DS.0.002; HH.0.001; DH.0.003. Lower portion of shaft missing. Head and shaft roughly circular in section.

F. Pins with conical heads. Shafts are straight or flaring and circular in section (ten examples). This type is widespread from the second to the fourth century.[90] Examples in metal of a similar type, with two superimposed cones, survive from the first cen-

tury A.D., and with a single cone from the fifth century A.D.[91] Palatine East examples are primarily
from contexts dated from the last quarter of the
third through the mid-fifth century.

THIRD CENTURY

310. Pin fragment. A135:VII/2450 (Pl. 31b)
L.0.040; DN.0.003; DS.0.005; HH.0.001;
DH.0.005. Head broken, two-thirds missing in
section. Lower portion of shaft missing. Irregular
flattened cone-shaped summit. Flaring shaft.

EARLY FOURTH CENTURY

311. Pin. A102:VIII/1824 (Fig. 24f; Pl. 32d)
L.0.062; DN.0.002; DS.0.005; HH.0.003;
DH.0.004. Horizontal crack below neck. Tip
missing. Flaring shaft. Stained brown.

312. Pin. A96:VIII/1807 (Fig. 24a; Pl. 32c)
L.0.036; DN.0.001; DS.0.015; HH.0.002;
DH.0.015. Tip missing. Head ogival in profile.
Flaring shaft.

313. Pin fragment. A94:VIII/1749 (Pl. 31a)
L.0.057; DN.0.002; DS.0.005; HH.0.002;
DH.0.005. Lower portion of shaft missing. Head
damaged at summit. Irregular rounded summit.
Flaring shaft.

314. Pin fragment. A38:VIII/1407 (Pl. 32e)
L.0.052; DN.0.002; DS.0.005; HH.0.003;
DH.0.005. Lower portion of shaft missing. Flaring
shaft.
St. Clair in Hostetter et al. 1994, 162, 165, Figs.
43, 46.

315. Pin fragment. A36:VIII/644 (Fig. 24d)
L.0.044; DN.0.001; DS.0.003; HH.0.004;
DH.0.005. Lower portion of shaft missing. Flaring
shaft.
St. Clair in Hostetter et al. 1994, 165, Fig. 46.

316. Pin fragment. A33:VIII/609 (Fig. 24b;
Pl. 32f)
L.0.036; DN.0.001; DS.0.002; HH.0.003;
DH.0.005. Lower portion of shaft missing. Flaring
shaft.

317. Pin. A22:VIII/313 (Fig. 24e)
L.0.065; DN.0.002; DS.0.002; HH.0.005;
DH.0.004. Straight shaft.
St. Clair in Hostetter et al. 1994, 162, Fig. 43.

MID-FOURTH TO MID-FIFTH CENTURY

318. Pin fragment. A20:VIII/193
L.0.046; DN.0.002; DS.0.003; HH.0.003;
DH.0.004. Lower portion of shaft missing.
Straight shaft.

319. Pin fragment. A20:VIII/258 (Fig. 24c)
L.0.045; DN.0.002; DS.0.003; HH.0.003;
DH.0.003. Lower portion of shaft missing. Flaring
shaft.

G. Pins with cylindrical heads and pyramidal or
cone-shaped summits. Shafts are straight or flaring
and generally circular in section (five examples). In
four of the five Palatine East examples, the heads
are roughly executed with preliminary faceting
clearly visible, raising the possibility that the type
represents a preliminary phase of carving.[92] Palatine
East examples occur primarily in second- and
third-century contexts.

SECOND TO THIRD CENTURY

320. Pin fragment. A123:V–VI/2369 (Fig. 25b;
Pl. 32b)
L.0.060; DN.0.003; DS.0.004; HH.0.007;
DH.0.005. Lower portion of shaft missing. Con-
ical summit. Shaft circular in section. Slightly
flaring shaft.

321. Pin fragment. A104:VII/1980 (Fig. 25a)
L.0.087; DN.0.002; DS.0.004; HH.0.006;
DH.0.005. Shaft has horizontal break at
midsection (modern). Head missing approximately
one-third in section. Conical summit. Head
retains preliminary faceting and appears
unfinished. Shaft circular in section. Flaring shaft.

322. Pin fragment. A144:VII/2507 (Fig. 25c)
L.0.051; DN.0.003; DS.0.004; HH.0.008;
DH.0.007. Unfinished. Lower portion of shaft

missing. Head and shaft polygonal in section and
retain preliminary faceting. Flaring shaft.

MEDIEVAL TO MODERN

323. Pin fragment. D32:XI–XII/2688 (Fig. 25d)
L0.048; DN.0.003; DS.0.005; HH.0.009;
DH.0.006. Lower portion of shaft missing. Conical summit. Head and flaring shaft polygonal in
section.

324. Pin fragment. ASF:XII/2360 (Pl. 32a)
L.0.086; DN.0.003; DS.0.003; HH.0.007;
DH:0.005. Shaft missing below neck. Head has
crack running diagonally from summit to base.
Head roughly ovoid in section with flattened conical summit. Shaft circular in section. Possible
discard.

H. Pins with spherical or subspherical heads
(height and maximum diameter of head differ by
0.001 or less). Shafts are straight or flaring and circular in section (twenty-nine examples). In most
cases, the diameter of the head exceeds that of the
shaft. This type is common throughout the empire
from the late first to the fifth century.[93] It survives,
with a straight shaft, in bronze as well.[94] The finest
Palatine East examples have heads and shafts that
are circular in section.[95] But frequently heads are
oval in section; some exhibit one flattened side on
which cancellous bone sometimes is visible. In
these cases, the shape is the result of the limited
thickness of the blank, which did not allow for a
fully realized circular head. The Palatine East examples begin in late third-century contexts and continue through the mid-fifth and beyond.

MID- TO LATE THIRD CENTURY

325. Pin fragment. A135:VII/2384 (Pl. 33a)
L.0.105; DN.0.003; DS.0.005; HH.0.006;
DH.0.006. Tip missing. Head chipped. Both head
and shaft ovoid in section. Flaring shaft.

326. Pin fragment. A135:VII/2372 (Fig. 26f)
L.0.033; DN.0.003; DS.0.003; HH.0.005;

DH.0.004. Lower portion of shaft missing. Head
roughly rectangular in section. Straight shaft.

327. Pin fragment. A93:VII/1667
L.0.029; DN.0.002; DS.0.003; HH.0.006;
DH.0.006. Lower portion of shaft missing. Head
ovoid in section with flat base. Flaring shaft.

EARLY FOURTH CENTURY

328. Pin fragment. A92:VIII/1681 (Fig. 26i)
L.0.057; DN.0.002; DS.0.004; HH.0.005;
DH.0.005. Lower portion of shaft missing. Flaring
shaft.

329. Pin fragment. A42:VIII/1746 (Fig. 26d)
L.0.048; DN.0.002; DS.0.004; HH.0.005;
DH.0.004. Lower portion of shaft missing. Head
ovoid in section. Flaring shaft.

330. Pin. A38:VIII/717 (Fig. 26j)
L.0.075; DN.0.002; DS.0.004; HH.0.005;
DH.0.005. Tip missing. Flaring shaft ovoid in sec-
tion near bottom.
St. Clair in Hostetter et al. 1994, 162, 165, Figs.
43, 46.

331. Pin fragment. A38:VIII/911
L.0.017; DN.0.003; HH.0.009; DH.0.008. Shaft
missing below neck.

332. Pin. A36:VIII/559
L.0.042; DN.0.002; DS.0.003; HH.0.003;
DH.0.003. Tip missing. Flaring shaft.

333. Pin. A36:VIII/787
L.0.087; DN.0.003; DS.0.004; HH.0.006;
DH.0.006. Slightly flaring shaft.

334. Pin fragment. A36:VIII/1033 (Fig. 26g)
L.0.042; DN.0.002; DS.0.002; HH.0.008;
DH.0.007. Lower portion of shaft missing.
Straight shaft unusually thin in relation to head.

335. Pin fragment. A34:VIII/634 (Fig. 26l)
L.0.065; DN.0.004; DS.0.005; HH.0.008;
DH.0.008. Lower portion of shaft missing. Head
flat on one side. Flaring shaft.
St. Clair in Hostetter et al. 1994, 162, 165, Figs.
43, 46.

336. Pin. A33:VIII/757 (Fig. 26e)

L.0.062; DN.0.003; DS.0.004; HH.0.006; DH.0.005. Tip missing. Head flat on one side. Flaring shaft.

337. Pin fragment. A22:VIII/287 (Fig. 26c)

L.0.027; DN.0.002; DS.0.003; HH.0.007; DH.0.007. Lower portion of shaft missing. Neck inset. Straight shaft.

338. Pin fragment. A16:VIII/500

L.0.068; DN.0.003; DS.0.004; HH.0.008; DH.0.007. Lower portion of shaft missing. Head slightly ovoid in section. Flaring shaft.

339. Pin fragment. A20:VIII/179 (Fig. 26b)

L.0.030; DN.0.002; DS.0.002; HH.0.005; DH.0.004. Lower portion of shaft missing. Straight shaft.

340. Pin fragment. A20:VIII/183 (Fig. 26m)

L.0.023; DN.0.004; HH.0.011; DH.0.010. Shaft missing below neck.

341. Pin fragment. A20:VIII/216

L.0.050; DN.0.002; DS.0.004; HH.0.005; DH.0.004. Lower portion of shaft missing. Head small in relation to shaft. Flaring shaft.

St. Clair in Hostetter et al. 1994, 165, Fig. 46.

342. Pin fragment. A20:VIII/264

L.0.020; DN.0.002; DS.0.003; HH.0.005; DH.0.006. Lower portion of shaft missing. Head has flat base. Flaring shaft.

343. Pin. B340:VIII/4141 (Fig. 26a; Pl. 33b)

L.0.070; DN.0.002; DS.0.003; HH.0.004; DH.0.003. Tip missing. Stained. Head small in relation to shaft. Slightly flaring shaft.

344. Pin. B294:VIII/3460 (Fig. 26k; Pl. 33c)

L.0.073; DN.0.003; DS.0.006; HH.0.009; DH.0.008. Light stain on tip. Cancellous tissue on neck and head. Flaring shaft.

345. Pin. A9:XI/82

L.0.071; DN.0.004; DS.0.004; HH.0.008; DH.0.008. Tip abraded. Straight shaft.

346. Pin fragment. B293:XI/3031

L.0.005; DN.0.002; DS.0.004; HH.0.005; DH.0.004. Lower portion of shaft missing. Head and flaring shaft have one flat side.

347. Pin fragment. D96:XI–XII/3671

L.0.062; DN.0.003; DS.0.005; HH.0.006; DH.0.006. Lower portion of shaft missing. Stained. Flaring shaft.

348. Pin fragment. C77:IX–XII/1384 (Fig. 26h)

L.0.035; DN.0.001; DS.0.003; HH.0.004; DH.0.004. Lower portion of shaft missing. Flaring shaft.

349. Pin. C106:IX–XII/1983

L.0.065; DN.0.002; DS.0.004; HH.0.005; DH.0.005. Tip missing. Flaring shaft.

350. Pin fragment. C113:IX–XII/2229

L.0.037; DN.0.002; DS.0.004; HH.0.006; DH.0.005. Lower portion of shaft missing. Flaring shaft.

351. Pin fragment. C115:IX–XII/2196

L.0.035; DN.0.002; DS.0.004; HH.0.005; DH.0.004. Head chipped. Lower portion of shaft missing. Head polygonal, flaring shaft ovoid in section.

352. Pin fragment. ASF:XII/2864

L.0.053; DN.0.002; DS.0.004; HH.0.006; DH.0.005. Lower portion of shaft missing. Head has one flat side. Flaring shaft.

353. Pin fragment. ASF:XII/3368

L.0.060; DN.0.002; DS.0.004; HH.0.005; DH.0.005. Lower portion of shaft missing. Head ovoid in section. Flaring shaft.

I. Pins with ovoid heads (height of head exceeds diameter by 0.002 or more). Shafts are flaring and generally circular in section (thirty-two examples). The type is common throughout the empire from the first to the late fifth or early sixth century.[96] As with Type H, the Palatine East examples often have heads that are ovoid in section and one flat side, reflecting the limited thickness of the blank. This type appears in contexts beginning in the last quarter of the third century and continuing through the fifth century and beyond.

354. Pin fragment. A153:VII/2855 (Fig. 27a)

L.0.038; DN.0.002; DS.0.003; HH.0.006; DH.0.004. Lower portion of shaft missing. Head and shaft polygonal in section.

355. Pin fragment. A153:VII/2856 (Fig. 27b)

L.0.028; DN.0.002; DS.0.003; HH.0.006; DH.0.004. Lower portion of shaft missing. Head and shaft polygonal in section.

356. Pin fragment. A148:VII/2698 (Fig. 27c)

L.0.032; DN.0.002; DS.0.004; HH.0.006; DH.0.004. Lower portion of shaft missing. Head and shaft polygonal in section.

357. Pin fragment. A124:VII/2200 (Fig. 27n)

L.0.048; DN.0.003; DH.0.006; HH.0.010; DH.0.006. Horizontal break below neck (modern). Lower portion of shaft missing. Head roughly triangular in section.

358. Pin fragment. A124VII/2201 (Fig. 27o)

L.0.055; DN.0.003; DS.0.005; HH.0.011 DH.0.009. Lower portion of shaft missing.

359. Pin fragment. A97:VII/2168 (Fig. 27m)

L.0.043; DN.0.003; DS.0.005; HH.0.010; DH.0.006; Lower portion of shaft missing. Shaft and ovoid head have one flat side.

St. Clair in Hostetter et al. 1994, 162, 165, Figs. 43, 46.

360. Pin fragment. A105:VIII/1868 (Fig. 27p)

L.0.053; DN.0.003; DS.0.005; HH.0.010; DH.0.007. Head encrusted. Lower portion of shaft missing. Head has one flat side.

361. Pin fragment. A96:VIII/1804

L.0.043; DN.0.003; DS.0.004; HH.0.009; DH.0.007. Horizontal break below neck (modern). Lower portion of shaft missing. Head ovoid in section with one flat side.

362. Pin fragment. A96:VIII/1861

L.0.048; DN.0.002; DS.0.004; HH.0.007; DH.0.004. Lower portion of shaft missing.

363. Pin fragment. A93:VII/1761 (Fig. 27k)

L.0.064; DN.0.002; DS.0.004; HH.0.009; DH.0.005. Horizontal break below neck (modern).Lower portion of shaft missing. Head flat on one side.

364. Pin fragment. A92:VIII/1668 (Fig. 27f)

L.0.046; DN.0.002; DS.0.003; HH.0.010; DH.0.005. Lower portion of shaft missing. Head ovoid in section.

365. Pin fragment. A67:VIII/1756

L.0.052; DN.0.003; DS.0.005; HH.0.009; DH.0.007. Lower portion of shaft missing.

366. Pin fragment. A36:VIII/639

L.0.035; DN.0.004; DS.0.004; HH.0.013; DH.0.007. Lower portion of shaft missing. Head ovoid in section with cancellous tissue on one side.

367. Pin fragment. A36:VIII/787 (Fig. 27j)

L.0.047; DN.0.002; DS.0.004; HH.0.006; DH.0.004. Lower portion of shaft missing.

368. Pin. A33:VIII/555 (Fig. 27i)

L.0.067; DN.0.002; DS.0.003; HH.0.006; DH.0.004. Tip missing. Head roughly ovoid in section with one concave side.

369. Pin fragment. A33:VIII/619 (Fig. 27g)

L.0.045; DN.0.002; DS.0.003; HH.0.006; DH.0.004. Lower portion of shaft missing.

370. Pin fragment. A33:VIII/758 (Fig. 27l)

L.0.041; DN.0.003; DS.0.004; HH.0.011; DH.0.007. Lower portion of shaft missing. Head flat on one side.

371. Pin fragment. A22:VIII/298

L.0.034; DN.0.002; DS.0.003; HH.0.008; DH.0.004. Lower portion of shaft missing.

372. Pin fragment. A16:VIII/414 (Fig. 27d)

L.0.045; DN.0.002; DS.0.003; HH.0.007; DH.0.004. Horizontal break below neck

(modern). Lower portion of shaft missing. Head
ovoid in section.

373. Pin. A16:VIII/437

L.0.079; DN.0.003; DS.0.005; HH.0.008;
DH.0.006. Tip missing. Upper shaft and head
ovoid in section.

MID-FOURTH TO MID-FIFTH CENTURY

374. Pin fragment. A20:VIII/211 (Fig. 27e)

L.0.068; DN.0.003; DS.0.004; HH.0.009;
DH.0.006. Head chipped. Lower portion of shaft
missing. Shaft flat on one side at midsection.

375. Pin fragment. A20:VIII/334

L.0.035; DN.0.003; DS.0.004; HH.0.008;
DH.0.005. Lower portion of shaft missing. Head
and upper shaft ovoid in section. Head flat on
one side.

376. Pin. A12:VIII/121 (Fig. 27h)

L.0.058; DN.0.002; DS.0.004; HH.0.008;
DH.0.005. Head ovoid in section.

SECOND HALF OF THE FIFTH CENTURY

377. Pin. B270:VIII/2534

L.0.071; DN.0.003; DS.0.005; HH.0.010;
DH.0.008. Tip missing. Head flat on one side.

378. Pin fragment. B270:VIII/2936

L.0.067; DN.0.002; DS.0.005; HH.0.009;
DH.0.007. Lower portion of shaft missing. Shaft
and head ovoid in section.

MEDIEVAL TO MODERN

379. Pin fragment. C6:IX–XII/130

L.0.032; DN.0.002; DS.0.005; HH.0.008;
DH.0.006. Lower portion of shaft missing. Head
flat on one side.

380. Pin. C77:IX–XII/1379 (Fig. 27q)

L.0.065; DN.0.004; DS.0.005; HH.0.010;
DH.0.008. Bottom of shaft damaged as though by
animal teeth. Head ovoid in section with flat base.

381. Pin fragment. C111:IX–XII/1993

L.0.047; DN.0.003; DS.0.005; HH.0.008;
DH.0.005. Lower portion of shaft missing. Shaft
ovoid in section below neck. Head flat on one side.

382. Pin fragment. C115:IX–XII/3518

L.0.041; DN.0.002; DS.0.004; HH.0.008;
DH.0.006. Lower portion of shaft missing. Head
ovoid in section with one flat side.

383. Pin fragment. C139:IX–XII/3118

L.0.036; DN.0.002; DS.0.003; HH.0.005;
DH.0.003. Lower portion of shaft missing. Head
flat on one side.

384. Pin fragment. C150/3372

L.0.086; DN.0.004; DS.0.005; HH.0.012;
DH.0.006. Lower portion of shaft missing. Head
flat on two sides. Lower shaft triangular in section.
Saw marks on shaft and head. Possibly unfinished.

385. Pin fragment. A3:XII/351

L.0.069; DN.0.002; DS.0.005; HH.0.015;
DH.0.010. Lower portion of shaft missing.

J. Pins with flat-topped ovoid or bulb-shaped heads.
Shafts are straight or flaring and generally circular
in section (fifteen examples). Examples survive from
third-century contexts in Italy and Pannonia, and a
similar type, but with faceted head, occurs at Corinth (fourth century) and in England (third to fifth
century).[97] As with Types H and I, the Palatine
East examples often have heads that are ovoid in
section and one flat side, reflecting the limited
thickness of the blank. This type begins in contexts
dated to the last quarter of the third century and
continues through the mid-fifth century.

MID- TO LATE THIRD CENTURY

386. Pin fragment. A152:VII/2863 (Fig. 28h)

L.0.009; DN.0.004; HH.0.006; DH.0.006. Shaft
missing. Head roughly cylindrical in profile.

EARLY FOURTH CENTURY

387. Pin fragment. A38:VIII/1390 (Fig. 28j)

L.0.027; DN.0.002; DS.0.002; HH.0.011;
DH.0.007. Lower portion of shaft missing. Head
flat on one side and at base. Straight shaft.

388. Pin. A38/782

L.0.086; DN.0.003; DS.0.004; HH.0.005;

DH.0.006. Head and shaft circular in section.
Straight shaft.

389. Pin fragment. A36:VIII/604

L.0.041; DN.0.002; DS.0.003; HH.0.010;
DH.0.006. Lower portion of shaft missing. Shaft
ovoid in section.

390. Pin fragment. A36:VIII/756 (Fig. 28e)

L.0.052; DN.0.004; DS.0.004; HH.0.008;
DH.0.007. Lower portion of shaft missing.
Straight shaft.

391. Pin. A34:VIII/633:VII (Fig. 28d)

L.0.062; DN.0.003; DS.0.005; HH.0.011;
DH.0.007. Tip worn and stained. Head flat on
two sides. Flaring shaft.

392. Pin fragment. A33:VIII/751 (Fig. 28i)

L.0.022; DN.0.003; DS.0.003; HH.0.014;
DH.0.008. Shaft missing below neck. Head ovoid
in section.

393. Pin fragment. A33:VIII/759 (Fig. 28a)

L.0.018; DN.0.002; HH.0.007; DH.0.006. Shaft
missing below neck. Head has vertical gouge running from summit to just above base.

394. Pin fragment. A22:VIII/305 (Fig. 28g)

L.0.054; DN.0.002; DS.0.004; HH.0.011;
DH.0.006. Lower portion of shaft missing. Head
ovoid in section. Flaring shaft.

395. Pin. A16:VIII/429 (Fig. 28c)

L.0.089; DN.0.002; DS.0.004; HH.0.080;
DH.0.006. Head ovoid in section. Flaring shaft.

396. Pin. A16:VIII/437 (Fig. 28b)

L.0.079; DN.0.003; DS.0.005; HH.0.008;
DH.0.006. Tip missing. Upper shaft and head
ovoid in section.

397. Pin fragment. A16:VIII/440 (Pl. 33e)

L.0.078; DN.0.002; DS.0.003; HH.0.008;
DH.0.006. Head has longitudinal break, one-
half missing in section. Tip chipped and
stained.

St. Clair in Hostetter et al. 1994, 162, 165, Figs.
43, 46.

398. Pin. A20:VIII/225 (Fig. 28f; Pl. 33d)

L.0.076; DN.0.002; DS.0.005; HH.0.011;

DH.0.008. Tip missing. Head flat on one side.
Flaring shaft.

MEDIEVAL TO MODERN

399. Pin fragment. B62:XI/792 (Fig. 28k)

L.0.021; DN.0.002; DS.0.003; HH.0.009;
DH.0.008. Lower portion of shaft missing. Head
ovoid in section.

400. Pin. A9:XI/58

L.0.068; DN.0.003; DS.0.005; HH.0.008;
DH.0.006. Head chipped. Head irregular in section with one flat side. Cancellous bone. Neck
inset. Shaft retains preliminary faceting.
Unfinished.

K. Pins with pointed ovoid heads. Shafts are
straight or flaring and circular in section. The
diameter of the head normally exceeds that of the
shaft (thirty-eight examples). This type is widespread from the late first through the fifth century.[98] As with Types H, I, and J, the Palatine East
examples often have heads that are ovoid in section
and one flat side reflecting the limited thickness of
the blank. The earliest examples are from contexts
dated to the first or second decade of the fourth
century, and the type continues through the late
fifth century and beyond.

EARLY FOURTH CENTURY

401. Pin fragment. A105:VIII/1869 (Fig. 29n)

L.0.063; DN.0.003; DS.0.005; HH.0.011;
DH.0.006. Lower portion of shaft missing. Shaft
encrusted. Flaring shaft.

402. Pin fragment. A96:VIII/1839

L.0.043; DN.0.002; DS. 0.003; HH.0.006;
DH.0.004. Lower portion of shaft missing.
Straight shaft.

403. Pin fragment. A67:VIII/1795 (Fig. 29i)

L.0.065; DN.0.003; DS.0.005; HH.0.010;
DH.0.007. Lower portion of shaft missing. Head
flat on one side with cancellous bone visible.
Flaring shaft.

404. Pin. A67:VIII/1743 (Fig. 29d)

L.0.078; DN.0.002; DS.0.003; HH.0.010;

DH.0.005. Tip missing. Head ovoid in section. Slightly flaring.

405. Pin. A67:VIII/1726

L.0.066; DN.0.002; DS.0.003; HH.0.006; DH.0.004. Flaring shaft. Lower shaft curves slightly in profile.

406. Pin. A49:VIII/1652

L.0.061; DN.0.003; DS.0.005; HH.0.011; DH.0.005. Tip missing. Head flat on two sides. Flaring shaft.

407. Pin. A42:VIII/1741

L.0.042; DN.0.003; DS.0.005; HH.0.008; DH.0.005. Tip missing. Flaring shaft. Lower shaft ovoid in section.

408. Pin. A38:VIII/1465

L.0.063; DN.0.003; DS.0.005; HH.0.010; DH.0.007. Tip worn and stained.

409. Pin fragment. A38:VIII/1387 (Fig. 29a)

L.0.029; DN.0.002; DS.0.003; HH.0.006; DH.0.004. Lower portion of shaft missing. Head ovoid in section. Straight shaft.

410. Pin fragment. A38:VIII/913

L.0.046; DN.0.003; DS.0.004; HH.0.017; DH.0.006. Lower portion of shaft missing. Head ovoid in section. Head flares slightly toward summit.

411. Pin fragment. A38:VIII/914

L.0.028; DN.0.005; HH.0.016; DH.0.008. Shaft missing below neck.

412. Pin fragment. A36/563

L.0.023; DN.0.003; DS.0.003; HH.0.011; DH.0.006. Lower shaft missing. Head chipped. Head ovoid in section.

413. Pin fragment. A36/642 (Fig. 29e)

L.0.056; DN.0.002 DS.0.004; DH.0.005; HH.0.010. Lower portion of shaft missing. Head ovoid in section with one flat side. Slightly flaring shaft.

414. Pin. A33:VIII/515 (Fig. 29b)

L.0.079; DN.0.002; DS.0.004; HH.0.011; DH.0.006. Tip missing.

St. Clair in Hostetter et al. 1994, 162, 165, Figs. 43, 46.

415. Pin fragment. A22:VIII/314

L.0.064; DN.0.002; DS.0.004; HH.0.011; DH.0.005. Lower shaft missing. Straight shaft.

416. Pin fragment. A16:VIII/419

L.0.024; DN.0.003; DS.0.003; HH.0.012; DH.0.005. Lower portion of shaft missing.

417. Pin. A16:VIII/422 (Fig. 29h; Pl. 34a)

L.0.069; DN.0.003; DS.0.005; HH.0.013; DH.0.008. Tip missing. Head ovoid in section with one flat side. Slightly flaring shaft.

St. Clair in Hostetter et al. 1994, 165, Fig. 46.

418. Pin fragment. B354:VIII/4556 (Fig. 29l)

L.0.060; DN.0.004; DS.0.005; HH.0.015; DH.0.009. Horizontal break below neck (modern). Lower portion of shaft missing. Head and shaft marked by short parallel incisions on one side, perhaps from a toothed chisel. Straight shaft. Unfinished.

MID-FOURTH TO FIFTH CENTURY

419. Pin fragment. A20:VIII/176 (Fig. 29j)

L.0.070; DN.0.004; DS.0.006; HH.0.015; DH.0.009. Lower portion of shaft missing. Head flat on two sides, one with cancellous bone visible. Flaring shaft.

420. Pin fragment. A20:VIII/180

L.0.050; DN.0.003; DS.0.004; HH.0.020; DH.0.007. Lower portion of shaft missing. Slightly flaring shaft.

421. Pin. A20:VIII/190 (Fig. 29f)

L.0.063; DN.0.003; DS.0.005 HH.0.011; DH.0.006. Tip missing. Shaft and head slightly ovoid in section. Flaring shaft.

422. Pin fragment. A20:VIII/201

L.0.050; DN.0.003; DS.0.005; HH 0.014; DH.0 006. Lower portion of shaft missing. Head flat on one side with cancellous bone visible.

423. Pin. A20:VIII/221 (Fig. 29k)

L.0.092; DN.0.003; DS.0.005; HH.0.012; DH 0.008. Tip missing. Neck ovoid in section. Head polygonal in section with two contiguous long sides and retains signs of preliminary faceting. Flaring shaft. Possibly unfinished.

424. Pin. A20:VIII/229 (Pl. 34b)

L.0.072; DN.0.002; DS.0.003; HH.0.008; DH.0.005. Tip stained. Flaring shaft.

St. Clair in Hostetter et al. 1994, 165, Fig. 46.

425. Pin fragment. A20:VIII/246

L.0.067; DN.0.004; DS.0.007; HH.0.011; DH.0.007. Lower shaft missing. Head has flat base. Flaring shaft.

426. Pin. A20:VIII/269

L.0.055; DN.0.002; DS.0.003; HH.0.009; DH.0.004. Tip missing. Flaring shaft.

427. Pin fragment. A20:VIII/275

L.0.052; DN.0.003; DS.0.005; HH.0.012; DH.0.009. Lower shaft missing. Flaring shaft.

428. Pin. A20:VIII/312

L.0.077; DN.0.003; DS.0.004; HH.0.014; DH.0.007. Tip missing. Head flat on one side with cancellous bone visible. Slightly flaring shaft.

429. Pin fragment. A12:VIII/147

L.0.047; DN.0.003; DS.0.005; HH.0.012; DH.0.007. Horizontal break at neck (modern). Lower portion of shaft missing. Head oval in section. Straight shaft.

430. Pin fragment. A12:VIII/126 (Fig. 29m)

L.0.048; DN.0.003; DS.0.005; HH.0.011; DH.0.008. Lower half of shaft missing. Stained. Head has vertical groove ca. 0.001 deep running from base to summit. Lower portion of shaft missing. Head oval in section.

431. Pin fragment. B342:VIII/4225 (Fig. 29g)

L.0.058; DN.0.003; DS.0.004; HH.0.008; DH.0.006. Lower portion of shaft missing. Head flat on one side. Slightly flaring shaft.

432. Pin fragment. B309:VIII/3739

L.0.058; DN.0.004; DS.0.005; HH.0.019; DH.0.006. Head has longitudinal break with upper third missing. Tip missing. Head and shaft flat on one side. Flaring shaft.

433. Pin fragment. B270:VIII/3633 (Pl. 34c)

L.0.061; DN.0.002; DS.0.003; HH.0.007;

DH.0.005. Ivory. Lower portion of shaft missing. Bulb-shaped head. Slightly flaring shaft.

MEDIEVAL TO MODERN

434. Pin. CSF:XII/1151

L.0.063; DN.0.003; DS.0.04; HH.0.012; DH.0.004. Tip missing. Head flat on one side and flares slightly toward summit.

435. Pin fragment. C115:IX–XII /3518

L.0.041; DN.0.002; DS.0.005; HH.0.008; DH.0.006. Lower portion of shaft missing. Head ovoid in section with one flat side.

436. Pin. A9:XI/90

L.0.062; DN.0.003; DS.0.005; HH.0.014 DH.0.008. Tip missing. Head flat on one side with cancellous bone visible.

437. Pin fragment. A35:XII/918 (Fig. 29c)

L.0.068; DN.0.003; DS.0.004; HH.0.011; DH.0.006. Lower shaft missing. Head ovoid in section. Slightly flaring shaft.

438. Pin fragment. A3:XII/382

L.0.041; DN.0.002; DS.0.003; HH.0.006; DH.0.004. Lower portion of shaft missing. Head and shaft flat on one side. Flaring shaft.

L. Pins with slightly flaring shafts, circular in section, decorated with incised concentric lines at or near the neck, and with spherical or ovoid heads (two examples). Scattered examples appear in contexts ranging from the first or second century (many with heads separate from bodies) to the fifth century.[99] The Palatine East examples are from a fifth-century and a later disturbed context with considerable residual material.

SECOND HALF OF THE FIFTH CENTURY

439. Pin. B296:VIII/3752 (Fig. 30a)

L.0.082; DN.0.003; DS.0.005; HH.0.011; DH.0.008. Tip missing. Shaft has two parallel, incised lines at the neck. Head ovoid with indentation at summit from lathe stock. Shaft flat on one side.

440. Pin. A9:XI/65 (Fig. 30b; Pl. 34d)

L.0.068; DN.0.004; DS.0.005; HH.0.011; DH.0.009. Tip missing. Bottom of shaft stained. Shaft polygonal in section with three irregular hand-carved incisions below neck. Head flat on one side with cancellous bone visible. Conical protrusion at summit partially undercut by a horizontal incision.

St. Clair in Hostetter et al. 1994, 162, 165, Figs. 43, 46.

M. Pin with flaring shaft and pointed ovoid head resting on a flange with concentric horizontal grooves (one example). The Palatine East example is ivory.

MID-FOURTH TO MID-FIFTH CENTURY

441. Pin. A20:VIII/210 (Fig. 30c; Pl. 35e)

L.0.044; DN.0.002; DS.0.005; HH.0.009; DH.0.006. Ivory. Shaft flaked vertically along the grain on one side. Head and shaft slightly ovoid in section.[100]

St. Clair in Hostetter et al. 1994, 162, 165, Figs. 43, 46.

N. Pins with straight or flaring shafts circular in section and ovoid or spherical heads resting on one or more reels (two examples). This type is present at a variety of sites, from the third to fifth century.[101] The Palatine East examples are highly polished with heads circular in section and appear to be lathe-turned.

EARLY FOURTH CENTURY

442. Pin. A36:VIII/622 (Fig. 30d; Pl. 35b)

L.0.066; DN.0.003; DS.0.004; HH (incl. reel).0.010; DH.0.007. Tip missing. Lower shaft stained. Ovoid head rests on two reels separated by a groove. Flaring shaft.

St. Clair in Hostetter et al. 1994, 162, 165, Figs. 43, 46.

443. Pin fragment. A33:VIII/507 (Fig. 30e; Pl. 35c)

L.0.055; DN.0.003; DS.0.004; HH (incl. reel)

.0.010; DH.0.007. Lower portion of shaft missing. Spherical head rests on a single reel. Straight shaft.

St. Clair in Hostetter et al. 1994, 162, 165, Figs. 43, 46.

O. Pins with flaring shafts, circular in section, decorated with bead and ring or reel motifs at the neck and ovoid or spherical heads (two examples). Bíró dates similar pins to the fourth century.[102] The Palatine East examples are from fifth-century contexts. One is ivory. The heads are spherical in section and appear to be lathe-turned.

SECOND HALF OF THE FIFTH CENTURY

444. Pin fragment. B186:VIII/2860 (Fig. 30f; Pl. 35f)

L.0.023; DN.0.004; HH.0.011; DH.0.008. Ivory. Shaft missing below neck. Pointed ovoid head rests on neck decorated with, from bottom, four narrow rings, a bead, and two wider rings.

445. Pin. B209:VIII/2171 (Fig. 30g; Pl. 35d)

L.0.054; DN.0.003; HH.0.005; DH.0.005. Spherical head rests on neck with, from bottom, a reel, bead, and narrow ring. Straight shaft.

P. Pins of large dimensions with straight or slightly flaring shafts circular in section (three examples). This type is widespread throughout the empire. It appears frequently in the first and second centuries, but scattered examples occur as late as the sixth or seventh century.[103] It has been suggested that these objects functioned as styli or spindles, as well as dress pins of the type *acus discriminalis*; their dimensions correspond to those in figural representations.[104] Béal suggests that examples with tips incised with rings may have been intended for the application of cosmetics, in the form of liquid or ointment.[105] One of the Palatine East examples is from a first-century context. None is complete, but the best preserved, which is missing the lower shaft, measures 0.106 in length. The heads are incomplete or missing, and it is possible that in some cases heads were attached separately.

446. Shaft fragment. D89:IV/3463 (Fig. 30h)

L.0.087; D.0.007

Upper portion of shaft missing. Broken along one side. Worn and stained. Lower portion of shaft tapering to point.

447. Pin fragment. B287:VIII:3342 (Fig. 30i; Pl. 35a)

L.0.106; DS.0.008. Lower portion of shaft missing. Summit chipped. Raised band encircles neck. Summit flat and roughly circular. Slightly flaring shaft.

448. Pin fragment. A122:X/1995 (Fig. 30j)

L.0.088; DS.0.007. Lower portion of shaft missing. Upper shaft is ovoid in section. Summit has projecting irregular knob above a raised band that encircles the shaft. Straight shaft. Possibly unfinished.

Q. Pin with hook shaped head. An example with a longer shaft survives from the Roman period from Saint-Romain-en-Gal (Vienne).[106]

449. Pin. A38:VIII/1403 (Fig. 30k)

L.0.049; W.0.007. Broken at one end. Circular in section. Diameter expands slightly toward curved end.

II. Pins with Decorated Heads

A. Pin with slightly flaring shaft, circular in section, and cone-shaped head formed by superimposed reels. Scattered examples with similar decoration, but in some cases lacking the cone-shaped profile, are found from the fourth or fifth century.[107]

450. Pin. A12:VIII/125 (Fig. 31a)

L.0.072; DN.0.004; DS.0.006; HH.0.009;

DH.0.006. Surface of shaft and tip worn. Head formed by three superimposed reels diminishing in diameter to form cone.

St. Clair in Hostetter et al., 164, 166, Figs. 44, 47.

B. Pin with straight or flaring shaft, circular in section, and pointed ovoid head decorated with concentric horizontal grooves that continue, sometimes in the form of more widely spaced bands, on the neck. The Palatine East example is ivory. The head and shaft were made separately. A similar two-part pin, dated to the first or second century, survives from Corinth.[108] Several separate shafts were found in the late antique contexts, however, and it is possible that two-part pins continued to be made during this period. Cruder one-piece bone examples survive from fourth or fifth century contexts at Carthage.[109]

451. Pin fragment. A 20:VIII/181 (Fig. 31b; Pl. 36f)

L.0.036; DN.0.003; DS.0.003; HH.0.012; DH.0.008. Ivory. Lower portion of shaft missing. Head has longitudinal fractures running from near summit to base caused by outward pressure of shaft inserted into base. Head circular in section and lathe-turned, with tightly spaced concentric grooves. Shaft, with concentric rings at neck, curves slightly in profile.

St. Clair 1996, 370, Fig. 7; St. Clair in Hostetter et al. 1994, 164, 166, Figs. 44, 47.

C. Pins with flaring shafts, circular in section, and pointed ovoid or bulb-shaped heads decorated with concentric horizontal grooves that continue on a flange at the neck (two examples). One example is from a fourth-century context; the other is ivory and from a disturbed context.[110]

452. Pin. A22:VIII/300 (Fig. 31c; Pl. 36b)

L.0.070; DN.0.004; DS.0.007; HH (with flange).0.018; DH.0.008. Tip missing. Lower portion of shaft stained. Ovoid head, circular in section, lathe-turned with tightly spaced concentric grooves that continue on flange. Flaring shaft.

St. Clair 1996, 370, Fig. 7; St. Clair in Hostetter et al. 1994, 164, 166, Figs. 44, 47.

MODERN

453. Pin. A14:XII/255 (Fig. 31d; Pl. 36d)

L.0.043; DN (below flange).0.003; DS.0.004; HH (incl. flange).0.010; DH.0.007. Ivory. Tip missing. Bulb-shaped head, circular in section, lathe-turned with tightly spaced concentric grooves that continue on flange. Slightly flaring shaft.

St. Clair 1996, 370, Fig.7; St. Clair in Hostetter et al. 1994, 166, Fig. 47.

D. Pins with flaring shafts that are circular in section and spherical or pointed ovoid heads decorated with concentric horizontal grooves and resting on a neck with a molding of bead and ring or reel motifs (two examples). Both Palatine East examples are ivory. One has a head made separately from the shaft. A similar bone pin, of unknown provenance, but presumably from Rome, is preserved in the Antiquarium Comunale, Rome.[111] Both Palatine East examples are from fifth-century contexts.

SECOND HALF OF THE FIFTH CENTURY

454. Pin. B209:VIII/2170 (Fig. 31e; Pl. 36c)

L.0.062; DN.0.004; DS.0.005; HH.0.012; DH.0.007. Ivory. Tip worn. Head circular in section, lathe-turned with tightly spaced horizontal grooves. Neck with lathe-turned bead flanked by rings.

St. Clair 1996, 370, Fig. 7.

455. Pin fragment. B276:VIII/2685 (Fig. 31f; Pl. 36e)

L.0.033; DN.0.003; DS.0.004; HH.0.010; DH.0.10; LN.0.005. Ivory. Head and upper portion of separate shaft preserved. Head has rectangular lacuna 0.004 long and 0.002 wide below a series of vertical cracks caused by outward pressure of shaft inserted into base. One side of head chipped (modern). Head originally circular

in section and lathe-turned with tightly spaced concentric grooves. Neck with lathe-turned bead between two reels.

St. Clair 1996, 370, Fig. 7.

E. Pin with flaring shaft and bulb-shaped head decorated with concentric bands or rings that begin on the head and continue on the neck.

FOURTH CENTURY

456. Pin fragment. B354:VIII/4373 (Fig. 31g; Pl. 37e)

L.0.055; DN.0.004; DS.0.005; HH.0.004. Ivory. Lower portion of shaft chipped. Tip missing. Portion of head missing. Lathe-turned concentric rings of varying widths begin on lower third of head and continue on neck above a bead and reel. Rings on head veer upward. Probable discard.

F. Pin with ovoid head decorated with concentric rings on the lower portion and topped by a cone formed by concentric rings and a knob (one example). Similar pins survive from Corinth dated to the first or second century.[112]

EARLY FOURTH CENTURY

457. Pin fragment. A33:VIII/505 (Fig. 31h; Pl. 37f)

HH.0.014; DH.0.007. Shaft missing. Encrusted. Head circular in section. Lathe-turned.

St. Clair in Hostetter et al. 1994, 164, 166, Figs. 44, 47.

G. Pin with straight shaft, circular in section decorated with incised lines at the neck and spherical head decorated with vertical incisions and topped by a knob. The head is a variant of the pomegranate type found at Corinth and in bronze at Delos.[113]

SECOND HALF OF THE FIFTH CENTURY

458. Pin fragment. B281:VIII/2710 (Fig. 31i; Pl. 37c)

L.0.47; DN.0.004; DS.0.004; HH.0.010; DH.0.10. Lower portion of shaft missing. Head and shaft made separately. Shaft with two parallel incised lines running obliquely beginning 0.002 below head. Head with knife carved v-shaped incisions, irregularly spaced, stopping short of summit and flat base. Knob at summit encircled by a groove 0.001 in width. Head and shaft ovoid in section.

H. Pin with straight shaft circular in section and ovoid heads decorated with incisions curving obliquely from base to summit. Similar pins, cruder in execution and of unknown provenance, are preserved in Rome and from fourth- or fifth-century contexts at Corinth and Leptis Magna.[114] The Palatine East example is from a late containing large amounts of residual material.

459. Pin. C9:IX–XII/421 (Fig. 31j; Pl. 37d)

L.0.052; DN.0.002; DS.0.003; HH.0.010; DH.0.006. Encrustation on neck and head. Tip missing. Head ovoid in section with knife carved, v-shaped incisions that vary in width. Straight shaft.

I. Pins with straight shafts circular in section decorated with horizontal grooves or rings at the neck and spherical or ovoid heads decorated with obliquely curving incisions and topped by a knob resting on a reel (three examples).[115] The Palatine East examples have separately made heads and shafts. All are from fifth-century contexts, suggesting that two-part pins continued to be made during this period.

460. Pin. B180:VIII/2179 (Fig. 31k; Pl. 37a)

L.0.087; DN.0.003; DS.0.003; HH.0.012; DH.0.012. Tip missing. Shaft with three parallel horizontal grooves beginning 0.003 below head. Separate head circular in section with flat base and knife carved tightly spaced v-shaped incisions.

461. Pin. B180:VIII/2182 (Fig. 31l; Pl. 37b)

L.0.078; DN.0.003; DS.0.003; HH.0.011;

DH.0.008. Tip slightly stained. Shaft with three horizontal groves beginning 0.002 below neck. Separate head slightly ovoid in section with flat base and knife carved tightly spaced v-shaped incisions.

462. Pin fragment. B186:VIII/2620 (Fig. 31m)

L.0.077; DN.0.003; DS.0.004; HH.0.012; DH.0.010. Lower portion of shaft missing. Shaft with four horizontal grooves that begin 0.002 below head. Separate head ovoid in section with one bulging side in profile and knife-carved, shallow v-shaped incisions. Shaft flares on one side.

J. Pins with flaring shafts that are circular in section and pointed ovoid heads decorated with obliquely curving incisions and resting on a reel (two examples). Similar pins survive in the Hungarian National Collections, and an example with two reels survives from Delos.[116]

463. Pin fragment. A38:VIII/908 (Fig. 31n; Pl. 38b)

L.0.047; DN.0.002; DS.0.004; HH (incl. reel).0.013; DH.0.005. Lower portion of shaft missing. Flaring shaft and head are ovoid in section. Knife-carved shallow v-shaped incisions. St. Clair in Hostetter et al. 1994, 164, 166, Figs. 44, 47.

464. Pin. A105:VIII/1828 (Fig. 32i; Pl. 38a)

L.0.065; DN.0.002; DS.0.004; HH (incl. reel).0.008; DH.0.005. Head flat on one side. Knife-carved, irregularly spaced v-shaped incisions.

K. Pin with flat-topped cylindrical head decorated with obliquely curving incisions, topped by and resting on a reel. Several examples of this type from Pannonia survive in the Hungarian National Collections.[117]

465. Pin fragment. A36:VIII/562 (Fig. 32a; Pl. 38e)

L.0.018; DN. 0.002; HH. 0.014; DH. 0.006. Shaft missing below neck. Top reel chipped. Head circular in section with knife-carved v-shaped incisions.

St. Clair in Hostetter et al. 1994, 164, 166, Figs. 44, 47.

L. Pin with flaring head decorated with obliquely curving incisions and topped by a reel.

466. Pin fragment. A113:VIII/1969 (Fig. 32b)

HH.0.007; DH.0.007. Shaft missing. Knife-carved v-shaped incisions.

M. Pins with ovoid heads decorated with obliquely curving incisions resting on a neck decorated with bead and ring or reel motifs (two examples). Similar pins survive from Pannonia in the Hungarian National Collections and from Corinth.[118] The Palatine East examples are from fourth- or fifth-century contexts. One is ivory.

467. Pin fragment. A12:VIII/157 (Fig. 32c; Pl. 38d)

L.0.016; DN.0.003; HH.0.010; DH.0.011. Shaft missing below neck. Neck with lathe-turned bead resting on two rings and topped by one ring. Head circular in section with irregularly spaced knife-carved v-shaped incisions and topped by a knob.

St. Clair 1996, 370, Fig.18; St. Clair in Hostetter et al. 1994, 164, 166, Figs. 44, 47.

468. Pin fragment. B270:VIII/3968 (Pl. 38c)

L.0.024; DN.0.002; HH.0.007; DH.0.006. Ivory. Lower portion of shaft missing. Upper shaft missing approximately one-third in section (modern break). Vertical crack runs through shaft and head. Pointed head with hand-carved obliquely curving lines resting on neck bead and reels.

N. Pin with ovoid head decorated with incised obliquely curving incisions and rings alternating with u-shaped grooves, topped by a knob.

469. Pin fragment. A105:VIII/1888 (Fig. 32d; Pl. 39c)

HH.0.012; DH.0.008. Shaft missing. Head ovoid in section with irregularly spaced knife-carved incisions interrupted by one ring flanked by grooves just below midsection and topped by two rings separated by grooves and a knob resting on a short stem.

St. Clair in Hostetter et al. 1994, 164, 166 Figs. 44, 47.

O. Pin with bulb-shaped head decorated with incised obliquely curving incisions resting on a base of lathe-turned concentric rings that continue on flange.

470. Pin fragment. A67:VIII/1745 (Fig. 32e; Pl. 39d)

L.0.017; DN.0.003; HH.0.006; DH.0.007. Shaft missing below flange. Head ovoid in section with knife-carved v-shaped incisions resting on three rings with sharply angled profiles. Flange with two rings that begin 0.002 from summit.

St. Clair in Hostetter et al. 1994, 164, 166, Figs. 44, 47.

P. Pin with straight shaft topped by a lathe-turned molding consisting of two rings, an inverted vase, a bobbin or spindle motif, and an ovoid summit. Scattered examples with variations in the molding motifs survive from first- or second-century contexts at Ostia and Corinth, and cruder versions survive from Pannonia in the Hungarian National Collections.[119] It has been suggested that such objects also may have functioned as parts of miniature furniture.[120] The Palatine East example is from a late context containing residual material.

471. Pin fragment. B51:XI/3004 (Fig. 32f; Pl. 39b)

L.0.61; DS.0.006; HH.0.025; DH.0.006. Broken

horizontally at neck (modern). Lower portion of shaft missing. Shaft ovoid in section with one flat side near summit. Circular indentation from lathe stock on summit.

Q. Large pin, exceeding 0.100 in length, with flaring shaft circular in section and pointed ovoid head with concentric horizontal grooves that continue on the neck in alternation with wider bands. This type is distinguished from Type II, B by its large size, comparable with that of large, undecorated pins (Type I). The Palatine East example is from a late containing significant amounts of residual material.

472. Pin. B255:X/2359 (Fig. 32g; Pl. 36a)
> L.0.118; DN.0.004; DS.0.007; HH.0.034; DH.0.010. Head chipped. Tip stained. Bone exceptionally light, almost white, in color and highly polished. Head and shaft circular in section. Lower shaft preserves evidence of preliminary faceting. Head with tightly spaced lathe-turned horizontal grooves that continue on the neck above and below two wider bands.
>
> St. Clair 1996, 370, Fig. 7.

III. Pins with Figural Decoration

A. Pin with flaring shaft, circular in section, and head in the form of a pinecone resting on a reel. The pinecone head was a popular motif from the first to the fourth century.[121]

473. Pin. A16:VIII/449 (Fig. 32h; Pl. 39a)
> L.0.081; DN.0.003; DS.0.004; HH (incl. reel).0.014; DH.0.006. Head encrusted. Head and shaft circular in section. Head cross-hatched with knife-carved shallow V-shaped incisions to suggest pinecone.
>
> St. Clair in Hostetter et al. 1994, 164, Fig. 44.

B. Shaft, oval in section, topped by a cloven hoof. Whether this form is associated with pins or another type of implement is uncertain. The same general form, although cruder, survives from several sites.[122]

474. Pin fragment? A196:III–IV/3993 (Fig. 32j)
> L.0.033; DS.0.004; Th.0.009 (head). Broken at bottom. Shaft with a summit in the form of a cloven hoof. Similar shafts survive, but with a cruder hooflike form at one end. The specific function of these objects is unclear.

C. Finial in the form of Aphrodite Anadyomene. This type, with Aphrodite depicted as a nude or half-nude figure with arms bent and one hand twisting or arranging locks of hair was popular throughout the Greco-Roman period and is common on late antique bone and ivory carvings as well as in other mediums.[123] Pins with Aphrodite finials were especially popular, and appropriate for an object associated with a woman's toilet. Typical of this type is the contrapposto, with the raised right shoulder and left hip, and relaxed right leg.

475. Aphrodite finial. D40:VIII/3396 (Fig. 32k; Pl. 40)
> H.0.024; W.0.007; Th.0.003. Broken at top and bottom. Despite losses, the figure is readily identifiable from the pose. Remains of drapery are visible behind the left leg. Given its small size the rendering of the anatomy is accomplished with both front and back carefully rendered. A similar figure, identified as a spoon or pin handle comes from Neronian contexts at Knossos.[124]

IV. Shafts

Approximately 500 shafts or shaft fragments were recovered. Examples are not individually catalogued. Many appear to be broken at the neck, and may be discards from the manufacturing process. In some cases they may have been intended to receive separately carved heads. Of the 77 decorated shafts or shaft fragments, 50 have necks or flanges with concentric horizontal grooves,[125] 26 have bead and reel decoration,[126] and 1 has a thin neck decorated with horizontal grooves separated from the shaft by a reel.[127] Approximately 180 undecorated shafts or shaft fragments appear to belong primarily to pins. Five examples have a diameter of 0.005 or more, and may be fragments of styli or needles. In 1 example the diameter of the shaft increases to a large conical point.[128] The number of small straight shafts (diameter 0.002 or less) increases in Sector A, contexts 36 and 38. Shafts in various stages of working, as well as rectangular and wedge-shaped blanks in bone and ivory, provide evidence of stages of manufacture. As with the pins, the fragments and blanks are most heavily concentrated in Sector A, contexts 20, 36, and 38, dating to the fourth or fifth century.

NEEDLES

Approximately fifty-five objects or fragments traditionally identified as needles were recovered. The shape and number of perforations, or "eyes, " which range from one to three, distinguish types.[129] While the function of single-perforation needles is not disputed, there is disagreement concerning the function of those with complex, and particularly triple, perforations. Most scholars identify complex examples as bodkins or needles designed to pull multiple cords or ribbons through previously made holes.[130] Bíró argues that examples with three perforations are dress pins and considers them the most frequent type of dress pin of the imperial age, replaced only in late antiquity by mass-produced fibulae.[131] While her reconstruction of the manner in which these objects might have been used is convincing, the existence of small-scale triple-hole examples that are

less likely dress pins, as well as of types with two holes, which are not discussed by Bíró, suggests that a study of the complete range of types is needed before the function of these objects can be decided with certainty.[132] Béal notes that examples with complex perforations, in particular three-holed examples, appear to be concentrated in contexts associated with the second century and later and suggests that they may indeed have had a specialized, though unknown, function because they are completely absent from certain sites.[133] This absence, however, also would seem to argue against Bíró's belief in their widespread use as dress pins.

The Palatine East examples have either single or triple perforations. In some cases the perforations are off-center or otherwise irregular; these needles are probably discards from the manufacturing process. The single-perforation types are grouped according to the shape of the perforation, either figure-eight or rectangular.[134] The shapes were achieved by joining two or more tangential circular holes. The needles with figure-eight-shaped perforations generally have pyramidal or conical summits, while those with rectangular or subrectangular holes have rounded or flat summits and heads that are flattened in section. Examples with triple perforations are characterized by a rectangular or subrectangular central perforation flanked by circular perforations. One example from a disturbed context has a central perforation in the form of a figure eight, a less common but widespread type as well.[135] All three types can be found in bone at a wide variety of sites from the first or second through the mid-fourth century, and it is difficult to devise a chronology based on types. Béal catalogued examples in Lyon and Nîmes with extensive references to comparative material.[136] In these cases, as with undecorated pins, references to comparative material include only a selection of sites to suggest the range of the type, with emphasis upon relevant material from Italy and more recent publications.

I. Needles with a Single Perforations

A. Needles that are oval or circular in section
with pyramidal or conical summits (eight examples). Figure-eight perforation formed by two tangential drilled holes. The type is widespread from
the second half of the first century through late
antiquity and beyond.[137] The Palatine East examples occur in contexts beginning in the second
century.

SECOND CENTURY

476. Needle fragment. D122:V/3979
     (Fig. 33b)
     L.0.050; D.0.004. Lower portion of shaft missing.
     Oval in section.
477. Needle. D165:V/4334 (Fig. 33e)
     L.0.064; D.0.005. Tip missing. Perforation
     angled and off-center. Oval in section.

MID- TO LATE THIRD CENTURY

478. Needle. A97:VII/2174 (Fig. 33c)
     L.0.65; D.0.005 Tip missing. Oval head tapers to
     shaft circular in section.

EARLY FOURTH CENTURY

479. Needle. A41:VIII/1876 (Fig. 33d; Pl. 41a)
     L.0.065; D.0.004. Tip missing. Oval head tapers
     to shaft circular in section.
480. Needle fragment. A112:VIII/1899
     (Fig. 33a)
     L.0.029; D.0.004. Lower portion missing. Cir-
     cular in section.

MEDIEVAL TO MODERN

481. Needle. C24:IX–XII/795 (Pl. 41b)
     L.0.060; D.0.004. Tip broken and stained. Oval
     head tapers to shaft circular in section.
482. Needle fragment. C85:IX–XII/2167
     L.0.0.036; D.0.005. Lower portion of shaft
     missing. Traces of cancellous bone on one side of
     shaft. Circular in section.

483. Needle. A9:XI/96 (Fig. 33f)
     L.0.082; D.0.005. Tip missing. Perforation breaks
     through sidewall of needle. Circular in section.
     Probably a discard.
     St. Clair in Hostetter et al. 1994, 164, 167, Figs.
     43, 48.

B. Needle with oval shaft tapering to head that is
flattened in section with rounded summit. Figure-eight perforation formed by two tangential
drilled holes. The single Palatine East example is
from a disturbed context. The type is present at
Salamis in a first- or second-century context, and
elsewhere.[138]

MODERN

484. Needle fragment. D73:XI–XII/3140
     (Fig. 33g; Pl. 41c)
     L.0.041; D.0.004 Th.0.001(head). Lower portion
     of shaft missing. Shaft oval in section.

C. Needles with shafts circular in section tapering
to flattened heads with rounded or flat summits
(eight examples). Shafts taper. Rectangular or
subrectangular perforations formed by tangential
perforations, usually three in number. The type is
common from the first through the fifth century
throughout the Greco-Roman world.[139] The Palatine East examples are concentrated in contexts
dated from the second half of the first to the first
half of the third century.

LATE FIRST TO SECOND CENTURY

485. Needle fragment. D89:IV/3458
     (Fig. 33h)
     L.0.052; D.0.004; Th.0.001 (head). Lower por-
     tion of shaft missing. Flat summit. Perforation
     retains curve of circular hole at bottom.
486. Needle fragment. D185:IV/4404 (Fig. 33m;
     Pl. 42c)
     L.0.064; D.0.005; Th.0.001 (head). Ivory. Lower
     portion of shaft missing. Rounded summit. Perfo-
     ration has rounded edges.

487. Needle. D219:IV/4768 (Pl. 42b)

L.0.086; D.0.007; Th.0.003 (head). Tip missing. Lower shaft chipped. Flat summit.

488. Needle fragment. D83:IV–V/3602 (Fig. 33k)

L.0.032; D.0.006; Th.0.001 (head). Lower shaft missing. Flat summit. Perforation has rounded edges.

489. Needle. D83:IV–V/3291 (Fig. 33j; Pl. 42a)

L.0.108; D.0.005 Th.0.001 (head). Tip slightly stained. Slightly rounded summit. Subrectangular perforation retains shape of three tangential holes.

490. Needle fragment. A158:V–VI/3255 (Fig. 33l)

L.0.039; D.0.007; Th.0.002 (head). Lower shaft missing. Slightly rounded summit. Perforation has rounded corners.

491. Needle fragment. C70:IX–XII/1142 (Fig. 33n)

L.0.064; D.0.007; Th.0.002 (head). Lower portion of shaft missing. Rounded summit.

492. Needle. A27:XI/510 (Fig. 33i)

L.0.092; D.0.007; Th.0.002 (head). Tip missing. Rounded summit.

St. Clair in Hostetter et al. 1994, 164, 167, Figs. 45, 48.

II. Needles with Triple Perforations

A. Needles with shafts circular in section tapering to flattened heads with rounded or pyramidal summits (four examples). Triple perforation in the form of a central rectangle or subrectangle flanked by circular perforations.[140] With one exception, the Palatine East examples are from second- through fifth-century contexts.

493. Needle. A156:V/3953 (Fig. 34a)

L.0.087; D.0.008; Th.0.003 (head). Tip missing. Rounded summit.

494. Needle fragment. A149:VII/2697 (Fig. 34b; Pl. 43b)

L.0.033; D.0.006; Th.0.001 (head). Shaft missing beginning at bottom of lower circular perforation. Rounded summit. Central and lower perforations off-center. Center perforation has rounded corners.

495. Needle. D15:VIII/2438 (Fig. 34c; Pl. 43a)

L.0.130; D.0.011; Th.0.004 (head). Pyramidal summit. Circular perforation at top is off-center.

496. Needle. C59:IX–XII/923 (Pl. 43c)

L.0.109; D.0.008; Th.0.001(head). Traces of cancellous tissue on one side of upper shaft. Rounded summit. Rectangular perforation and lower circular perforation are off-center.

B. Needle with circular shaft tapering to flattened heads with rounded summit. Triple perforation in the form of a figure eight flanked by circular perforations. The Palatine East example is from a medieval context with considerable residual material. The type is less common than II.A, but known from the second through the fifth century and beyond.[141]

497. Needle. C59:IX–XII/1141

L.0.038; D.0.004; Th.0.001. Lower portion of shaft missing. Rounded summit. Central perforation formed by two tangential perforations.

III. Needle Shafts

The approximately thirty shafts that appear to belong to needles were not individually catalogued. They were concentrated in Sectors A and D, in second- and third-century deposits.

UTENSILS WITH SPATULATE OR BOWL-SHAPED TERMINALS

Shafts with flat or bowl-shaped heads served a variety of purposes, and there is little agreement on nomenclature or descriptive terminology. For the purposes of this catalogue they are divided into three categories.

I. Ligulae

Objects of this type are characterized by long, usually pointed, shafts and flat palette-like heads set at an angle to the shaft. They are common in metal as well as bone from at least the first century and undoubtedly served a variety of purposes.[142] In English they are variously identified as unguent or perfume spoons, ear scoops, or spatulae. The undecorated Palatine East examples are concentrated in late first- and second-century contexts and appear to be hand-carved. The two decorated examples are from later contexts.

A. Undecorated Ligulae

The Palatine East examples are for the most part fragmentary, with the lower shaft missing (seven examples). With two exceptions that may be residual, they occur in first- and second-century contexts, perhaps a reflection of their popularity during this period, although the type appears elsewhere in later contexts in both bone and metal.[143]

LATE FIRST TO SECOND CENTURY

498. Ligula fragment. D89:IV/3454 (Fig. 35b)
L.0.048; DS.0.004; DN.0.002; HH.0.005; DH.0.005. Lower portion of shaft missing. Scratched.

499. Ligula fragment. D98:IV/3688 (Fig. 35f)
L.0.048; DS.0.004; DN.0.002; HH.0.004; DH.0.004. Lower portion of shaft missing.

500. Ligula fragment. D103:IV/3743
L.0.046; DS.0.003; DN.0.002; HH.0.004; DH.0.005. Ivory. Lower portion of shaft missing. Stained.

501. Ligula. D129:IV/3998 (Fig. 35c; Pl. 44d)
L.0.076; DS.0.004; DN.0.002; HH.0.005; DH.0.004. Tip chipped and stained.

502. Ligula fragment. D83:IV–V/3293 (Fig. 35d)
L.0.080; DS.0.004; DN.0.002; HH.0.005; DH.0.005. Lower portion of shaft missing.

503. Ligula fragment. A176:V/3290 (Fig. 35a)
L.0.057; DS.0.003; DN.0.002; HH.0.005; DH.0.005. Lower portion of shaft missing.

MEDIEVAL TO MODERN

504. Ligula. A9:XI/78
L.0.098; DS.0.005; DN.0.002; HH.0.005; DH.0.005. Tip missing.
St. Clair in Hostetter et al. 1994, 164, 167, Figs. 45, 48.

505. Ligula. C10:IX–XII/322 (Fig. 35e; Pl. 44c)
L.0.086; DS.0.004; DN.0.002; HH.0.007; DH.0.005 Tip broken and stained.

B. Decorated Ligulae

Two examples, from late antique or late contexts, are decorated with spiral bands at the neck. Decorated ligulae are less common than undecorated, but examples are preserved from late antique Carthage.[144]

SECOND HALF OF THE FIFTH CENTURY

506. Ligula. B281:VIII/2709 (Fig. 35g; Pl. 44b)
L.0.088; DS.0.005; DN.0.003; HH.0.005; DH.0.005. Tip worn. Decoration of spiral bands framed by rings beginning at neck and extending 0.025 on shaft. A cruder, but similar example survives from Carthage.[145]

507. Ligula. B276:VIII 2618 (Fig. 35h; Pl. 44a)
L.0.123; DS.0.004; DN.0.003; HH.0.005; DH.0.005. Decoration of narrow spiral bands beginning below neck and extending 0.016 down shaft.

II. Spatulae

Most often identified as spoons for unguent, or perfume in solid form, they are characterized by circular shafts with pointed or ogival tips and elongated tear-shaped or flattened heads that are formed by hollowing the shaft to form a bowl ending in a ∨ at the base. A longitudinal incision sometimes extends from the base of the bowl along the shaft. The form exists in metal as well, but in bone examples both the shafts and bowls are generally shorter. Examples are known from the first century B.C. through the fifth century, but as at Palatine East they are associated primarily with the first and second centuries.[146] No. 511, with a flat head may belong to this general category.

508. Spatula fragment. D137:IV or III–IV/4543 (Fig. 36b)

 L.0.081; DS.0.004; HH.0.012; DH.0.005. Top of spoon and lower portion of shaft missing. Incision extends from base of bowl along shaft.

509. Spatula. D153:IV/4233 (Fig. 36a)

 L.0.097; DS.0.004; HH.0.037; DH.0.005. Tip chipped.

LATE FIRST TO SECOND CENTURY

510. Spatula shaft. D65:IV–V/3395

 L.0.031; DS.0.003. Head and lower part of shaft missing. Incision extends from base of bowl along shaft.

511. Spatula. D209:IV/4508 (Fig. 36d; Pl. 45a)

 L.0.116; DS.0.004; HH.0.017; DH.0.005. Small shallow bowl. Tip missing.

512. Spatula head fragment? D103:IV/4389 (Fig. 36f)

 L.0.017; W.0.012; Th.0.002. Lower head and shaft missing. Flat with oval summit.

513. Spatula head. A177:V/3389 (Fig. 36c)

 L.0.033; DH.0.007. Shaft missing below head.

SECOND HALF OF THE THIRD CENTURY

514. Spatula fragment. A135:VII/2394 (Fig. 36e; Pl. 45b)

 L.0.051; DS.0.005; HH.0.015. Lower shaft missing. Incision extends from base of bowl along shaft.

MEDIEVAL TO MODERN

515. Spatula. C10:IX–XII/322

 L.0.098; DS.0.005; DN.0.002; HH.0.005; DH.0.005. Tip broken and stained.

III. Spoon

Spoons with circular bowls and a handle ending in a point are common throughout the Greco-Roman world in bone and in metal, and spoons of the Palatine East type are documented from the third century B.C. through the Merovingian period.[147] They undoubtedly served a variety of uses, including consummation of shellfish and eggs (the pointed handle was employed to pierce the shell).[148]

SECOND HALF OF THE SECOND TO EARLY THIRD CENTURY

516. Spoon. A133:V–VI/3144 (Fig. 36g; Pl. 46)

 L.0.090; DS.0.007; DH.0.010 Tip of shaft missing. Circular bowl. Handle decorated with chevron design on front banded by two horizontal incisions at bottom. Back decorated with incised ✗ framed by parallel, incised lines.

STUDS

Buttons pierced with multiple holes are generally thought to be unknown prior to the medieval period, and they are associated only with medieval and modern contexts at Palatine East.[149] Two studs, characterized by disk, plano-convex or dumbbell-shaped terminals connected by a short stem survive from first- and third-century contexts.

They are paralleled by examples from late antique
Carthage.[150]

SECOND HALF OF THE FIRST CENTURY

517. Stud. A188:IV/4771 (Fig. 37a)

L.0.008; D.0.006. Disk-shaped terminal connected by stem to plano-convex terminal with
indentation from lathe stock.

SECOND HALF OF THE THIRD CENTURY

518. Stud. A148:VII/2694 (Fig. 37b)

L.0.023; D.0.010. Dumbbell-shaped terminals
with incised lines encircling bases connected by
short stem. One terminal has indentation from
lathe stock.[151]

COMBS

Combs are characterized as one-piece, made from a
single block of material, or composite, with separate elements joined by rivets.[152] Two of the surviving combs from Palatine East are single piece, the
third is possibly a fragment from a composite
comb. One-piece bone combs were limited in size
by the dimensions and mechanical properties of the
material; the teeth had to be cut with the grain.
Roman combs usually have two rows of teeth, with
one set coarser than the other. Except in the case of
large so-called liturgical combs, single-piece combs
were largely eclipsed by composite combs in the
late Roman period, although single-piece combs
returned to popularity by the eleventh century. All
of the fragments from Palatine East are from medieval to modern contexts that contained significant
amounts of residual material. Two are without distinctive features that would allow dating. A third,
however, compares well with late antique Merovingian and Lombard examples. Recent excavations at
the site of the Crypta Balbi in Rome suggest that
such items may have been manufactured in Rome
and exported.[153]

I. One-Piece Combs

MEDIEVAL TO MODERN

519. Comb fragment. B18:XII/59 (Fig. 38a)

L.0.023; H.0.056; Th.0.003. Broken along one
end and side. Stained along longitudinal break at
center. One tooth remains. Reserve is decorated on
front and back with a central motif of incised circles containing ring and dot motifs flanked by
curving converging lines that extend onto the ends
with two pairs of ring and dot motifs. Both the
shape and decoration correspond to Merovingian
and Lombard examples dated to the sixth or seventh century.[154]

520. Comb fragment. D45:XI/3016

L.0.012; H.0.042; Th.0.003. One end and a small
portion of length remain. Teeth broken.
One-piece construction with coarse and fine teeth.

II. Composite Combs

MEDIEVAL TO MODERN

521. Comb fragment. CSF:XII/1682

L.0.011; H.0.056; Th.0.004. Broken at both ends.
Some teeth missing. Semicircular cut on one edge
of reserve suggests that this was part of a composite comb.[155]

522. Comb sideplate fragment? C59:IX–XII/966,
971, 972 (Fig. 38b)

L.0.022, 0.029, 0.020; W.0.011; Th.0.003.
Broken into three pieces. Incised decoration of half
ring and dot motifs alternating with parallel lines
running horizontally and obliquely. Remains of
three holes stained from metal along center axis.
Probable sideplate for a composite comb.

HANDLES

Handles of ivory and bone in association with tools
and utensils, including cutting implements, are
mentioned by ancient authors, and they undoubtedly served other functions as well—for example,
for fans and fly switches.[156] There are three basic

types: one-piece, into which the pointed tang was inserted; two-piece, with plates riveted on either side of the tang; and slotted, for folding knives. All three types survive from Palatine East. Cylindrical handles made from the hollow shafts of long bones were plugged with wood or another material to hold the tang firmly. The tang also could be secured with a washer at either end. None of the Palatine East examples retains its blade, but in several the tang remains in place. In two cases fragmentary blades appear to fit handles from the same context, although it is not certain that they belonged together.[157]

I. One-Piece Handles

FIRST CENTURY

523. Handle. D137:III–IV/4590 (Fig. 39c; Pl. 47c)

L.0.060; W.0.014; Th.0.005. Chipped. Corrosion from metal on surface. Rectangular one-piece handle with inset u-shaped "waist" above rimmed base. Roughly oval in section. Front and back surfaces retain natural longitudinal grooves with traces of cancellous tissue. Tang in place and visible at top and bottom. Similar forms are attested in Britain and Gaul, where the type is associated with the first and second century A.D. and later.[158] The "waist" provided space for a metal binder to hold the tang in place, and also a convenient finger hold.

SECOND CENTURY

524. Handle. D204:V/4773 (Fig. 39b; Pl. 47b)

L.0.046; W.0.012; Th.0.004. Bottom chipped stained. Green and brown stain from tang continues as shadow 0.032 up shaft. Rectangular one-piece handle, plano-convex in section. Summit decorated with knobs at sides and on summit. A knife blade was uncovered from this context hat appears to fit this handle. A similarly shaped decorated example, dated to the Byzantine period, survives from Istanbul.[159]

MID-FOURTH TO FIFTH CENTURY

525. Handle fragment. A12:VIII/129 (Fig. 39d; Pl. 48b)

L.0.057; W.0.018; Th.0.014. Hole: D.0.006; L.0.032. Ivory. Broken longitudinally into two pieces (modern). Lower portion missing. Sides worn. Brown stain from tang. One-piece handle approximately square in section with summit rounded in profile. Summit encircled by narrow raised band. Patterns of wear suggest that the handle was held between the fingers on the sides.[160]

526. Handle fragment. A20:VIII/235 (Fig. 39a; Pl. 48c)

L.0.083; W.0.029; Th.0.006; Hole: D.0.003. Broken horizontally into two pieces (modern). Chipped along one side. Oblique break in lower wall exposing 0.026 of hole for tang. Rectangular handle decorated with two convex longitudinal bands framed by narrow bands. Handle shows no obvious signs of wear.

527. Handle fragment. B270:VIII/3640 (Fig. 40a; Pl. 48a)

L.0.081; D.0.019. Top and bottom missing. Shaft chipped toward bottom. Handle formed from long bone. Bottom circular in section, decorated with three narrow incised bands. Upper half oval in section with crude incised cross-hatching framed by incised bands. A similar handle fragment survives from Istanbul dated to the seventh century or late and has been tentatively identified as a fly switch or fan handle.[161]

MEDIEVAL TO MODERN

528. Handle fragment. C59:IX–XII/969 (Pl. 49b)

L.0.053; D.0.018. Broken approximately in half longitudinally. Upper portion missing. Stain from tang on inner surface beginning at base and continuing upward 0.024. Surface decorated with alternating crudely incised horizontal lines and Xs along longitudinal edges.[162] The shape is similar to examples tentatively identified as fans or fly switches.[163]

529. Handle. C151:IX–XII/3610 (Fig. 40b; Pl. 49a)

L.0.072; W.0.021; Th.0.008. Hole: D.0.002. Bottom missing. Oblique break in lower wall revealing hole for tang. Rectangular with rounded inset summit, probably for metal band. Oval in section. Front decorated with four double ring and dot motifs.[164]

530. Handle. C85:IX–XII/2601 (Fig. 39e)

L.0.060; W.0.019; Th.0.007. Hole: D.0.003. Handle in form of rooster, tapering from rectangular to square in section. Hole for tang in base. Probably unfinished.[165]

II. Two-Piece Handle

SECOND HALF OF THE FIFTH CENTURY

531. Handle fragment. B270:VIII/3650 (Fig. 40c)

L.0.070; W.0.030; Th.0.008. Ivory. One-half (longitudinal) preserved. Surface black to gray-blue as a result of burning. Chipped and flaked. Half of rectangular handle. Plano-convex in section. Summit retains traces of decoration in the form of alternating convex and concave bands above two narrow bands. Indentation for tang visible on back extending approximately 0.025 from base. The handle was probably formed by two separate pieces riveted or banded together, but the poor condition makes certainty impossible. A knife blade that may fit this handle was uncovered in this context.

III. Handle for Folding Knife

EARLY FOURTH CENTURY

532. Handle for folding knife. A67:VIII/1748 (Fig. 40d; Pl. 47a)

L.0.060; D.0.011. Ivory. Broken into three pieces (modern). Chipped at top and bottom. Green and brown stain visible around hole for tang in base. Lathe-turned one-piece handle in form of baluster topped by a ball and reel resting on two raised bands above a base pierced horizontally for attach-

ment of a pin to secure a ferrule.[166] Vertical slot, rectangular in section, approximately 0.002 wide, extends from base to reel on summit. Slot becomes deeper toward base. A similar groove or slot is present on turned bone handles with knobbed terminals from third- and sixth-century contexts in Britain.[167]

JEWELRY

Segments of rings made from transverse slices of bone and ivory survive in a variety of sizes. Depending on their size, such rings are generally identified as bracelets or finger rings, but the wide range of sizes suggests that smaller examples may have served various functions, ranging from jewelry for humans, statuettes, and dolls to more prosaic pulls for furniture and boxes.[168] Bracelets were among the most popular means of adornment in the Greco-Roman world. They survive in a variety of materials and are depicted on upper and lower arms and on ankles in Roman art.[169] Both ivory and bone bracelets in the form of unbroken circles survive from throughout the Roman world. Elephant tusks provided a suitable diameter even for adult bracelets, while the size of bone rings was limited by the smaller diameter of the material. Alternatively, segments or semicircles of ivory or bone could be joined by sleeves of metal held in place by rivets and linked by a joint and pin fastener.[170] Most of the Palatine East examples appear to have been originally unbroken circles, but two ivory examples (nos. 536, 547) belonged to the composite type. The Palatine East examples are oval, plano-convex, or domed in section, with the flat surface on the interior. Five ivory examples are decorated with simple bands or incised patterns. One ivory bead, pierced for suspension, was uncovered in a late antique context.

The Palatine East finds are associated almost

exclusively with third- and fourth-century contexts and reflect the late antique fashion for ivory and bone noticeable elsewhere as well. Rings of bone, and occasionally of ivory, are among the most numerous objects associated with burials in the catacombs, where they were pressed into the cement that sealed the graves.[171]

I. Rings and Bracelets

A. Undecorated

LATE THIRD CENTURY

533. Ring Fragment. A152:VII /not accessioned

Projected D.0.030; Th.0.003 Ivory. Less than one-quarter remains. Plano-convex in section.

EARLY FOURTH CENTURY

534. Ring fragment. A36:VIII /637

Projected D.0.022; Th.0.003. Approximately one-quarter remains. Oval in section.
St. Clair in Hostetter et al. 1994, 170, Fig. 51.

535. Ring fragment. A36:VIII/658 (Fig. 41g; Pl. 50d)

Projected D.0.070; Th.0.005. Ivory. Approximately one-fifth remains. Oval in section.
St. Clair in Hostetter et al. 1994, 170, Fig. 51.

536. Bracelet or necklace fragment. A36:VIII/754 (Pl. 50f)

Projected D.0.080; Th.0.004. Ivory. Broken on one end. Approximately square tapering to oval in section. Segment from complex bracelet or necklace, tapered at one end to receive metal sleeve.
St. Clair in Hostetter et al. 1994, 170, Fig. 51.

537. Ring fragment. A38:VIII/915 (Fig. 41c; Pl. 50b)

Projected D.0.021; Th.0.002. Approximately one-half remains. Highly polished. Domed in section with flat inner surface.
St. Clair in Hostetter et al. 1994, 170, Fig. 51.

538. Ring fragment. A38:VIII/1246

Projected D.0.015; Th.0.005. Ivory. Less than one-quarter remains. Broken in four pieces (modern). Domed in section with slightly concave inner surface.

539. Ring fragment. A38:VIII/1471 (Fig. 41f; Pl. 50a)

Projected D.0.020; Th.0.003. Approximately one-half remains. Domed in section with flat inner surface.

540. Ring fragment. A48:VIII/1669 (Fig. 41e)

Projected D.0.042; Th.0.003. Domed in section with flat inner surface.

541. Ring fragment. A67:VIII/1740 (Fig. 41b)

Projected D.0.040; Th.0.003. Approximately one-half remains. Plano-convex in section.

FOURTH TO FIFTH CENTURY

542. Ring fragment. D111/3861:VIII (Fig. 41d)

Projected D.0.032; W.0.005; Th.0.004. Ivory. Slightly less than one-half remains. Approximately rectangular in section. Grain of ivory clearly visible on outer surface.

MODERN

543. Ring fragment. CSF:XII/1168 (Fig. 41a)

Projected D.0.060; Th.0.003. Ivory. Less than one-fifth remains. Oval in section.

B. Decorated

EARLY FOURTH CENTURY

544. Bracelet fragment. A33:VIII /528 (Fig. 41j; Pl. 50c)

Projected D.0.040; Th.0.005. Ivory. Less than one-quarter remains. Oval in section. Decorated with spiral bands.
St. Clair in Hostetter et al. 1994, 170, Fig. 51.

545. Bracelet fragment. A38:VIII/1464 (Fig. 41h)

Projected D.0.045; W.0.005; Th.0.003. Ivory. Approximately one-half remains. Roughly rectangular in section with smooth inner surface. Outer surface decorated with incised concentric band flanked by v-shaped hatch marks.

546. Bracelet fragment. A67:VIII /1751

> Projected D.0.070; Th.0.005. Ivory. Less than
> one-fourth remains. Stained brown. Decorated
> with horizontal incisions.

547. Bracelet fragment. A20:VIII/234 (Fig. 41i;
Pl. 50e)

> Projected D.0.070; Th.0.005. Ivory. Broken at
> one end. Domed in section with flat inner surface.
> Finished end encircled by four concentric incisions
> and pierced through the side 0.004 from end by
> hole 0.001+ in diameter, an indication that seg-
> ments joined together by means of a sleeve
> attached with rivets formed the bracelet. Outer
> surface decorated with incised crosshatch pattern.
> Inner surface flat in section.
>
> St. Clair in Hostetter et al. 1994, 170, Fig. 51.

548. Bracelet fragment. B222:VIII/2267
(Fig. 41k)

> Projected D.0.070; Th.0.005. Ivory. Less than
> one-fifth remains. Chipped. Stained brown. Oval
> in section. Decorated with raised spiral bands.

II. Bead

549. Bead. A102:VIII/1826 (Fig. 41l)

> D.0.008; H.0.011. Ivory. Stained brown. Ball
> decorated with concentric incisions set on a
> foot and topped by a pierced hanger for
> suspension.[172]

ARTICULATED DOLLS

Among the most interesting finds from Palatine
East are the bone remains of limbs and torsos of
articulated dolls, some of which are unfinished.
They can be associated with a type that is usually
dated to the third and fourth centuries, although
manufacture may have continued after this date.
The type is associated primarily with burials in the
catacombs.[173] The dolls are highly stylized, with
summary modeling of the anatomy. Limbs were
attached with pins through the shoulders and
through a flange at the base of the body. Many of
the Palatine examples appear to be unfinished, and
all of the bodies are broken at the neck.[174] Because
bodies and heads are of one piece in all preserved
examples, these are probably discards from the
carving process. The remains are from contexts
dated from the second through the fifth century,
with scattered examples in later contexts containing
large amounts of residual material.

I. Bodies

550. Blank for doll's body. A34:VIII/799
(Fig. 42e)

> L.0.091; W.0.017; Th.0.006. Broken along
> pierced channel for arms. Circular indentation
> indicating navel. Saw marks on front and back.
>
> St. Clair in Hostetter et al. 1994, 171, Fig. 53.

551. Doll body. A20:VIII/198 (Fig. 42a)

> L.0.073; W.0.017; Th.0.009. Encrusted. Broken
> at neck. Breasts rounded and demarcated by inci-
> sions on torso. Torso pierced for attachment of
> arms at breast level. Pubis indicated by V-shaped
> incision, navel by circular indentation. Flange
> pierced for attachment of legs.
>
> St. Clair 1996, 371, Fig. 10; St. Clair in Hostetter
> et al. 1994, 171, Fig. 53.

552. Doll body. A20:VIII/205 (Fig. 42f;
Pl. 52b)

> L.0.075; W.0.019; Th.0.007. Broken at neck.
> Flange chipped. Pierced for attachment of arms
> below area associated with breasts on most exam-
> ples. Pubis indicated by V-shaped incision, navel

by circular indentation. Flange pierced for attachment of legs.

St. Clair 1996, 371, Fig. 10; St. Clair in Hostetter et al. 1994, 171, Fig. 53.

553. **Doll body.** A20:VIII/461 (Fig. 42b; Pls. 51, 52a)

L.0.085; W.0.019; Th.0.007. Broken at neck. Breasts modeled and demarcated by oblique incisions. Pubis indicated by V-shaped incision, navel by circular indentation. Flange pierced for attachment of legs. Back has marks of claw chisel.

St. Clair 1996, 371, Fig. 10; St. Clair in Hostetter et al. 1994, 171, Fig. 53.

554. **Doll body fragment.** B/186:VIII/2804

L.0.039; W.0.018; Th.0.004. Broken at top and bottom. Lower half of torso with pubis indicated by V-shaped incision and navel by circular indentation. Nutrient foramina visible on surface along left edge and at top break. Cancellous tissue on back surface.

MEDIEVAL TO MODERN

555. **Doll body fragment.** C1:IX–XII/546

L.0.045; W.0.021; Th.0.007. Broken at top. Lower half of torso with pubis indicated by V-shaped incision. Flange pierced for attachment of legs.

556. **Doll body fragment.** C115:IX–XII/2199 (Fig. 42g)

L.0.074; W.0.024; Th.0.009. Broken at both ends along pierced channel for arms and legs. Chipped in area of breast. V-shaped incision indicating pubis extends to flange on one side. Navel indicated by circular indentation.

557. **Doll body.** C139:IX–XII/3478 (Pl. 52c)

L.0.047; W.0.006; Th.0.006. Broken at neck. Pierced for attachment of arms below protrusions usually associated with breasts. Pubis indicated by V-shaped incision. Navel absent. Flange pierced for attachment of legs. Possibly unfinished.

St. Clair 1996, 371, Fig. 10.

II. Limbs

A. Legs

SECOND TO FIRST HALF
OF THE THIRD CENTURY

558. **Leg.** A123:V–VI/2364 (Fig. 43e)

L.0.072; W.0.005; Th.0.005. Chipped. Roughly square in section tapering to point. Inset at top. Unfinished.

EARLY FOURTH CENTURY

559. **Leg.** A105:VIII/1863

L.0.056; W.0.007; Th.0.005. Oval in section tapering to "foot." Inset to receive flange and pierced for attachment.

560. **Leg.** A36:VIII/1034 (Fig. 43d)

L.0.079; W.0.009; Th.0.008. Rectangular to flattened oval in section tapering to "foot." Inset to receive flange. Saw marks. Unfinished.

St. Clair in Hostetter et al. 1994, 170, Fig. 53.

561. **Leg fragment.** A16:VIII/416 (Fig. 42d; Pl. 51)

L.0.047; W.0.005; Th.0.004. Broken at bottom. Chipped. Roughly triangular in section tapering to "foot." Inset to receive flange and pierced for attachment.

St. Clair in Hostetter et al. 1994, 171, Fig. 53.

MID-FOURTH TO MID-FIFTH CENTURY

562. **Leg.** A12:VIII/1722 (Fig. 43c; Pl. 51)

L.0.045; W.0.006; Th.0.005. Broken at top. Roughly rectangular in section tapering to band at "ankle" and pointed "foot."

St. Clair in Hostetter et al. 1994, 171, Fig. 53.

563. **Leg fragment.** A20:VIII/200 (Pl. 52i)

L.0.083; W.0.008; Th.0.007. Broken horizontally in two pieces (modern) and at top. Chipped at bottom. Roughly triangular in section tapering to band at "ankle" and "foot."

St. Clair 1996, 371, Fig. 10; St. Clair in Hostetter et al. 1994, 171, Fig. 53.

564. **Leg.** A20:VIII/474 (Fig. 43a; Pls. 51, 52h)

L.0.075; W.0.008; Th.0.005. Roughly oval in sec-

tion tapering to tip. Inset to receive flange and
pierced for attachment. Chisel marks from preliminary shaping. Possibly unfinished.

St. Clair 1996, 371, Fig. 10; St. Clair in Hostetter
et al. 1994, 171, Fig. 53.

565. Leg. A20:VIII/491 (Pl. 51)

L.0.052; W.0.008; Th.0.005. Broken at top and
bottom. Roughly oval in section tapering to band
at "ankle."

St. Clair in Hostetter et al. 1994, 171, Fig. 53.

566. Leg fragment. A20:VIII/775 (Fig. 42c)

L.0.033; W.0.005; Th.0.005. Bottom half
missing. Roughly triangular in section. Inset at
top. Pierced for attachment to flange.

B. Arms

LATE THIRD CENTURY

567. Arm fragment. A160:VII/3037 (Fig. 51)

L.0.040; W.0.007; Th.0.007. Unfinished. Broken
at both ends. Roughly oval in section with chisel
marks indicating preliminary carving stage. Horizontal band flanked by notches indicating wrist.

568. Arm fragment. A93:VII/1790

L.0.039; W.0.005; Th.0.005. Broken at both
ends. Oval in section flattening toward shoulder
where pierced for attachment.

EARLY FOURTH CENTURY

569. Arm fragment. A26:VIII/1893 (Fig. 43g;
Pl. 52g)

L.0.079; W.0.007; Th.0.006. Broken at top and
bottom. Oval in section tapering toward wrist.
Pierced at top for attachment.

St. Clair 1996, 371, Fig. 10.

570. Arm fragment. A33:VIII/655

L.0.045; W.0.005; Th.0.0.002. Broken at top.
Rectangular in section with V-shaped incision at
"wrist." Probably unfinished.

MID-FOURTH TO FIFTH CENTURY

571. Arm. A12:VIII/1720 (Fig. 43f; Pls. 51, 52f)

L.0.055; W.0.006; Th.0.003. Rectangular in sec-

tion tapering toward "wrist," indicated by notch.
Saw marks on all surfaces. Cancellous tissue along
one edge. Unfinished.

St. Clair 1996, 371, Fig. 10.

572. Arm fragment. A12:VIII/1721 (Fig. 43i;
Pl. 52d)

L.0.032; W.0.007; Th.0.004. Broken at top.
Chipped. Roughly rectangular in section with
notch indicating wrist and two oblique incisions
suggesting fingers.

St. Clair 1996, 371, Fig. 10; St. Clair in Hostetter
et al. 1994, 171, Fig. 53.

573. Arm. B186:VIII/2715 (Fig. 43k)

L.0.053; W.0.006; Th.0.004. Polygonal in section. Saw and chisel marks from preliminary
shaping. Notched at wrist. Two V-shaped incisions suggesting fingers. Possibly unfinished.

574. Arm. B209:VIII/2266 (Fig. 43j; Pl. 52e)

L.0.044; W.0.006; Th.0.004. Chipped at bottom.
Roughly polygonal in section with chisel marks
from preliminary working. Notched at wrist. Two
V-shaped incisions suggest fingers. Pierced at top
for attachment. Possibly unfinished.

St. Clair 1996, 371, Fig. 10.

575. Arm. B340:VIII/4136

L.0.050; W.0.006; Th.0.007. Roughly rectangular
in section with saw marks on all surfaces. Two
oblique incisions at bottom. Pierced for attachment at top. Unfinished.

576. Arm fragment. D203:VIII/3024 (Fig. 43h)

L.0.030; D.0.004. Top and bottom missing.
Bracelet at wrist. Arm round in section; "hand"
oval.

MEDIEVAL TO MODERN

577. Arm fragment. D96:XI–XII/3716

L.0.026; W.0.005; Th.0.0005. Broken at top.
Chipped and worn. Notched at "wrist."

GAMING PIECES
AND COUNTERS

Gaming pieces and counters are typically carved from longitudinal slices of bone or ivory.[175] Bones in their natural shapes, including knucklebones (*astragali*) from sheep or goats, phalangeal bones, and fish vertebrae, were used as well.[176] Most disk-shaped counters are bone and produced on a lathe or with a center bit. Types are distinguished by the form or by the decoration on the obverse. The range includes flat, countersunk or dished, plano-convex, and lathe-turned with concentric rings. Counters and gaming pieces are sometimes marked with crude letters or symbols on the reverse, but this is the exception, and the graffiti provide little evidence of function. It is likely that identical counters were used in a variety of games and that different types were used in a single game. They were undoubtedly used in commerce and as gambling tokens as well.[177] The Palatine East examples are unmarked, as might be expected if they formed part of a manufacturer's inventory. Chronological distinctions between the types have not been successfully drawn, although at Palatine East, flat-topped counters appear in the first- and second-century contexts whereas plano-convex examples appear only in the later contexts.[178] Flat-topped examples with straight or a V-shaped sidewalls survive in various materials from throughout the Roman world. As at Palatine East, the bone examples are generally small, with a diameter of 0.018 or less, and have undecorated surfaces that are frequently highly polished. Most have an indentation on one surface from the lathe stock or center bit. The type is common in the first century A.D. elsewhere, but occurs as well in second- and third-century contexts in bone, and in stone from the first through the third century.[179] Flat-topped disks of elephant and walrus, ivory are rarer, and very few examples survive with a known provenance.[180] The two ivory Palatine East examples, although fragmentary, provide excellent examples of this type of large gaming piece with incised decoration (nos. 582, 583). These large pieces are difficult to date. They were undoubtedly prized in antiquity and may be older than the contexts in which they were found. Comparable disks, preserved in museums, are presumed to be medieval.[181] Two similar disks were unearthed from twelfth- and thirteenth-century contexts in the exedra of the Crypta Balbi in Rome.[182] The use of large diskoid counters has been associated with the game, or series of games, of tables, attested in the eleventh century.[183] Small undecorated plano-convex counters or gaming pieces, usually under 0.030 in diameter, survive from throughout the Roman world in a variety of materials and, as at Palatine East, are especially common in late antique contexts.[184] Gaming pieces or counters with lathe-turned decoration are also common throughout the Roman world. The simplest are diskoid with a concave depression surrounded by a flat border, allowing the pieces to be moved easily with a finger.[185] More elaborate examples feature concentric concave and convex designs.[186] A few have central perforations. The most elaborate type of lathe-turned gaming piece is composite, and domed in shape.[187] Domed gaming pieces were cut from transverse sections of long bones that were closed at top and bottom by bone plugs.[188] The Palatine East examples are closely paralleled by examples from late antique Carthage and from a seventh-century context in the Crypta Balbi in Rome.[189] The type occurs at Saraçhane in Istanbul as well.[190] One of the Palatine East examples is from a late fifth-century context. The rest are from medieval or modern deposits that contained considerable amounts of residual material. Undoubtedly prized, they are difficult to date.

I. Flat-Topped Counters or Gaming Pieces

A. Undecorated

FIRST CENTURY

578. Counter or gaming piece. D137:III–IV/4504

   D.0.008; Th.0.003. Highly polished. Straight wall.

SECOND CENTURY

579. Counter or gaming piece. D43:V/2926

   D.0.017; Th.0.006. Highly polished. V-shaped wall. Central indentation on one surface.

580. Counter or gaming piece. D123:V/4439 (Fig. 44d)

   D.0.018; Th.0.005. V-shaped wall. Saw marks on both top and bottom. Central indentation on one surface.

581. Counter or gaming piece. A173:V/3261 (Fig. 44b)

   D.0.016; Th.0.004. V-shaped wall. Central indentation on one surface.

B. Decorated

FIFTH CENTURY

582. Gaming piece fragment. B329:VIII/3952 (Fig. 44a; Pl. 53a)

   Projected D.0.043; Th.0.010. Ivory. Slightly less than one-half missing. Top surface chipped and cracked. Bottom surface rough and pitted. Straight wall. Pierced by circular hole 0.005 in diameter at center. One surface decorated with three incised concentric circles and ring and dot motif. Two similar pieces were uncovered in twelfth- and thirteenth-century contexts in the exedra of the Crypta Balbi in Rome.[191]

583. Gaming piece fragment. B186:VIII/2686 (Fig. 44c; Pl. 53b)

   Projected D.0.040; Th.0.008. Ivory. Fragmentary. Approximately one-half missing. Top and bottom pitted. Pierced by hole 0.004 in diameter. Top and bottom surfaces decorated with incised concentric circles in pairs. The type is the same as no. 582.

II. Plano-Convex Counters or Gaming Pieces

EARLY FOURTH CENTURY

584. Counter or gaming piece. A20:VIII/252 (Pl. 54d)

   D.0.020; Th.0.008. Bottom surface chipped. Central indentation from lathe stock.

   St. Clair in Hostetter et al. 1994, 170, Fig. 51.

585. Counter or gaming piece? A67:VIII/1739 (Fig. 44e)

   D.0.021; Th.0.007. Chipped on bottom and on one side. Pierced by hole 0.004 in diameter. This piece may well have served as a mount.

SECOND HALF OF THE FIFTH CENTURY

586. Counter or gaming piece. B186:VIII/2689 (Pl. 54c)

   D.0.022; Th.0.007. Highly polished with no central indentation.

587. Counter or gaming piece. B309:VIII/3748 (Fig. 44f; Pl. 54a)

   D.0.027; Th.0.006. Highly polished. Summit has nipple with central indentation. Saw marks and cancellous tissue on back. Chatter marks from lathe turning on outer edge. This example is paralleled by a gaming piece in Lyon.[192]

MEDIEVAL TO MODERN

588. Counter or gaming piece. C50:IX–XII/749 (Pl. 54b)

   D.0.025; Th.0.008. Bottom surface and one wall chipped. Saw marks and traces of cancellous tissue on bottom. No central indentation.

III. Counters or Gaming Pieces with Lathe-Turned Decoration

THIRD CENTURY

589. Counter or gaming piece. A 160:VII/2995 (Fig. 44g)

   D.0.023; Th.0.005. Bottom chipped. Flat outer border with central concave depression. Hole at center.[193]

590. Counter or gaming piece. C72:IX–XII/973
     (Fig. 44h)

     D.0.022; Th.0.002. Top surface and walls cor-
     roded and chipped. Bottom chipped and worn.
     Decorated with six concentric incisions within
     wide rim. Central indentation.[194]

591. Counter or gaming piece. B18:XII/1690

     D.0.034; Th.0.002. Surfaces pocked and worn.
     Chipped. Decorated with alternating concave and
     convex concentric bands around central indentation
     from lathe stock.[195] Cancellous tissue on bottom.

IV. Domed Gaming Pieces

SECOND HALF OF THE FIFTH CENTURY

592. Domed gaming piece fragment.
     B270:VIII/3135 (Fig. 45a; Pls. 55b, 56b)

     D.0.025; H.0.027; Plug D.0.007; L.0.006.
     Approximately one-third of wall missing. Plug
     broken at top. Highly polished surface decorated
     with lathe-turned concentric circles that continue
     on plug at top and on the bottom surface. Central
     cavity approximately circular in section with
     smoothed walls. Plug roughly circular in section.
     Saw marks on bottom. The natural longitudinal
     groove characteristic of long bones formed by the
     fusion of two digits extends 0.020 from base.[196]

     St. Clair 1996, 370, Fig. 8.

593. Domed gaming piece. C77:IX–XII/1437
     (Fig. 45b; Pls. 55a, 56a)

     D.0.030; H.0.029. Plug D.0.015. Edge of base
     chipped. Two longitudinal cracks, one extending
     through base. Saw marks visible on top. Body
     decorated with two concentric lathe-turned cir-
     cles at top. Roughly oval plug with one concave
     side, topped by knob with indentation from
     lathe stock on summit. Lower plug inset approxi-
     mately 0.002, revealing cancellous tissue on inner
     walls. As on no. 593, natural longitudinal groove
     extends approximately 0.020 from base.[197]

     St. Clair 1996, 370, Fig. 8.

594. Domed gaming piece. C22:IX–XII/800
     (Fig. 45d; Pls. 55c, 56c)

     D.0.023; H.0.028. Top plug: D at base.0.009; at
     top.0.013; L.0.019. D Bottom plug: L.0.005,
     D.0.012. Broken into three pieces (modern).
     Green stain on summit. Surface decorated with
     series of oblique knife-cut incisions above plain
     base. Top decorated with lathe-turned concentric
     circles. Saw marks on bottom. Top plug roughly
     oval with one concave side and topped by a knob.
     Indentation from lathe stock on summit. Bottom
     plug has indentation from lathe stock and incised
     circle from lathe turning.[198]

     St. Clair 1996, 370, Fig. 8.

595. Domed gaming piece fragment. A9:XI?/72
     (Fig. 45c)

     D.0.029; H.0.025. Plug and section of wall
     missing. Saw marks on base. Incised ring around
     opening on top. Central cavity approximately cir-
     cular in section with smooth walls.

596. Plug for domed gaming piece. CSF:XII/2353

     L.0.011; W.0.007. Roughly oval with one concave
     side. Topped by circular knob. Cancellous tissue
     on surface.

DICE

Cubical six-sided dice in bone and ivory, which
were used in games as well as for casting lots, are
common throughout the Greco-Roman world
from at least the seventh century B.C.[199] Most bone
dice are small in size, due to the dimensional limitations of the material. Cutting a transverse section
from the shaft of a long bone and closing the
medullary cavity with a bone plug to produce a
more or less solid cube created larger bone dice.[200]
On cubical dice, values were marked with dots,
drilled holes that could be filled with colored paste,
or ring and dot motifs. Double ring and dot motifs
are by far the most common. The values were
commonly arranged so that opposite faces total

seven (6–1, 5–2, 4–3). Dice are rarely perfectly cubical in shape, and values are often not regularly spaced. A number of examples from Palatine East are unfinished or discards from the manufacturing process. One rectangular example, marked with ring and dot motifs, may be a parallelepiped die, a type largely replaced by cubical dice in the Roman world by the second century A.D.[201] One cubical die, probably a discard, has drilled values and one partially hollowed out face, apparently for weighting with lead or another material (no. 597). In this case the weight would have caused the die to fall on the one spot, thus favoring the six. The Palatine East examples decorated with ring and dot motifs are paralleled at sites throughout the Greco-Roman world.[202]

I. Dice with Drilled Holes

FIRST TO SECOND CENTURY

597. Die. D83:IV–V/3229 (Fig. 46a; Pl. 57b)
L.0.013; W.0.013; Th.0.013. Broken on one side. Unfinished. Break on side of one spot reveals hollowed interior extending inward approximately 0.002 to surface parallel to wall. Opposite wall blank. Other walls drilled with two spots.
St. Clair 1996, 370, Fig. 9.

II. Dice with Ring and Dot Motifs

A. Single Ring and Dot Motifs

FIRST CENTURY

598. Die. D137:III–IV/4554
L.0.010; W.0.011; Th.0.011. Ivory. Cracked. One corner chipped.

LATE FIRST TO SECOND CENTURY

599. Die. A187:IV–V/3789 (Fig. 46b; Pl. 57c)
L.0.011; W.0.009; Th.0.010. Chipped and abraded.
St. Clair 1996, 370, Fig. 9.

600. Die. A176:V/3258
L.0.011; W.0.009; Th.0.010.

MID- TO LATE THIRD CENTURY

601. Die. A140:VII/2448
L.0.006; W.0.007; Th.0.007.
602. Die. A140:VII/2449 (Pl. 57a)
L.0.007; W.0.006; Th.0.008. Values irregularly spaced.
St. Clair 1996, 370, Fig. 9.
603. Die. A160:VII/2994 (Pl. 57f)
L.0.010; W.0.009; Th.0.010. Ivory. Values irregularly spaced. One spot off center.
St. Clair 1996, 370, Fig. 9.

EARLY FOURTH CENTURY

604. Die. A22:VIII/278 (Pl. 57d)
L.0.013; W.0.013; Th.0.014.
St. Clair 1996, 370, Fig. 9; St. Clair in Hostetter et al. 1994, 170, Fig. 51.
605. Die. A36:VIII/180
L.0.006; W.0.006; Th.0.007.
606. Die. A62:VIII/358
L.0.010; W.0.008; Th.0.009. Ivory.
607. Die. A36:VIII 560
L.0.008; W.0.007; Th.0.008.

FOURTH TO FIFTH CENTURY

608. Die. D111:VIII/3969
L.0.008; W.0.008; Th.0.008. Chipped.

B. Double Ring and Dot Motifs.

SECOND HALF OF THE FIRST TO SECOND CENTURY

609. Die. D19:IV/2437
L.0.008; W.0.008. Chipped at one corner.
610. Die. D83:IV–V/3282 (Pl. 57i)
L.0.015; W.0.014; Th.0.015. Ivory. Cracked.
St. Clair 1996, 370, Fig. 9.

611. Die. A140:VII/2413

L.0.007; W.0.008; Th.0.008. Chipped along one edge.

612. Die. A99:VII/1791 (Fig. 46c)

L.0.014; W.0.010; Th.0.013. Rectangular.

EARLY FOURTH CENTURY

613. Die. A105:VIII/1897

L.0.007; W.0.007; Th.0.007. Chipped along one side. Saw marks.

614. Die. A36:VIII/560

L.0.007; W.0.007; Th.0.007.

615. Die. A36:VIII/648 (Fig. 46h)

L.0.009; W.0.00009; Th.0.010. Surface abrasion. Saw marks.

616. Die. A36:VIII/649

L.0.008; W.0.008; Th.0.008.

617. Die. A36:VIII/561

L.0.007; W.0.006; Th.0.006. Edges uneven. Values crude and irregularly spaced.

St. Clair in Hostetter et al. 1994, 170, Fig. 51.

618. Die. A38:VIII/881

L.0.007; W.0.008; Th.0.008.

619. Die. A38:VIII/889

L.0.008; W.0.008; Th.0.008.

St. Clair in Hostetter et al. 1994, 170, Fig. 51.

620. Die. A38:VIII/781

L.0.008; W.0.007; Th.0.007. Chipped. Edges rough and uneven.

621. Die. A38:VIII/1408

L.0.008; W.0.007; Th.0.007. Chipped at one corner. Encrusted. Saw marks.

622. Die. A33:VIII/504

L.0.009; W.0.008; Th.0.009.

623. Die. A33:VIII/511

L.0.010; W.0.010; Th.0.010.

St. Clair in Hostetter et al. 1994, 170, Fig. 51.

624. Die. A33:VIII/656

L.0.009; W.0.008; Th.0.009.

625. Die. A34:VIII/508

L.0.009; W.0.008; Th.0.008.

626. Die. A35:XII/963

L.0009; W.0.009; Th.0.009. Chipped at one corner.

627. Die. A48:VIII/1670 (Fig. 46f)

L.0.013; W.0.012; Th.0.013. Cancellous tissue on side with three spot necessitated moving spots off center.

628. Die. A62:VIII/558

L.0.010; W.0.009; Th.0.009. Edges uneven.

629. Die. A67:VIII/1842

L.0.008; W.0.008; Th.0.008. Four spot has irregular gouges associated with two rings, possibly associated with movement of center bit.

MID-FOURTH TO FIFTH CENTURY

630. Die. B351:VIII/4534

L.0.008; W.0.0.008; Th.0.005. Broken and unfinished with one blank side.

631. Die. A20:VIII/203

L.0.010; W.0.009; Th.0.010.

632. Die. B220:VIII/2272

L.0.011; W.0.010; Th.0.012. Ivory. Cracked. Chipped along one edge.

633. Die. B186:VIII/2713

L.0.009; W.0.009; Th.0.009.

634. Die. B270:VIII/2439 (Pl. 57e)

L.0.009; W.0.008; Th.0.009. Chipped. One spot off center. Values irregularly spaced.

St. Clair 1996, 370, Fig. 9.

635. Die. B287:VIII/3129 (Fig. 46e; Pl. 57g)

L.0.014; W.0.014; Th.0.013. Ivory. Unfinished. Cracked on three surfaces. Six spot missing. Two one spots. Probable discard.

St. Clair 1996, 370, Fig. 9.

636. Die. B294:VIII/3404

L.010; W.0.011; Th.0.011. Ivory. Cracked. One corner missing. Unfinished. Surface of six spot chipped with two spots missing. One side blank (one spot). Three spot side missing one spot. Probable discard.

637. Die. B342:VIII/4226

L.0.010; W.0.010; Th.0.010.

638. Die. C48:IX–XII/1468

L.0.007; W.0.008; Th.0.008. Encrusted on two surfaces. Chipped at one corner.

639. Die. C59:IX–XII/962

L.0.009; W.0.009; Th.0.009. Cracked. Chipped at one corner.

640. Die. C115:IX–XII/2285

L.0.012; W.0.012; Th.0.011. Ivory. Broken along one edge. Cracked. Unfinished. One blank surface (one spot). Probable discard.

641. Die. C145:IX–XII/3179

L.0.007; W.0.008; Th.0.009.

642. Die. A9:XI/73(Fig. 46d; Pl. 57h)

L.0.011; W.0.013; Th.0.012. Ivory. Chipped at one corner. Unfinished. Two blank sides (one and six spots). Side for one spot has slight central indentation marking site for drill or center bit. Two, four, and six spots indicated by lightly incised single circles and dots. Five spot indicated by double ring and circles.

St. Clair 1996, 370, Fig. 9; Hostetter et al. 1994, 170, Fig. 51.

C. Triple Ring and Dot Motifs

EARLY FOURTH CENTURY

643. Die. A67:VIII/1821(Fig. 46g)

L.0.007; W.0.006; Th.0.007.

III. Parallelepiped Die

SECOND HALF OF THE FIFTH CENTURY

644. Parallelepiped die or blank. B294:VIII/3451 (Fig. 44i)

L.0.029; W.0.010; Th.0.010. Horizontal crack on one side. Roughly rectangular piece tapering slightly in profile. All sides sawn. Almost square in section. Drilled with three double ring and dot

motifs on front surface and two on rear. Crack suggests possible discard. While parallelepiped dice are known from the Roman period, they are usually made from the shafts of small long bones, and the numbers 1 and 2 are usually omitted.[203] Even when solid, as with this example, the ends usually are left blank.

LETTERS OF THE ALPHABET.

Both Quintilian and Jerome mention letters of boxwood or ivory that were given to children in the guise of toys, as an aid to learning.[204] Remains of this type have usually been identified as inlay, however.[205] The three bone examples from Palatine East are associated with late antique contexts and are fragmentary.

FOURTH TO FIFTH CENTURY

645. Letters of alphabet fragment. D40:VIII /2805 (Fig. 47b, Pl. 58a)

L.0.036; W.0.020; Th.0.004. Broken on three sides. Fragment of two letters, separated by an incision. Cancellous tissue on back surface. Probably unfinished. Letters would have been broken apart along incision.

646. Letter of alphabet fragment. B270:VIII /3651 (Fig. 47a, Pl. 58c)

L.0.014; W.0.013; Th.0.002. Broken in two pieces (modern). Chipped along one edge. Letter A?

647. Letter of alphabet. D15:VIII /2680 (Fig. 47c, Pl. 58b)

L.0.034; W.0.010; Th.0.001. Letter I. Saw marks on one side. Traces of claw chisel on other.[206]

WHISTLE

The Latin word for flute, *tibia,* has a clear anatomical allusion, and many simple flutes and whistles were made from this and other bones from a variety of animals, as well as from the pneumatic limb bones of large birds.[207] Roman flutes that served as musical instruments are generally lathe-turned and of composite construction, but simple end blown instruments served less sophisticated purposes, as they do today. In the Roman period, they are frequently found in association with military camps.[208]

648. Whistle fragment. D7:V/2602 (Fig. 47d)
L.0.075; D.0.010. Broken at both ends. Shaft tapers slightly. Two holes 0.003 in diameter sited in the natural longitudinal groove formed by the fusion of two digits.

FIGURES AND PLATES

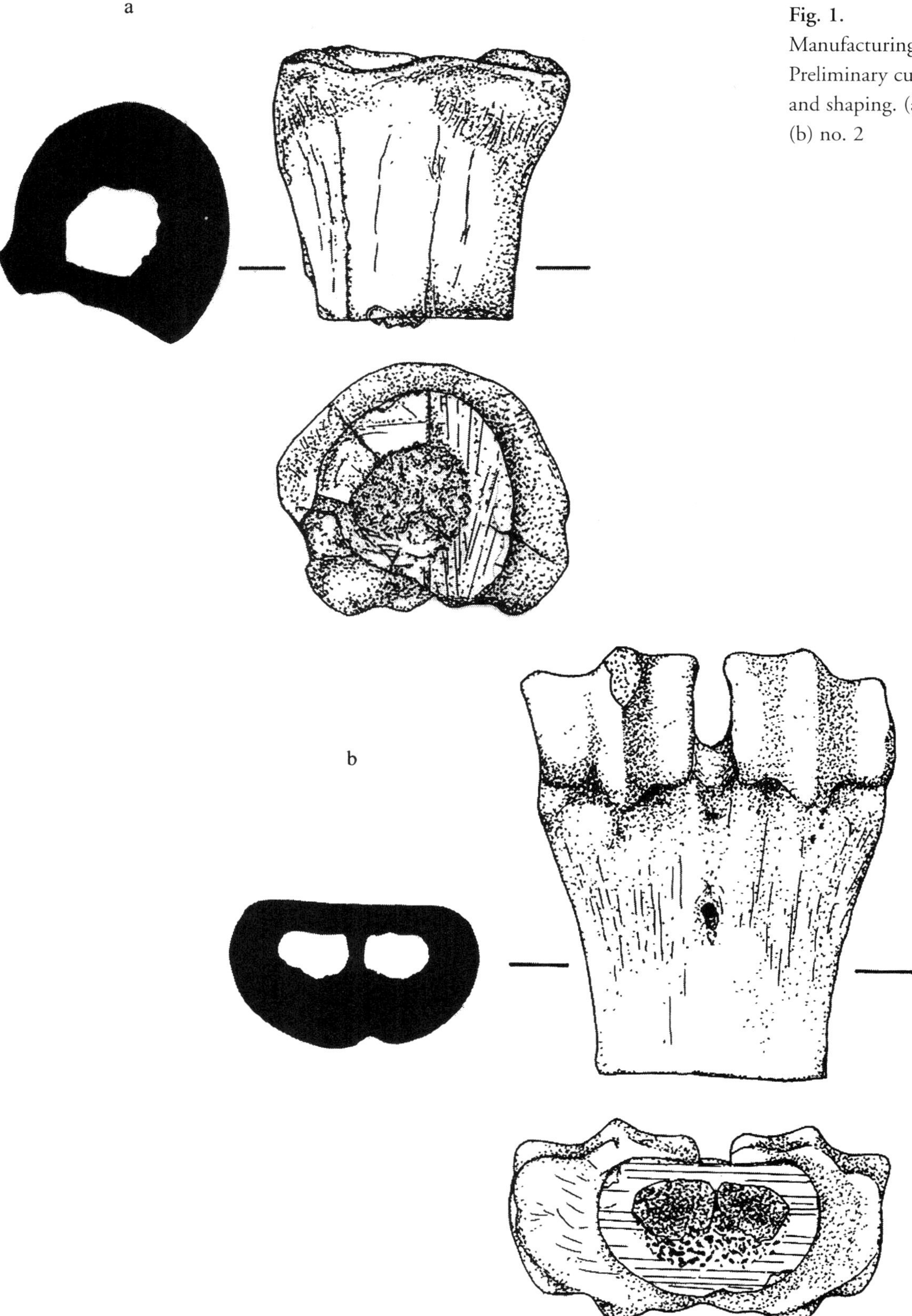

a

b

Fig. 1.
Manufacturing evidence:
Preliminary cutting
and shaping. (a) no. 4;
(b) no. 2

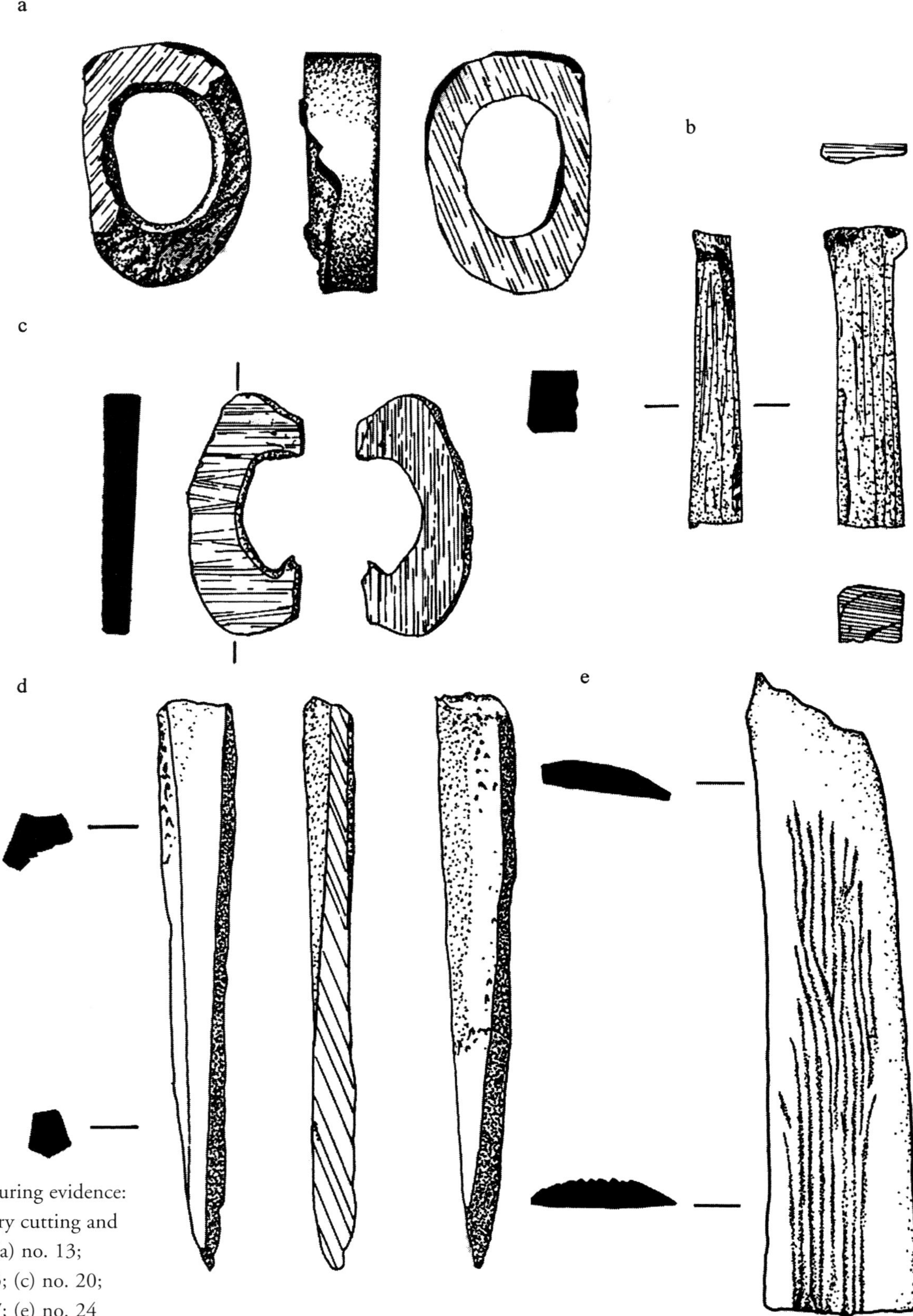

Fig. 2.
Manufacturing evidence:
Preliminary cutting and
shaping. (a) no. 13;
(b) no. 73; (c) no. 20;
(d) no. 47; (e) no. 24

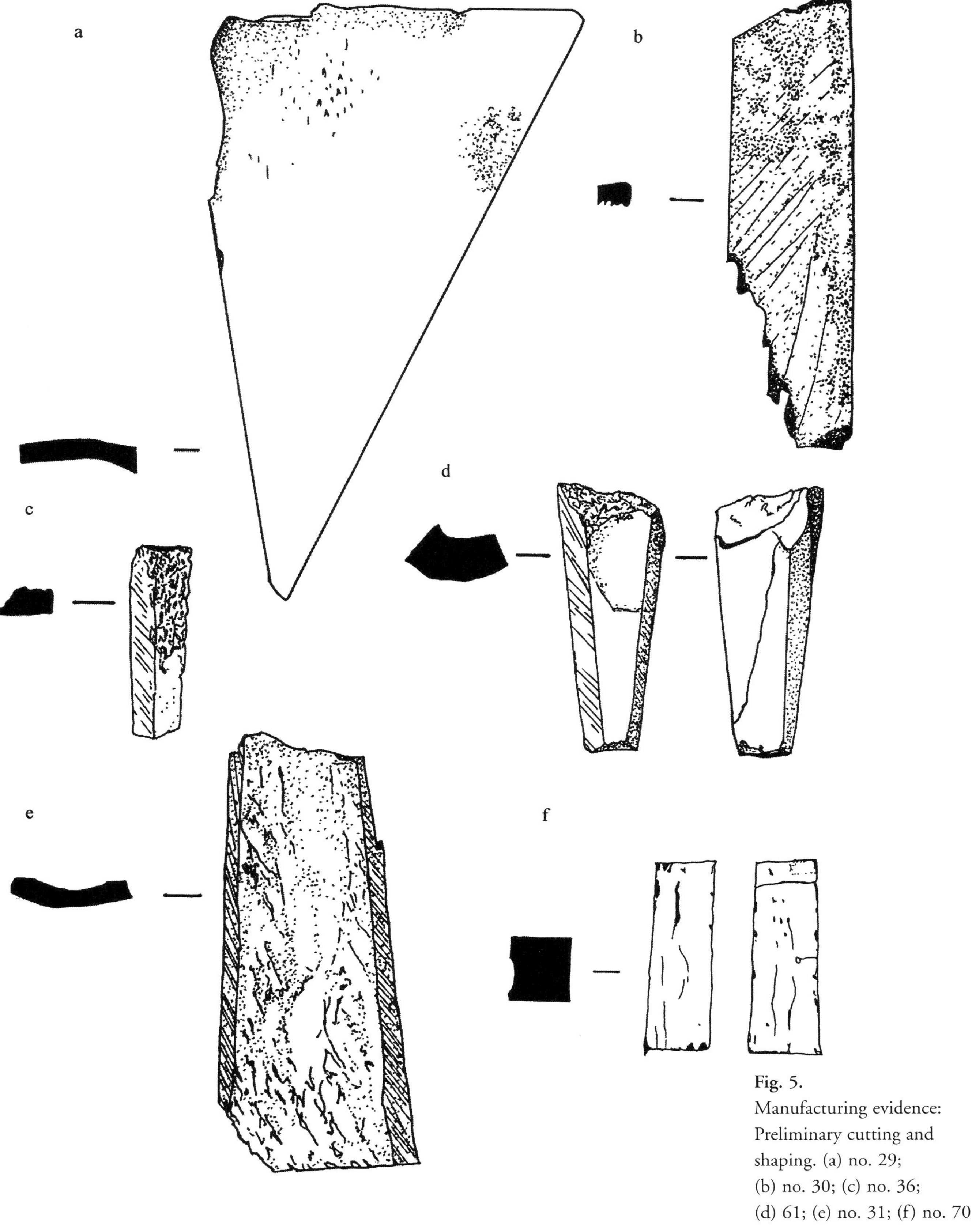

Fig. 5.
Manufacturing evidence:
Preliminary cutting and
shaping. (a) no. 29;
(b) no. 30; (c) no. 36;
(d) 61; (e) no. 31; (f) no. 70

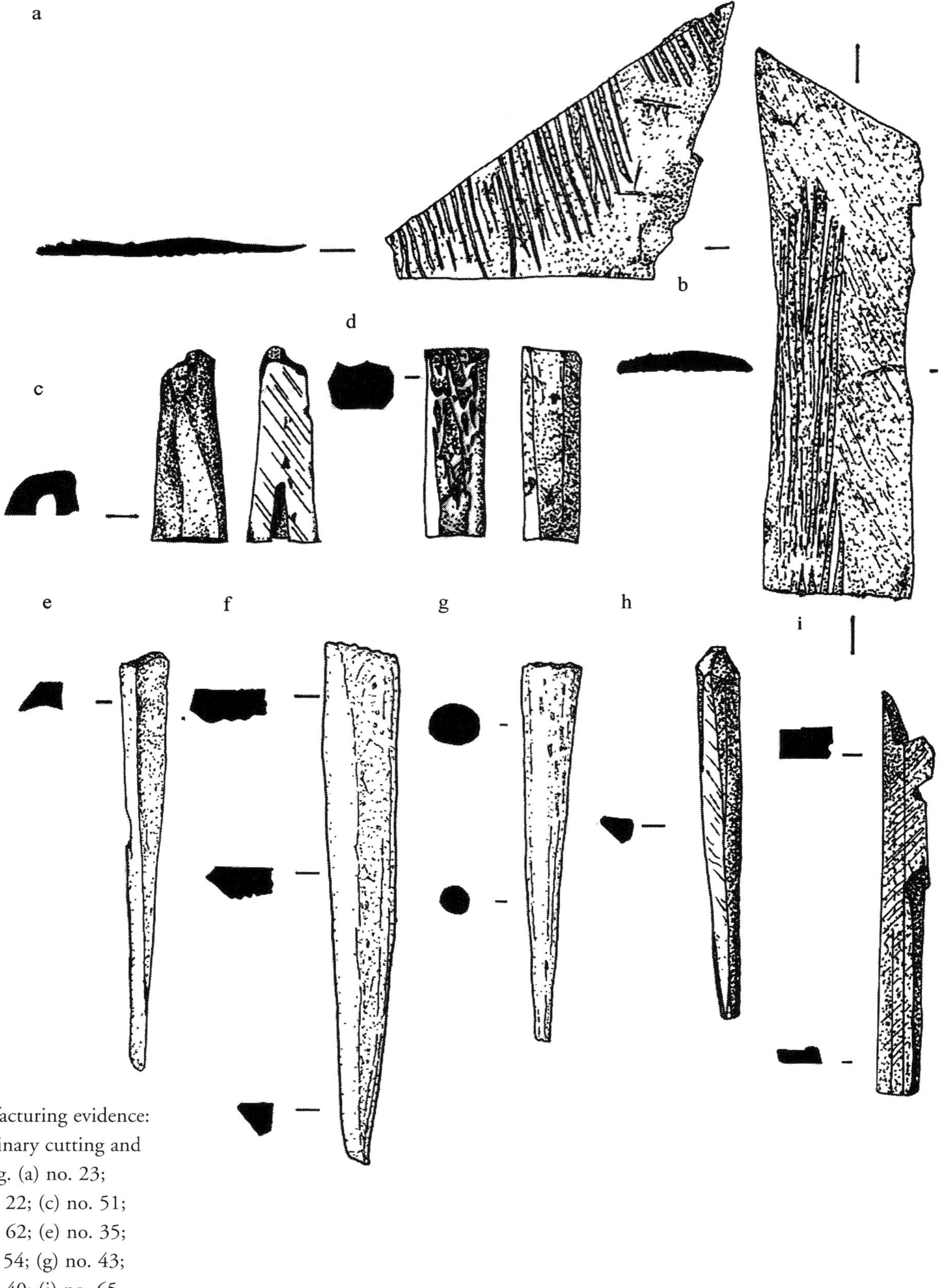

Fig. 6.
Manufacturing evidence:
Preliminary cutting and
shaping. (a) no. 23;
(b) no. 22; (c) no. 51;
(d) no. 62; (e) no. 35;
(f) no. 54; (g) no. 43;
(h) no. 40; (i) no. 65

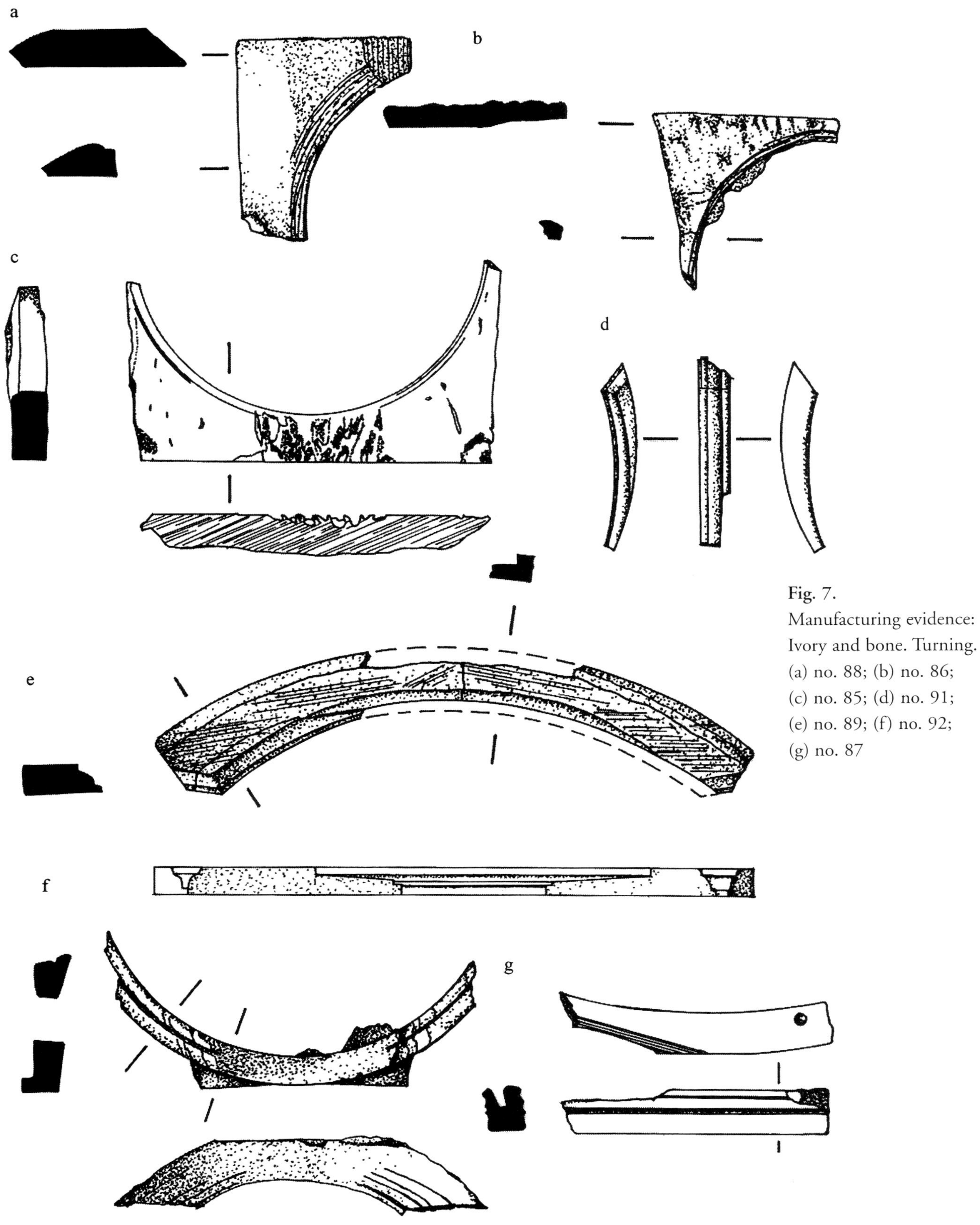

Fig. 7.
Manufacturing evidence:
Ivory and bone. Turning.
(a) no. 88; (b) no. 86;
(c) no. 85; (d) no. 91;
(e) no. 89; (f) no. 92;
(g) no. 87

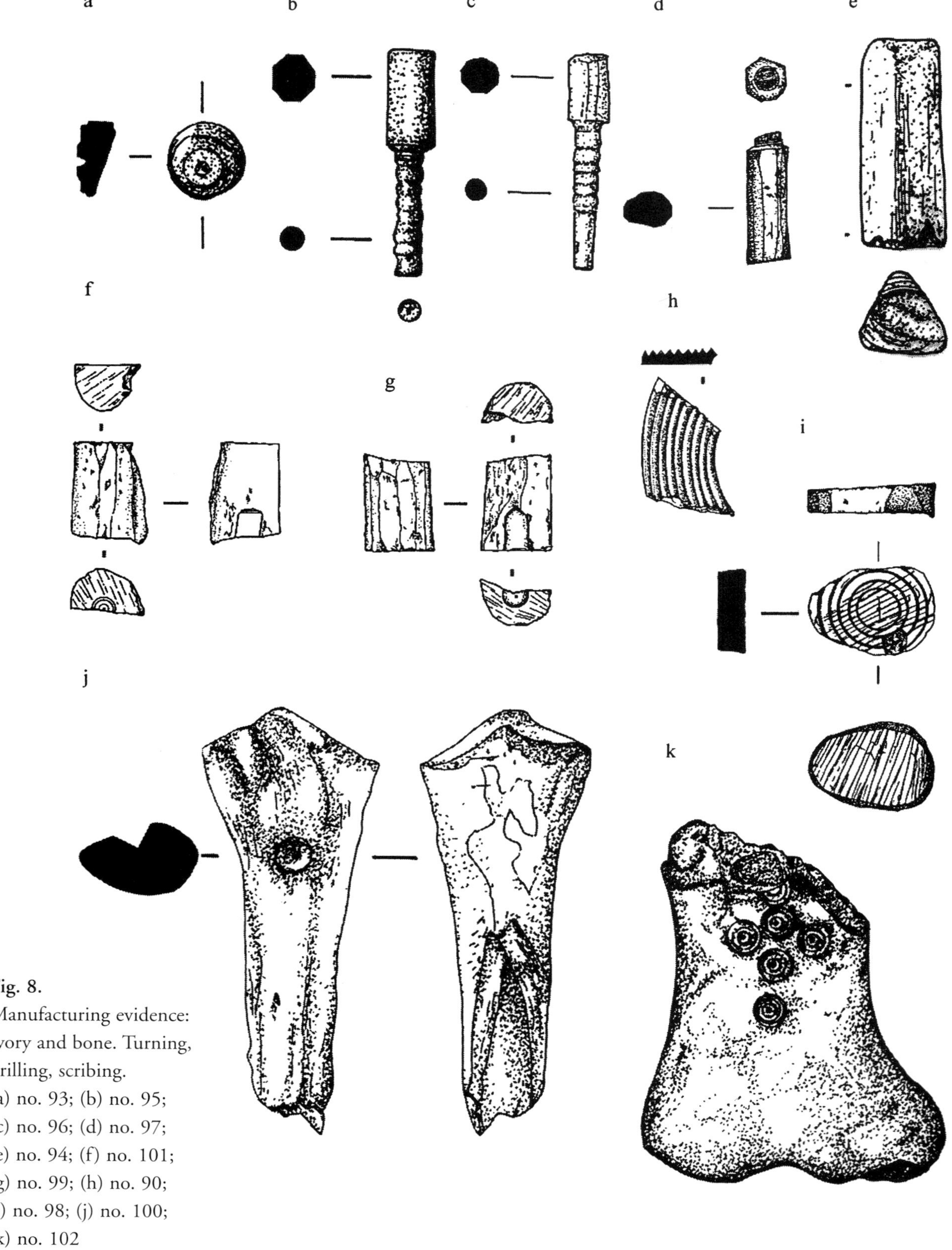

Fig. 8.
Manufacturing evidence:
Ivory and bone. Turning,
drilling, scribing.
(a) no. 93; (b) no. 95;
(c) no. 96; (d) no. 97;
(e) no. 94; (f) no. 101;
(g) no. 99; (h) no. 90;
(i) no. 98; (j) no. 100;
(k) no. 102

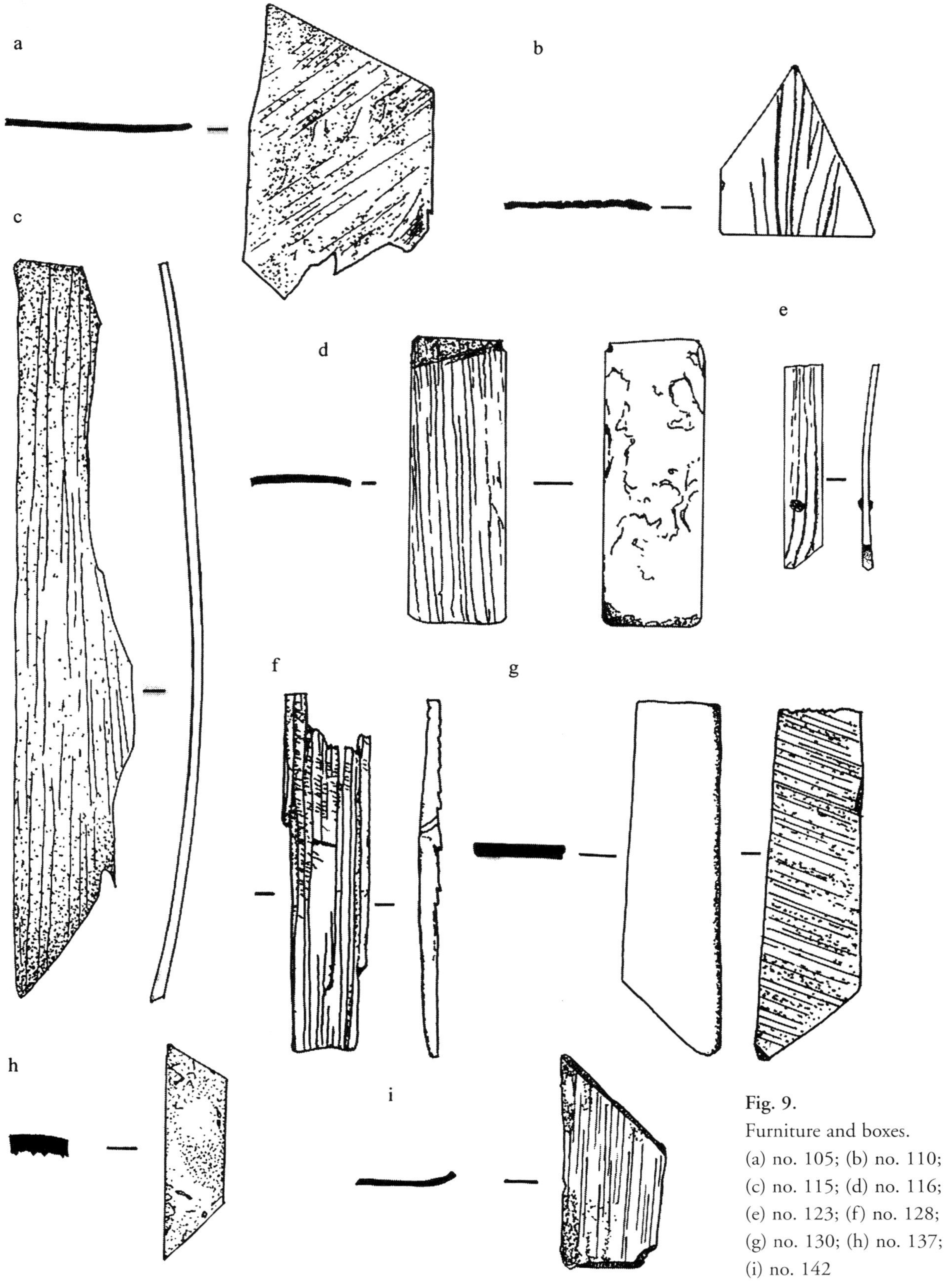

Fig. 9.
Furniture and boxes.
(a) no. 105; (b) no. 110;
(c) no. 115; (d) no. 116;
(e) no. 123; (f) no. 128;
(g) no. 130; (h) no. 137;
(i) no. 142

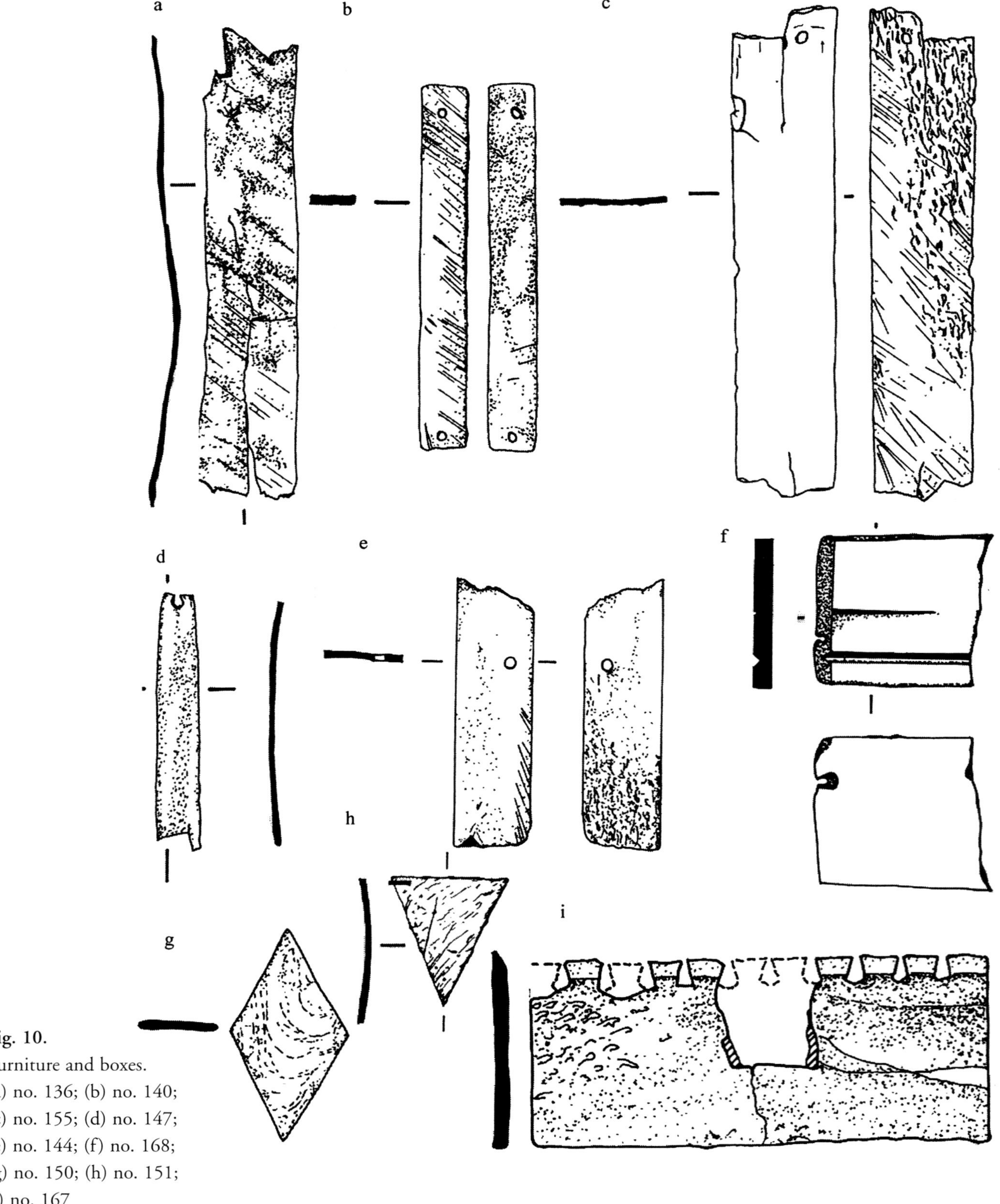

Fig. 10.
Furniture and boxes.
(a) no. 136; (b) no. 140;
(c) no. 155; (d) no. 147;
(e) no. 144; (f) no. 168;
(g) no. 150; (h) no. 151;
(i) no. 167

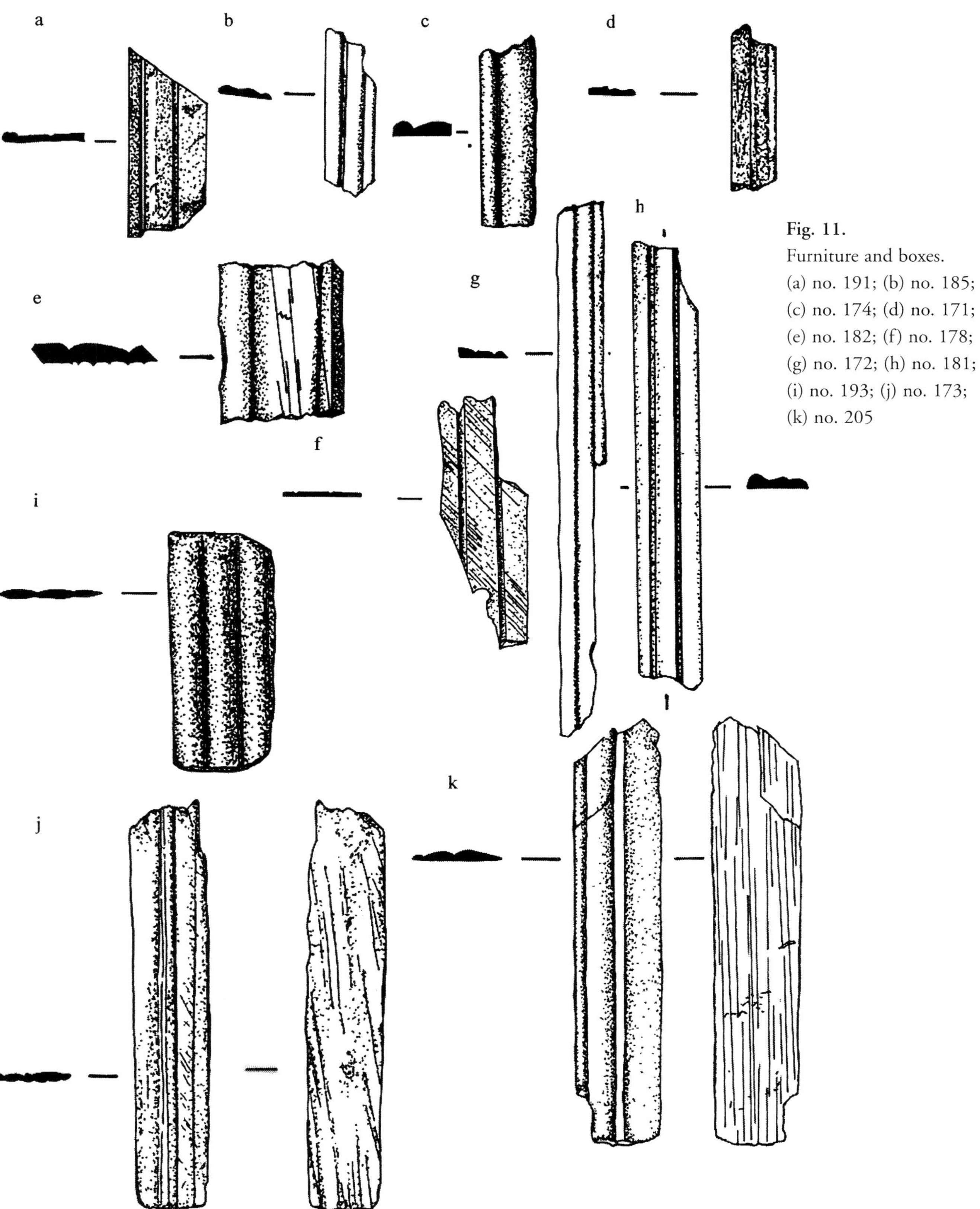

Fig. 11.
Furniture and boxes.
(a) no. 191; (b) no. 185;
(c) no. 174; (d) no. 171;
(e) no. 182; (f) no. 178;
(g) no. 172; (h) no. 181;
(i) no. 193; (j) no. 173;
(k) no. 205

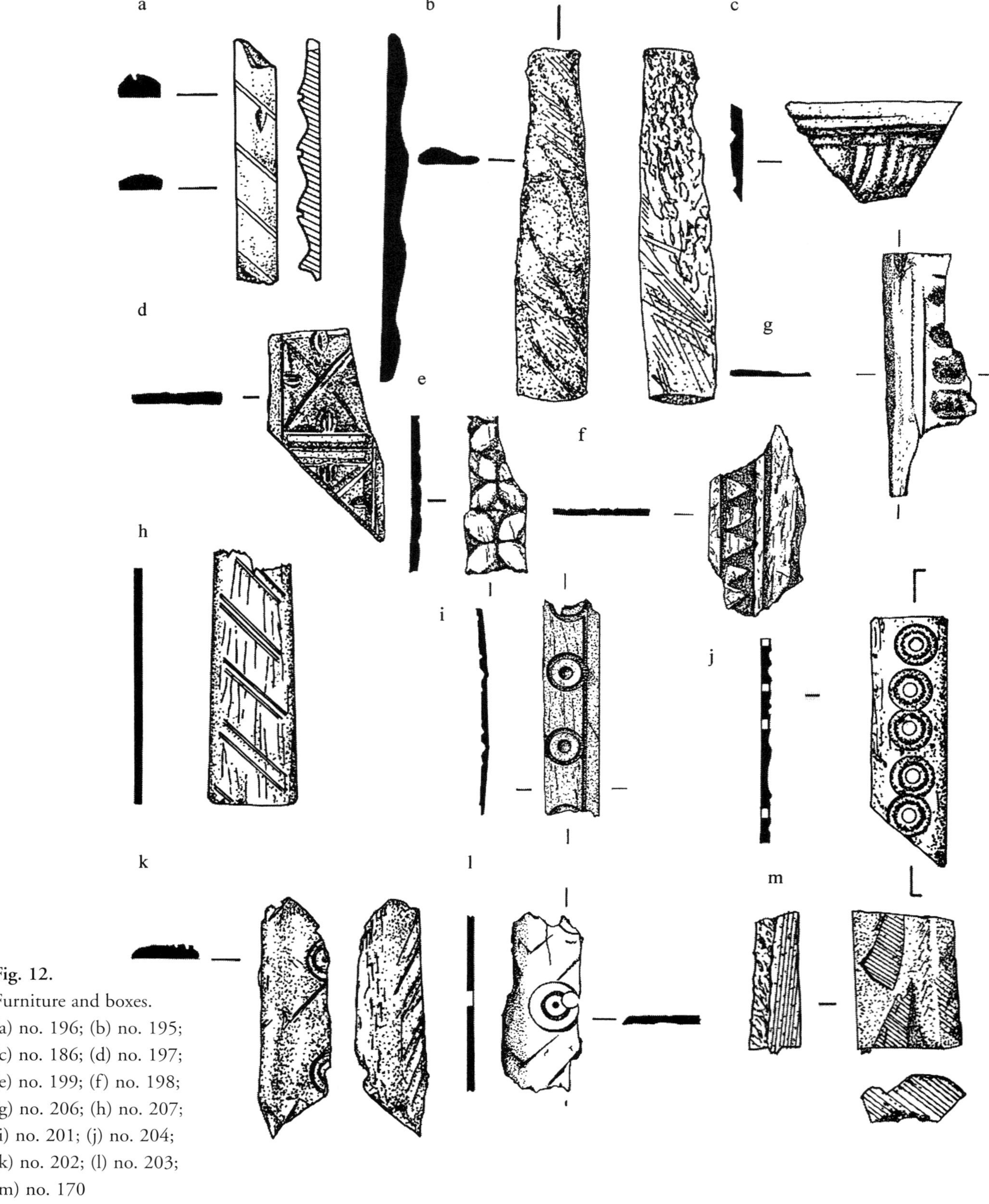

Fig. 12.

Furniture and boxes.
(a) no. 196; (b) no. 195;
(c) no. 186; (d) no. 197;
(e) no. 199; (f) no. 198;
(g) no. 206; (h) no. 207;
(i) no. 201; (j) no. 204;
(k) no. 202; (l) no. 203;
(m) no. 170

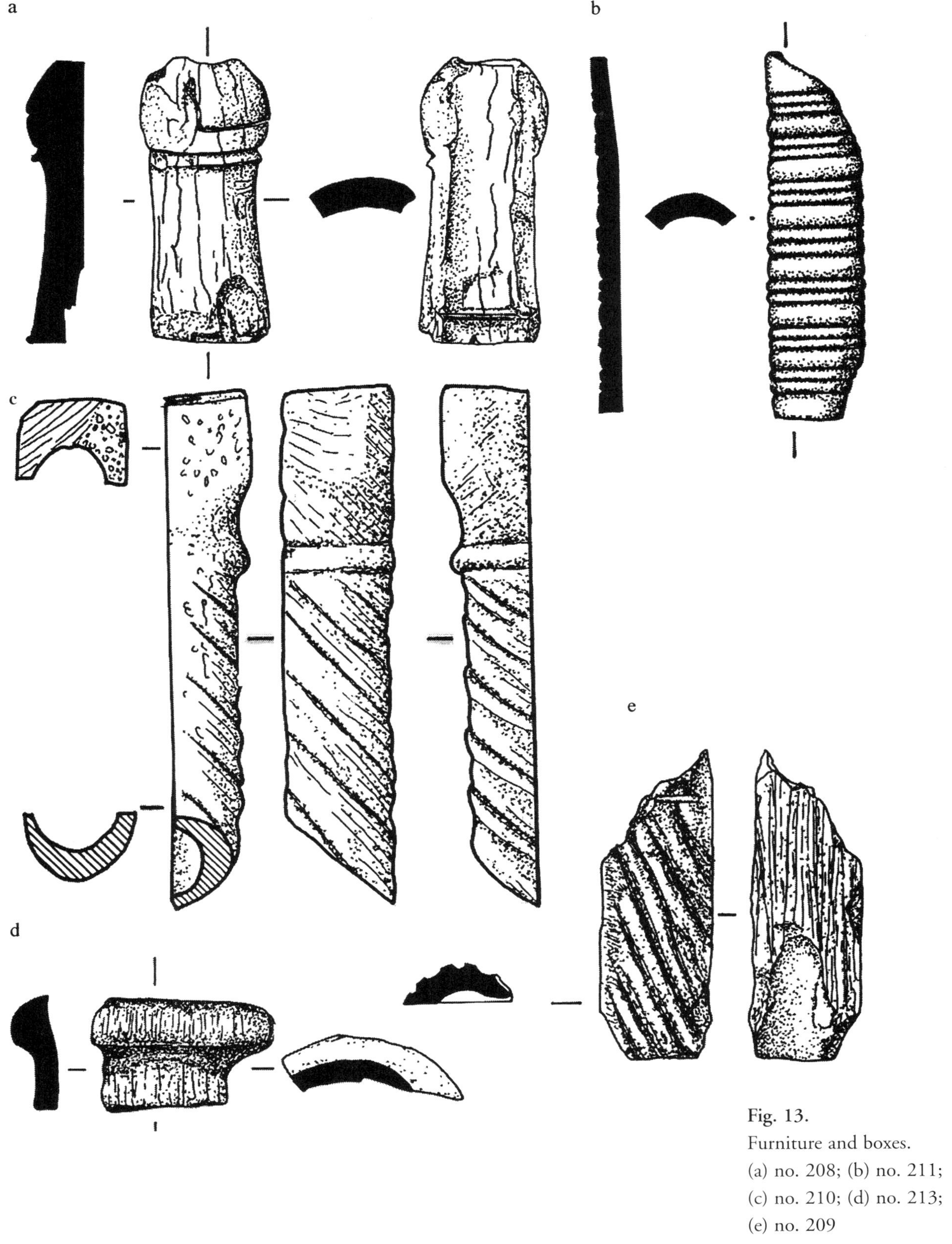

Fig. 13.
Furniture and boxes.
(a) no. 208; (b) no. 211;
(c) no. 210; (d) no. 213;
(e) no. 209

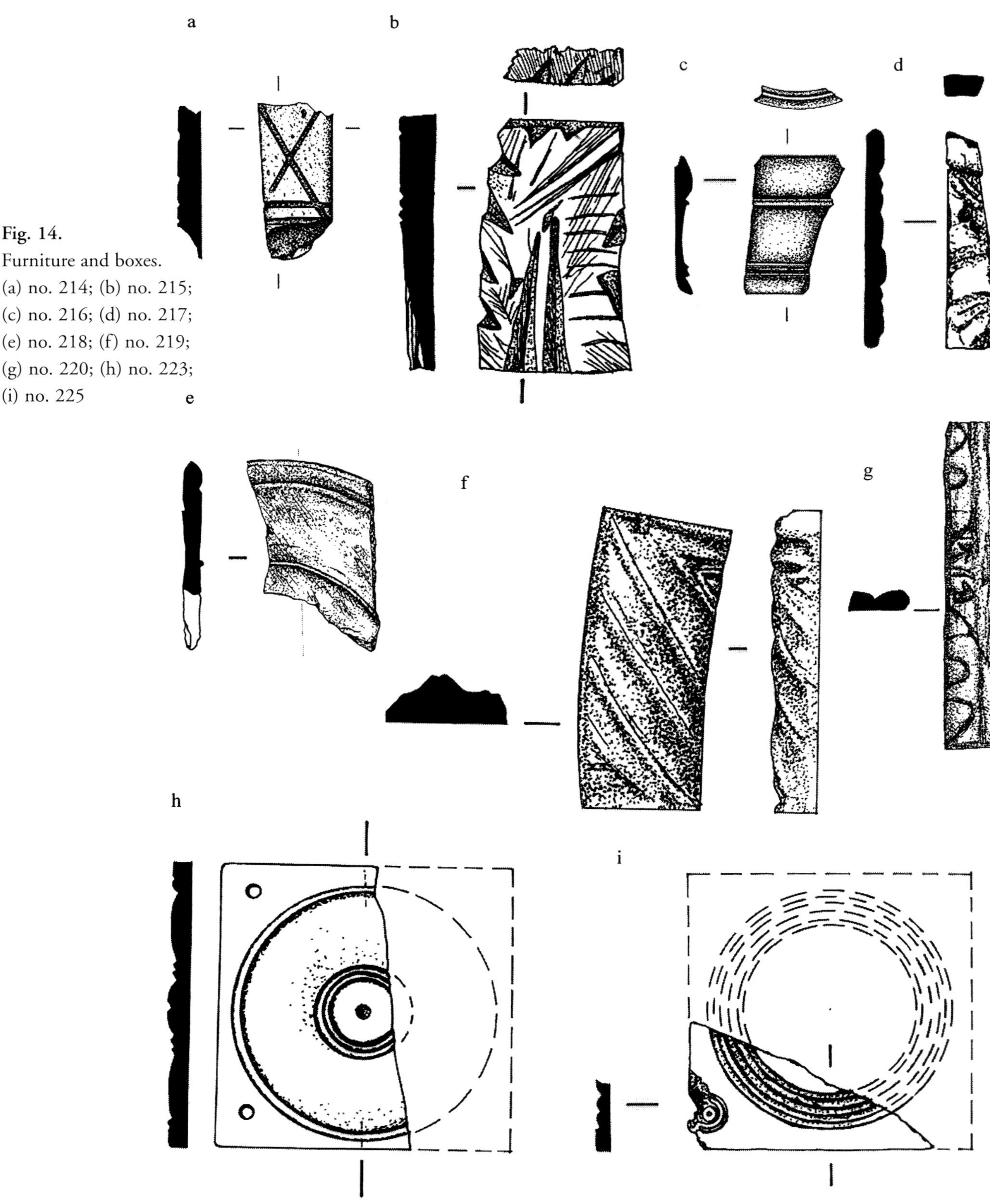

Fig. 14.
Furniture and boxes.
(a) no. 214; (b) no. 215;
(c) no. 216; (d) no. 217;
(e) no. 218; (f) no. 219;
(g) no. 220; (h) no. 223;
(i) no. 225

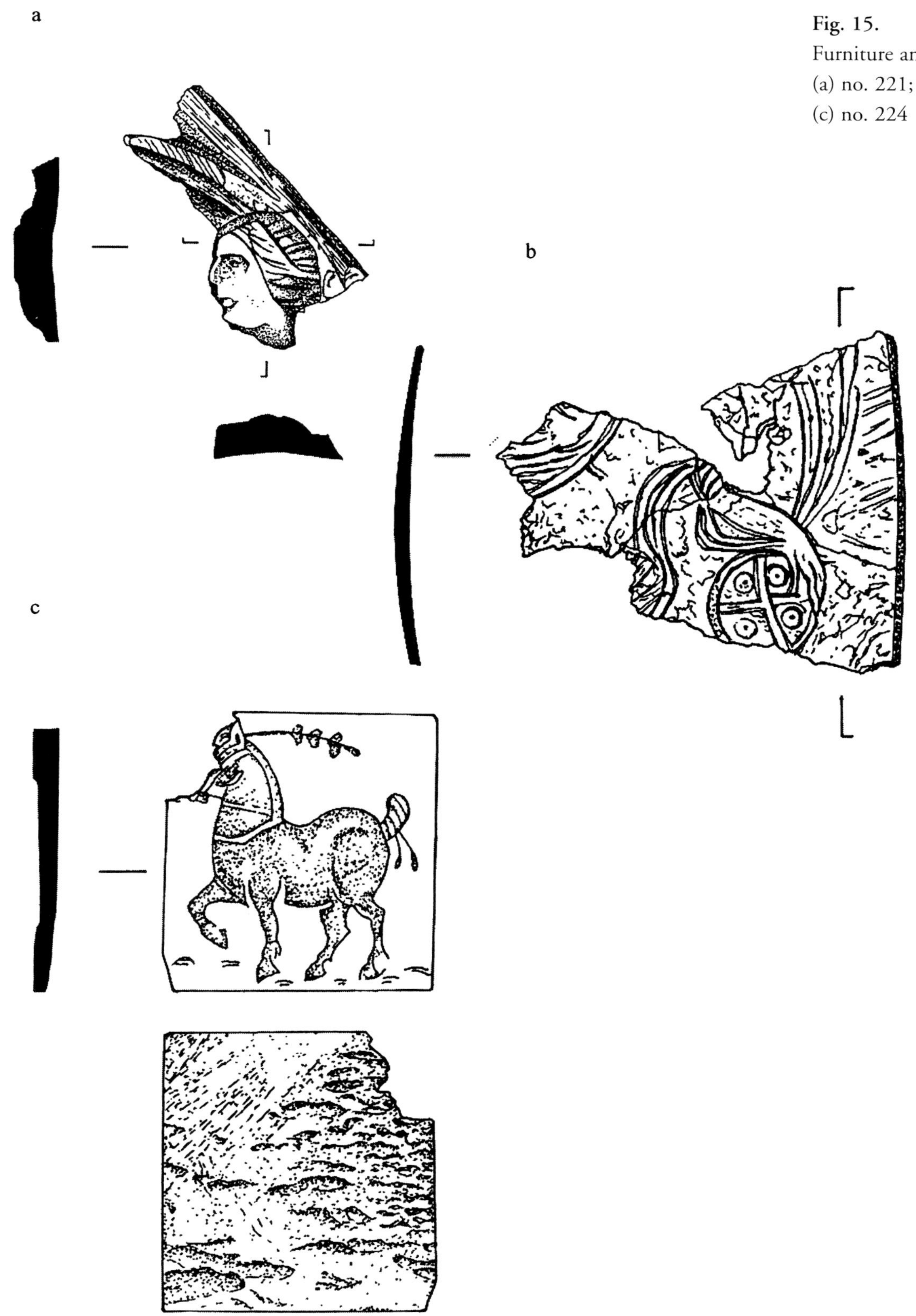

Fig. 15.
Furniture and boxes.
(a) no. 221; (b) no. 222;
(c) no. 224

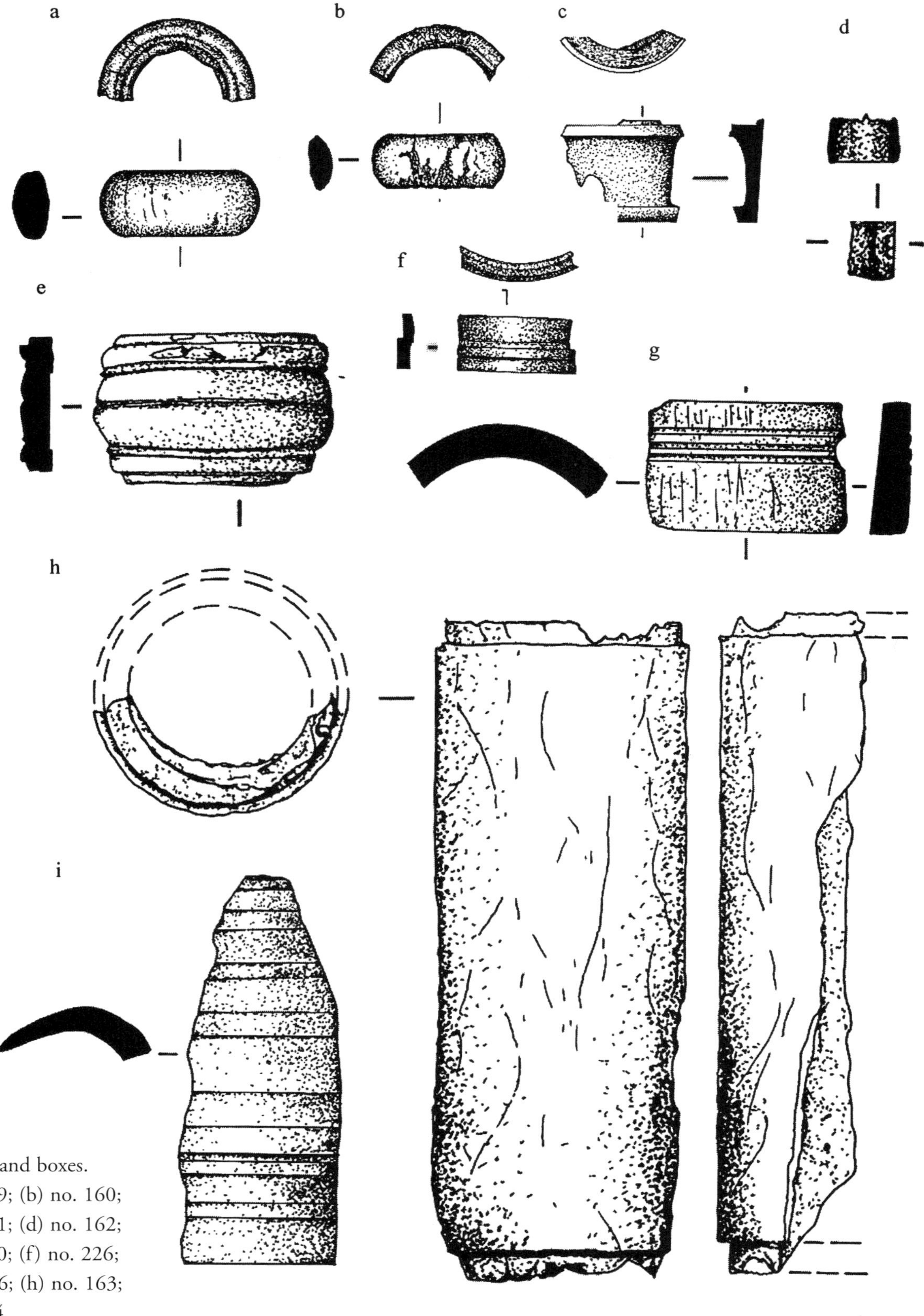

Fig. 16.
Furniture and boxes.
(a) no. 159; (b) no. 160;
(c) no. 161; (d) no. 162;
(e) no. 230; (f) no. 226;
(g) no. 246; (h) no. 163;
(i) no. 164

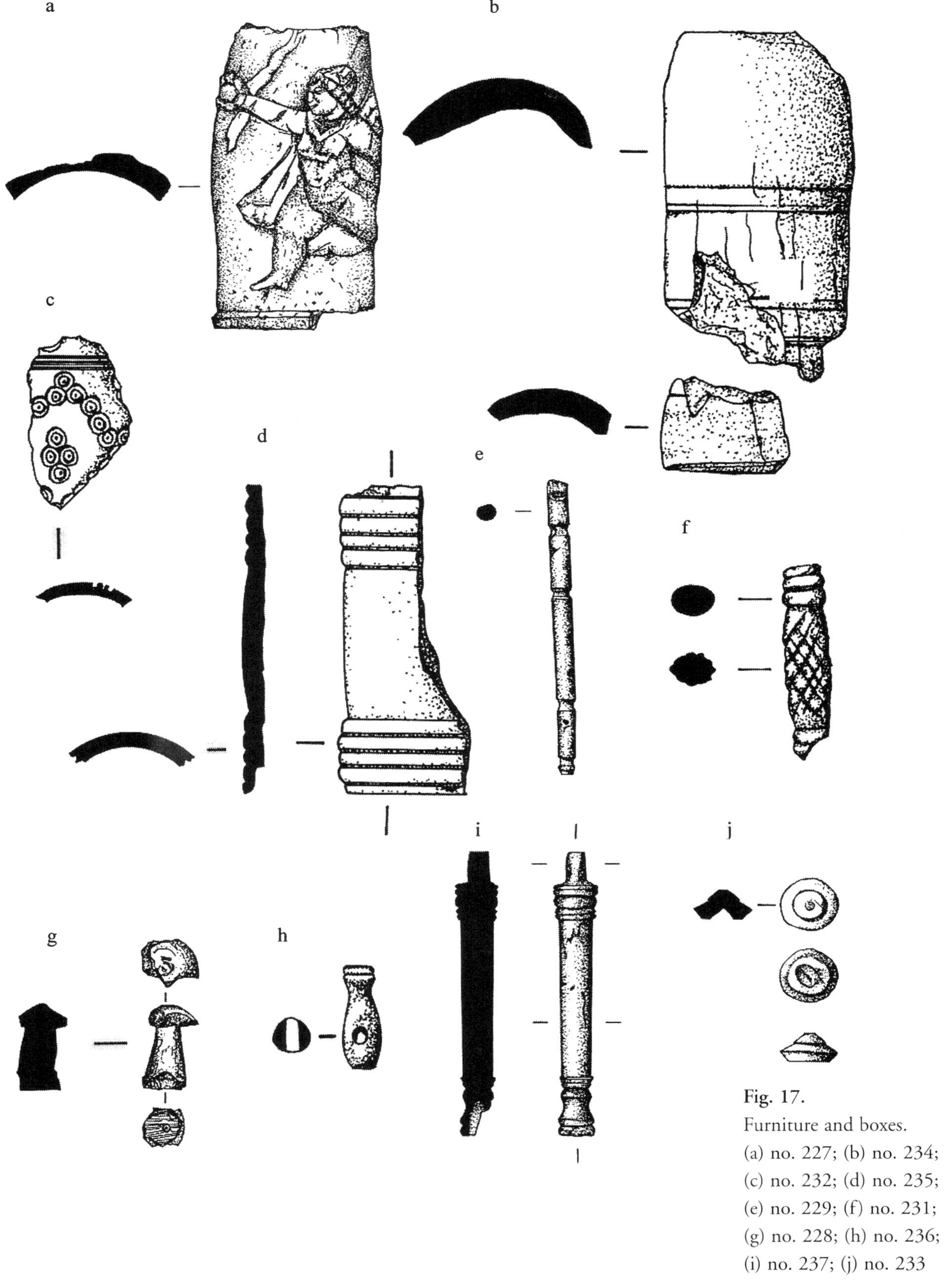

Fig. 17.
Furniture and boxes.
(a) no. 227; (b) no. 234;
(c) no. 232; (d) no. 235;
(e) no. 229; (f) no. 231;
(g) no. 228; (h) no. 236;
(i) no. 237; (j) no. 233

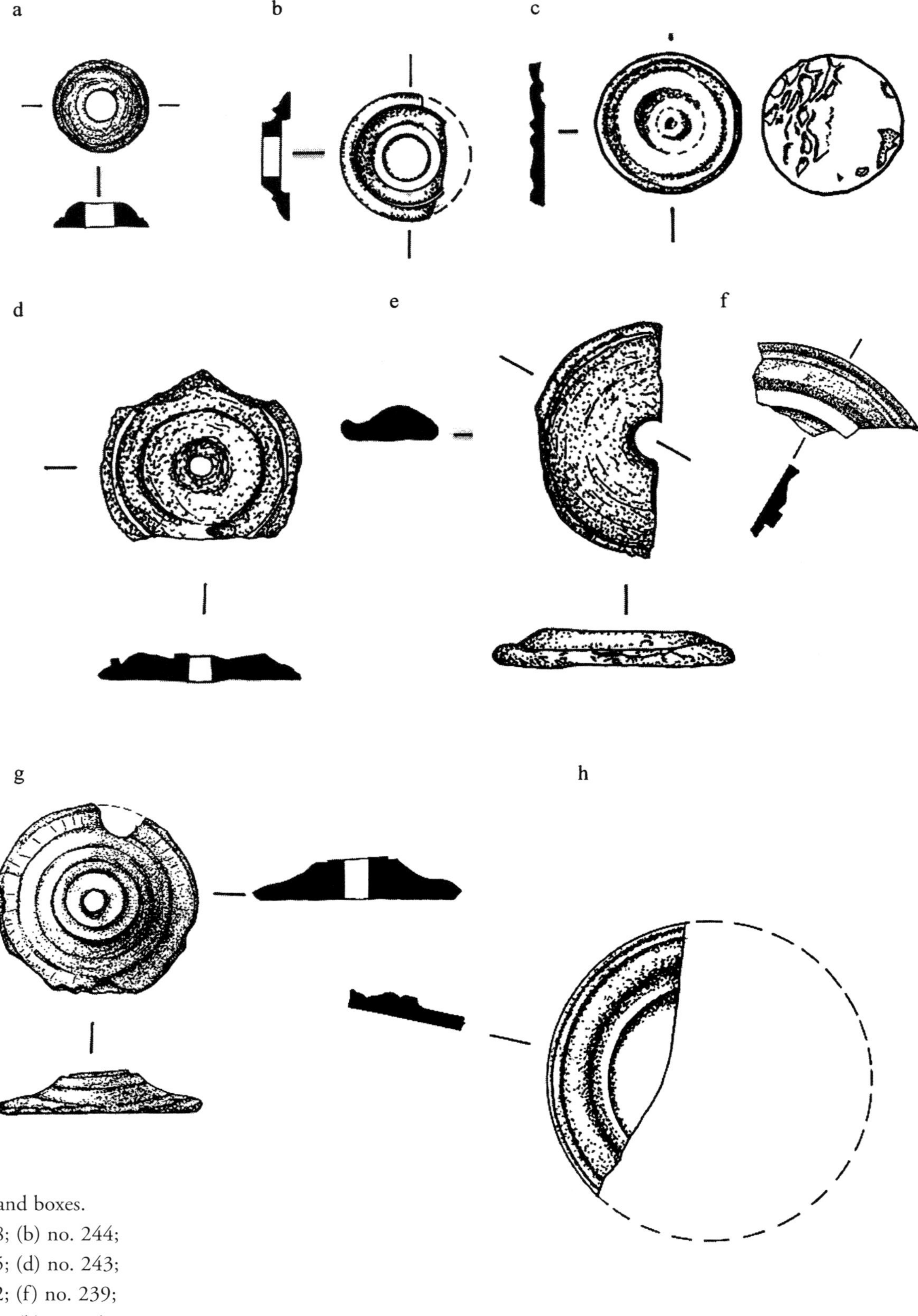

Fig. 18.
Furniture and boxes.
(a) no. 238; (b) no. 244;
(c) no. 245; (d) no. 243;
(e) no. 242; (f) no. 239;
(g) no. 241; (h) no. 240

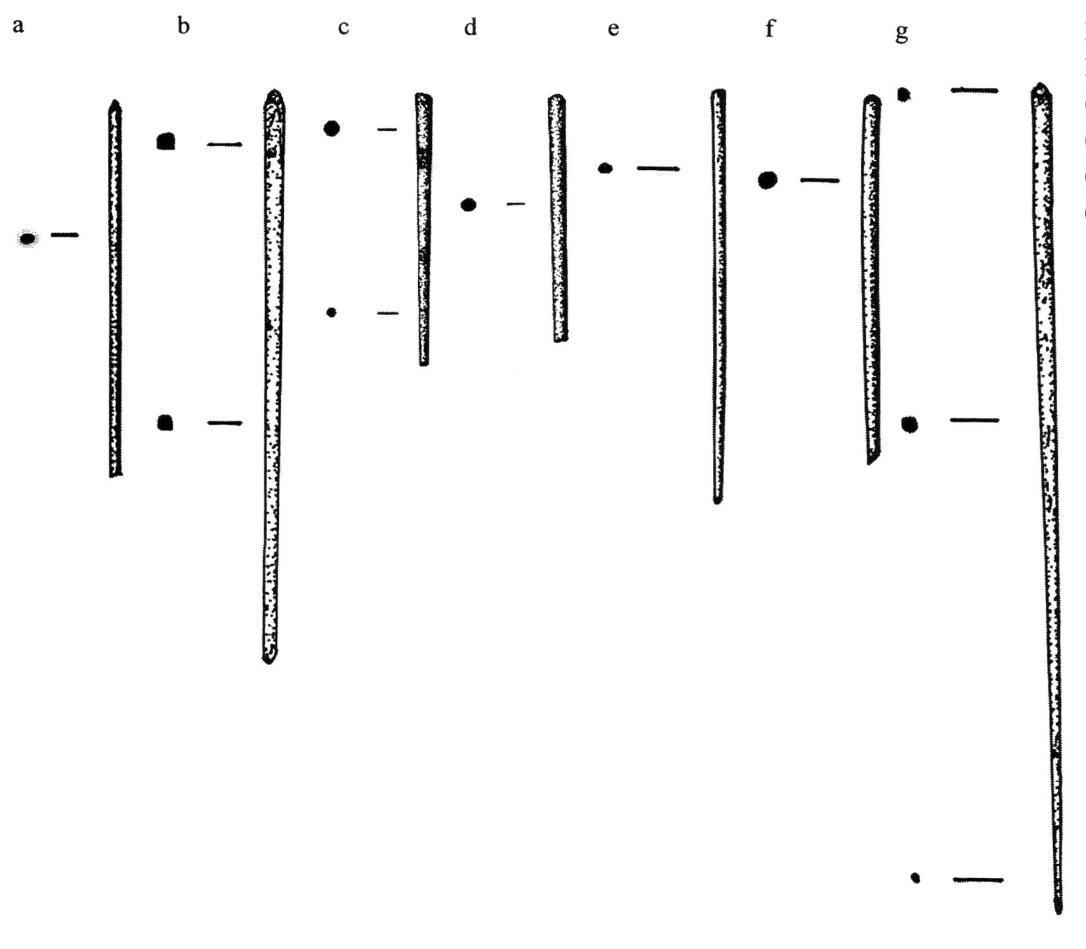

Fig. 19.
Pins: Type I, A.
(a) no. 248; (b) no. 251;
(c) no. 264; (d) no. 253;
(e) no. 255; (f) no. 256;
(g) no. 257

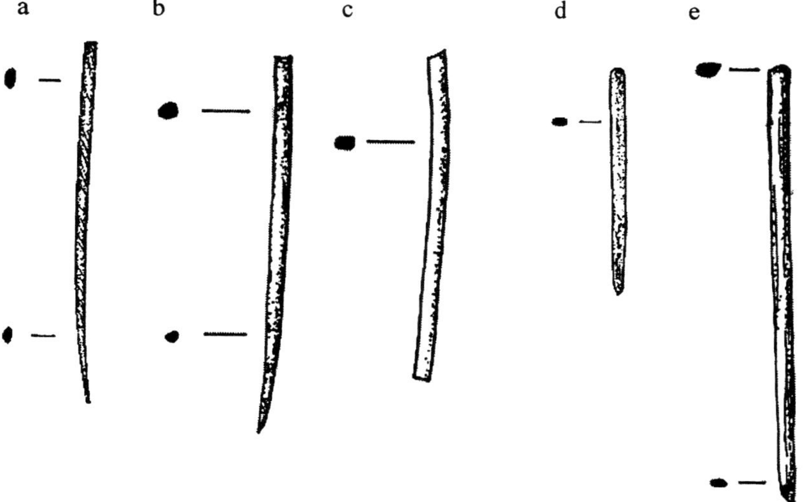

Fig. 20.
Pins: Type I, B.
(a) no. 267; (b) no. 269;
(c) no. 270; (d) no. 271;
(e) no. 272

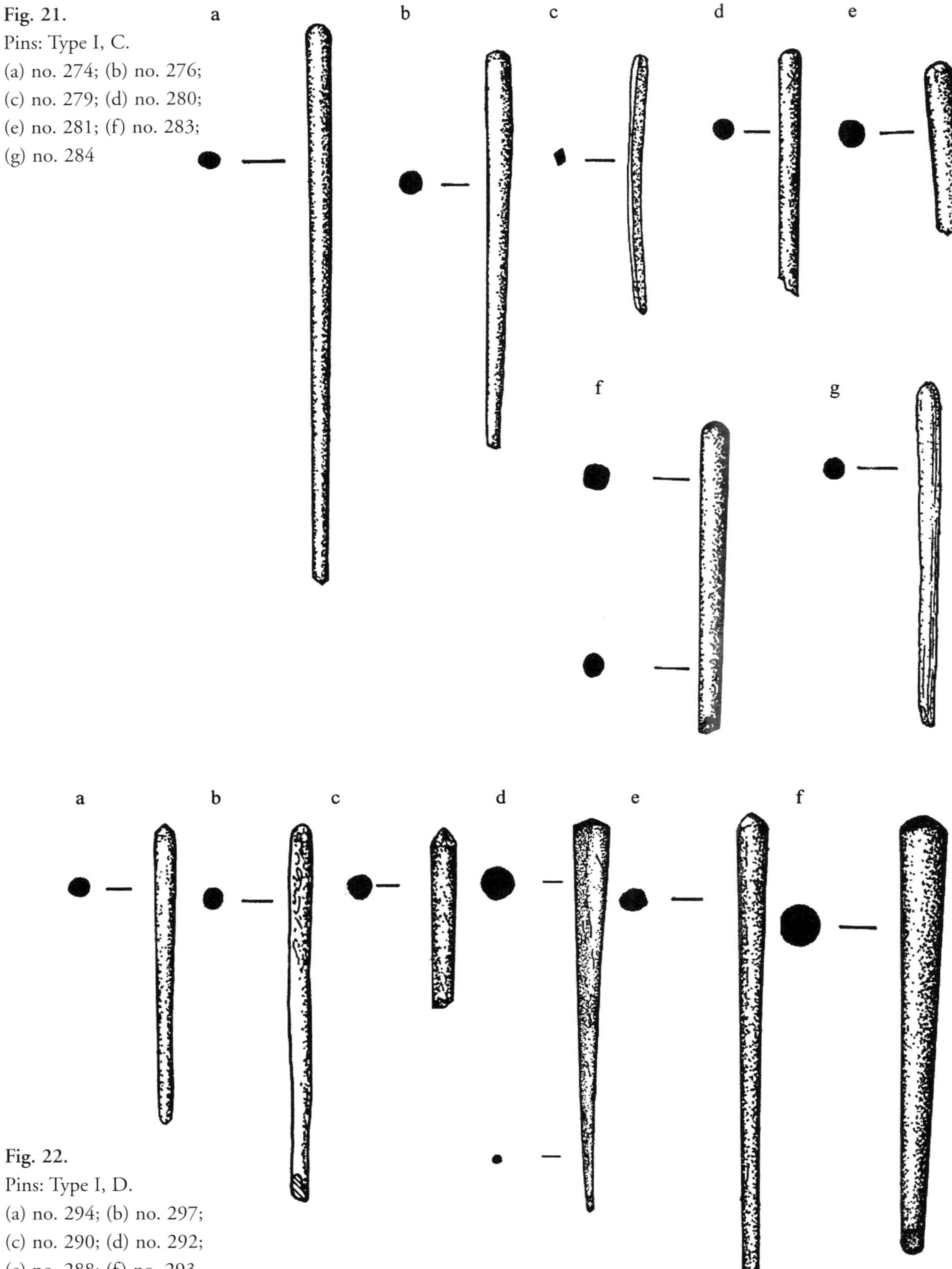

Fig. 21.
Pins: Type I, C.
(a) no. 274; (b) no. 276;
(c) no. 279; (d) no. 280;
(e) no. 281; (f) no. 283;
(g) no. 284

Fig. 22.
Pins: Type I, D.
(a) no. 294; (b) no. 297;
(c) no. 290; (d) no. 292;
(e) no. 288; (f) no. 293

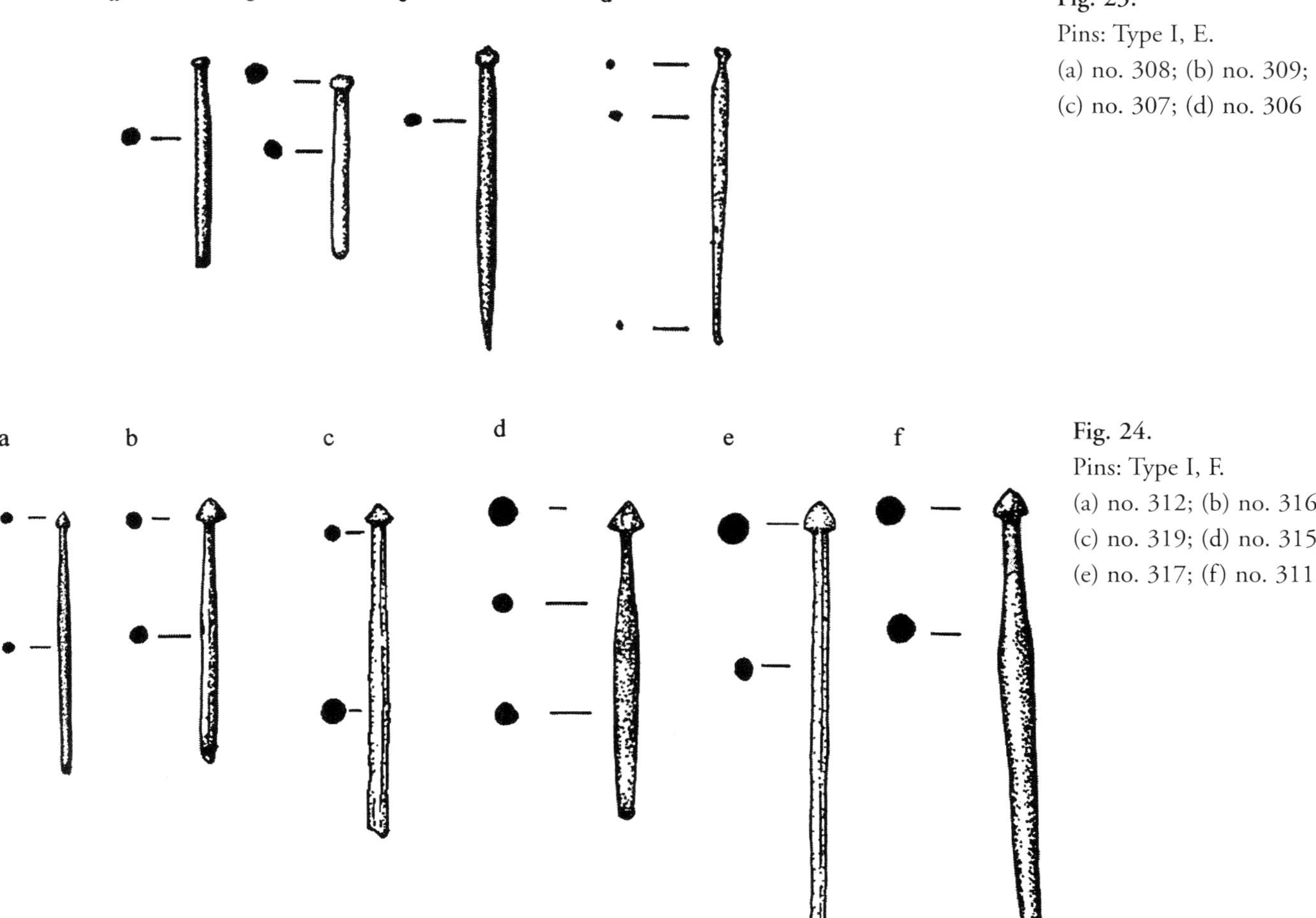

Fig. 23.
Pins: Type I, E.
(a) no. 308; (b) no. 309;
(c) no. 307; (d) no. 306

Fig. 24.
Pins: Type I, F.
(a) no. 312; (b) no. 316;
(c) no. 319; (d) no. 315;
(e) no. 317; (f) no. 311

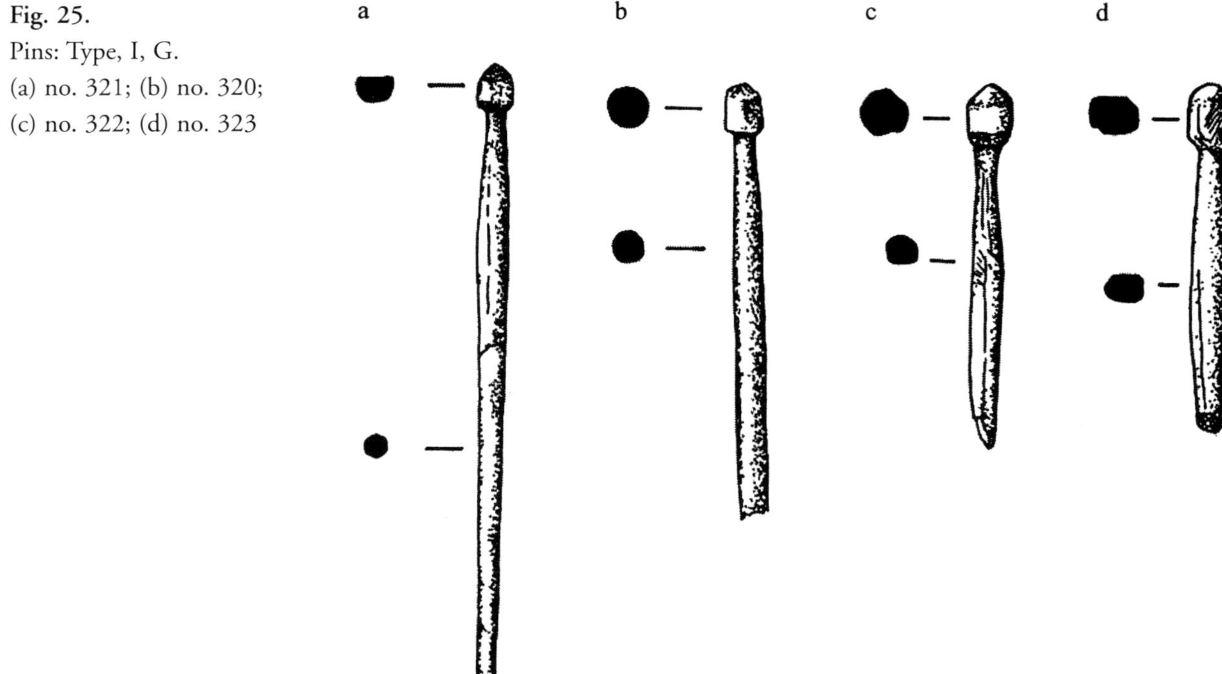

Fig. 25.
Pins: Type, I, G.
(a) no. 321; (b) no. 320;
(c) no. 322; (d) no. 323

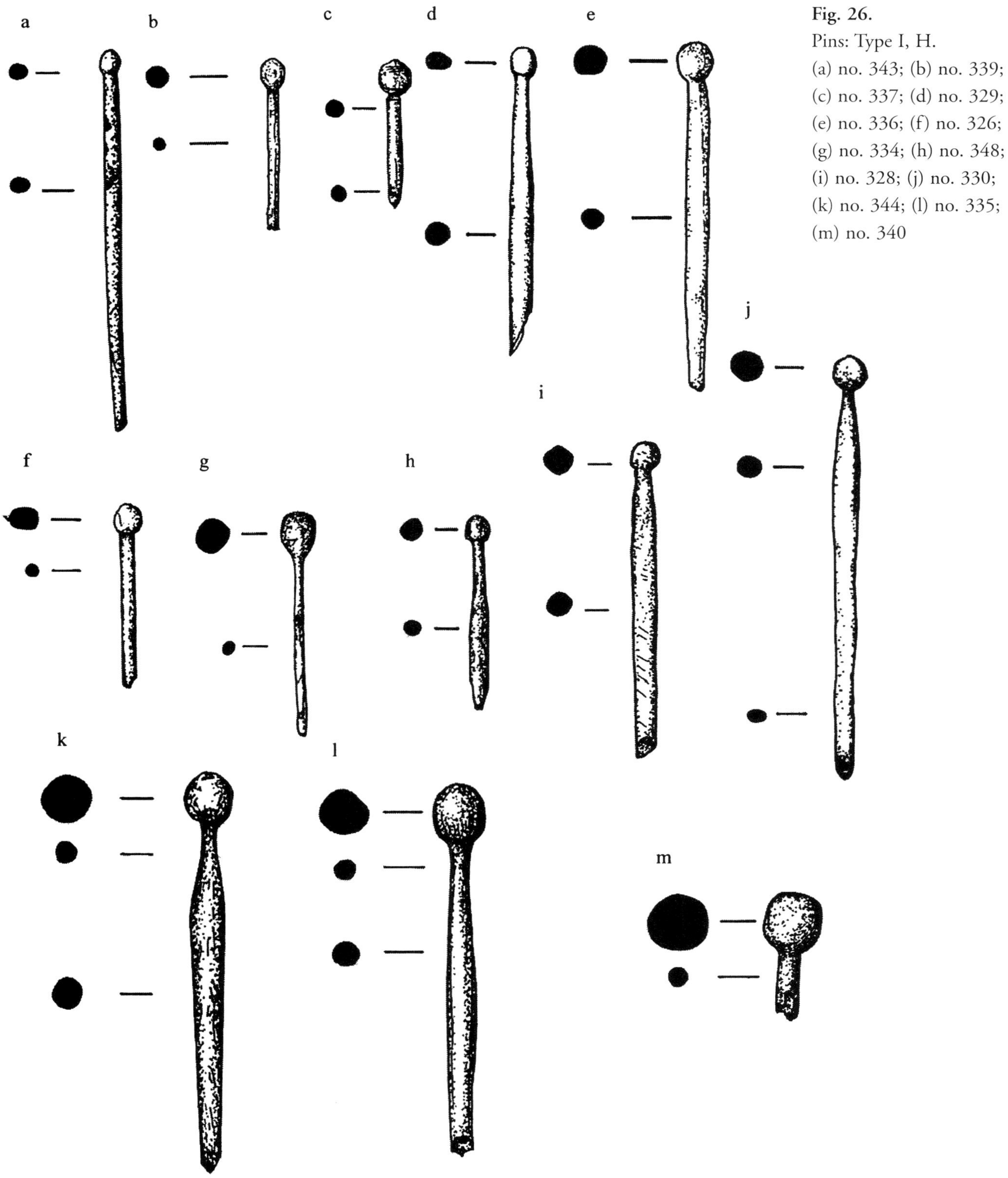

Fig. 26.
Pins: Type I, H.
(a) no. 343; (b) no. 339;
(c) no. 337; (d) no. 329;
(e) no. 336; (f) no. 326;
(g) no. 334; (h) no. 348;
(i) no. 328; (j) no. 330;
(k) no. 344; (l) no. 335;
(m) no. 340

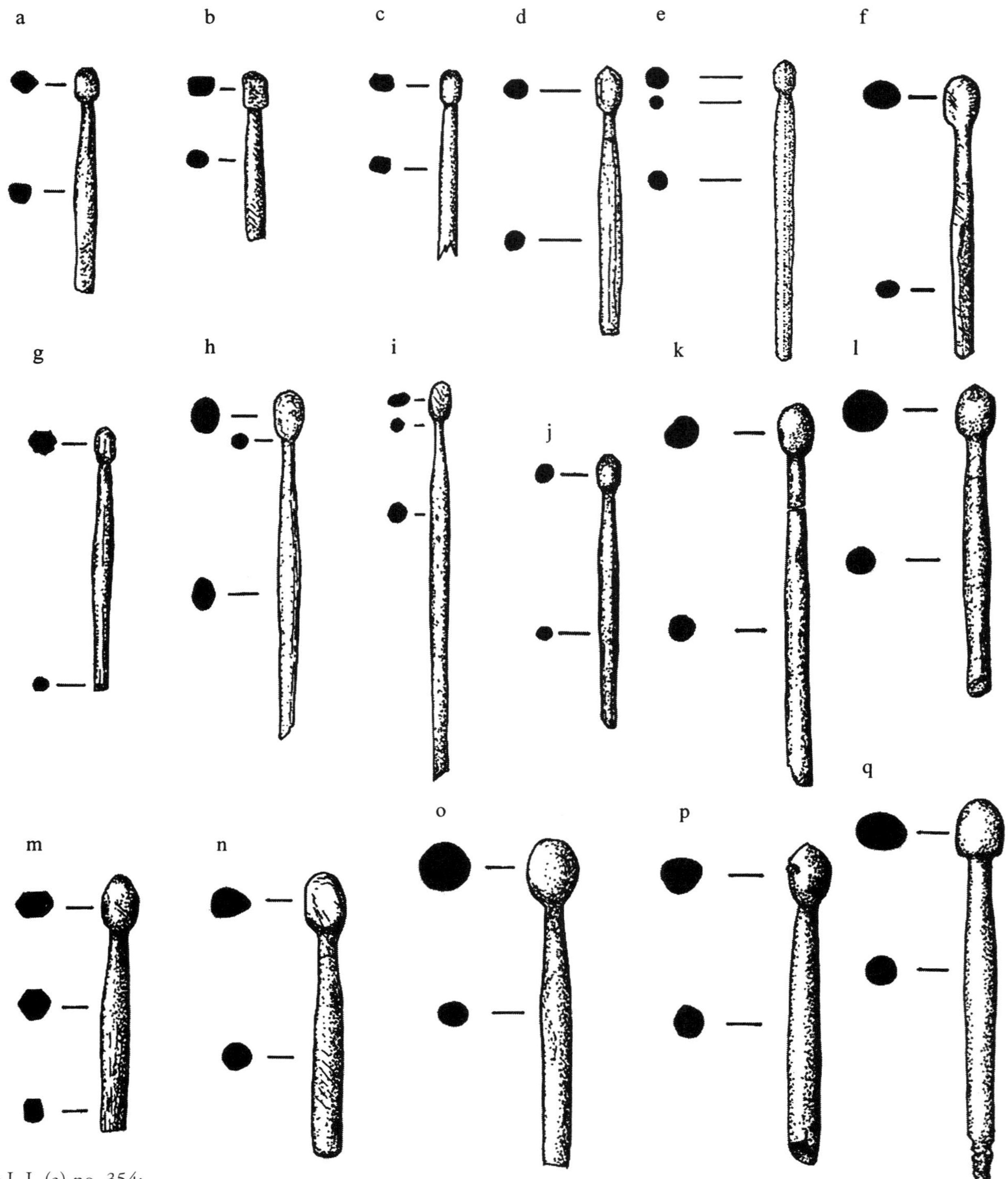

Fig. 27.
Pins: Type I, I. (a) no. 354;
(b) no. 355; (c) no. 356; (d) no. 372;
(e) no. 374; (f) no. 364; (g) no. 369;
(h) no. 376; (i) no. 368; (j) no. 367;
(k) no. 363; (l) no. 370; (m) no. 359;
(n) no. 357; (o) no. 358; (p) no. 360;
(q) no. 380

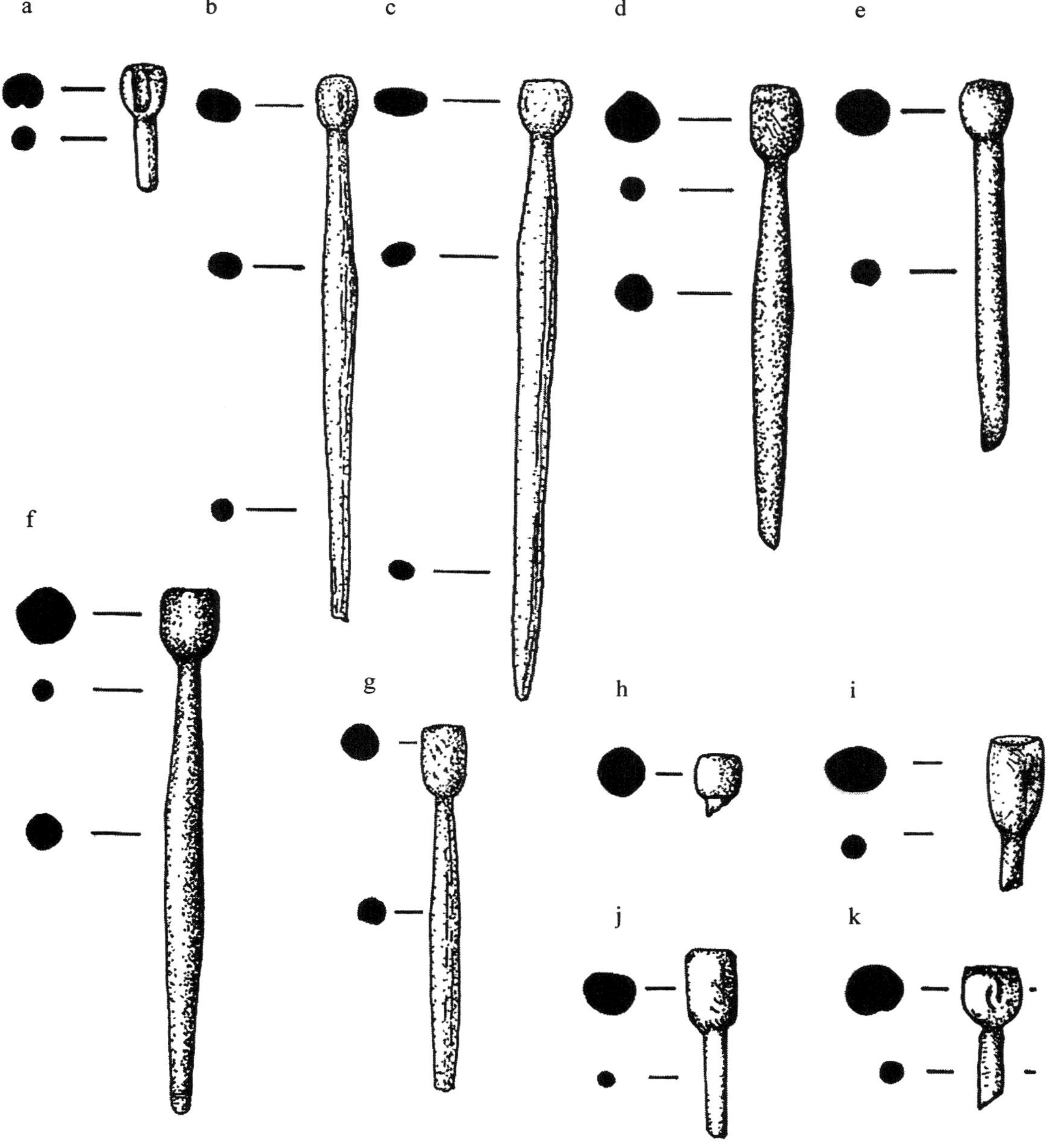

Fig. 28.

Pins: Type I, J.
(a) no. 393; (b) no. 396;
(c) no. 395; (d) no. 391;
(e) no. 390; (f) no. 398;
(g) no. 394; (h) no. 386;
(i) no. 392; (j) no. 387;
(k) no. 399

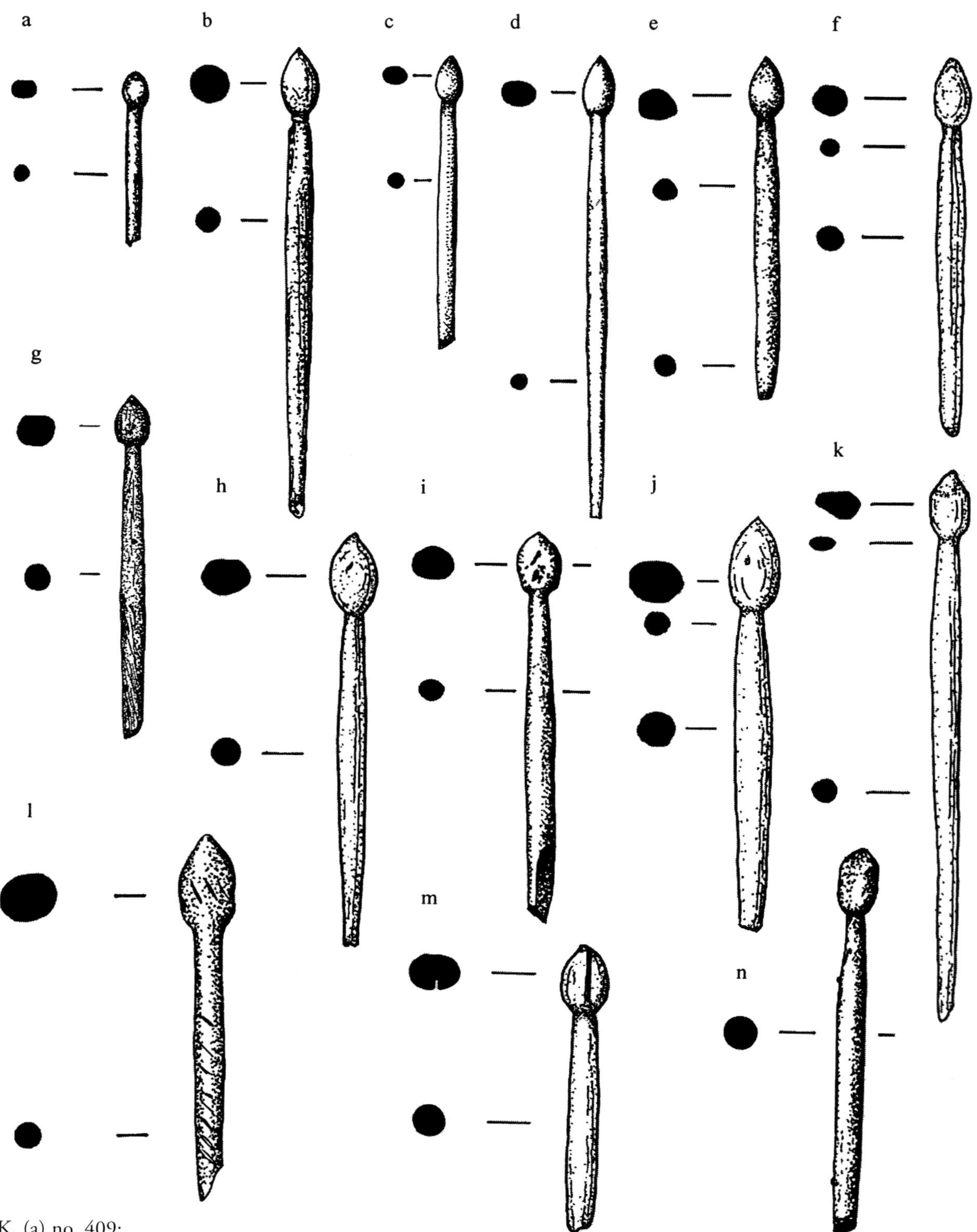

Fig. 29.
Pins: Type, I, K. (a) no. 409;
(b) no. 414; (c) no. 437; (d) no. 404;
(e) no. 413; (f) no. 421; (g) no. 431;
(h) no. 417; (i) no. 403; (j) no. 419;
(k) no. 423; (l) no. 418; (m) no. 430;
(n) no. 401

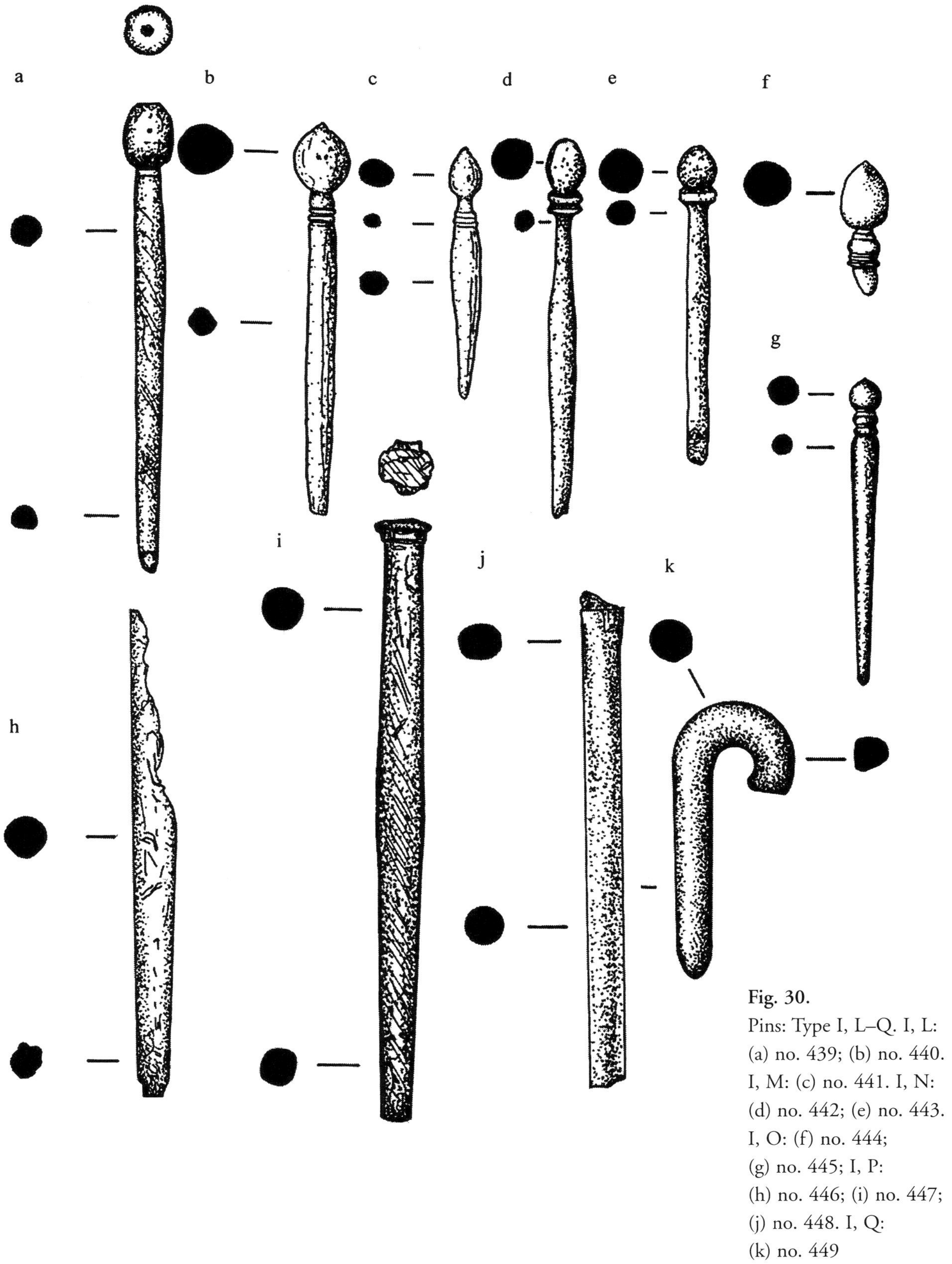

Fig. 30.
Pins: Type I, L–Q. I, L:
(a) no. 439; (b) no. 440.
I, M: (c) no. 441. I, N:
(d) no. 442; (e) no. 443.
I, O: (f) no. 444;
(g) no. 445; I, P:
(h) no. 446; (i) no. 447;
(j) no. 448. I, Q:
(k) no. 449

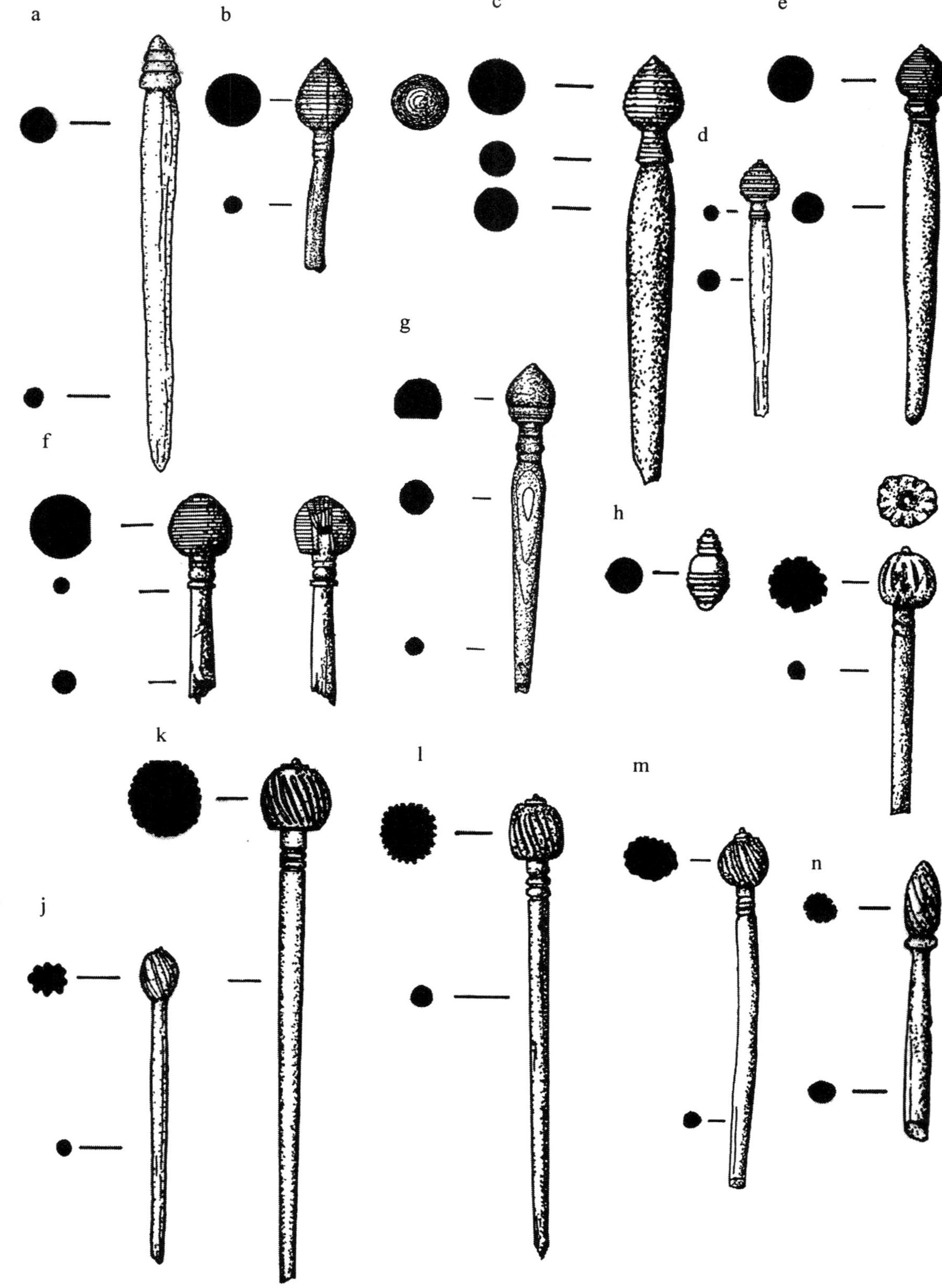

Fig. 31.
Pins: Type II, A–J.
II, A: (a) no. 450.
II, B: (b) no. 451.
II, C: (c) no. 452;
(d) no. 453. II,
D: (e) no. 454;
(f) no. 455. II,
E: (g) no. 456.
II, F: (h) no. 457.
II, G: (i) no. 458.
II, H: (j) no. 459.
II, I: (k) no. 460;
(l) no. 461;
(m) no. 462. II,
J: (n) no. 463

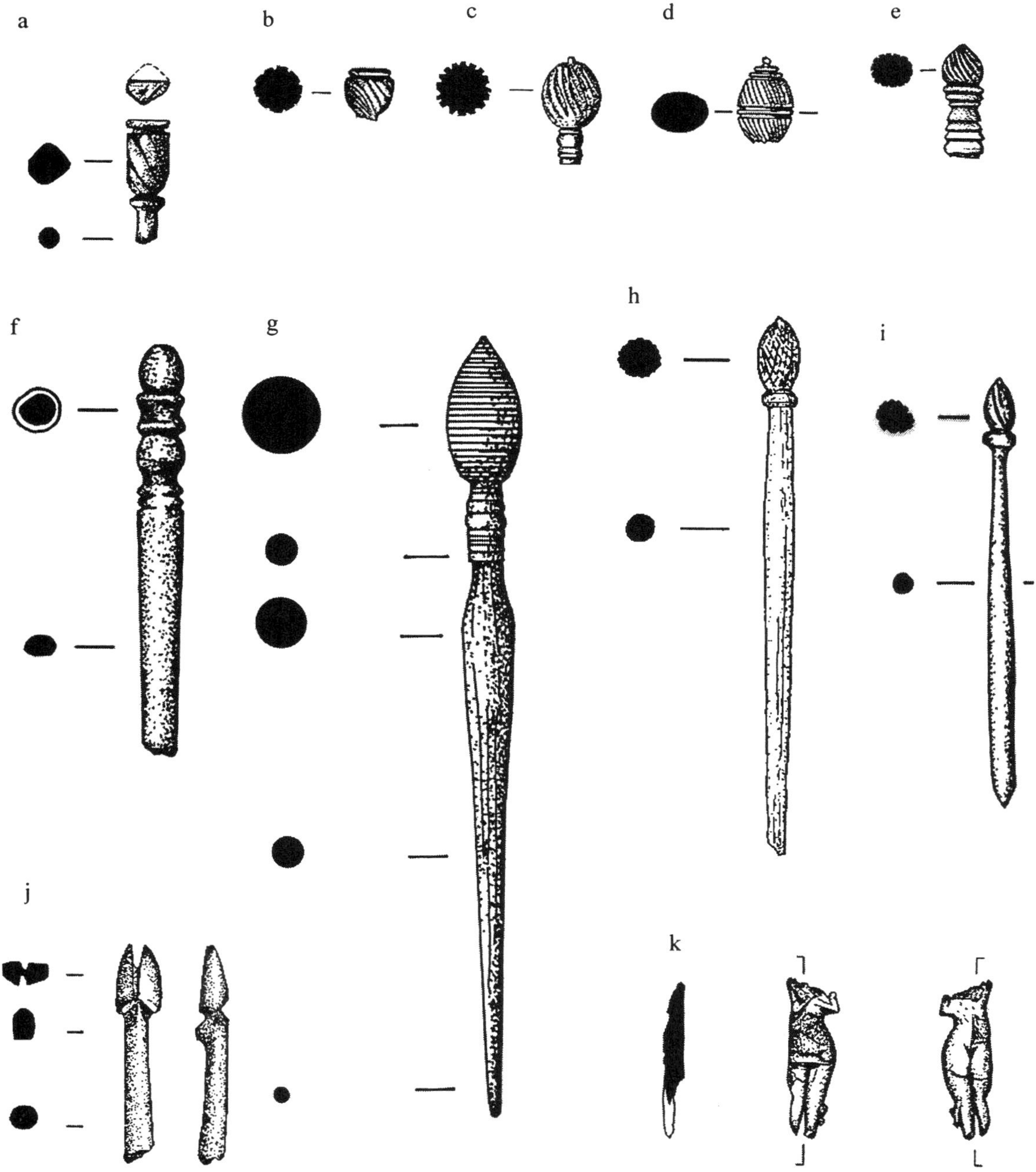

Fig. 32.
Pins: Types II, K–Q, III, A–C.
II, K: (a) no. 465. II, L: (b) no. 466.
II, M: (c) no. 467. II, N: (d) no. 469.
II, O: (e) no. 470. II, P; (f) no. 471.
II, Q: (g) no. 472. III, A: (h) no. 473.
III, B: (i) no. 464; (j) no. 474. III,
C: (k) no. 475

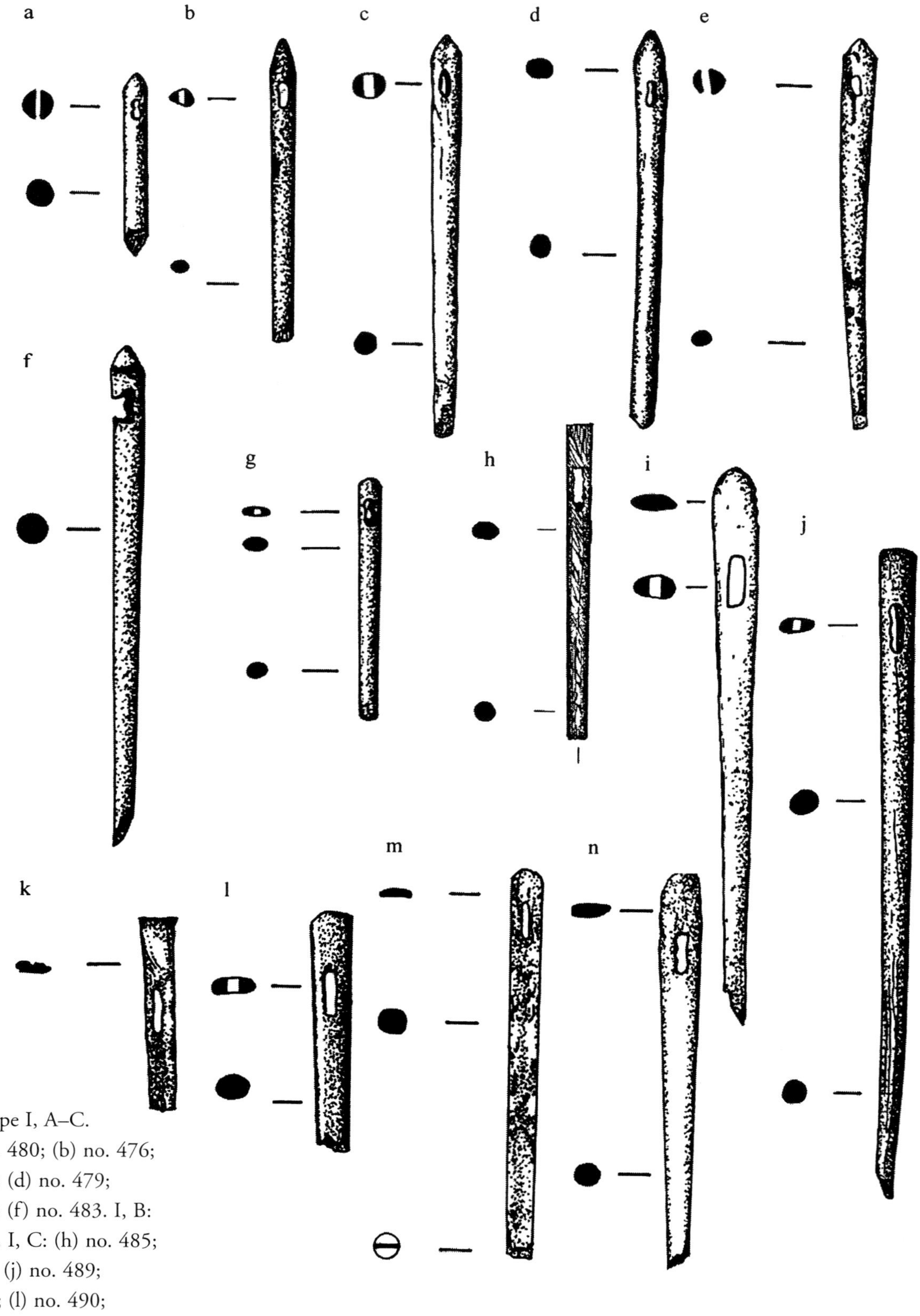

Fig. 33.
Needles: Type I, A–C.
I, A: (a) no. 480; (b) no. 476;
(c) no. 478; (d) no. 479;
(e) no. 477; (f) no. 483. I, B:
(g) no. 484. I, C: (h) no. 485;
(i) no. 492; (j) no. 489;
(k) no. 488; (l) no. 490;
(m) no. 486; (n) no. 491

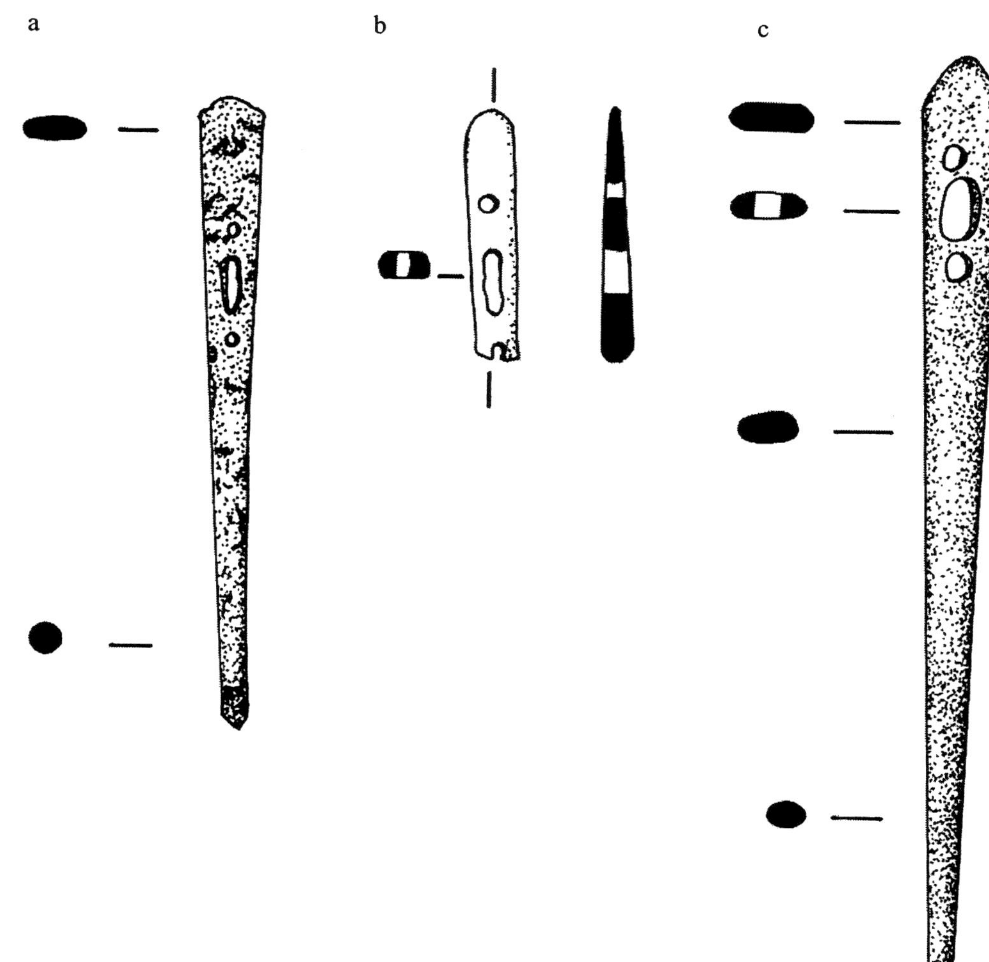

Fig. 34.
Needles: Type II, A.
(a) no. 493; (b) no. 494;
(c) no. 495

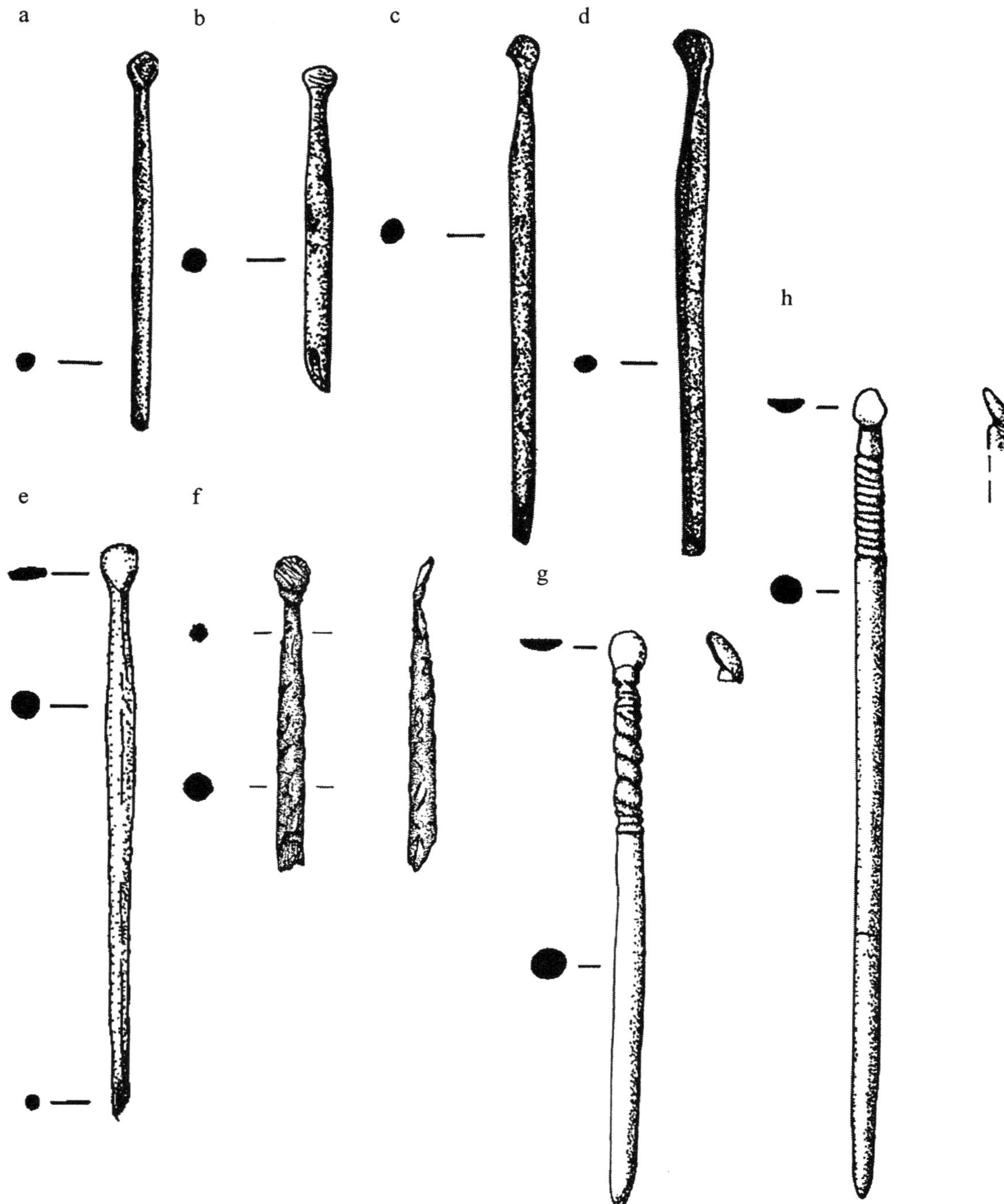

Fig. 35.
Utensils with spatulate or
bowl-shaped terminals:
Type I, A, B (Ligulae).
I, A: (a) no. 503;
(b) no. 498; (c) no. 501;
(d) no. 502; (e) no. 505;
(f) no. 499. I, B:
(g) no. 506; (h) no. 507

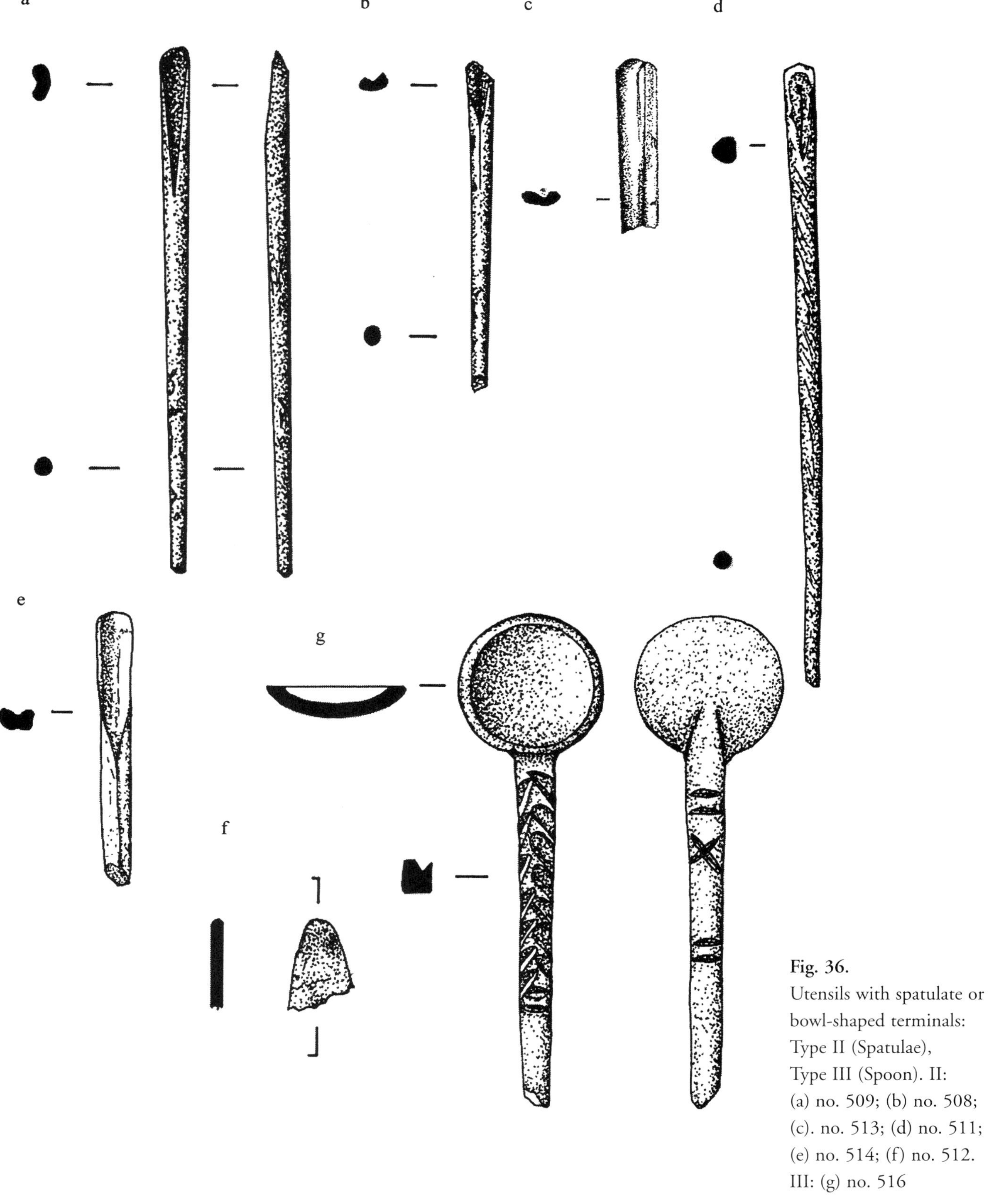

Fig. 36.
Utensils with spatulate or
bowl-shaped terminals:
Type II (Spatulae),
Type III (Spoon). II:
(a) no. 509; (b) no. 508;
(c). no. 513; (d) no. 511;
(e) no. 514; (f) no. 512.
III: (g) no. 516

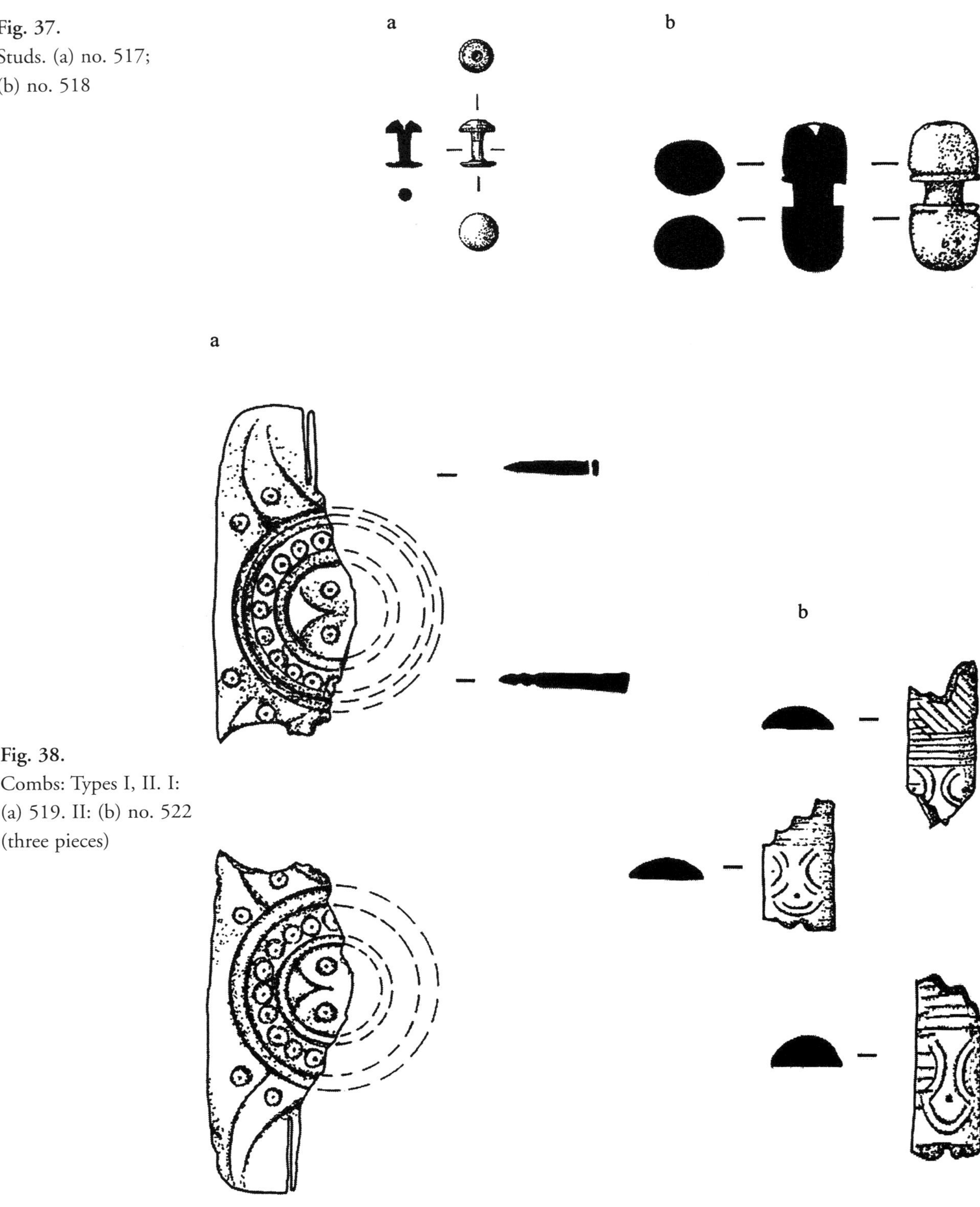

Fig. 37.
Studs. (a) no. 517;
(b) no. 518

Fig. 38.
Combs: Types I, II. I:
(a) 519. II: (b) no. 522
(three pieces)

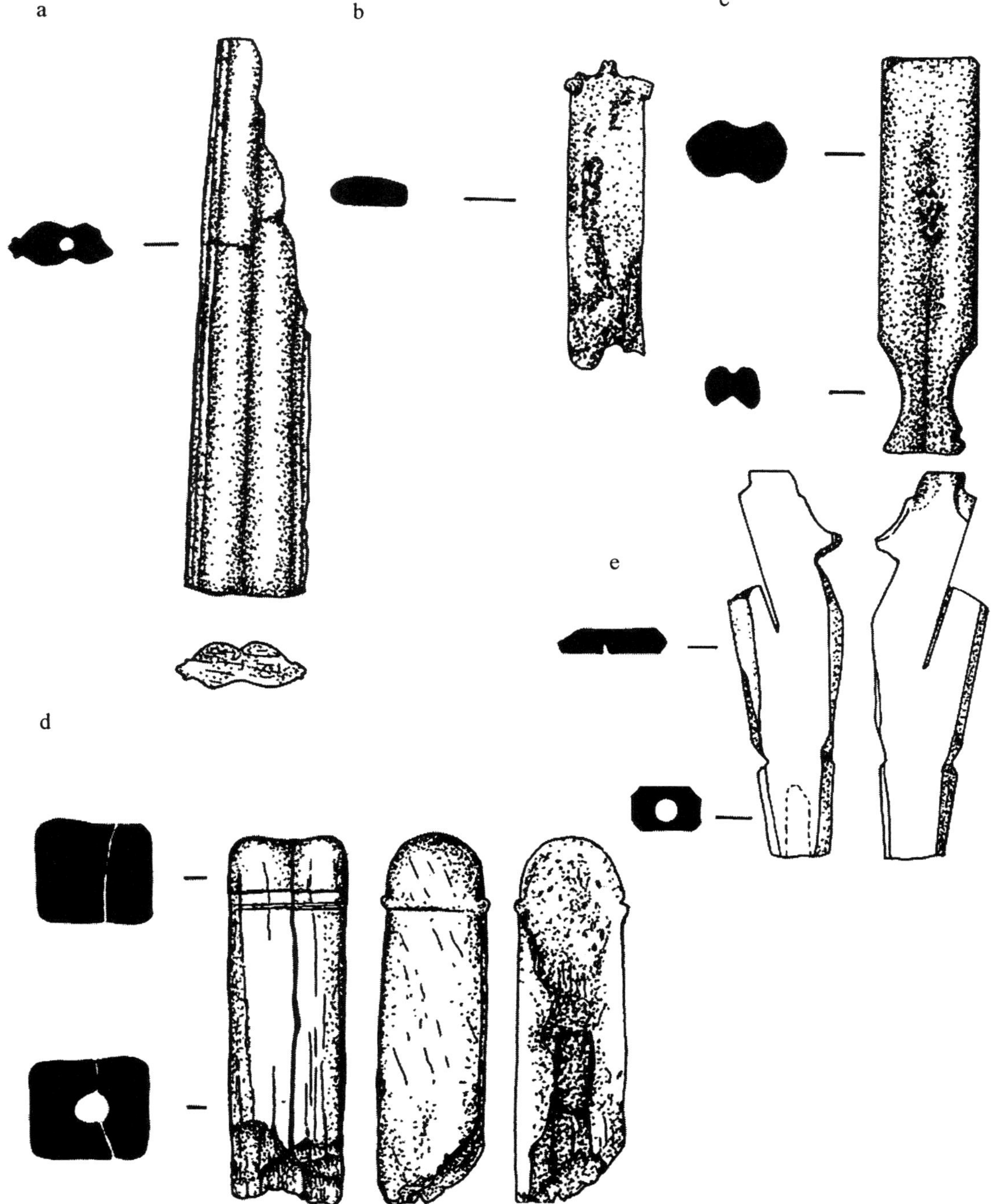

Fig. 39.
Handles: Type I.
(a) no. 526; (b) no. 524;
(c) no. 523; (d) no. 525;
(e) no. 530

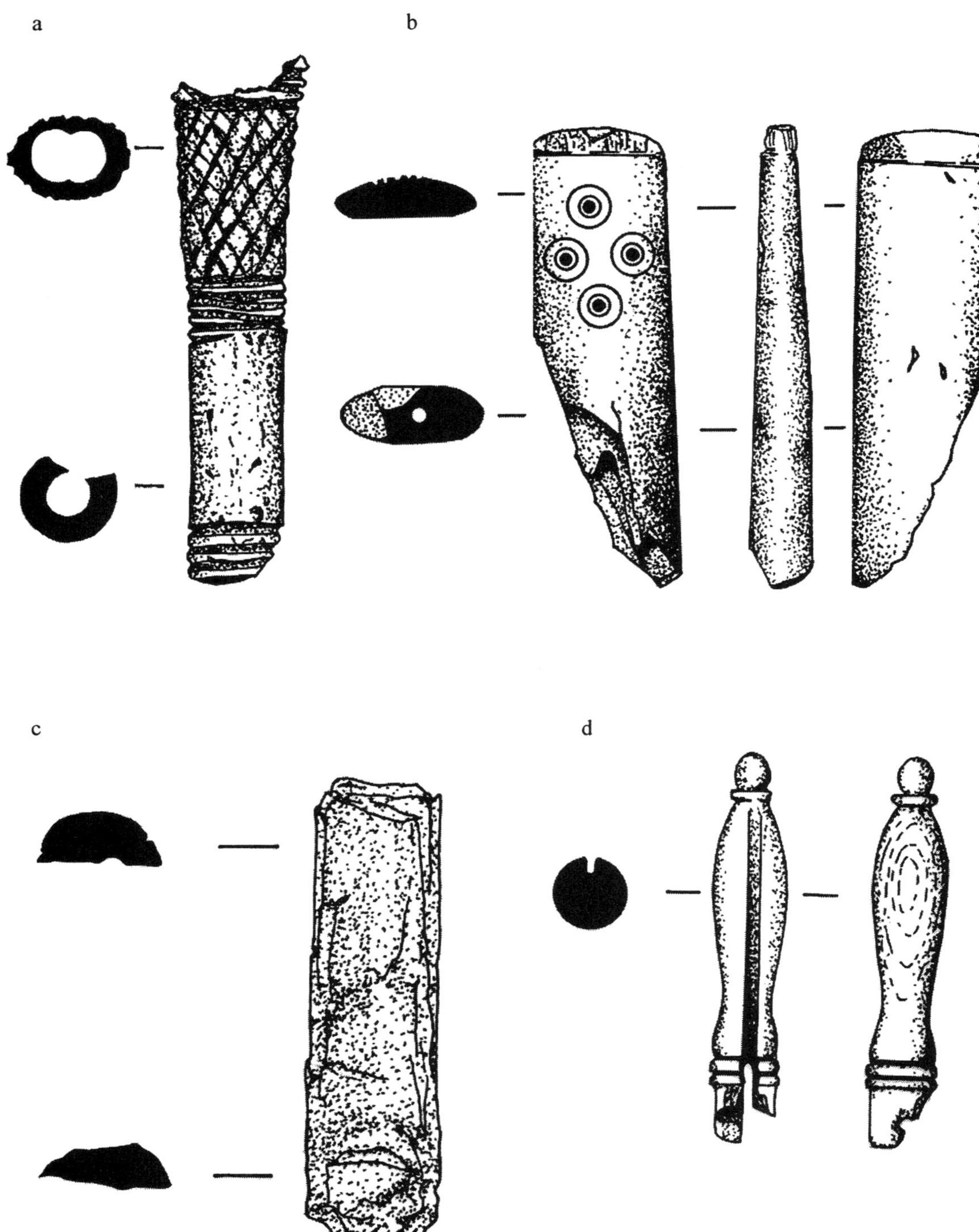

Fig. 40.
Handles: Types I–III. I:
(a) no. 527; (b) no. 529.
II: (c) no. 531. III:
(d) no. 532

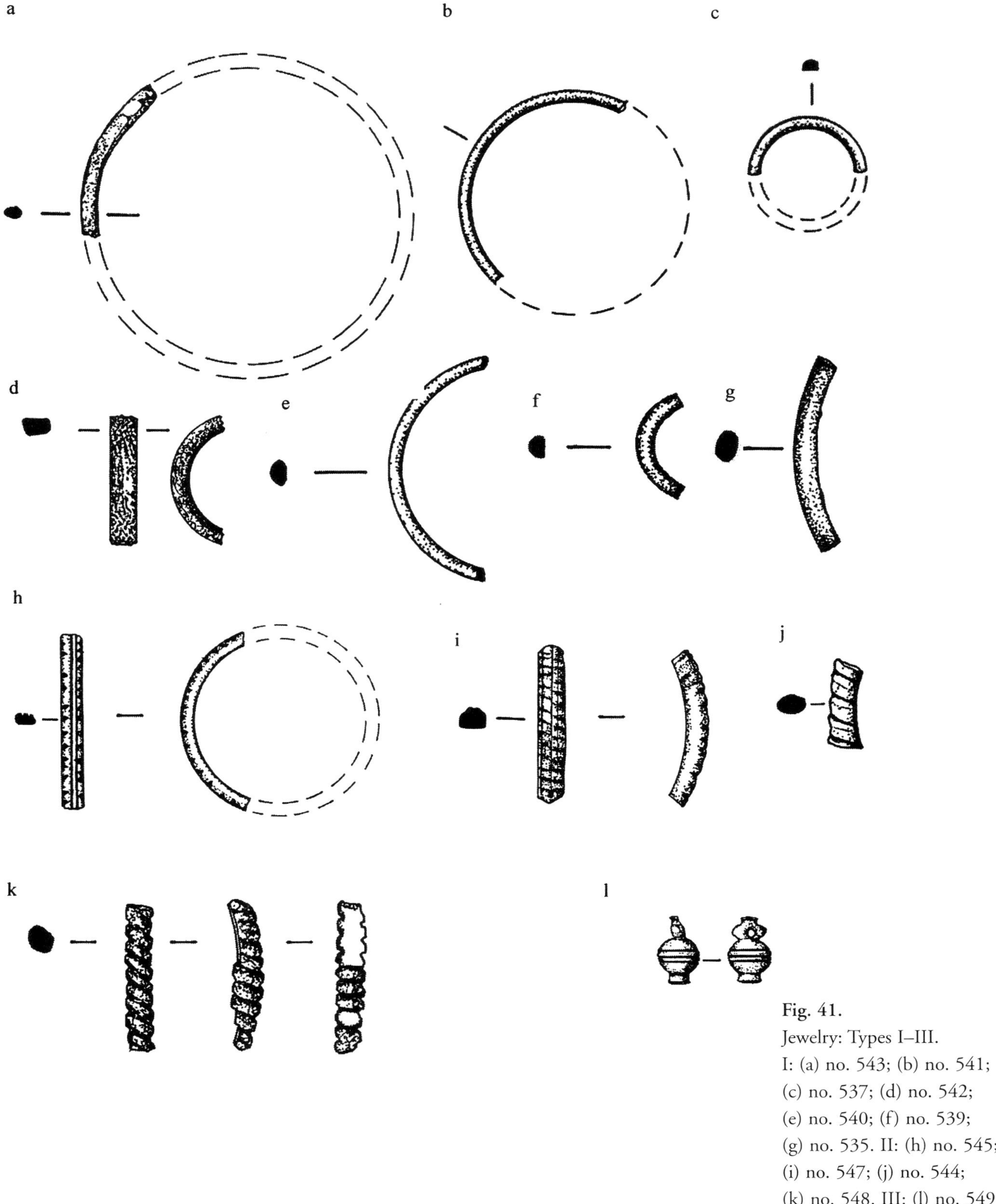

Fig. 41.
Jewelry: Types I–III.
I: (a) no. 543; (b) no. 541;
(c) no. 537; (d) no. 542;
(e) no. 540; (f) no. 539;
(g) no. 535. II: (h) no. 545;
(i) no. 547; (j) no. 544;
(k) no. 548. III: (l) no. 549

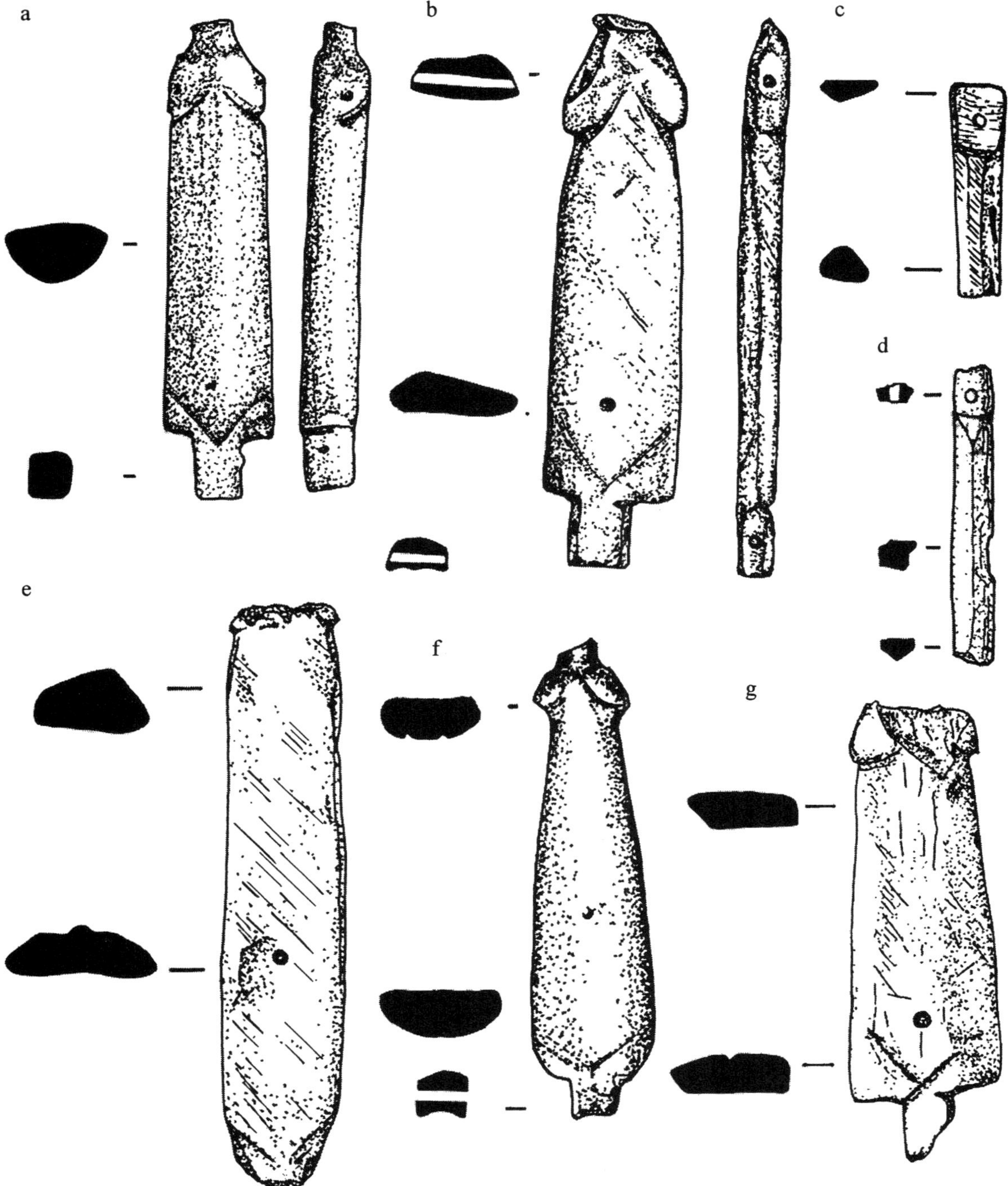

Fig. 42.
Articulated dolls: I,
Bodies II, Limbs I:
(Bodies) (a) no. 551;
(b) no. 553; (Legs)
(c) no. 566; (d) no. 561;
(Bodies) (e) no. 550;
(f) no. 552; (g) no. 556

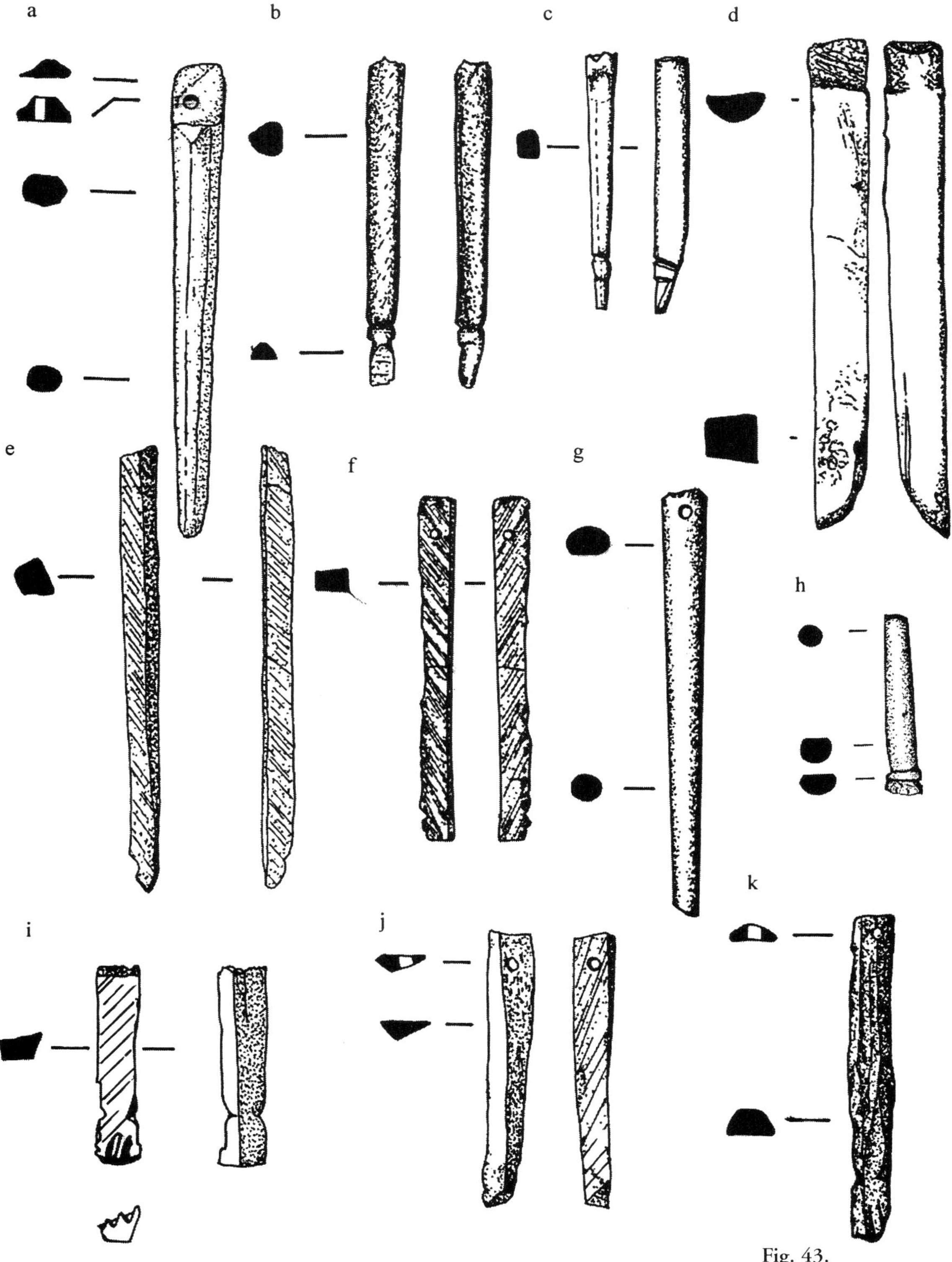

Fig. 43.
Articulated dolls: II, Limbs II: (Legs)
(a) no. 564; (b) no. 563; (c) no. 562;
(d) no. 560; (e) no. 558; (Arms)
(f) no. 571; (g) no. 569; (h) no. 576;
(i) no. 572; (j) no. 574; (k) no. 573

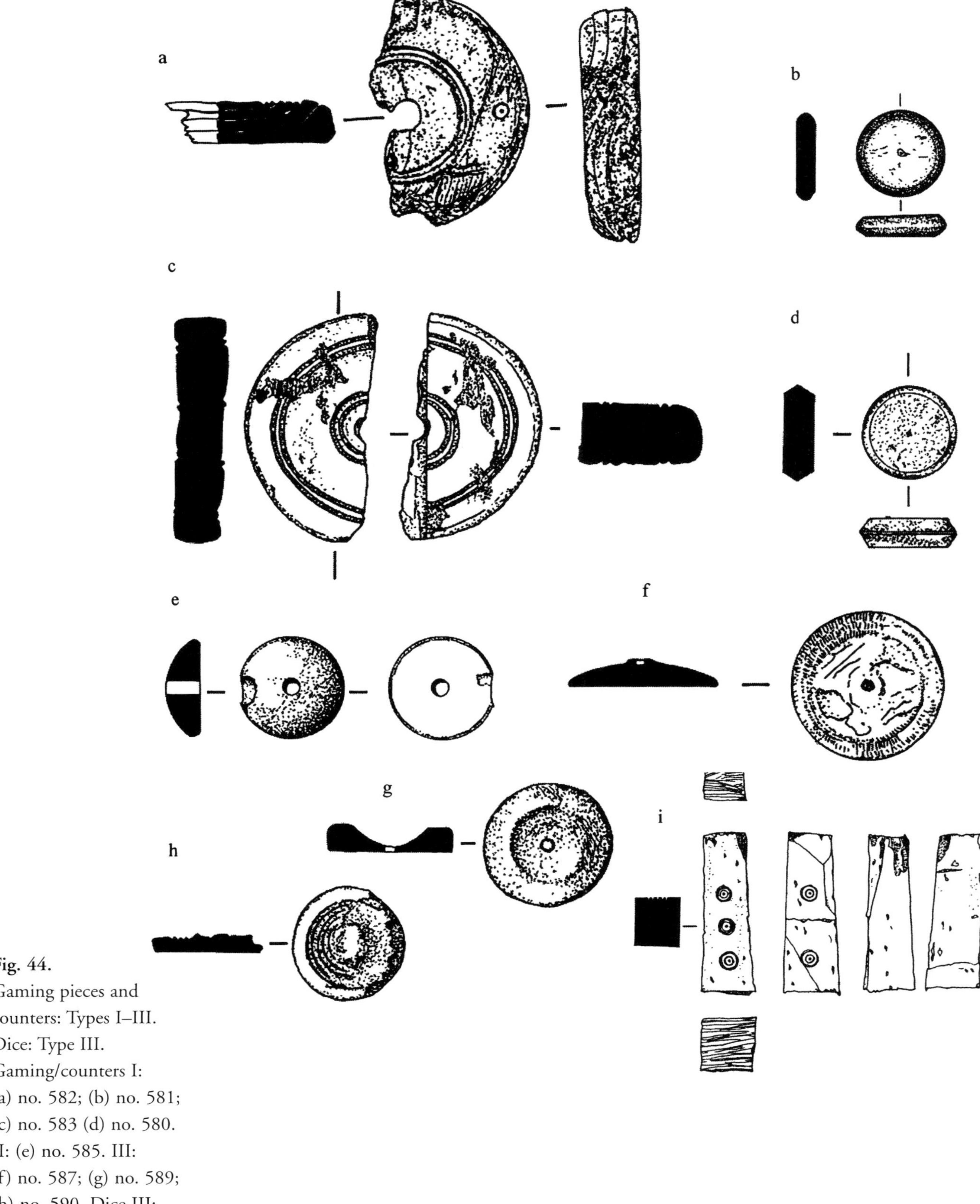

Fig. 44.
Gaming pieces and
counters: Types I–III.
Dice: Type III.
Gaming/counters I:
(a) no. 582; (b) no. 581;
(c) no. 583 (d) no. 580.
II: (e) no. 585. III:
(f) no. 587; (g) no. 589;
(h) no. 590. Dice III:
(i) no. 644

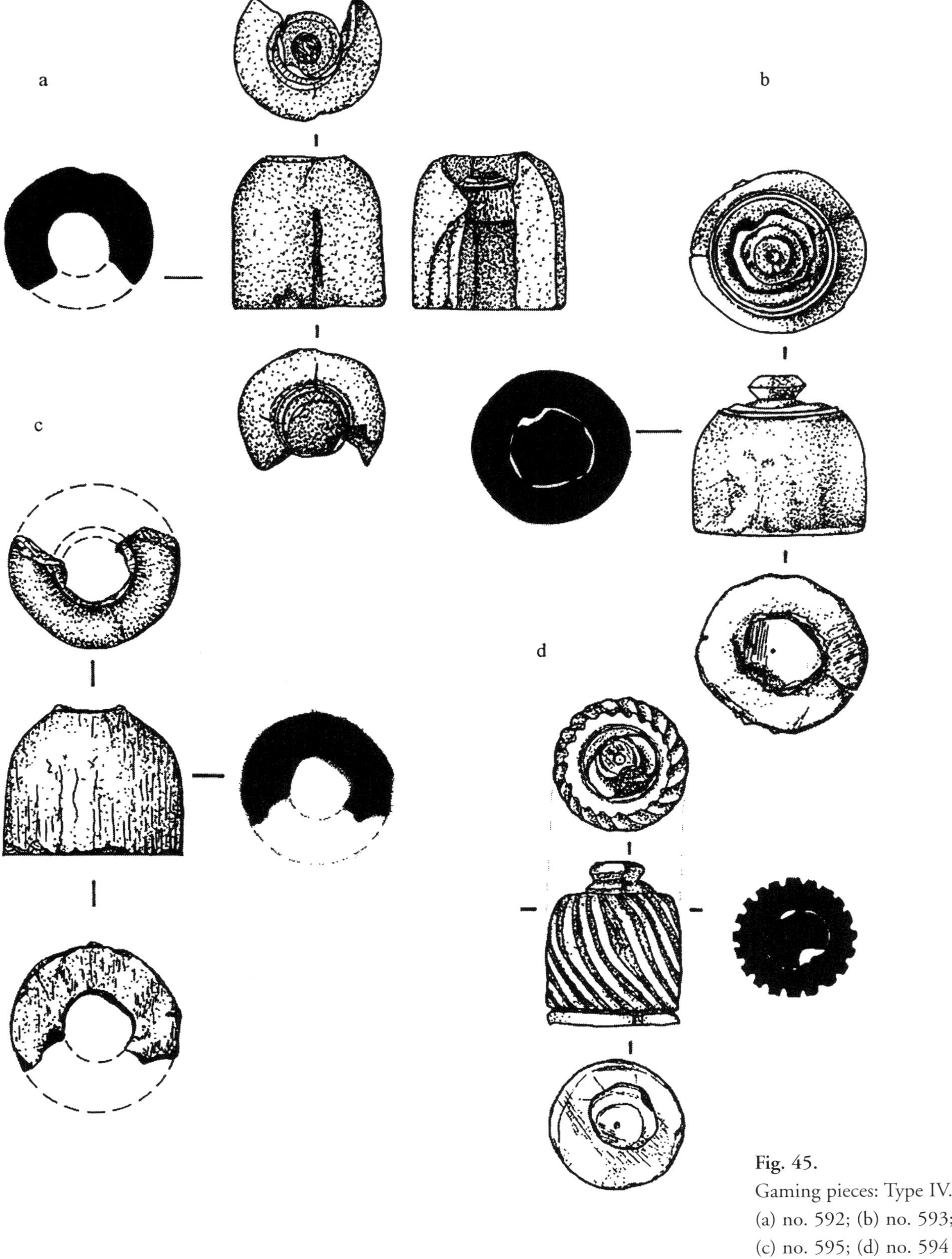

Fig. 45.
Gaming pieces: Type IV.
(a) no. 592; (b) no. 593;
(c) no. 595; (d) no. 594

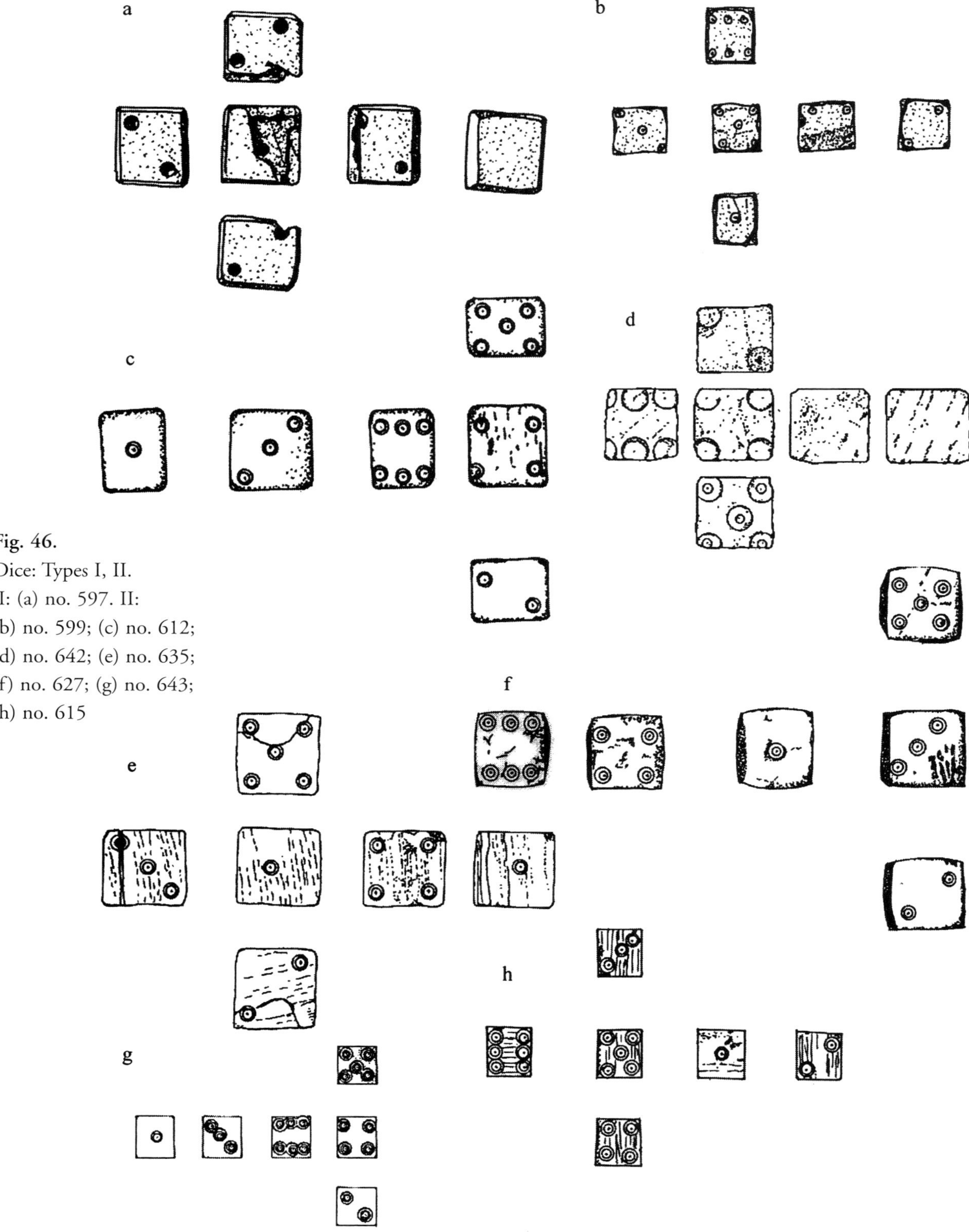

Fig. 46.
Dice: Types I, II.
 I: (a) no. 597. II:
(b) no. 599; (c) no. 612;
(d) no. 642; (e) no. 635;
(f) no. 627; (g) no. 643;
(h) no. 615

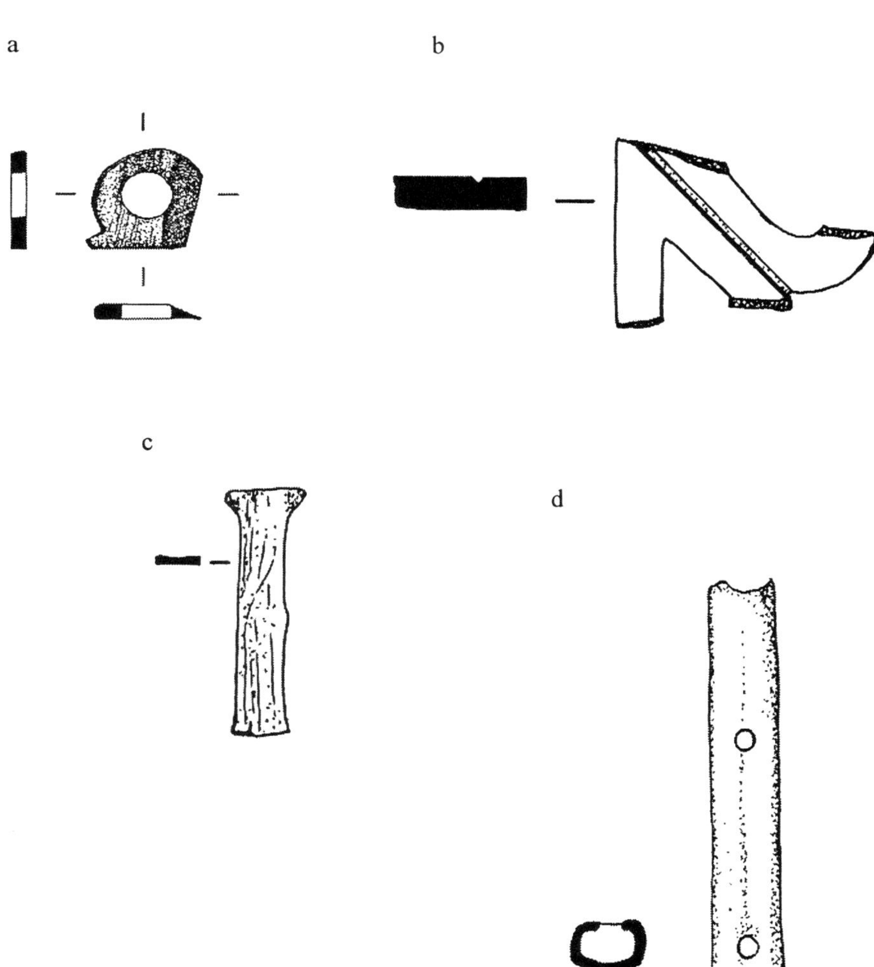

Fig. 47.
Letters of the alphabet.
Whistle. Letters:
(a) no. 646; (b) no. 645;
(c) no. 647. Whistle:
(d) no. 648

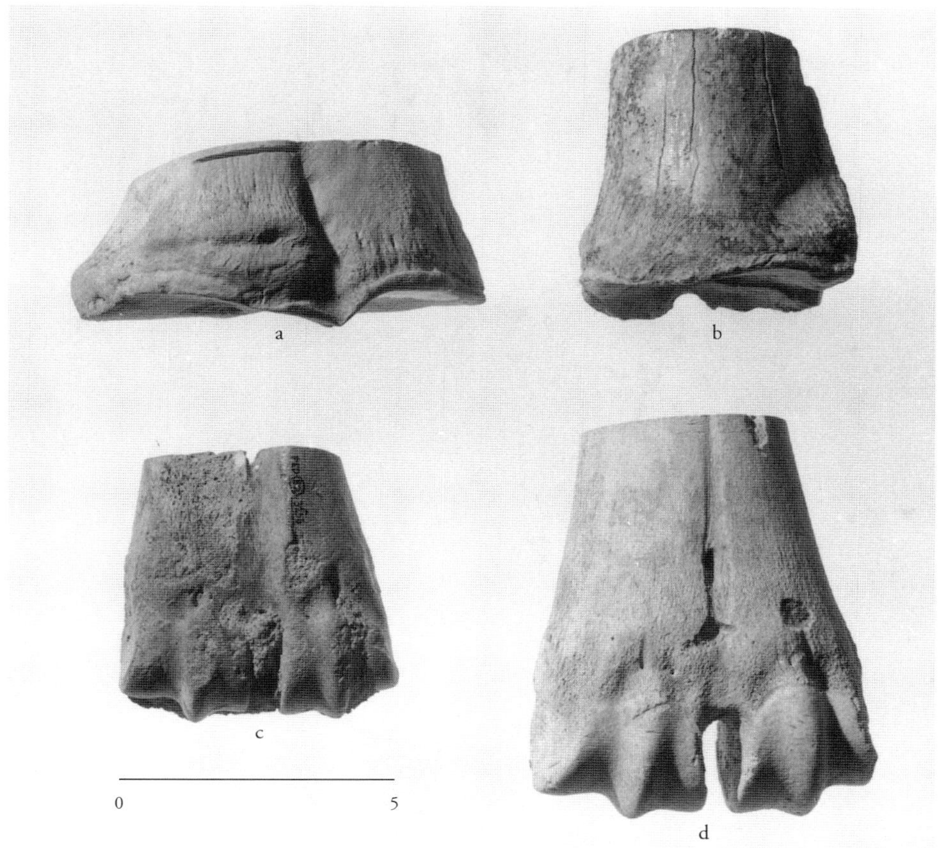

Plate 1.
Manufacturing evidence.
(a) no. 5; (b) no. 4;
(c) no. 1; (d) no. 3

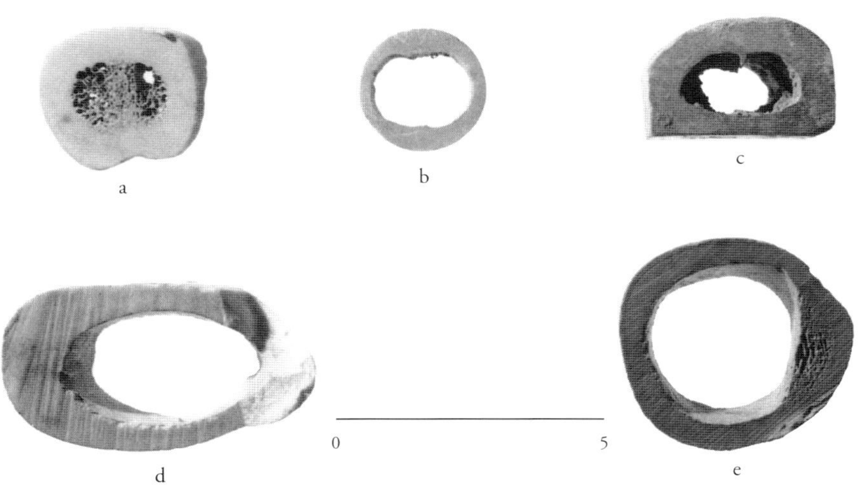

Plate 2.
Manufacturing evidence.
(a) no. 18; (b) no. 17;
(c) no. 6; (d) no. 16;
(e) no. 9

Plate 3.
Manufacturing evidence.
(a) no. 44; (b) no. 60;
(c) no. 49; (d) no. 46

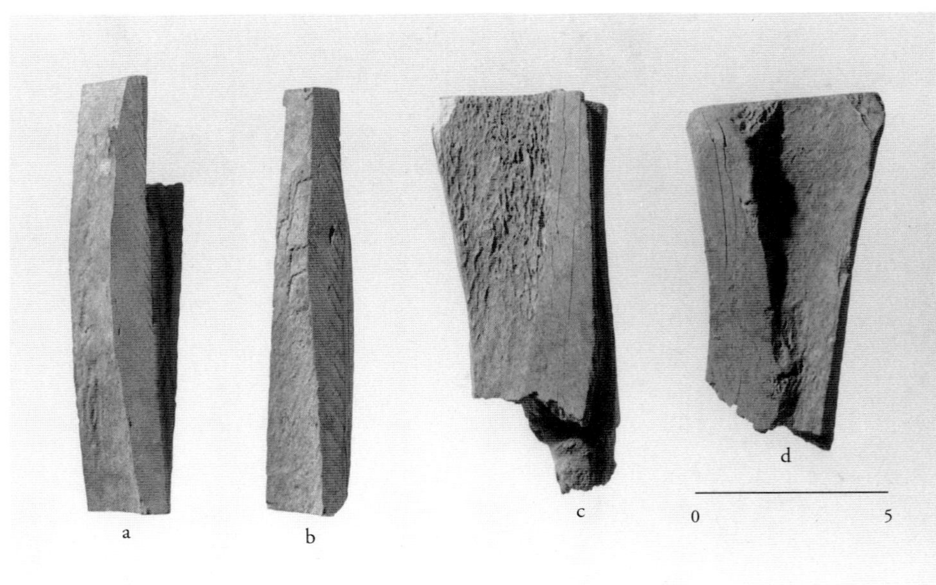

Plate 4.
Manufacturing evidence.
(a) no. 27; (b) no. 26;
(c) no. 28; (d) no. 29

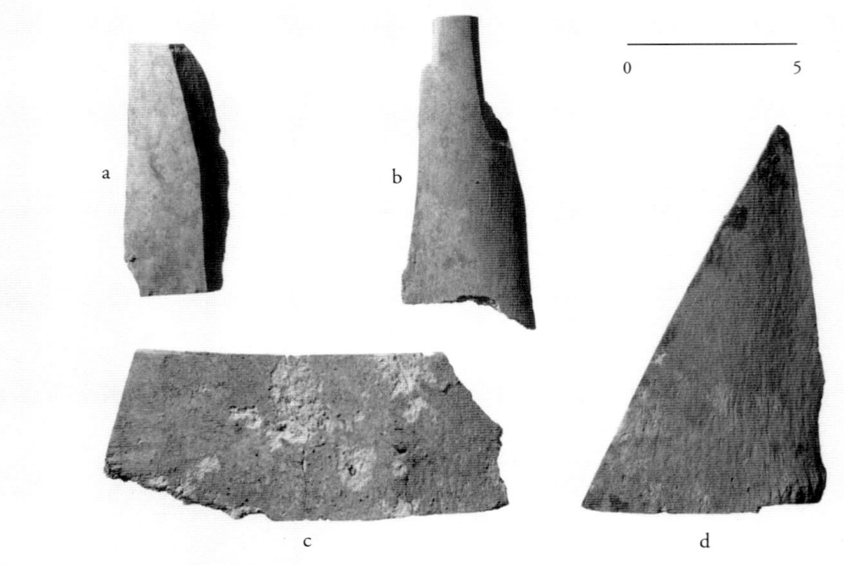

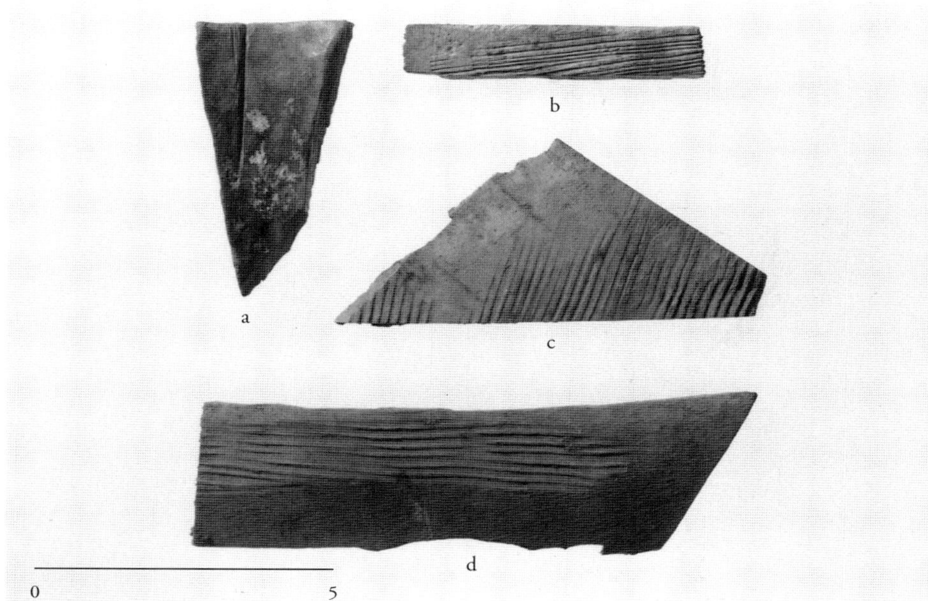

Plate 5.
Manufacturing evidence.
(a) no. 33; (b) no. 58;
(c) no. 23; (d) no. 22

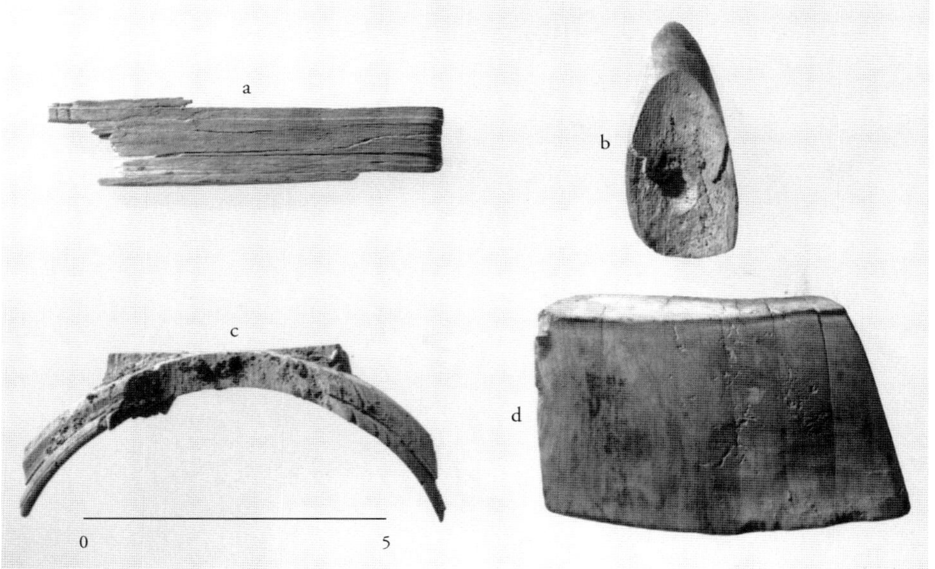

Plate 6.
Manufacturing evidence,
ivory. (a) no. 128;
(b) no. 50; (c) no. 92;
(d) no. 64

Plate 7.
Manufacturing evidence,
ivory. (a) no. 87;
(b) no. 32; (c) no. 65;
(d) no. 38; (e) no. 89

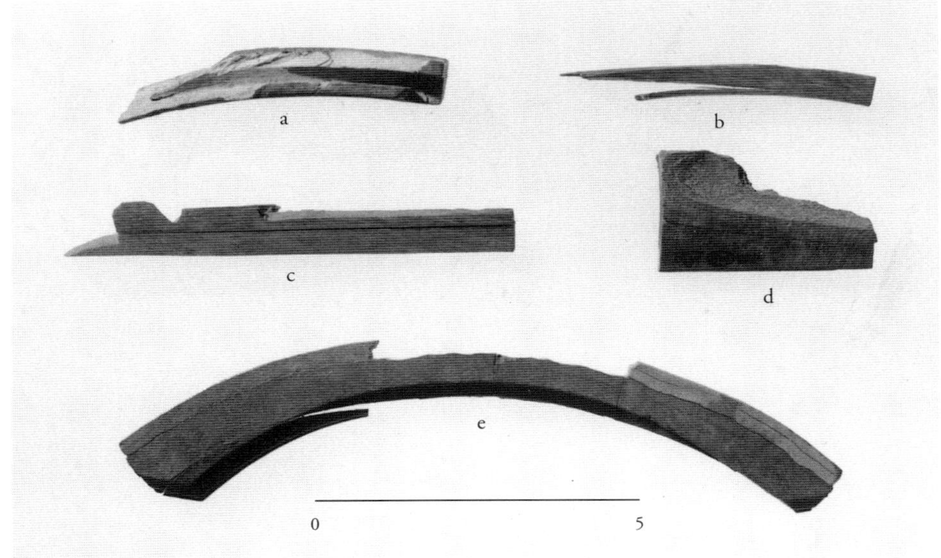

Plate 8.
Manufacturing evidence,
ivory. (a) no. 52;
(b) no. 67; (c) no. 94;
(d) no. 66

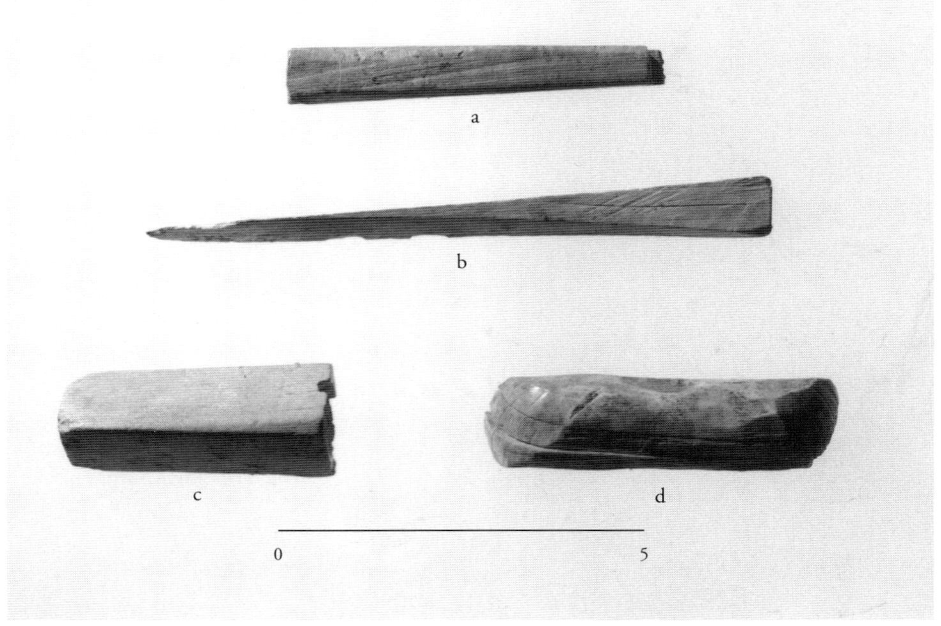

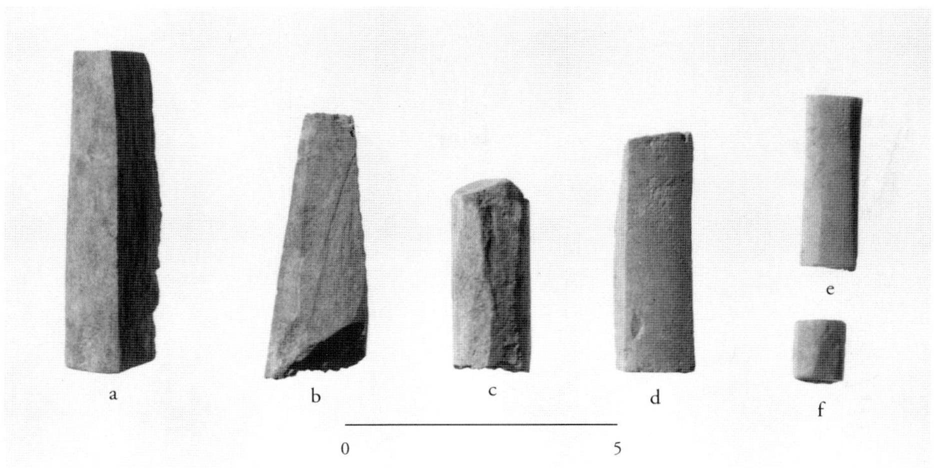

Plate 9.
Manufacturing evidence.
(a) no. 21; (b) no. 61;
(c) no. 34; (d) no. 56;
(e) no. 62; (f) no. 63

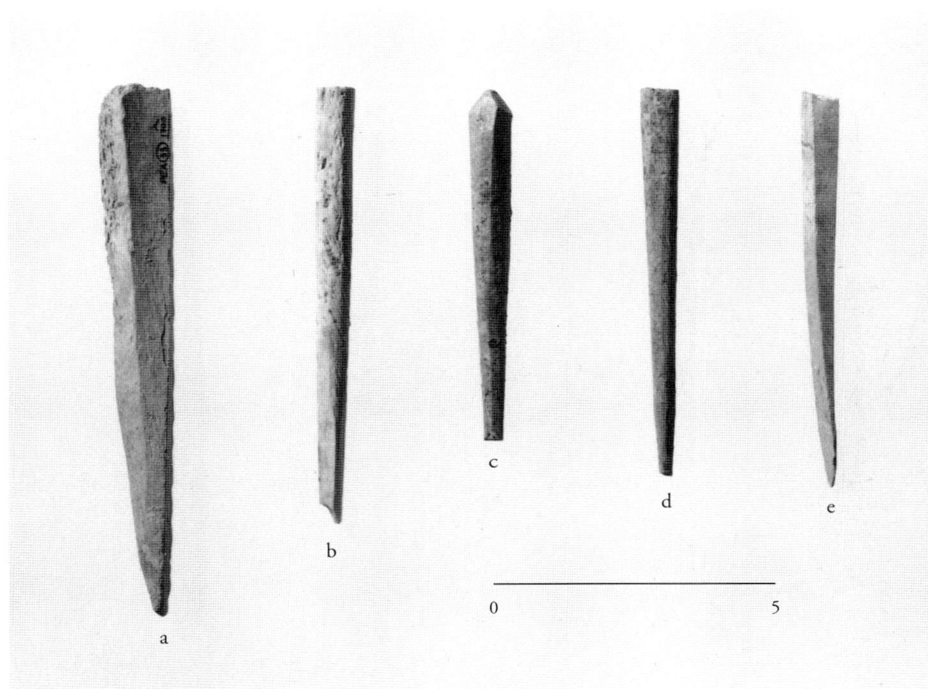

Plate 10.
Manufacturing evidence.
(a) no. 47; (b) no. 53;
(c) no. 40; (d) no. 72;
(e) no. 35

Plate 11.
Manufacturing evidence.
(a) no. 82; (b) no. 80;
(c) no. 86; (d) no. 83;
(e) no. 85

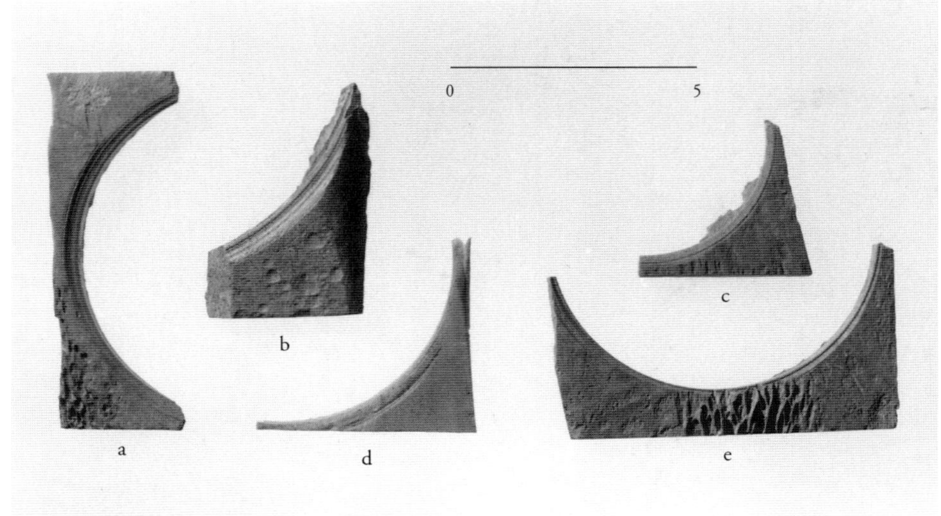

Plate 12.
Manufacturing evidence.
(a) no. 95; (b) no. 96;
(c) no. 93; (d) no. 99;
(e) no. 98 (f). no. 101

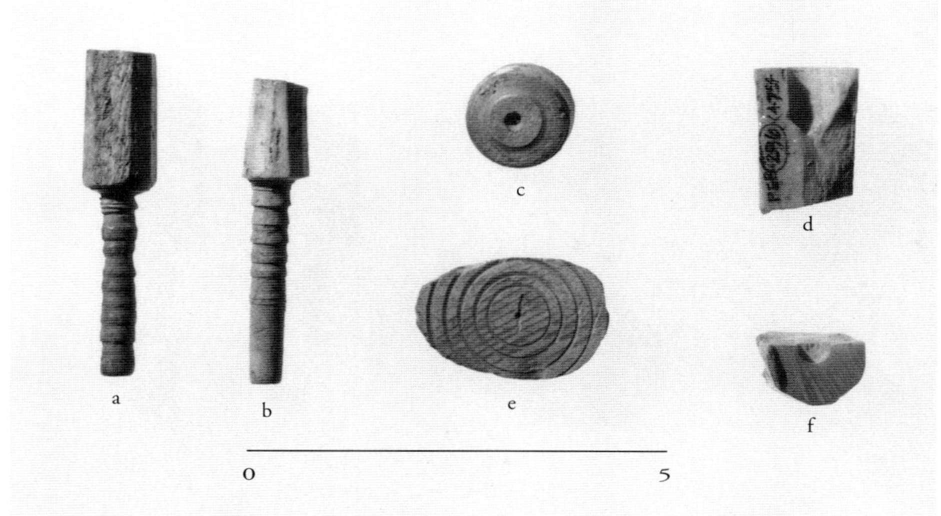

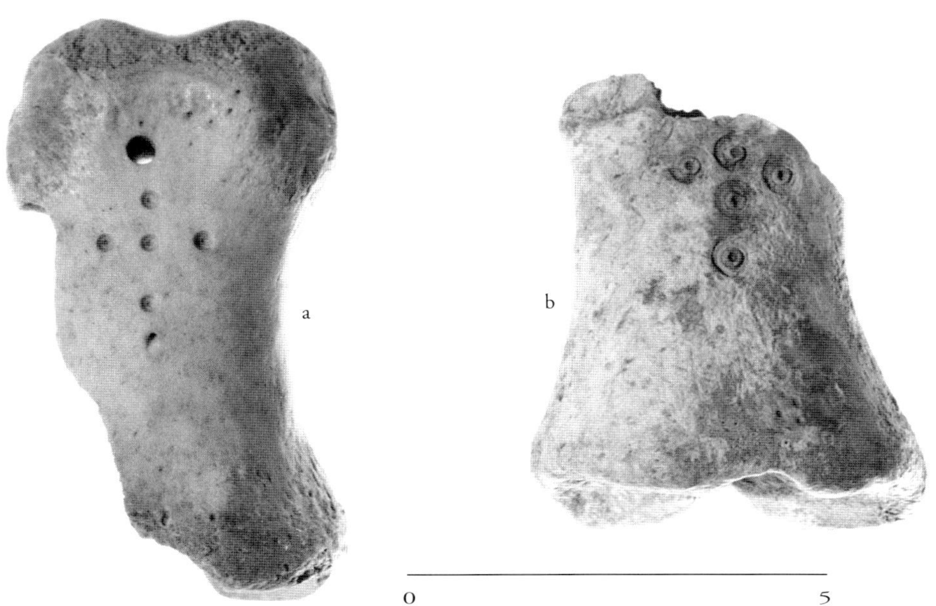

Plate 13.
Manufacturing evidence.
(a) no. 103; (b) no. 102

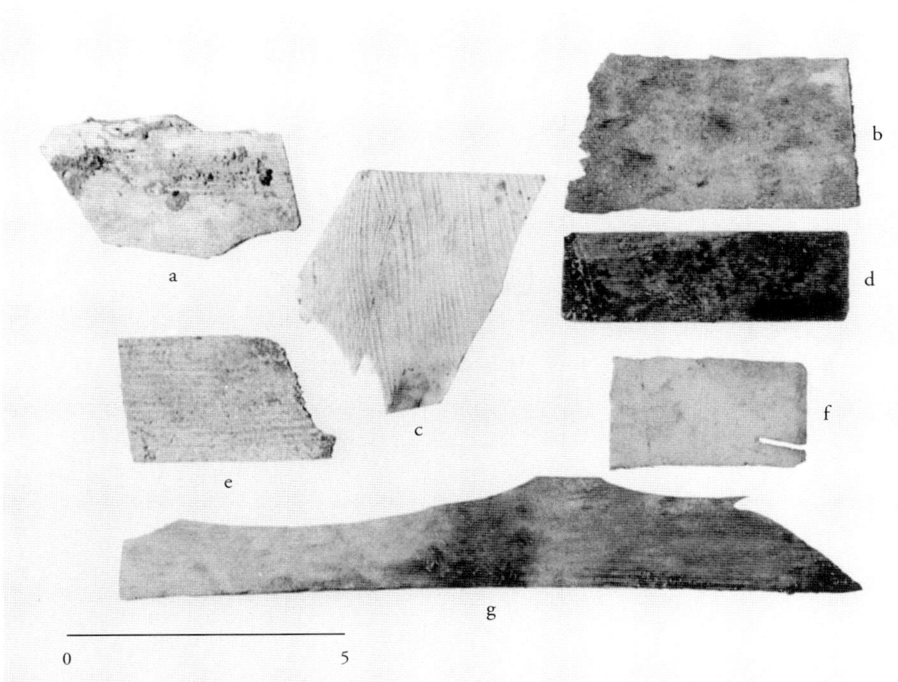

Plate 14.
Furniture and boxes.
(a) no. 112; (b) no. 106;
(c) no. 105; (d) no. 116;
(e) no. 117; (f) no. 118;
(g) no. 115

Plate 15.
Furniture and boxes.
(a) no. 144; (b) no. 148;
(c) no. 140; (d) no. 147;
(e) no. 145

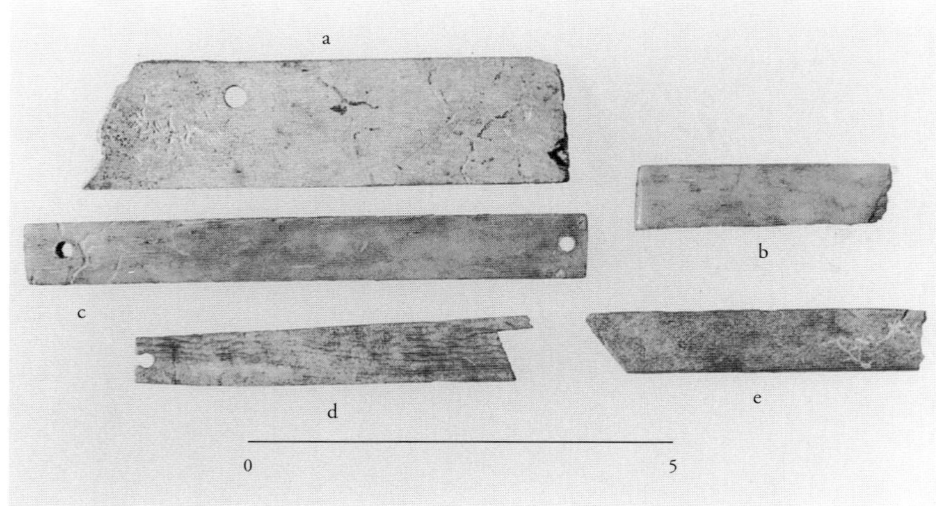

Plate 16.
Furniture and boxes.
(a) no. 155; (b) no. 158;
(c) no. 156; (d) no. 157;
(e) no. 151; (f) no. 150

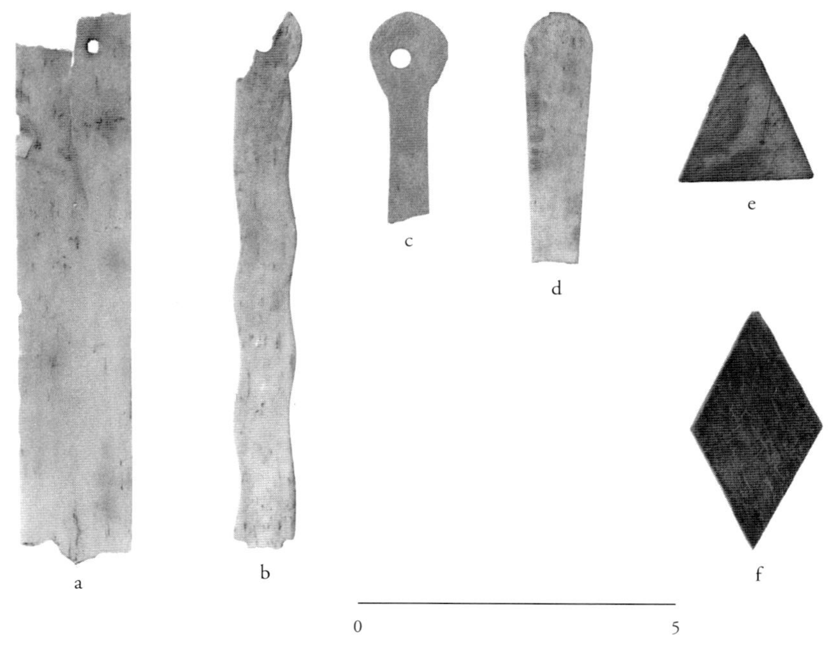

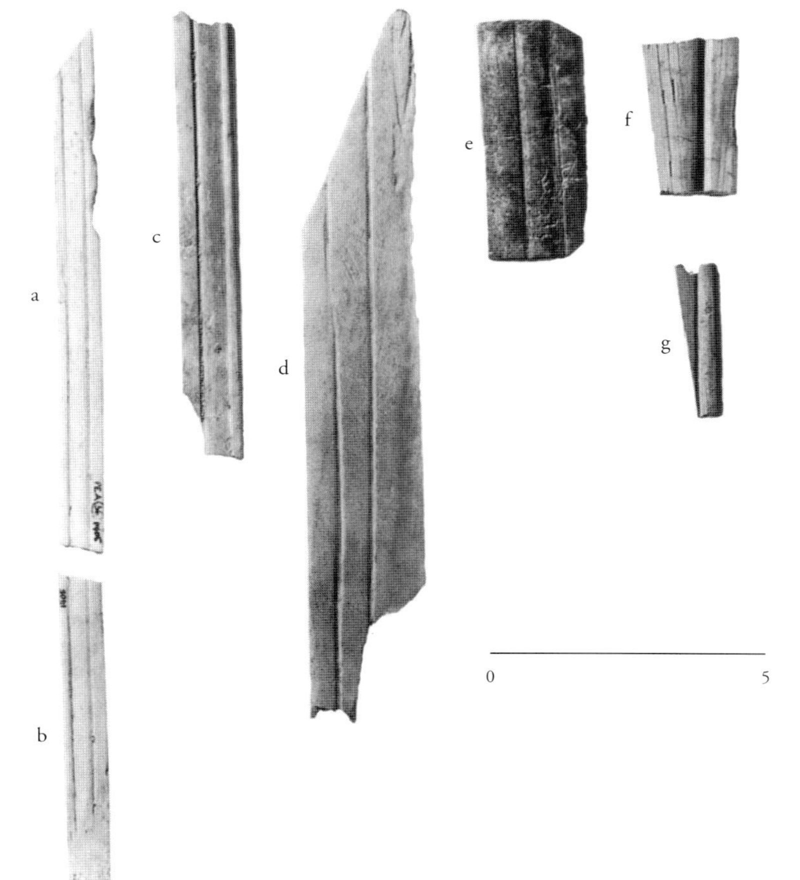

Plate 17.
Furniture and boxes.
(a) and (b) no. 180;
(c) no. 181; (d) no. 192;
(e) no. 193; (f) and
(g) no. 182

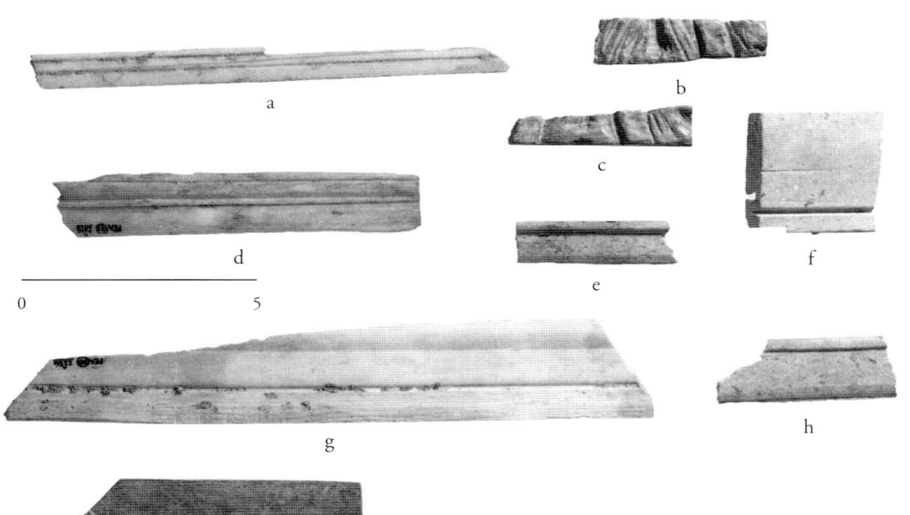

Plate 18.
Furniture and boxes.
(a) no. 172; (b) and
(c) no. 217; (d) no. 173;
(e) no. 174; (f) no. 168;
(g) no. 184; (h) no. 176;
(i) no. 130

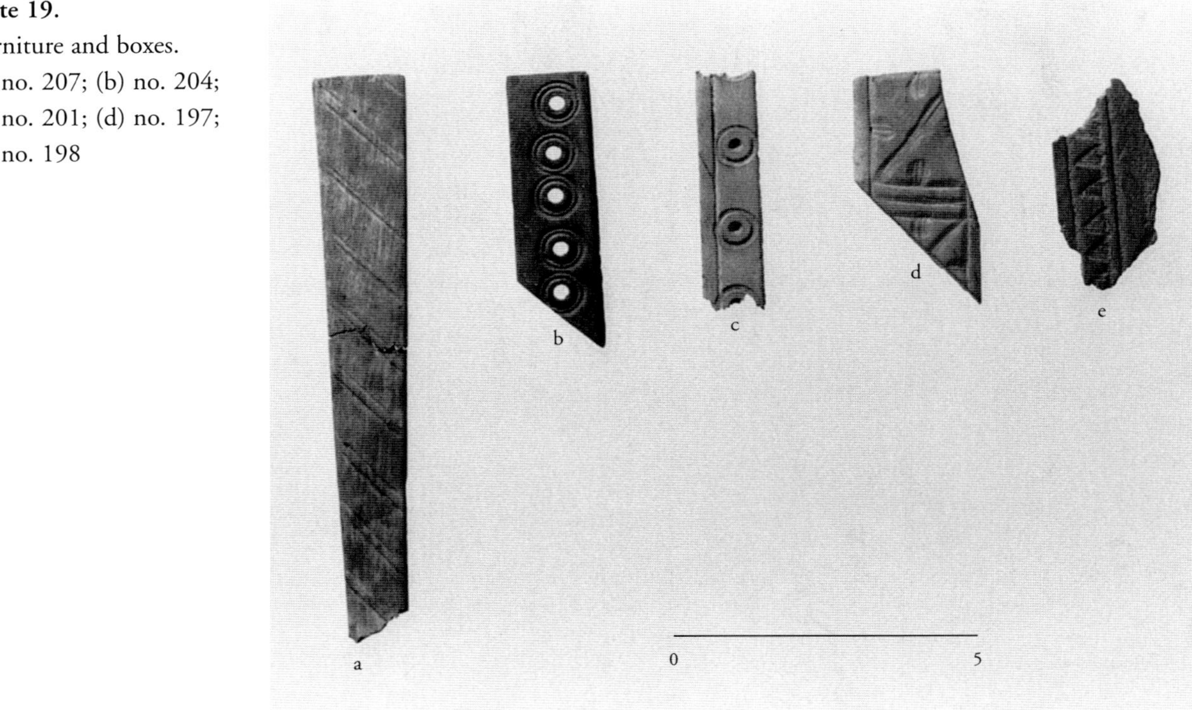

Plate 19.
Furniture and boxes.
(a) no. 207; (b) no. 204;
(c) no. 201; (d) no. 197;
(e) no. 198

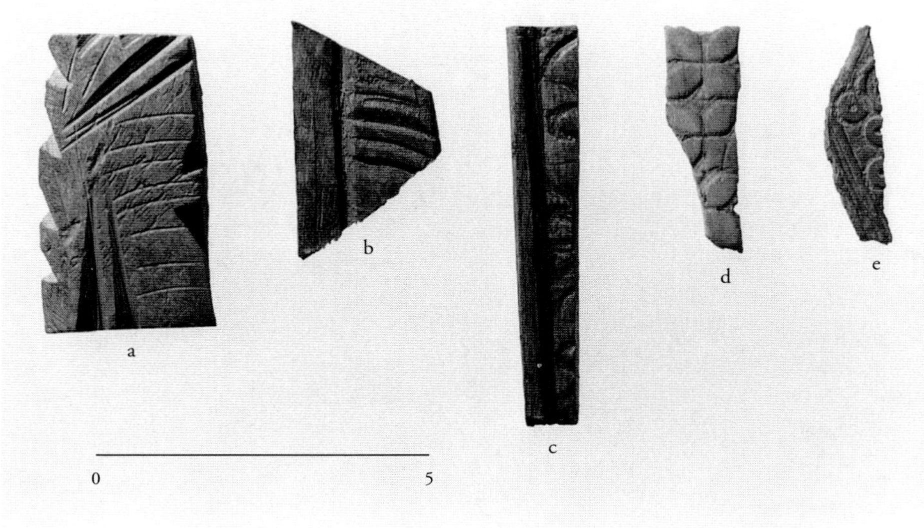

Plate 20.
Furniture and boxes.
(a) no. 215; (b) no. 186;
(c) no. 220; (d) no. 199;
(e) no. 200

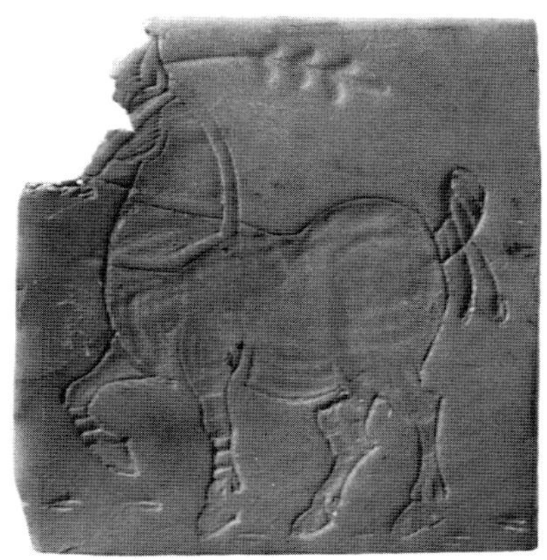
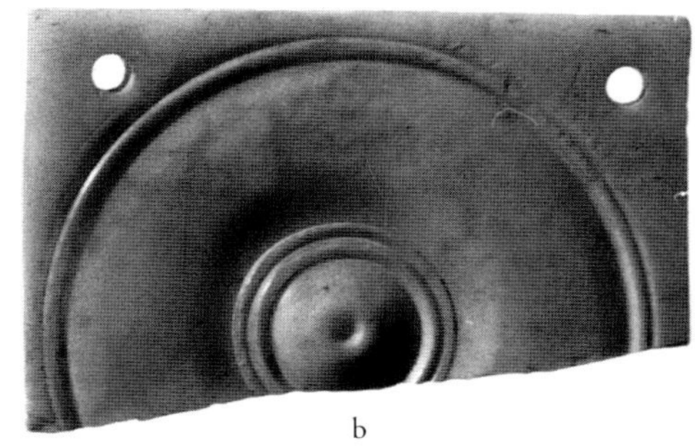

a

b

0   5

Plate 21.
Furniture and boxes.
(a) no. 224; (b) no. 223

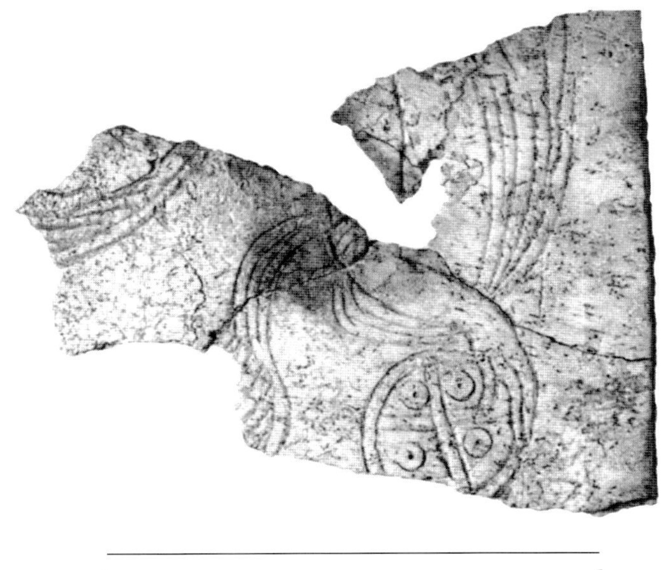

0   5

Plate 22.
Furniture and boxes.
no. 222

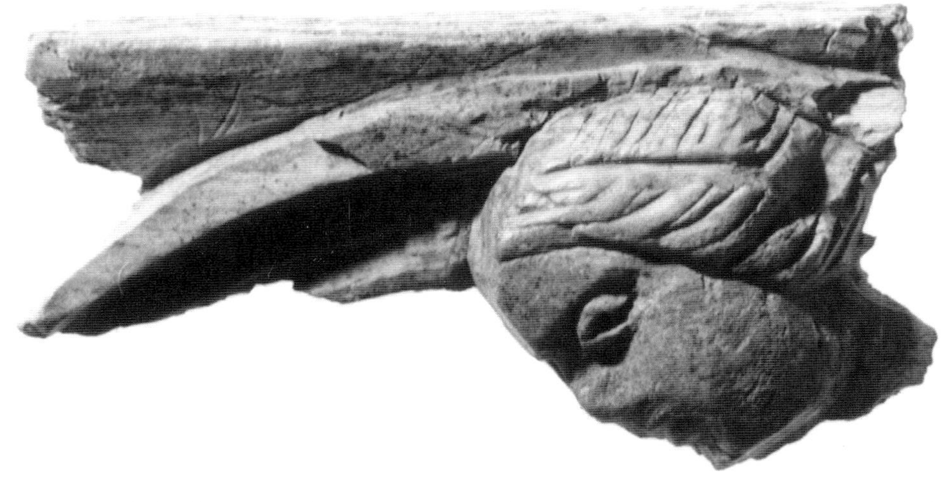

Plate 23.
Furniture and boxes.
no. 221

0   5

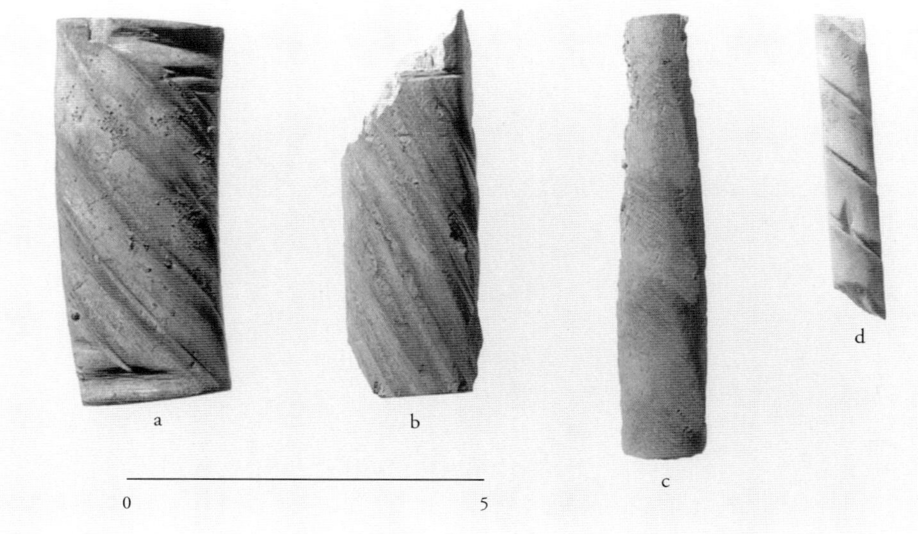

Plate 24.
Furniture and boxes.
(a) no. 219; (b) no. 209;
(c) no. 195; (d) no. 196

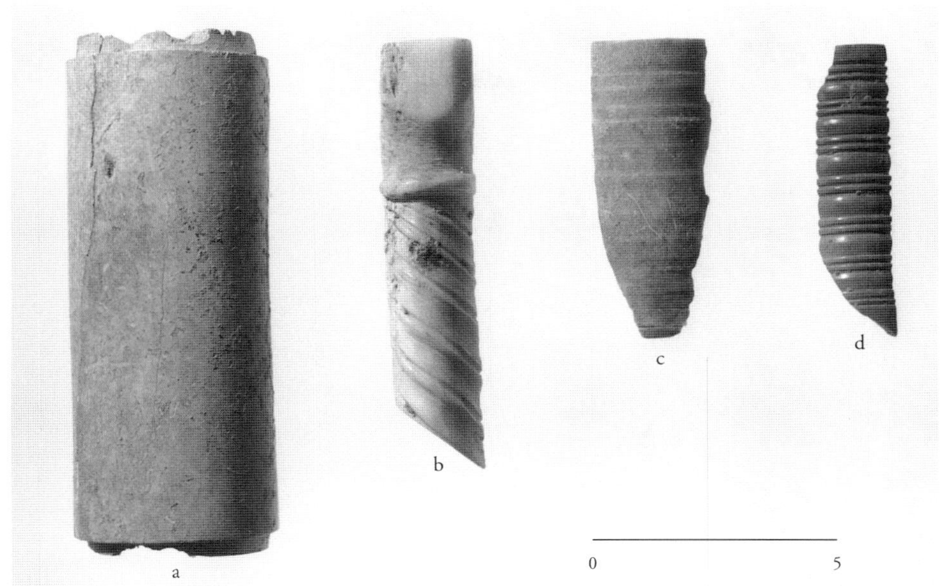

Plate 25.
Furniture and boxes.
(a) no. 163; (b) no. 210;
(c) no. 164; (d) no. 211

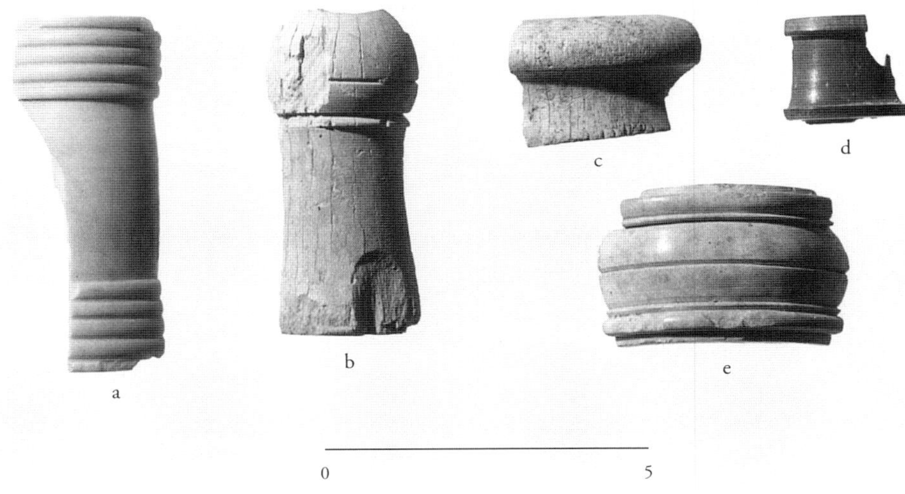

Plate 26.
Furniture and boxes.
(a) no. 235; (b) no. 208;
(c) no. 213; (d) no. 161;
(e) no. 230

Plate 27.
Furniture and boxes.
(a) no. 242; (b) no. 238;
(c) no. 244; (d) no. 243;
(e) no. 241

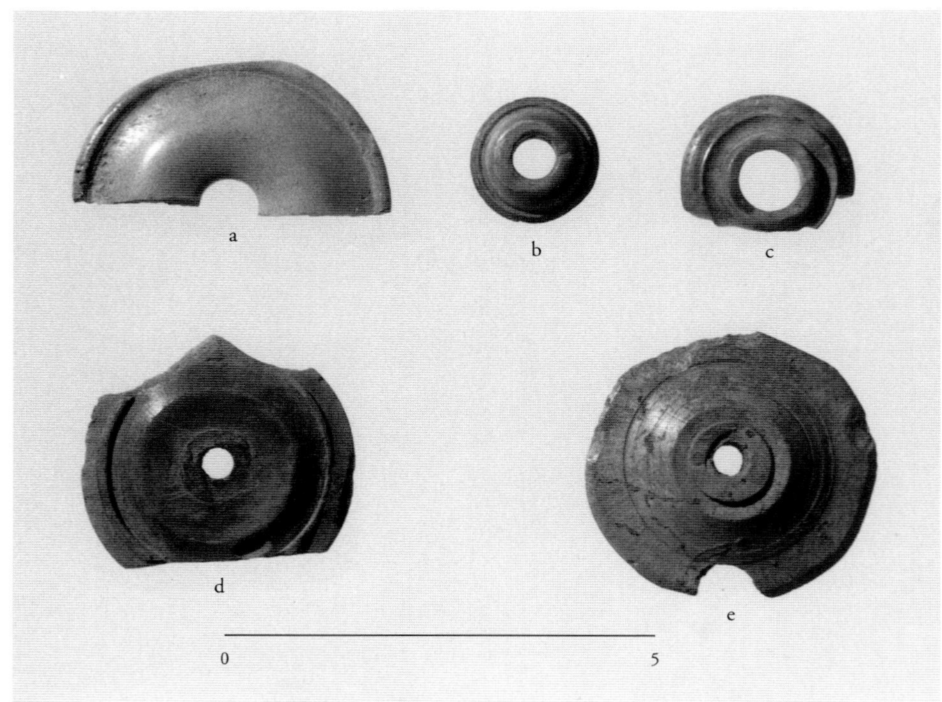

Plate 28.
Furniture and boxes.
no. 227

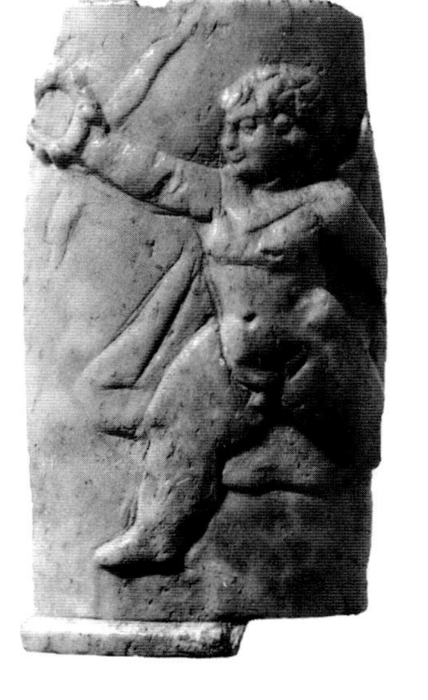

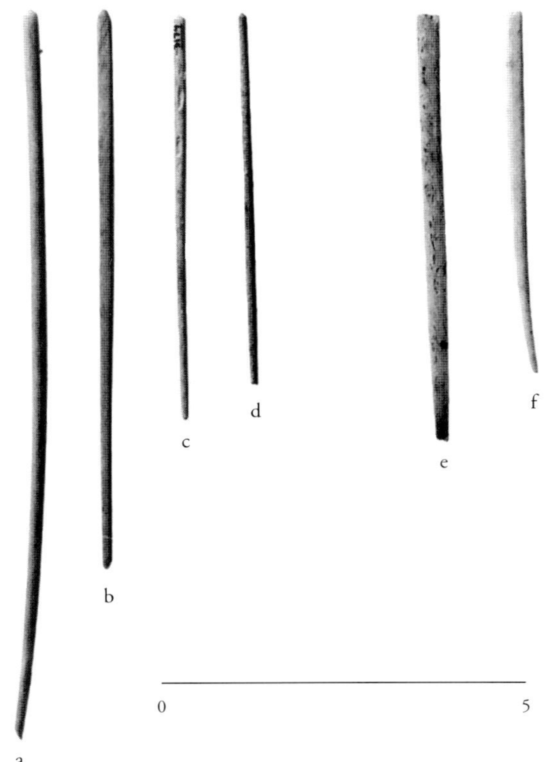

Plate 29.
Pins. (a) no. 257;
(b) no. 251; (c) no. 255;
(d) no. 248; (e) no. 272;
(f). no. 269

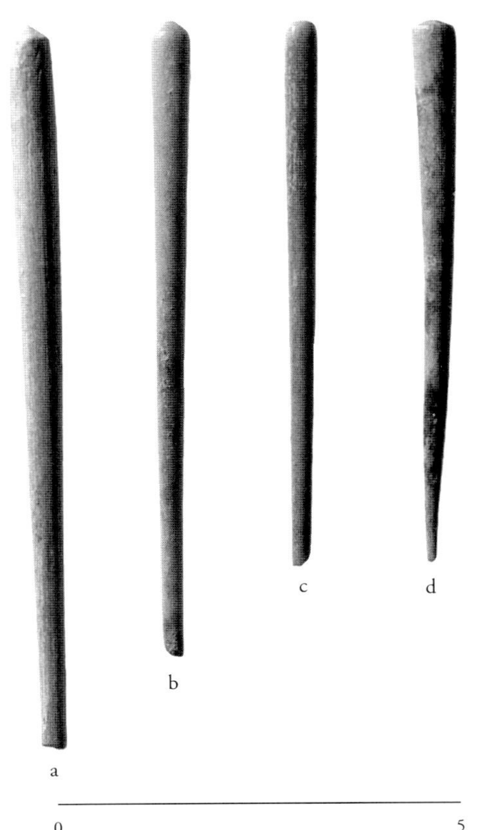

Plate 30.
Pins. (a) no. 291;
(b) no. 288; (c) no. 276;
(d) no. 292

Plate 31.
Pins. (a) no. 313;
(b) no. 310; (c) no. 307;
(d) no. 306

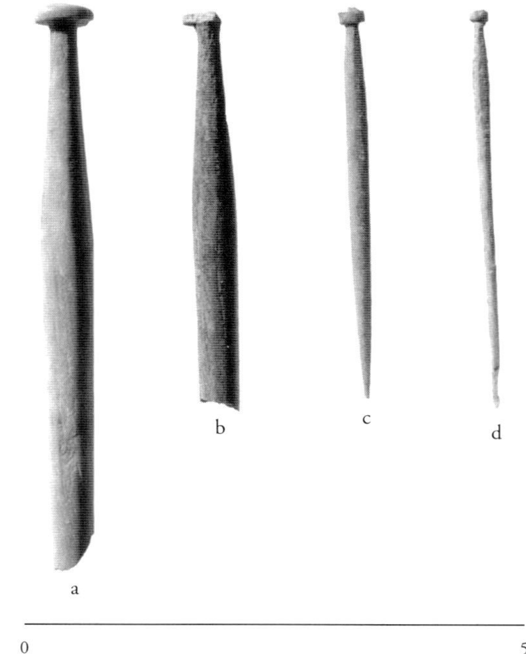

a
b
c
d
0
5

Plate 32.
Pins. (a) no. 324;
(b) no. 320; (c) no. 312;
(d) no. 311; (e) no. 314;
(f). no. 316

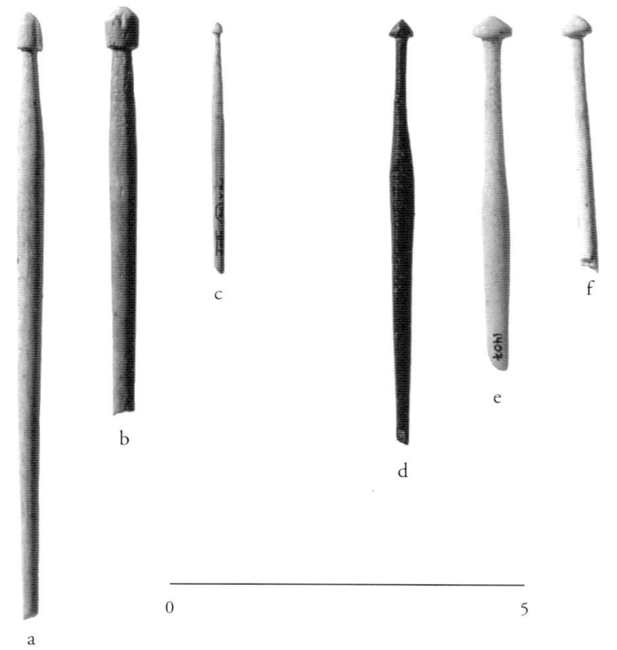

a
b
c
d
e
f
0
5

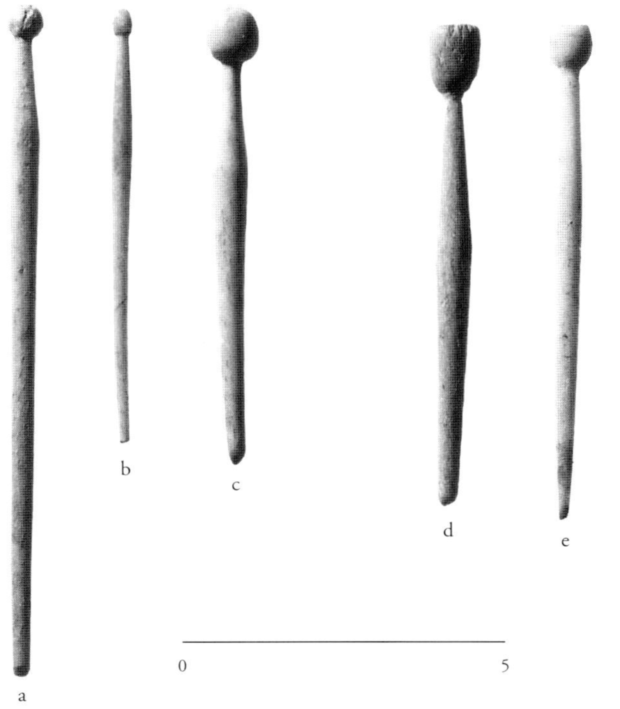

Plate 33.
Pins. (a) no. 325;
(b) no. 343; (c) no. 344;
(d) no. 398; (e) no. 397

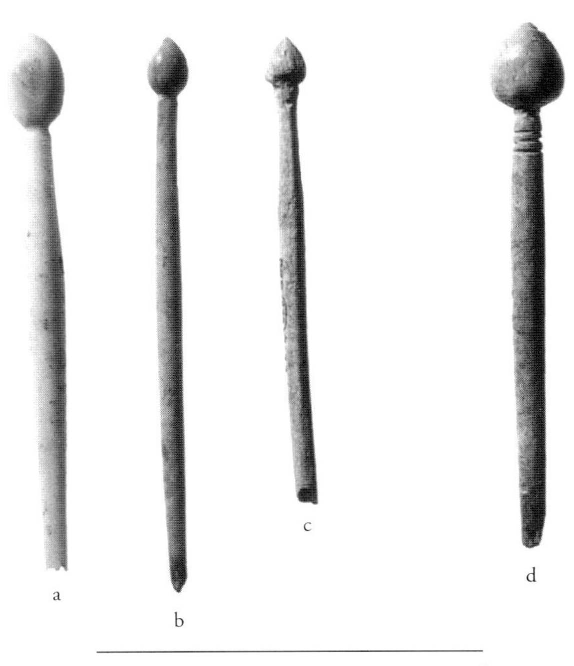

Plate 34.
Pins. (a) no. 417;
(b) no. 424; (c) no. 433;
(d) no. 440

Plate 35.
Pins. (a) no. 447;
(b) no. 442; (c) no. 443;
(d) no. 445; (e) no. 441;
(f). no. 444

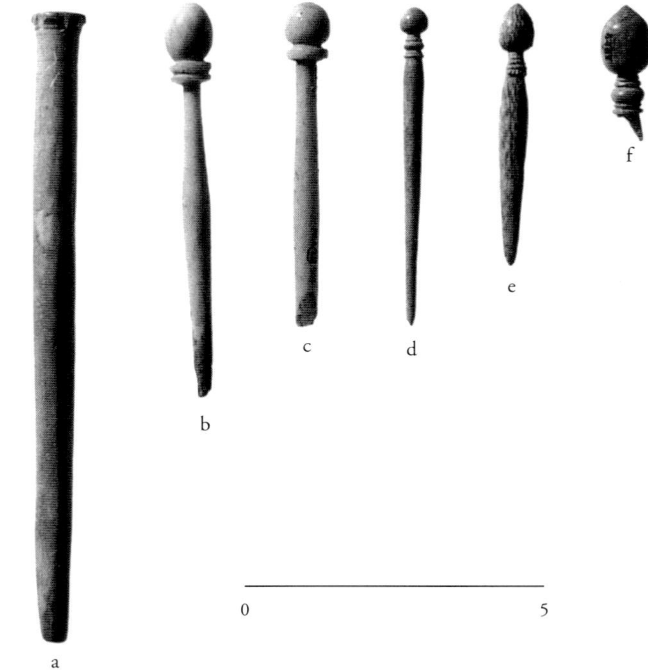

Plate 36.
Pins. (a) no. 472;
(b) no. 452; (c) no. 454;
(d) no. 453; (e) no. 455;
(f). no. 451

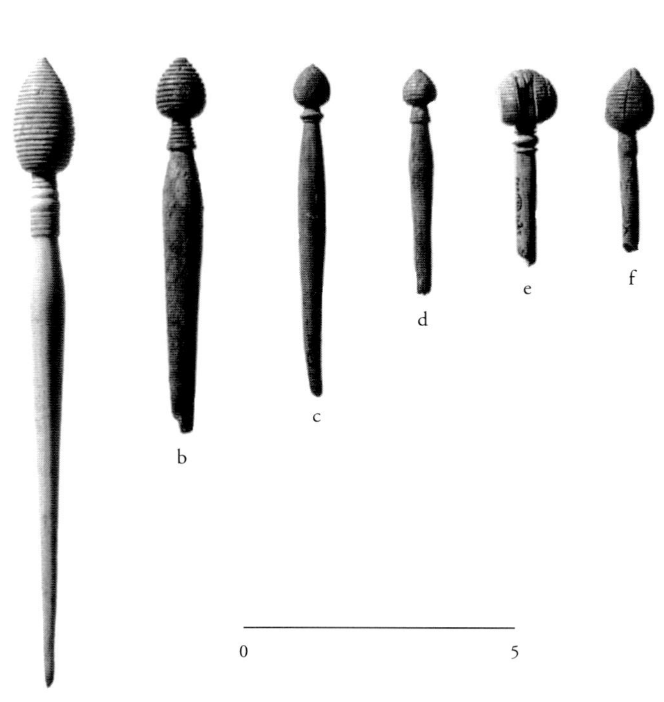

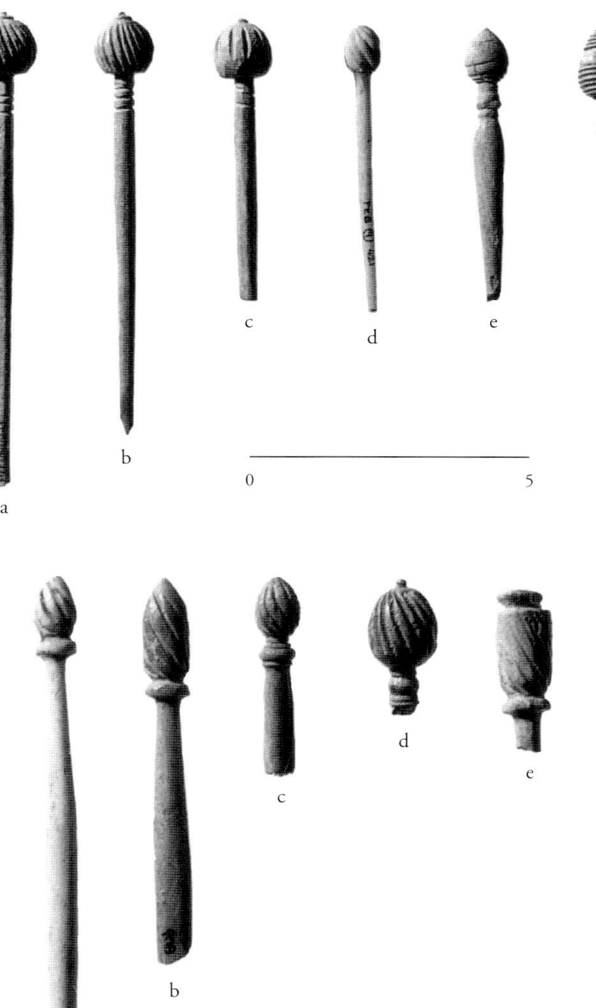

Plate 37.
Pins. (a) no. 460;
(b) no. 461; (c) no. 458;
(d) no. 459; (e) no. 456;
(f). no. 457

Plate 38.
Pins. (a) no. 464;
(b) no. 463; (c) no. 468;
(d) no. 467; (e) no. 465

Plate 39.
Pins. (a) no. 473;
(b) no. 471; (c) no. 469;
(d) no. 470

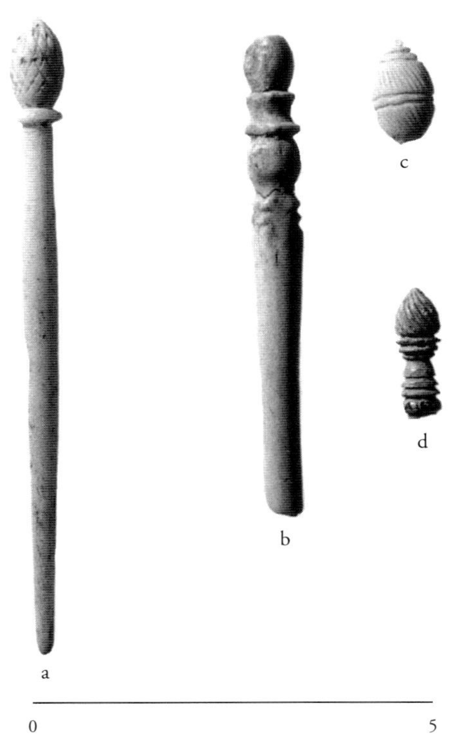

Plate 40.
Pins. no. 475

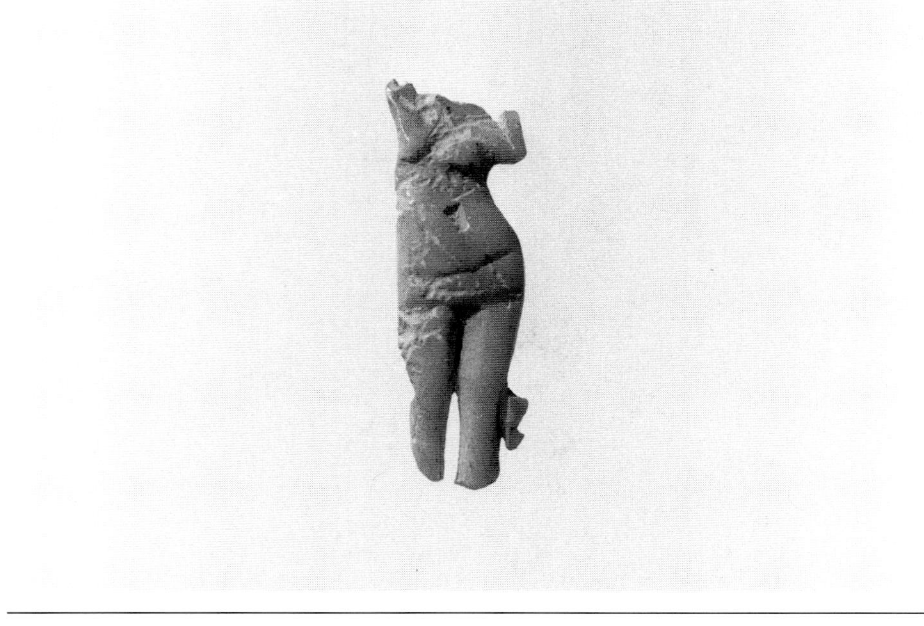

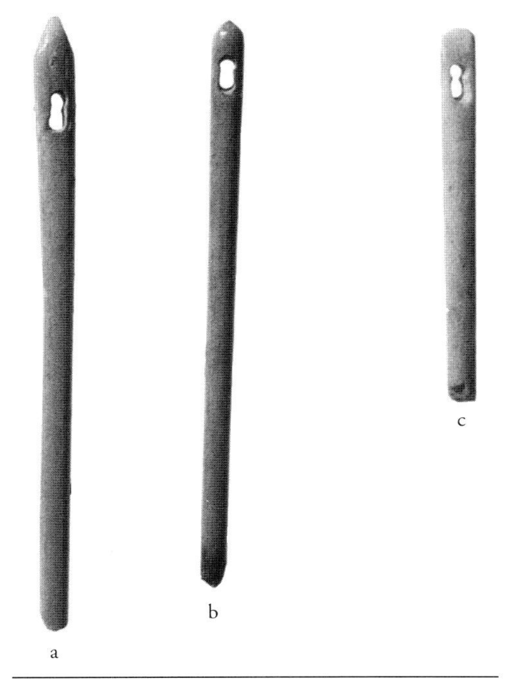

Plate 41.
Pins. (a) no. 479;
(b) no. 481; (c) no. 484

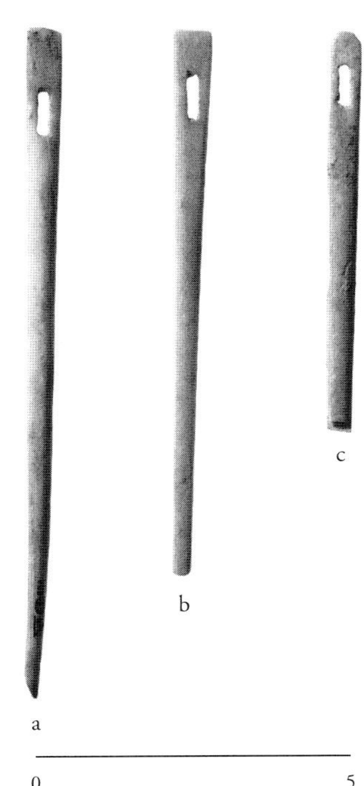

Plate 42.
Needles. (a) no. 489;
(b) no. 487; (c) no. 486

Plate 43.
Needles: (a) no. 495;
(b) no. 494; (c) no. 496

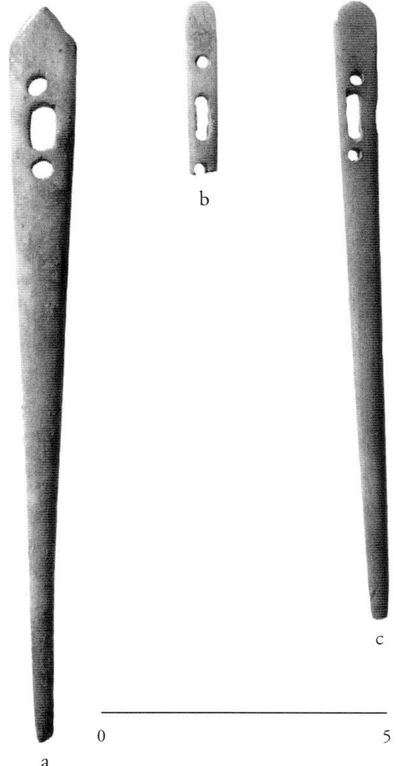

Plate 44.
Ligulae. (a) no. 507;
(b) no. 506; (c) no. 505;
(d) no. 501

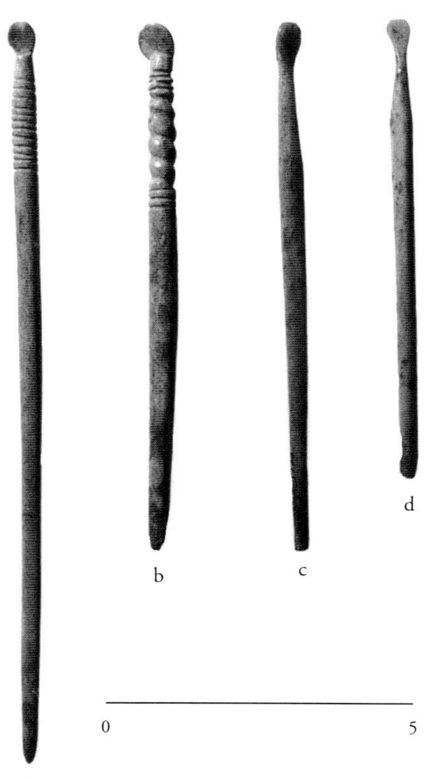

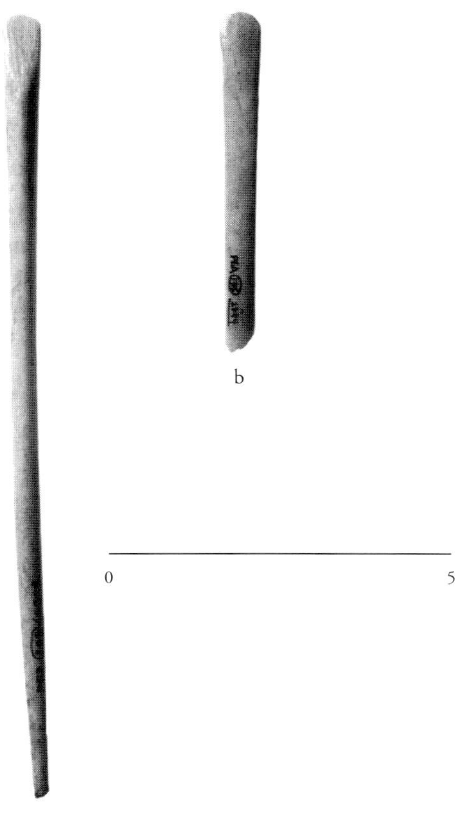

Plate 45.
Spatulae. (a) no. 511;
(b) no. 514

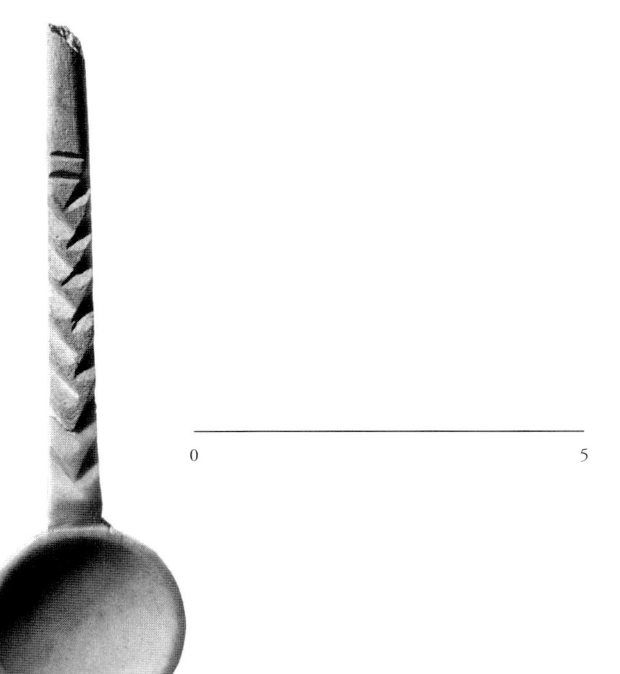

Plate 46.
Spoon. no. 516

Plate 47.
Handles. (a) no. 532;
(b) no. 524; (c) no. 523

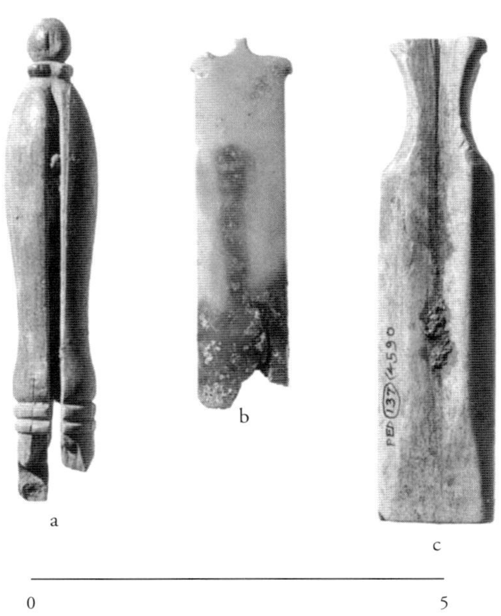

Plate 48.
Handles. (a) no. 527;
(b) no. 525; (c) no. 526

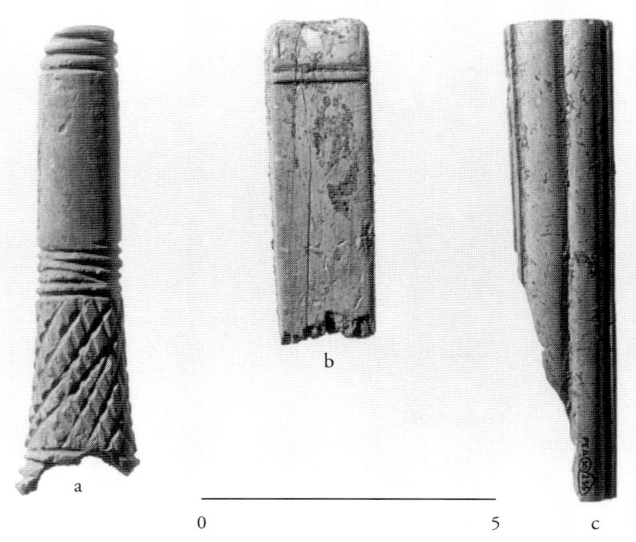

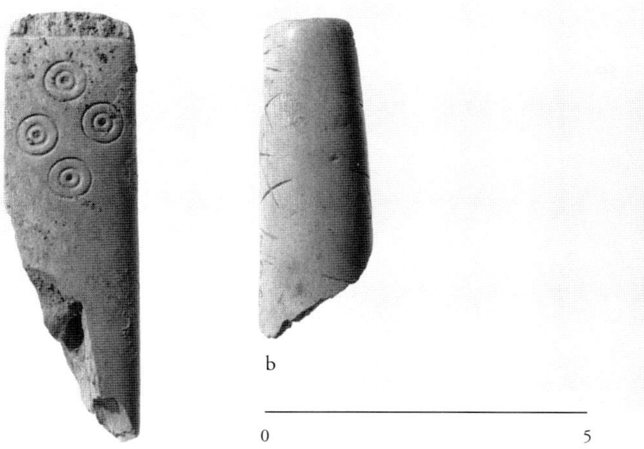

Plate 49.
Handles. (a) no. 529;
(b) no. 528

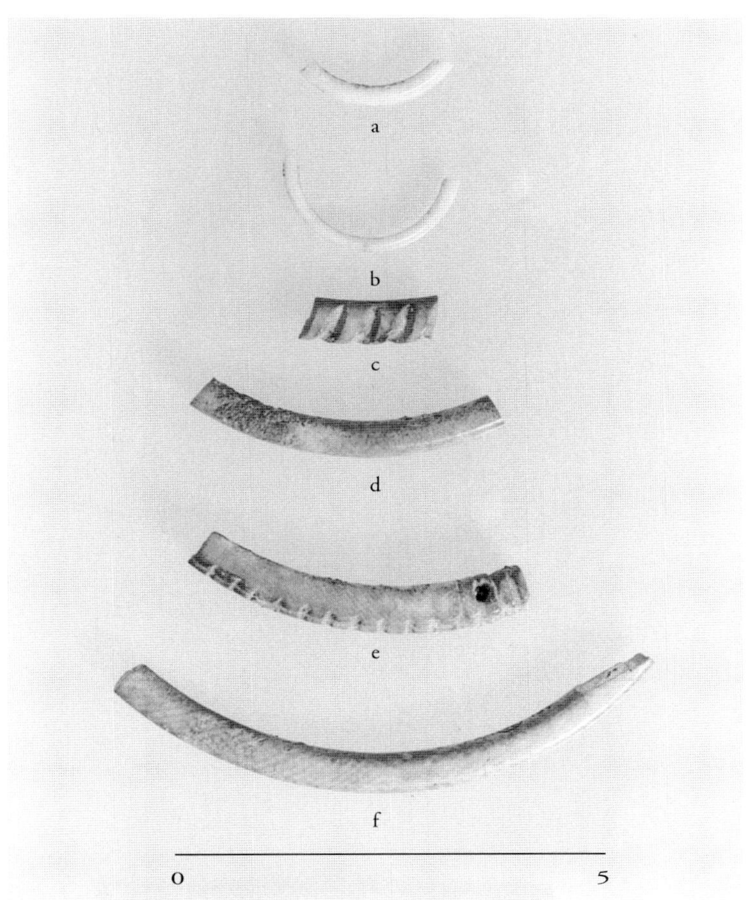

Plate 50.
Jewelry. (a) no. 539;
(b) no. 537; (c) no. 544;
(d) no. 535; (e) no. 547;
(f) no. 536

Plate 51.
Articulated doll. Approximate reconstruction using separately excavated body parts (body, no. 553; legs, nos. 562, 564, 565; arms, nos. 567, 571)

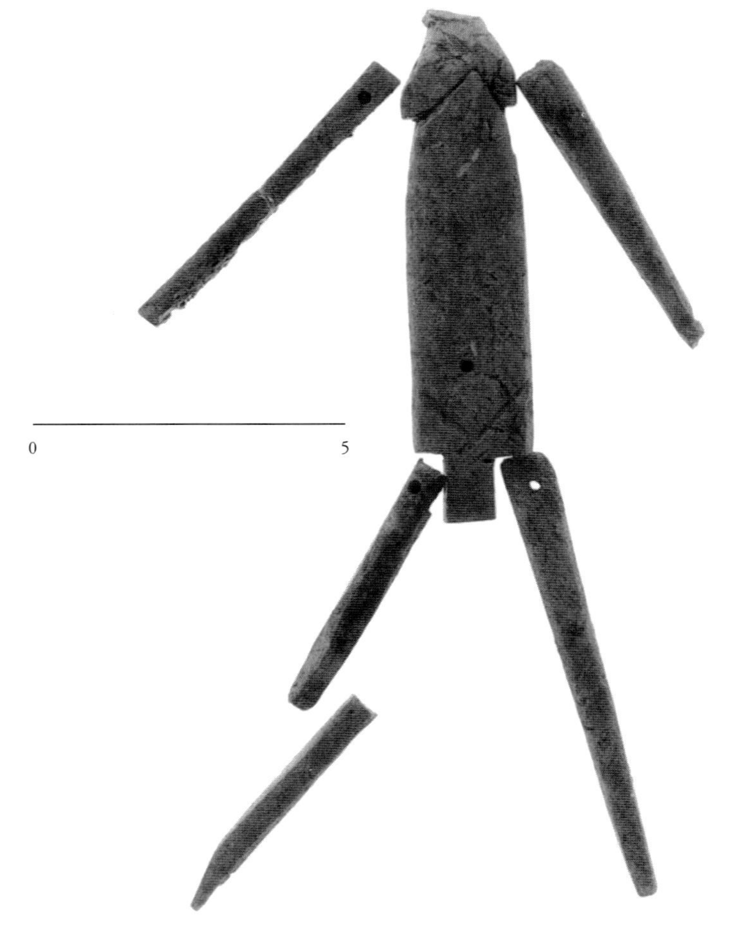

Plate 52.
Articulated dolls.
(a) no. 553; (b) no. 552;
(c) no. 557; (d) no. 572;
(e) no. 574; (f) no. 571;
(g) no. 569; (h) no. 564;
(i) no. 563

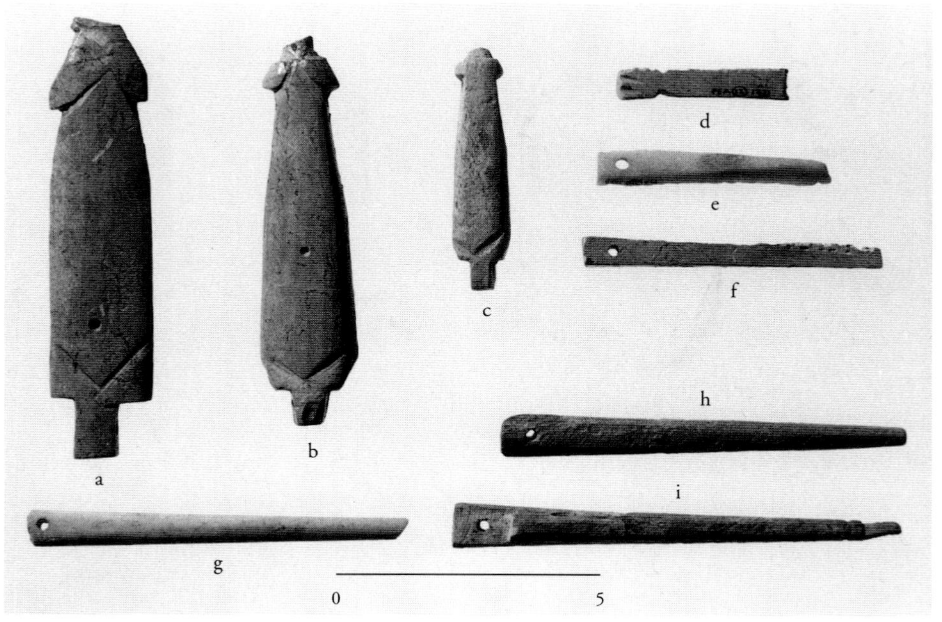

190   CATALOGUE

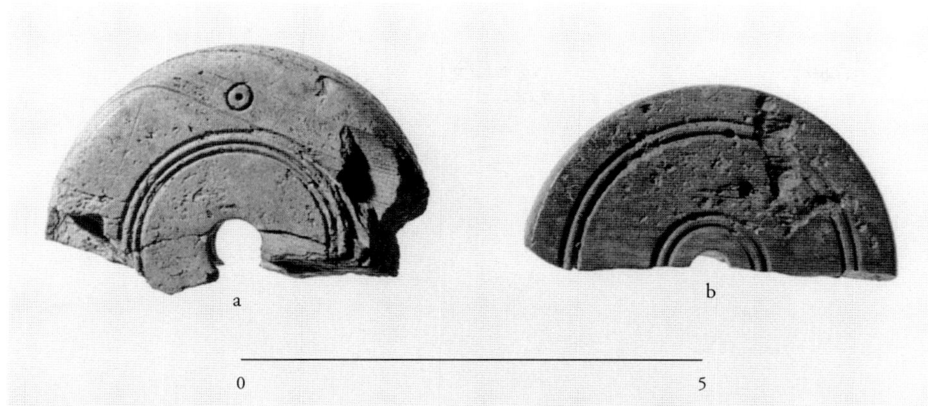

Plate 53.
Gaming pieces, ivory.
(a) no. 582; (b) no. 583

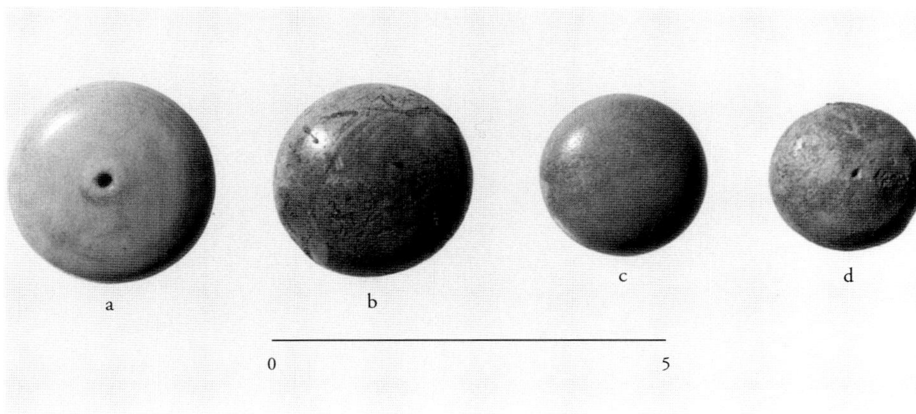

Plate 54.
Gaming pieces and
counters. (a) no. 587;
(b) no. 588; (c) no. 586;
(d) no. 584

Plate 55.
Gaming pieces.
(a) no. 593; (b) no. 592;
(c) no. 594

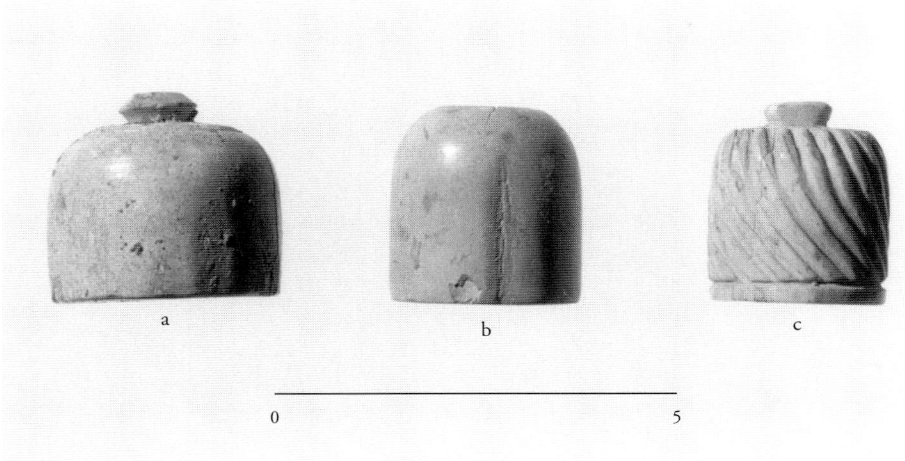

Plate 56.
Gaming pieces.
(a) no. 593; (b) no. 59;
(c) no. 594

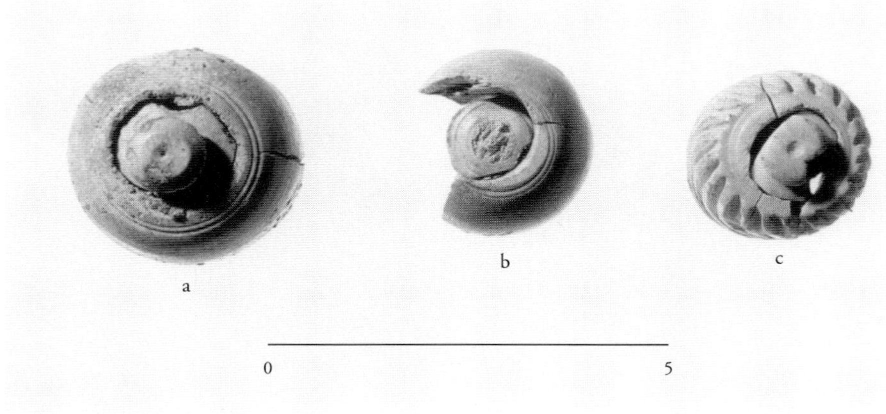

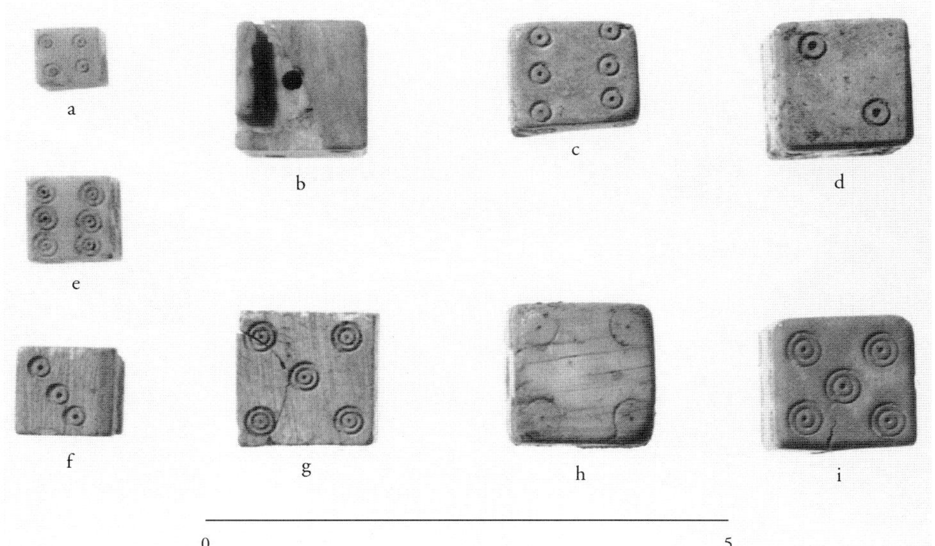

Plate 57.
Dice. (a) no. 602;
(b) no. 597; (c) no. 599;
(d) no. 604; (e) no. 634;
(f). no. 603; (g) no. 635;
(h) no. 642; (i) no. 610

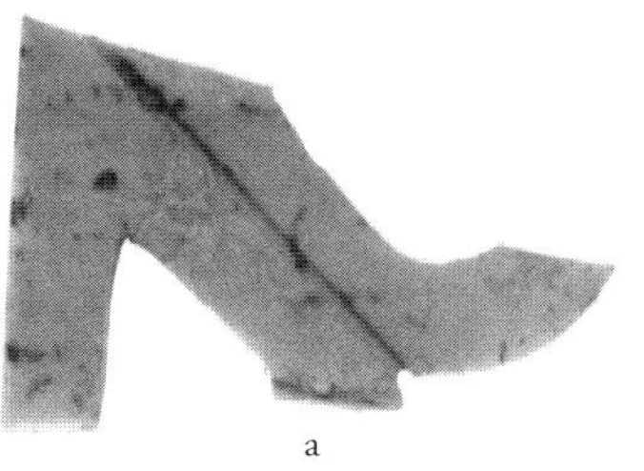

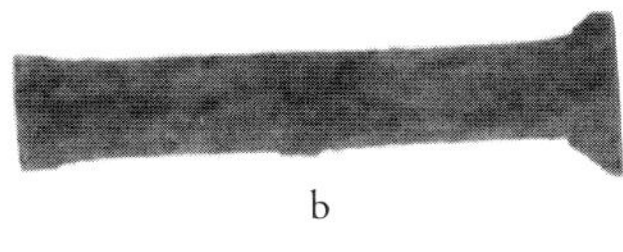

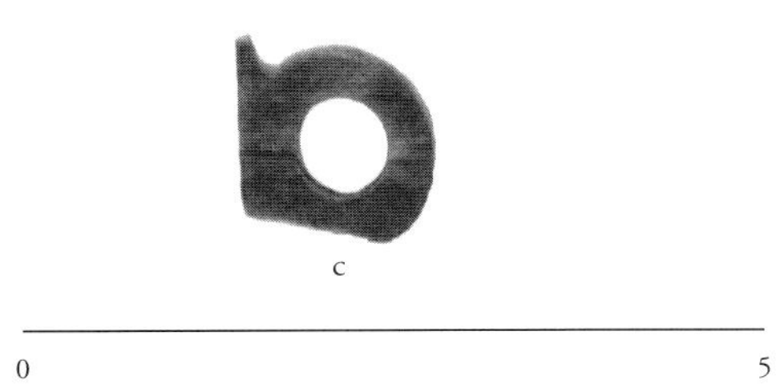

Plate 58.
Letters. (a) no. 645;
(b) no. 647; (c) no. 646

APPENDIX

CHRONOLOGICAL LIST OF OBJECTS BASED ON CONTEXT DATES

*Period
and Category*   *Catalogue Number*

III–IV: First century

Manufacturing	6–7, 21, 23–25, 78–80
Furniture	104–112, 159–160, 169, 226–227, 246
Pins	248–250, 273, 288, 446
Needles	485–487
Ligulae	498–501
Spatulae	508–509, 511–512
Handle	523
Gaming	578, 598, 609

IV–V: Mid-first–second century

Manufacturing	8, 9, 26–31, 81–86
Furniture	113–117, 161, 214–216, 228–229, 238
Pins	251–252, 289, 306
Needles	488–489
Ligula	502
Spatula	510
Gaming	597, 599, 610

V: Second century

Manufacturing	10, 32–34, 58
Furniture	118–122, 165, 170
Pins	253–254, 267, 290–292, 307–308
Needles	476–477, 493
Ligula	503
Spatula	513

Handle	524
Gaming	579–581
Whistle	648

V–VI: Second–first half of the third century

Manufacturing	35–37
Pins	255–257, 320
Needle	490
Spoon	516
Doll	558

VII: Mid–late third century

Furniture	123, 171–173, 230
Pins	258–259, 268, 274–279, 293–294, 310, 321–322, 325–327, 354–359, 363, 386
Needles	478, 494
Spatula	514
Stud	518
Dolls	567–568
Gaming	580, 601–603, 611–612

VIIIa: Late third–fourth century

Manufacturing	3, 11–13, 39–51, 87–91, 94
Furniture	124–130, 162, 166–167, 174–186, 209–211, 217, 231–232, 239–241
Pins	269–272, 280–284, 295–298, 311–317, 328–338, 360–373, 387–397, 401–418, 442–443, 449, 463–466, 469–470, 474, 475
Needles	479–480
Handle	532
Jewelry	534–541, 544–546, 549
Dolls	550, 559–561, 569–570
Gaming	584–585, 604–607, 613–629, 643

VIIIb: Mid-fourth–fifth century

Manufacturing	52–73, 92, 95–98
Furniture	131–149, 163–164, 187–201, 218–222
Pins	299, 318–319, 323, 339–342, 374–376, 398, 419–430
Needle	495
Handles	525–527
Jewelry	547
Dolls	551–559, 562–566, 571–576
Gaming	608, 630–637
Letters	645–647

VIIIc: Second half of the fifth century

Manufacturing	4, 16–17, 99
Furniture	150–151, 212–213, 234, 242
Pins	343–344, 377–378, 431–433, 439, 444–445, 447, 454–455, 458, 460–462
Ligulae	506–507
Handle	531
Jewelry	548
Gaming	582–583, 586–587, 592, 644

IX–XII: Medieval–modern

Manufacturing	18–20, 74–77, 100–103
Furniture	152–158, 168, 202–207, 223–225, 235–237, 243–245, 247
Pins	265–266, 300–305, 323–324, 379–385, 399–400, 434–438, 440, 448, 453, 459, 471–472
Needles	481–484, 491–492, 496–497
Ligula	504
Spatulae	505, 515
Combs	520–522
Handles	528–530
Jewelry	542
Dolls	555–557, 577
Gaming	588, 590–591, 593–596, 638–642

LIST OF IVORY OBJECTS BY CATEGORY

Category	*Object Number*
Manufacturing	25, 32, 34, 38, 41–42, 50, 52, 57–58, 64–68, 89, 91–92, 94
Furniture	127–128, 141, 150, 154, 175, 182, 187–188, 213, 217, 226, 238, 244
Pins	433, 441, 451, 453–456, 468
Needles	486
Ligulae	500
Handles	525, 531–532
Jewelry	533, 535–536, 538, 542–549
Gaming	582–583, 603, 606, 610, 632, 635–636, 640, 642

NOTES

1. The Materials

1. The structure and mechanical properties of bone and ivory have been analyzed in several studies. For bone see MacGregor and Currey 1983; MacGregor 1985, 1–9, 23–29; Ayalon and Sorek 1999, 8–10; Krzyskowska 1990; St. Clair and McLachlan 1989, 1–4; Cutler 1985a, 17–19, and 1993, 172–175. Useful studies of ivory include MacGregor 1985, 14–19; Cutler 1985a, 1–19, and 1993, 172–175; Krzyskowska 1990; St. Clair and McLachlan 1989, 1–6; Gaborit-Chopin 1978; Penniman 1952.

2. Bending strength, modulus of elasticity, and work to break of bone, particularly in comparison to antler, are discussed in MacGregor and Currey 1983, 73–76. See also MacGregor 1985, 23–29.

3. MacGregor 1985, 23.

4. MacGregor 1985, 30–32. For camel see Wapnish 1991; E. Rodziewicz 1995, 406.

5. For a discussion of selection by craftsmen based on analysis of assemblages from Saxon sites see Driver 1984.

6. See MacGregor 1985, 135–136, Fig.72c.

7. Jourdan 1976, 110, 113; Béal 1983a, 21.

8. Cf. a metapodial from Pheidias's workshop at Olympia measuring 0.270 meter in length (Schiering 1991, 161, n. 137). A fragmentary bone pyxis in the Louvre measuring 0.145 meter in diameter is a notable exception, and may have been cut from the metapodial of an elephant or hippopotamus. See Cutler 1993, 170–171, Figs. 5–6.

9. Béal 1983a, 21, 62, no. 67, Pl. IX.

10. See MacGregor 1985, 203–205.

11. See St. Clair 1995–1996, 33.

12. See Béal 1983a, 374, no. 1329, Pl. LXI.

13. MacGregor 1985, 63–65.

14. It has been suggested that the unique dentine structure seen in elephant tusks was developed in response to stress imposed by the weight of the tusks and the manner in which they are used. See MacGregor 1985, 17; Thornton 1981.

15. Pausanius, *Description of Greece* VIII, 46, 4. A number of other types of ivory exist, including warthog and related members of the boar family, sperm whale, and narwhal. See Randall 1985, 13–16; MacGregor 1985, 17–19; Espinosa and Mann 1992.

16. MacGregor 1985, 17. Differences between African and Indian tusks, especially as regards their maximum diameter, are debated. See Cutler 1985a, 27–29; Von Bargen 1994, 56–62.

17. Cox 1946, 30.

18. The use of fossilized ivory from mammoth tusks may explain the presence of ivory bag rings in fifth and sixth century Saxon graves. See MacGregor 1985, 39–40. For "marsh ivory" (fossile ebor) see Theophrastus, *De Lapidus* 37; Pliny, *Nat. Hist.* XXXVI, 29, 134; Philostratus, *Life of Apollonius* II, 13.

19. Von Bargen 1994, 63. Cf. Cutler 1985a, 25–28, Fig.25c (Dionysus and Tyche box). For plaques see Volbach 1976, 28–63.

20. Currey 1970; MacGregor 1985, 25–29, with explanatory diagrams.

21. Bronze and iron pins with ivory heads survive from as early as the tenth century B.C. in Greece, and examples with bone as well as ivory heads are common at sites such as Sparta. See Dawkins 1929, 226–227, Pl. CXXXVI. For bone shafts with separately attached heads from the Roman period see Desborough 1972, 198, n. 5.

22. Baer et al. 1971; Baer, Appelbaum, and Indictor 1971.

23. MacGregor (1985, 110) notes that some ivory bag rings from post-Roman graves in England had delaminated before burial, and were repaired with bronze plates. See also Gaborit-Chopin 1978; Penniman 1952; Cutler 1985a, 13–15.

24. Lapatin 1997, 675–679, and 2001, 75–78. These experiments were carried out on strips of ivory that were not "raw," and which may have been previously treated, altering their structure. Cox (1946, 110) reported that the Chinese softened ivory for carving in a solution of phosphate acid, but that this process was unsatisfactory for bending.

25. See Lapatin 1997, 679–682, and 2001, 73–76, who argues that the technique was available in antiquity. MacGregor (1985, 65–66) notes that a similar procedure may have allowed the creation of plaques used by eighteenth-century portrait painters.

2. Literary Evidence

1. Pliny, *Nat. Hist.* XI, 87, 215; XVII, 24, 109. See also Vergil, *Georgics* II, 193; Propertius, *Elegiae* IV, 6, 8; Philostratus, *Life of Apollonius* V, 21; Columella, *De re rustica* XII, 14, 1 and 47, 4.

2. "[Q]uamquam nuper ossa etiam in laminas secari coepere paenuria, etenim rara amplitudo iam dentium praeterquam ex India reperitur, cetera in nostro orbe cessere luxuriae." *Nat. Hist.* VIII, 4, 7, trans H. Rackham (Loeb ed.) (Cambridge and London 1940), 3:7.

3. "[A]deo nulla uncia nobis est eboris, nec tessellae nec calculus ex hac materia, quin ipsa manubria cultellorum ossea." *Satires* XI, 131–134, trans. G. G. Ramsey (Loeb ed.) (Cambridge and London 1957), 230.

4. *An vitiositas ad infilicitatem sufficiat* 499E.

5. For the most complete list of references to ivory in the ancient sources see Pauly-Wissowa, II, cols. 2356–2365 ("elfenbein").

6. For Lucius Cornelius Scipio see Livy, *History of Rome* XXXVII, 59, 3. For Seneca see Dio Cassius, LXI, 10, 3.

7. "[A]rborea et simulacra numinum fuere nundum pretio excogitato beluarum cadaveri atque ut, a diis nato ure luxuriae, eodem ebore numinum ora spectarentur et mensarum pedis." *Punica* VIII, 486–487, trans. J. D. Duff (Loeb ed.) (New York and London 1934), 428–429.

8. " . . . Democritum invenisse, quemadmodum ebur molliretur, quemadmodum decoctus calculus in zmaragdum converteretur." *Epistle* XC, 33, trans. R. M. Gummere (Loeb ed.) (London and New York 1920), 2:421.

9. See Pausanius, *Description of Greece* V, 12, 2; Plutarch *An vitiositas as infelicitatem sufficiat* 499E, and *Pericles* 12,6; Oppian, *Cynergetica* III, 514; Dioskourides, *De materia medica* 2, 87 and 4, 76. Methods mentioned in ancient and medieval literature are discussed in Lapatin 1994, 185–188, and 1997, 675–679.

10. Pausanias, for example, refers to the "horns of oxen and elephants" being straightened and shaped by fire [*Description of Greece* V.12.2]. For horn working see St. Clair and McLachlan 1989, 18–20.

11. For a discussion of these sources and of Africa and India as suppliers see Gill 1992, 233–237; Cutler 1985a, 22–23.

12. Cutler 1983, 937–938. On Ptolemy Philadelphus see Tarn 1928.

13. Harrauer and Sijpestein 1985, 1329 (verso, ii, 4–10), 134, 146–147, cited in Lapatin 1994, 28.

14. Diocletian's Edict of Maximum Prices 16.6a. Cutler (1983, 937–945; 1985a, 22–26) demonstrated that ample supplies were available in the eastern empire until at least the sixth century A.D.

15. The elephant was adopted on coin issues by later generations of Metelli. See Crawford 1974, I, 287. For Lucius Cornelius Scipio, see Livy, *History of Rome* XXXVII, 59, 3.

16. *MGH,* AA, XI.2, 213.21–22.

17. Rehm 1958, no. 394, cited in Scullard 1974, 61–62.

18. Cicero, *Verrine Orations* II, 4, 46, 103 (along with ivory statues); Pliny, *Nat. Hist.*VIII, 10, 1; Plutarch *Antony* LXXIV, 2.

19. Pausanius, *Description of Greece* II, 22, 5: VIII, 46, 4. See Lapatin 2001, 56.

20. Pausanius, *Description of Greece* I, 24, 5–7, and V, 11. For the statues see Lapatin 2001, 63–90; Stevens 1955, 240–76, and 1957, 350–61; Pfeiffer 1941.

21. Pausanius, *Description of Greece* V, 20, 10. See Lapatin 2001, 115–119.

22. Theocritus, XVII, 121–125.

23. Jupiter: Pliny, *Nat. Hist.* XXXVI, 40 (Jupiter Stator); Chalcidius, *Platonis Timaeus* CXXXVIII (Capitoline); Julius Caesar (57 B.C.): Dio Cassius XLIII, 45, 2–4; Germanicus (A.D. 17): Tacitus, *The Annals* II, 83; Britannicus (A.D. 79–81): Suetonius, *The Deified Titus* II. The temple statue of Mars Ultor was likely chryselephantine as well. See Zanker 1988,198. Evidence for chryselephantine statuary in Rome is discussed by Lapatin 2001, 121–126, who attributes the ivory foot in the Metropolitan Museum (MMA 25.78.43) to the first or second century A.D. (130–132).

24. Pliny, *Nat. Hist.* XV, 32.

25. Josephus, *The Jewish War* VII, 150–152.

26. Pliny the Younger, *Epistle* IV, 7, 1.

27. Pausanius, *Description of Greece* I, 18, 6 and 40, 4; Philostratus, *Lives of the Sophists* 2,550.

28. According to the fourth-century *Curiosum Urbis* (Jordan and Hülsen 1907, 2:572). By the sixth century, the number had declined to sixty-six. See Lapatin 2001, 122.

29. Homeric allusions to furniture ornamented with ivory most likely reflect the Mycenean rather than Homer's own age. See Carter 1985, 7–21.

30. *Inscriptiones Graecae* IV, 2, and I, 102 (Epidaurus); Diodorus Siculus, V, 46, 6; Propertius, II.31, 12. It has been suggested that in Homer's famous remarks concern-

ing the superiority of horn gates over ivory (*Odyssey* 19, 562–567), horn should be understood as bone, but recent scholarship rejects this hypothesis. See Amory 1966, 45–57; Miller 1994, 15–16. Additional references are discussed by Connor (1998, 61–62) and Oliver (1992, 227–232).

31. *Verrine Orations* II, 4, 67, 124.

32. Pausanius, *Description of Greece* V, 17–20. For Kolotes see Lapatin 2001, 96–98.

33. Pausanius, *Description of Greece* VI, 20; Athenaeus, *Deipnosophistae* V, 202B.

34. *Scholia in Equites* 532. Cf. Photius, *Lexicon*, s.v. *elektrai* (9th c.); Eustathius, *Comentarii ad Homeri Iliadem* IV.73 (12th c.), cited in Mastrocinque 1991, 8.

35. *Stichus* 377. See also Livy, *History of Rome* XXXIX, 6, 7.

36. Herodian, IV, 2–11.

37. Suetonius, *The Deified Julius,* 84,1.

38. Dio Cassius, LVI, 34, 1, 4:42, 1; LXXV, 4, 2–4.

39. Herodian, III, 15, 7; IV, 2.

40. Ovid, *Fasti* I, 82, V, 51(curule chairs); Plautus, *Stichus 377*; Horace, *Satires* II , 6, 103 (couches inlaid with ivory); Martial, *Epigrams* XIV, 91; Juvenal, *Satires* XI, 123–127 (tables with ivory legs).

41. Propertius, *Elegies* II, 13, 17–21. Dio Cassius, LXI, 10, 3.

42. Clement of Alexandria, *Paidagogos* II. 3. 8 (*PG* 6, col. 239b); John Chrysostom, *Hom. In Mattheum*, 83.4 (*PG* 58, col.750), cited with additional references in Cutler 1983, 971, n. 29.

43. *Acta Conciliorum Oecumenicorum* 1.4. 224–225. See Batiffol 1911, 251–252, 260–261. This report, perhaps unwisely given the possible confusion between ivory and bone, has been used to argue for the continued flourishing of the ivory industry in Alexandria during this period. See Cutler 1985a, 20.

44. Demosthenes, *Against Aphobus* I, 9–10; Diogenes Laertius, *Lives of Eminent Philosophers* VIII, 1, 5.

45. Livy, *History of Rome* XLII, 14 (scepters); Martial, *Epigrams* XIV.5 (tablets), 12 (boxes), 14 (dice), 77 (bird cage), 78 (medicine chest), 83 (back scratcher), 91 (tusks). Quintilian, *Institutio Oratoria* I, I, 26; Jerome *Epistle* CVII (letters of the alphabet). See *DA*, "ebur," II, 444–9.

46. *Codex Theodosianus* XV, 9, 1. See Cameron 1982, 126–129. Widespread distribution is confirmed by Symmachus, *Epistulae* II, 81, and V, 56.

47. *CIL* VI, 37374, 37793, 7885, 9375, 9397, 33423, 7655. See G. Vergantini in Panciera 1987, 92–94; Morel 1987, 164–165. Five are associated with the area between the Porta Salaria and the Porta Pinciana, suggesting a possible early concentration of ivory workers in that area. For the tombs see Gatti 1905.

48. *Faber eborarius: CIL* VI, 33423, 9397; *Politor eborarius:* VI, 7885,7952. Horace (*Epistles* II, 196) uses the term *eboris faber.* The inscriptions are discussed in Morel 1987, 164–165.

49. G. Vergantini in Panciera 1987, 92–94. See Morel 1987, 144, 164–165.

50. *Nat.Hist.* XXXV, 40, 147–148. Given that bone carving was also practiced as a household skill, it would not be surprising if craftspeople were of both sexes. For women metalworkers see *CIL* V, 7044; VI, 6939, 2911; III, 2117, cited in Kampen 1982, 72.

51. Petropoulos 1939, 413, cited in Barnett 1982, 95, n. 81.

52. Oppian, *Cynergetica* III, 514.

53. *Inscriptiones Christianae* II, 6111, cited in Fiocchi Nicolai et al. 1999, 162.

54. Graziosi 1912, 211; Karageorghis 1968. Citrus wood tables with ivory legs are mentioned by Martial (*Epigrams* XIV, 91).

55. Order of A.D. 337 addressed in the name of Constantine I to Valerius Maximus on the Danube frontier. *Codex Theodosianus* XIII, 4, 2 (1952, 390–391).

56. *Life of Apollonius* V, 20, trans. W. C.Wright (Loeb ed.) (London and New York 1992), 506, 507: ἡ δὲ ἀγαλματοποιία ἡ ἀρχαία οὐ τοῦτο ἔπραττεν, οὐδὲ περιήεσαν τὰς πόλεις ἀποδιδόμενοι τοὺς θεούς, ἀλλ᾿ ἀπάγοντες μόνον τὰς αὑτῶν χεῖρας καὶ ὄργανα λιθουργὰ καὶ ἐλεφαντουργά, ὕλην τε παρατιθέμενοι ἀργόν, ἐν αὐτοῖς τοῖς ἱεροῖς τὰς δημιουργίας ἐποιοῦντο.

57. Demosthenes, *Against Aphobus* I, 9–10, 30–32.

58. Meiggs and Lewis, 1969, no. 54. Pheidias was accused of embezzling the precious materials for the Parthenos statue and died in prison. See Barnett 1982, 63.

59. Lucian, 51, 17–24: ὅλως δέ, νομιστέον τὸν ἱστορίαν συγγράφοντα Φειδίᾳ χρῆναι ἢ Πραξιτέλει ἐοικέναι ἢ Ἀλκαμένει ἢ τῳ ἄλλῳ ἐκείνων—οὐδὲ γὰρ οὐδὲ ἐκεῖνοι χρυσὸν ἢ ἄργυρον ἢ ἐλέφαντα ἢ τὴν ἄλλην ὕλην ἐποίουν, ἀλλ᾿ ἡ μὲν ὑπῆρχε καὶ προϋποβέβλητο Ἠλείων ἢ Ἀθηναίων ἢ Ἀργείων πεπορισμένων, οἱ δὲ ἔπλαττον μόνον καὶ ἔπριον τὸν ἐλέφαντα καὶ ἔξεον καὶ ἐκόλλων καὶ ἐρρύθμιζον καὶ ἐπήνθιζον τῷ χρυσῷ, καὶ τοῦτο ἦν ἡ τέχνη αὐτοῖς ἐς δέον οἰκονομήσασθαι τὴν ὕλην.

60. *Nat. Hist.* XXXV, 41, 149, and IX, 14, 40. He mentions radishes as polishing agents as well (*Nat. Hist.* XIX, 26,87). Ancient and medieval texts referring to color and to the care of ivory are discussed in Connor 1998, 47–65.

61. Pausanius, *Description of Greece* V, 11, 10–11; VII, 27, 2. For the effects of such procedures see Gaugler and Hamill 1989; Lapatin 2001, 85–86.

62. Vergil, *Georgics* I, 480; Ovid, *Metamorphoses* XV, 792.

63. Martial, *Epigrams* IV, 62, VII, 12, and VIII, 28; Propertius, IV, 7, 82; Silius Italicus, *Punica* XII, 29. Pliny (*Nat. Hist.* XXXVI, 22, 98) mentions light and cool breezes as beneficial.

64. Publications include Strzygowski 1902, 1904; Marangou
1976; Loverdou-Tsigarida 1986; Bonacasa Carra 1995.
For the history of scholarship and the dating of some of
the pieces in the Hellenistic period see Marangou 1976,
19–28, 71–75.

65. Marangou 1976, 80.

66. Studies include Italy: Mocchegiani Carpano 1982, 25–27;
St. Clair in Hostetter et al. 1994, 161–171; De Grossi
Mazzorin and Minniti 1995; St. Clair 1996b; Cavallo in
Pantò 1996, 215–221; Pergamum: Driesch and
Boessneck 1982, 563–74; Egypt: M. Rodziewicz 1984;
Carthage: Hutchinson and Reese in Humphrey 1989,
549–594; Ashkelon: Wapnish 1991, 54–57; Ayalon and
Sorek 1999; Knossos: Sackett 1992, 379–389; Sagalassos:
De Cupere et al. 1993, 269–278; Kenchreai: Stern 2000.
Davidson 1952, 174, 278, Pls.147b, 148b, published
bone utensil blanks from Corinth.

67. See esp. Bíró 1994; MacGregor 1985; Béal 1983a,
1983b, 1984; Allason-Jones and Miket 1984; Crummy
1981; Holdsworth 1976; Lányi 1972; Schmid 1968.

68. See esp. Cutler 1985a, 1994. A secondary benefit of Cutler's studies of ivory carving based on observation of
finished objects has been the revelation of bone carvings
of high quality wrongly identified as ivory.

69. See Bianchi 2000; St. Clair 1996b; Cutler 1993, 170–
171, Figs. 5–6; Talamo 1987–1988.

70. See esp. Cutler 1983, 945–953, 1985a, 20–26. Valuable
overviews are provided by Canby, Buitron, and Olivier in
Randall 1985, chaps. 2–4; Barnett 1982, chaps. 6–10.
More specific studies include Lapatin 2001; Gill 1992,
233–237; Haywood 1990, 103–109.

71. For Bronze Age sites see Evely 1992, 7–16; Krzyskowska
1992, 25–35; Reese and Krzyskowska 1996, 324–326;
Tournavitou 1992, 37–42. For Olympia see Schiering
1991. For the prehistoric period see Poplin 1974a,b,
1977a,b. Studies of finished objects include Von Bargen
1994; Melucco Vaccaro 1993; Cutler 1993, 1991, 1985a,
1985b, 1985c, 1983; Engemann 1987; Gill 1992, 233–
237. Connor (1998) examines color on late antique and
Byzantine ivories. For chryselephantine statuary see
Lapatin 1997 and 2001.

3. Material Remains: The Greco-Roman World

1. Bone: St. Clair 1996b; terra-cotta: Bailey 1996. Identical
male heads appeared in Roman contexts in Lyon and in
Haltern in bone and at Tác in clay. See Bíró 1994,12.

2. Pausanius, *Description of Greece* VIII, 46, 5. Smilis, who
created chryselephantine statues for the Heraion at Olympia, restored the wooden xoanon of Hera there. See Pausanius: *Description of Greece* V, 17, 1 and VII, 4, 4, 7;
Clement of Alexandria, *Exhortation to the Greeks* 40, 41.
References to chryselephantine statues are collected in
Lapatin 2001, appendix 1, 193–197.

3. A Samian sculpture of a pair of lovers carved in wood,
unfortunately lost, closely resembled ivory work of the
period. See Akurgal 1966, Pl. 64. For wooden artifacts
see Donati 1996, 259, nos. 139–140 (writing tablets);
Virgili and Viola 1990, 111–112, nos. 221.5–6 (pyxides);
Kleiner and Matheson 1996, 155, no. 98 (writing tablet).

4. Vetters 1981, 139, Pl.1, and 1982, 65, Pl.1; Bammer
1982, 67, Pl.16b,c.

5. MacGregor 1985, 113; Ricci 1985, 69, 71, Pl.18, 2
(Trajanic-Hadrianic).

6. Béal 1983a, 19.

7. Dawkins 1929, 196, 198–199, 224–225, Pls. LXXI–
LXXIV, esp. LXXXIIc,d,h,m.

8. Dawkins 1929, 199, Pl. LXXXIIs.

9. Corinth: Davidson 1952, 277–278; Delos: Déonna
1938, 275–282.

10. Cutler (1983, 1985a, 20–37) discusses the ready availability of ivory and its relatively low cost in comparison
to other luxury materials from at least the late third
through the sixth century.

11. Lányi 1972; Bíró 1994, 12–13, 26, 30–31.

12. Cutler 1994, 56–65.

13. See Bíró 1987b, 53–54; 1994, 27.

14. Joly et al. 1992, 206 and n. 14.

15. See DeSantis 1994, 33–51; Felle et al. 1994, 114–120.

16. Pliny, *Nat. Hist.* XXIX, 36, 113; Barnett 1982, 14, n. 49.
This notion has been recently revived by E. Rodziewicz
(1992, 319) to explain the lack of evidence in Alexandria.

17. Kunze 1930; Lapatin 2001, 44–45. There is disagreement as to whether there were four or five female figures
originally. It has been suggested that they were cut from a
single tusk, and probably carved in Greece after Near
Eastern models. See Carter 1985, 1–7, and 40, n. 6;
Dunbabin 1957, 27. Four ivory heads were unearthed in
the geometric-archaic cemetery at Eleutherna. See
Stampolidis 1992.

18. Knigge 1976, 7–10, 60–83.

19. Andronikos 1978, 40, Figs. 16–20, and 1984, 122–127,
202–206. The remains include miniature portraits that
may depict the royal family. For small-scale portraits on
furniture see E. Rodziewicz 1968, 257–265.

20. Etruria: Mastrocinque 1991; Germany: Fischer 1990,
115–118, Fig. 1. The most celebrated witnesses to such
trade are ivory veneer fragments, dated to the fifth or
fourth century B.C. and probably from a couch, excavated
at Kul-Oba, on the hellenized peninsula of Kertch in the
Crimea. See Minns 1912, 200–206, Figs. 100–103;
Vaulina and Wasowicz 1974, Pls. VIII–XI, LVI–LVII.

21. For the site see Dawkins 1929, 12–27. For the bone and
ivory see Carter 1985; Marangou 1969.

22. Hogarth 1908; Lapatin 2001, 48–50, 145–146, nos. 23,
25–27; Bammer 1992, 185–204. There is no consensus
that the Ephesian ivories are all Greek. See Barnett 1982,

58–59. For dating problems see Carter 1985, 225–248. Other sites that produced smaller amounts of material, but relied apparently primarily on imports, include: the Heraions at Samos (Dawkins 1929; Marangou 1969; Freyer-Schauenburg 1966; Sinn 1982; Brize 1992); Argos (Waldstein 1905, 351–354, Pl. CXXIX); and Perachora, where a small amount of waste material suggests work done at the site (Payne and Dunbabin 1962, 437, no. A194, Pl. 185; 447, nos. A381, A385, Pl. 189). A well at on the acropolis at Rhodes produced twenty-two ivory and six bone carvings (Hogarth 1908,178–181, Pls. 28–31; Schofield 1992).

23. Dawkins 1929, 241, Pl. CLXX, 6.

24. Carvers of the intaglio reverses on disk and four-faced seals in ivory and bone, for example, also carved plaques and fibulae. See Carter 1985, 149–51.

25. See Dawkins 1929, 211–215, Pl. CVI, 3; 217–218, Pl. CXVI, 2.

26. Pipili 1987, 43–44. For the figures see Dawkins 1929, 218–219, Pls. CXVII–CXX; Marangou 1969, 151–163, nos. 88–108, Figs. 113–133, 136; Carter 1985, 202.

27. Similar truncated figures held by children depicted on Attic grave reliefs, traditionally identified as dolls, have recently been reinterpreted as cult figures by Reilly 1997. For Roman examples see St. Clair 1995–1996, 30–49. Smaller-scale bone pendants in the form of *kore* survive from an archaic sanctuary at Anagni. See Ruffo 1994–1995 102, Figs. 66, 69.

28. Dawkins 1929, 237, 243, Pls. CLXII, 12; CLXIV–CLXV, classed as "purpose unknown."

29. Hammond 1995–1996, 59.

30. Dawkins 1929, 220–221, Pls. CXXII–CXIII. Two examples (221, Pls. CXXIV–CXXV) depicting seated pairs are ivory.

31. Combs: Dawkins 1929, 222–224, Pls. CXXVI–CXXXI; Marangou 1969, 93–111, nos. 40–57. The largest ivory example is 0.080 meter in length. Spectacle and eagle fibulae: Dawkins 1929, 224–226, Pls. CXXXII–CXXXIV. The size range is 0.045–0.160 meter.

32. Dawkins 1929, 228–230, Pls. CXXXIX–CXLVII.

33. Payne and Dunbabin 1962, 410–411. Barnett (1948, 12) suggests that some were seals of office for priests or other officials, perhaps dedicated on completing a term of office.

34. Dawkins (1929, 219–220, Pls. CXXI–CXXII, 1–4) believed that the heads depict Orthia. Marangou (1969, 130–135, nos. 73–83, Figs. 93–105) discusses nine examples and believes that at least one of the heads is male.

35. Dawkins 1929, 220, Pls. CXXI, 3; CXXII, 1, 4; Marangou 1969, 132, nos. 76, 81, 83, Figs. 95a–b, 96a–b, 104a–c.

36. Dawkins 1929, 220, Pl. CXXI, 5; Marangou 133, no. 78, Fig. 105a–c.

37. Dawkins 1929, 230–235, Pls. CXLVIII–CLX. Carter 1985, 62–101; Marangou 1969, 112–124, nos. 58–71, Figs. 84–89, dates some to the 640s. Ten are on circular bases (diam. 0.017–0.030 meter) the remainder on rectangular bases (L.0.030–0.045 with a few exceptional examples of L.0.080).

38. Dawkins 1929, 204–218, Pls. CXII–CXVI. For question of dating see Marangou 1969, 168–177, nos. 112–121, Figs. 140–145, 163; Carter 1985, 118–73, esp. 169–172.

39. Probably by flood. For the history of the temple site see Dawkins 1929, 12–27.

40. See Carter 1985, 172–173; Barnett 1982, 60.

41. Carter 1985, 289–90.

42. Mastrocinque 1991, 6–10.

43. Dawkins 1929, 213–214, Pl. CVI, 3; Marangou 1969, 70–71, no. 3, Fig. 48.

44. Dawkins, 1929, 216–217, Pls. CXIII–CXV.

45. Dawkins 1929, 217–218, Pl. CXVI, 2.

46. See Dawkins 1929, 218, Pl. CXVI, 3; Carter 1985, 172, Fig. 69; Marangou 1969, 175–177, no. 120, Fig. 163. For two other plaques that were joined together see Dawkins 1929, 216, Pl. CXII, 1; Marangou 1969, 171–174, nos. 117, 118, Figs. 145a,b. Carter (1985, 169–71) believes that these were part of a larger composition including plaques now in the National Museum at Athens.

47. For the ivory plaques see Dawkins 1929, 217, Pls. CXVI, 1, 2.

48. See Pausanius, *Description of Greece* III, 16, 7–9. The cult images of Artemis Orthia at Sparta, Hera at Samos, Athena Polias at Athens, and Artemis at Brauron were wooden. Such statues were transportable, and routinely carried in processions. On Greek wooden statuary see Donohue 1988; Romano in Hägg et al. 1988, 127–134.

49. See Chapter 2, p. 12, and note 56. The situation was probably fluid. While many of the surviving remains from Perachora appear to be imports, the presence of an unfinished fibula plaque and of two pieces of ivory, perhaps blanks or waste, suggest that some carving was done at the site as well, perhaps by itinerant craftspeople. See Payne and Dunbabin 1962, 437, no. A194, Pl.185; 447, nos. A381, A385, Pl.189.

50. Dawkins 1929, 224–225, Pls. CXXXII–CXXXIV.

51. Dawkins 1929,198, Pl. LXXXIIa,b,e,j,i,k; Payne and Dunbabin 1962, 433.

52. Dawkins 1929, 226–227, Pls. CXXXVI–CXXXVIIa–e. Because eighty-five disk heads were discovered but only twenty-four shafts, presumably the shafts were primarily metal.

53. See Amandry 1939; *Guide de Delphes* 1991, 206–219; Lapatin 2001, 57–60, 147–148, no. 33. Carter 1989, 355–78, suggested that the ajouré reliefs decorated a chest and posited a Spartan carver.

54. Amandry 1939, 91, 93, 94; Lapatin 2001, 58, 147, no. 33.1, fig. 116.

55. Early Greek ivory fragments from composite statues are discussed in Lapatin 2001, 42–60.

56. Pausanius, *Description of Greece* V, 15,1. For the dating of the remains and their association with the statue see Mallwitz and Schiering 1964, 272–277; Mallwitz 1972, 255–263; Schiering 1991; Lapatin 2001, 79–83. Fink's (1967, 65–77) rejection of the evidence has not won acceptance. A fragmentary cup with "of Pheidias" scratched on its base was found at the site. See Kunze 1959, 281, Figs 18–33.

57. Mallwitz and Schiering 1964, 16–47, 74–101.

58. Kunze 1959, 280.

59. Technical analyses revealed that the molds were not used for shaping gold sheets for drapery as originally supposed, but to create positives in glass. See Schiering 1991, 17–22.

60. Schiering 1991, 161–163, Pls. 54, 57d.

61. Kunze (1959, 291, 293–294, Figs. 32, 33) suggested that along with a bronze goldsmith's hammer, they were used for working the thin sheets of gold that made up the drapery of the figure.

62. Schiering (1991, 161, Pl. 52b) suggests that the bone leaves alternated with glass.

63. Schiering 1991, 162, Pl. 55a.

64. Athens: Knigge 1976, 64; Mycenae: Sakellarakis 1979, 373, Figs. 88, 89–91; Italy: Bianchi 2000, 75–76, no. C.b.1.

65. Schiering 1991, Pl. 52c. One rectangular fragment has a more elaborate design of superimposed keyholes, probably representing a preliminary stage in the carving process.

66. E. Rodziewicz 1992; Lapatin 2001, 150–151, no. 51.

67. Ancient and modern evidence for the construction of the Athena Parthenos is collected in Lapatin 2001, 63–74. See also Lapatin 1997, 667; Stevens 1957, 350–361. Precedents for the use of metal struts and for statues formed of wooden cores covered with sheets of metal on a small scale are known from Delphi (Amandry 1939, 109–110, Fig. 13). The precise form of such cores is unknown. Lucian's remarks in the second century suggest scaffolding (*Juppiter Tragoedus* 8), rather than the solid blocks of wood envisioned by Stevens.

68. *Description of Greece* I, 40, 4.

69. Lapatin 1997, 672–675. Cf. 2001, 74–78.

70. See Chapter 2 and note 60.

71. For the use of celloid gum, bitumen, and fish glue see Barnett 1982 14. Cf. Lapatin 2001, 77–78. A Roman glue-boiling site has been identified at Augst. See Schmid 1968, 194; 1972, 48.

72. Knigge 1976, 71–73, Figs. 22, 28, 29. In the case of the couch, ivory plaques 0.150–0.200 meter long, 0.040–

73. Andronikos 1978, 40, Figs. 16–20; 1984, 123.

74. For the appearance and development of turned legs see Faust 1989, 22–28, Fig.1, with previous bibliography.

75. See Richter 1966, 56, Fig. 298; Ransom 1902, 133–134, and 1905, 39–41; Faust 1989. For bronze examples see esp. Greifenhagen 1930, 137–165. For sculptural fragments in ivory and in bone that have been identified as belonging to such furniture see Faust 1992; E. Rodziewicz 1968; Hill 1963, 293–300; Buitron and Olivier in Randall 1985, 54–78; Floriani Squarciapino in Floriani Squarciapino et al.1958, 11–20; Graeven 1903, 49, 100, Pls. 31, 61.

76. For examples see Mütz 1972, 166–167, Figs. 487–490; Richter 1966, 57; Ransom 1905, 48–49; Hill 1963, 293–294.

77. The basic study of the couches and catalogue is Letta 1984. A more recent overview of the material and bibliography is provided in Bianchi 2000. Other important studies include Nicholls 1979; Talamo 1987–1988, 1992; Béal 1991. For discoveries in Italy see Bianchi 2000, 125–128; Mollo-Mezzena in Cappelli 1992, 158–169; Monacchi 1994; Simone 1991; Saronio 1990; Rossi 1988–1989. The numerous fragments from tombs in Ostia, usually referred to in the literature as *avori* are discussed by Floriani Squarciapino 1958, 11–20.

78. For the use of glass inlay see Letta 1984, 38, 40–42, nos. 86, 97, 102–103, 116; Nicholls 1979, 15, 24, no. 17. For the glass inlay on the reconstructed bone couch in the Metropolitan Museum see Bacchelli et al. 1995, 447–466; Saguì 1998, 33–34.

79. For examples see Nicholls 1979, 10; Béal 1986, 113, Fig. 2, and 1991, 291, Fig. 3; Bianchi 2000, 27, 31. For the Egyptian examples see Barnett 1982, 13. On some couches (Nicholls 1979, 27) larger sculpture is carved in a single layer over a wooden maquette.

80. Pausanius, *Description of Greece,* VIII, 46, 4; Diogenes Laertius, *Lives of Eminent Philosophers* VIII, 1, 5.

81. Cf. M. v. Solodkoff in Schiering 1991, 160.

82. Lapatin 1997, 678–679, Fig.10. Cf. 2001, 76. He does not indicate whether the prefabricated strips he used for softening experiments had been previously treated, an important distinction because initial softening for "unscrolling" may have altered the structure of the material. Softening of skeletal materials is discussed in MacGregor 1985, 63–66, with bibliography.

83. Tombs with bone and ivory remains include: Barberini, Castellani, and Barnaedini Tombs at Praeneste; Regolini-Galassi Tomb at Cerveteri; "Tomba del Duce" at Vetulonia (7th c. B.C.). See Aubet 1970, 39–64. For furniture remains from Quinto Fiorentino see Mastrocinque 1991; Schäfer 1989, 48–50, Pls. 1, 1–3, and 2, 1. For unworked blocks of ivory found in association with grave circles see Huls 1957,

135, 208. Evidence for the carving of plaques and other objects in bone and antler was uncovered near the archaic sanctuary at Murlo. See Nielson and Phillips 1983, 17–24.

84. Sheep and goats occasionally were used as well. See Ayalon and Sorek 1999, 15–17, Figs. 2–6; 20, Fig. 4; 24, Fig. 12; 28, Fig. 23; 42, Fig. 52; 49, Fig. 62; 56, Fig. 76; 62, Fig. 89; 63, Fig. 88; Wapnish 1991, 54.

85. Vercoutter 1962.

86. One of the rhyta bore a Greek inscription, suggesting the involvement of Greek or Greek-trained artisans. See Masson and Pugacenkova 1982, esp. 19; Bernard 1970, 327–43; Pugachenkova 1948, 161–171. A similar piece of furniture was found at Ai Khanum, a Greek city on the Oxus River in Bactria. See Bernard 1970, 312.

87. Hackin 1939, 63–117, nos. 315–345; 1954, 19–54, 157–253, nos. 5–58. The trade with Italy is confirmed by the discovery in Pompeii of an elaborately carved Indian statuette. See During Caspers 1979, 10–29.

88. For ivory statuettes from the Hellenistic period see E. Rodziewicz 1974, 88, Fig. 6. She (1968) identified a variety of small-scale sculptures as belonging to furniture decoration from as early as the archaic period but concentrated in the Hellenistic and early Roman periods. Ivory remains of furniture decorated with portraits and mythological reliefs are preserved from a tomb near Lefkadia dated 250–140 B.C. See Rhomiopoulou 1973, 87–92. For a relief from a second century B.C. tomb on the Esquiline see Cicerchia et al. 1976, 29–31. For Roman examples see Graeven 1903, 113, Pls. 14, 53, 54, 69, 75. A collection of this type of material is in the Walters Art Museum. See Buitron and Olivier in Randall 1985, 64–74.

89. Vermeule 1989.

90. Ivory examples were found in tombs and in habitations. Letta (1984, 90–92) believed that bone was limited to funerary contexts, but examples from habitations in Gaul contradict this theory. See Béal 1986,116; Nicholls 1979, 25–26; Hill 1963, 298–300.

91. See note 77.

92. For the pattern of distribution see Bianchi 2000, 130–131, Figs. 32–33. For individual examples see Letta 1984, 96–97, 110–111, nos. 25–28, 177–186; For Gaul see Béal 1986, 1991, Béraud and Gébara 1986; Fouet and Labrousse 1952.

93. Letta 1984, 97–111. Nos. 34–74 follow ivory models, nos. 75–126, bronze models. Talamo (1987–1988, 78) questions Letta's classifications, but does not contradict the main ideas. For a recent evaluation see Bianchi 2000, 95–124.

94. See Chapter 3, p. 16.

95. Talamo 1987–88; Bonacasa Carra in Ensoli and La Rocca 2000, 353–354; Letta 1984, 93–94.

96. Letta 1984, 93; Nicholls 1979, 26.

97. Eckinger 1929, 256; Holliger and Holliger Wiesmann 1993, 26; Béal 1991, 313.

98. Béal 1991, 313. Cf. Bianchi 2000, 95–100, 129.

99. Gianfrotta 1986, 215, Fig. 368; Faust 1989, no. 529.

100. With one exception (Letta 1984, 97, no. 34), the bone remains from second through first century tombs in Ostia, excavated in the early twentieth century, have not survived in a form that would allow for reconstruction. See Letta 1984, 98, 105–106, 108, nos. 38, 108–113, 128–136; Floriani Squarciapino in Floriani Squarciapino et al. 1958, 11–20.

101. Antiquarium Comunale inv. no. 18741. The fragment is carved with Dionysiac imagery. See Cicerchia et al. 1976, 29–31.

102. For an ivory Trajanic relief from Ephesus, depicting the emperor and his military retinue, see Lessing and Oberleitner 1978, Pl. 9; Dawid and Dawid 1972–1975; Dawid 1980, Pls. 15–17. For ivory panels carved in relief and bone box parts dated to the second and third centuries in the Walters Art Museum see Buitron and Olivier in Randall 1985, 70–71, nos. 75, 77a–b). For small-scale sculpture in ivory see Barnett 1982, 70; Cutler 1985a, 8–11, 40–41, Figs. 12, 39, 40. Statuettes with a known provenance include Shear 1937, 349–351, Figs. 13–14 (Athens, 3rd c.), Inan and Alföldi-Rosenbaum 1979, 191–194, nos. 157, 159–161, Pls. 120, 122, 123 (Ephesus, 3rd c.).

103. See Bacchelli et al. 1995, 447–466; Saguì 1998, 33–34.

104. Cutler 1983; 1985a, 20–37; 1985b; 1987; 1993.

105. See Volbach 1976, 28–56, nos. 1–65a.

106. St. Clair 1996a. A bone medallion incised with an apostle, dated to the fourth century, is in the Metropolitan Museum (inv. 1979.401).

107. Marangou 1976, 87, no. 3, Pl. 2a, and Volbach 1976, 60, nos. 73–74, Pl. 42; Randall 1985, 100, no. 171, and Volbach 1976, 93–94, no. 140, Pls. 72–74. The stylistic similarities were noted by Cutler (1993, 174, n. 49).

108. See Volbach 1976, 93–94, no. 140, Pls. 72–74 (Cathedra of Maximianus); 85, no. 120, Pl. 64 (Pola casket); 77, no. 107, Pl. 57 (Brescia casket); 84–85, no. 119, Pl. 63 (Milan Diptych); 47–48, no. 48, Pl. 26 (so-called Barberini Diptych); 69–76, 103–121, nos. 89–106, 161–201 (pyxides). On the making and function of the five-part Barberini plaque, which was probably not a diptych, see Cutler 1991, esp. 337–338.

109. See, for example, Loverdou-Tsigarida 1986; Marangou 1976; Buitron, Olivier, and Randall in Randall 1985, 54–112. Large numbers of reliefs in bone and ivory have been published by Strzygowski (1902, 1904); Wulff (1909); and Volbach (1976), among others.

110. For the remains see Stern 2000; Scranton et al. 1978, 68–69; Scranton and Ramage 1967, 141–146. The final report by Stern is forthcoming.

111. See, for example, Randall 1985, 98–99, nos. 164, 165.

112. Findspots indicate that such objects were created primarily for domestic and official contexts, rather than specifically for funerary use. See Aiosa 1997, 144–148.

113. The collection was acquired primarily from dealers and sales of private collections in Alexandria and Cairo. Material of this type in the Walters Art Museum is similarly difficult to date and in most cases of unknown provenance. See Buitron, Olivier, and Randall in Randall 1985, 54–112.

114. See Bonacasa Carra 1995, 281, Pl. XXXVI; Bonacasa Carra in Ensoli and La Rocca 2000, 353–358.

115. Wace 1949, 151–156. The site is near the crossing of the Via Canopica and the Via Sema or Soma. For the history of excavations carried at Kom el Dikka and in the vicinity see Dabrowski 1960; Lipinska 1966, 182–184; M. Rodziewicz 1984, 11–16. Earlier excavations in Alexandria by von Sieglin uncovered bone plaques along with other bone objects, several of which appear unfinished. See Pagenstecher 1913, 168–170, 229–236, Pls. 54–60.

116. See Shenouda 1973; M. Rodziewicz 1976, 1984; E. Rodziewicz 1969, 1978. For a history of the bone and ivory discoveries see E. Rodziewicz 1992, 317–318.

117. M. Rodziewicz 1984, 17–58. See also E. Rodziewicz 1992, 317–319.

118. M. Rodziewicz 1984, 198–208.

119. See M. Rodziewicz 1976, 204–207; 1984, 141–143, 148, 241–245; 1991, 214; and E. Rodziewicz 1969, 151–152.

120. See E. Rodziewicz 1978, 317–336; M. Rodziewicz 1976, 204–205, and 1984, 243–245.

121. For plaques of this type with known provenances in Egypt see Loverdou-Tsigarida 1986.

122. E. Rodziewicz 1995. Englebach, who catalogued the Saqqara finds, believed that most were exports from Alexandria. Cf. Petrie and Mackay 1915, 43.

123. Engemann 1987. Alexandria seems to have been the major supplier of St. Menas ampullae as well. See Kiss 1973.

124. See Ayalon and Sorek 1999; Wapnish 1991.

125. See Davidson 1952, 132–136, nos. 940–966, Pls. 68–70; Reese 1987, 261–262.

126. Knossos: Sackett 1992; Carthage: Hutchinson and Reese in Humphrey 1989, 549–594. The remains include inlay strips, plaques decorated with simple geometric forms and a single fragmentary incised plaque with a standing figure. Bone offcuts and debris were also discovered on Avenue du President Habib Bourgiba in contexts containing largely residual material. See Henig in Hurst and Roskams 1984, chap. 11. For Sagalassos see De Cupere 1994.

127. Egypt: E. Rodziewicz 1995; Marangou 1976, 22–23. Palestine: Rosenthal 1976; Goldfuss and Bowes 2000 (ancient Elusa). Leptis Magna: Joly et al. 1992; Aiosa 1997.

128. Remains from Saraçhane are difficult to date securely and include material from Roman times up to the twentieth century. They include mounts and framing strips associated with furniture, utensils, and gaming pieces in bone and ivory. See Gill in Harrison 1985, 226–63.

129. A box imported to Gaul is discussed by Fouet and Labrousse 1952. See also Melucco Vaccaro 1993, 12–16.

130. Hassal and Rhodes 1974, 15–100. For other remains of this type, several with late Roman inscriptions see MacGregor 1985, 197–203; Allason-Jones and Miket 1984, 61–62.

131. Crummy 1981.

132. Crummy 1981, 285. Tournavitou (1992, 42) suggests that there may have been separate joiners' workshops in Mycenae.

133. The state of scholarship is summarized with bibliography in Melucco Vaccaro, 1993, 16–19.

134. Ibrahim et al. 1976; for the Egyptian provenance see 259–269. See also Scranton and Ramage 1967, 141–146.

135. Melucco Vaccaro 1993, 11–13. Cf. Cutler on ivory remains attributed to Brescia (1993, 176). Evidence for commerce in ivory and bone relief plaques of the so-called Alexandrian school with Pannonia is provided by objects from Dunapentele and Tác. See Bíró 1994, 59–60, 106–107, nos. 599–622.

4. Material Remains: Palatine East

1. A small amount of related material, including bone- and ivory-carving debris, was uncovered in an adjacent first-century context between the Meta Sudans and the Colosseum. See De Grossi Mazzorin and Minniti 1995.

2. See Hostetter et al. 1994, 131–153, and the forthcoming final report.

3. See Chapter 2, p. 12, and Chapter 3, pp. 35–36.

4. For the Meta Sudans see Panella 1996. For the Vigna Barberini see M. Royo, in Royo et al. 1997, 11–30. For the Velian see Collini 1983. For the Via Sacra and forum area see Morel 1987, 145–155.

5. For the locations of artisanal and commercial activities in Rome and imperial attempts to regulate them see Morel 1987. In addition to defined market areas, such as the Macellum Magnum and the Markets of Trajan, small-scale tabernae that housed shops as well as artisanal and industrial activities flourished throughout the city, including the area around the Atrium Vestae, for example, along the south side of the Via Nova, and along the clivus Palatinus and the Via di San Gregorio.

6. The term "workshop" and its various definitions are discussed by Rudolph 1988, 524–35.

7. Evidence for bone working on a small scale has been published from numerous Roman excavations, especially in Britain and northern Europe. See MacGregor 1985, 44–54.

8. See Peña in Hostetter et al. 1994, 154–60; Peña 1998.

9. Cf. Carthage (Hutchinson and Reese in Humphrey 1989, 549–51) where bone-working evidence comes from a series of dumps outside the back wall of the circus. For a sculptor's "workshop" at Aphrodisias see Rockwell 1991.

10. See Chapter 3, pp. 31–32.

11. Esquiline: Talamo 1987–1988, 60, Fig. 70; Cambridge: Letta 1984, 98, no. 42; Nicholls 1979, 7, 12, Fig. 3, Pl. VIa. See also Cremona: Letta 1984, 106, no. 121; Bianchi 2000, 73–74, nos. C.a.3–5; Cologne: Letta 1984, 97–98, 111, nos. 37, 46, 182; Talamo 1987–1988, 78, Fig.106; Vindonissa: Letta 1984, 98, 107, nos. 43, 44, 125; Talamo 1987–1988, 89, 91, 93, Fig. 3.115, 116, 117 (all 1st c. B.C.–A.D.).

12. Béal 1991, 303–304, nos. 54–55, Fig. 14. For similar molding on the couch from Aosta see Letta 1984, 98, nos. 40–41; Talamo 1987–1988, 85, Fig. 113.

13. An almost identical plaque surfaced in association with small amounts of bone- and ivory-carving debris in an adjacent first-century context between the Meta Sudans and the Colosseum. See De Grossi Mazzorin and Minniti 1995, 372, 374, Fig. 2.8.

14. Cucuron: Béal 1986, 112–113, Fig. 4; 1991, 303–304, Figs. 13, 14, no. 52. For Aosta, Vindonissa, and Cologne see Letta 1984, 97, 98, 107, 111, nos. 37, 40, 41, 43, 44, 125, 182, Pl. IX; Talamo 1987–1988, 78, Fig. 106; 85, Fig. 113; 95, Fig. 118.

15. Cf. Nicholls 1979, 27, n. 7, Pl. VIa.

16. Gaul: Béraud and Gébara 1986, 193, nos. A1–A33, Figs. 6–7; Aosta: Letta 1984, 98, nos. 40–41; Talamo 1987–1988, 85, Fig. 113; Chieti: Talamo 1987–1988, 87, Fig.114; Vindonissa: Letta 1984, 98, 107, nos. 43, 44, 125; Talamo 1987–1988, 89, Fig. 115. Similar examples survive from Pheidias's workshop as well; see Schiering 1991, 162, Pl. 55a.

17. Béraud and Gébara 1986, 193, nos. B44–B57, Fig. 7:10.

18. Cf. Cremona and Abruzzo: Letta 1984, 104, 106, nos. 93–96, 121; Bianchi 2000, 101–104, Fig. 2.

19. Aielli: Letta 1984, 96, no. 20; Nicholls 1979, 21, no. 3. Cambridge: Letta 1984, 98, no. 42; Nicholls 1979, 20, 21, Fig. 7, Pl. Xb.

20. See Bianchi 2000, 27, 31; Nicholls 1979, 4, 7, 10, nos. A3, A11a, Fig. 1.

21. Cambridge: Letta 1984, 98, no. 42; Nicholls 1979, 4, no. A7, Pl. Va,c, Fig. 1; Cremona: Letta 1984, 106, no. 121; Bianchi 2000, 25, 29–30, nos. A.b.I.4, A.b.II.7, A.b.II.13–14; Vindonissa: Letta 1984, 98, 107, nos. 43, 44, 125; Talamo 1987–1988, 89, Fig. 115; Gaul: Béal 1986, 113–114, Figs. 2, 5, 6; Béal 1991, 287–288, no. 2, Fig. 1.2; Cologne: Letta 1984, 97, 98, 111, nos. 37, 46, 182; Talamo 1986–1987, 78, Fig. 106.

22. See Nicholls 1979, 5–6, no. A11, Figs. 3, 4, Pl. VIb; Gaul: Béal 1991, 311, Fig. 16; Aosta: Letta 1984, 98, nos. 40–41; Talamo 1987–1988, 85, Fig. 113; Vindonissa: Letta 1984, 98, 107, nos. 43, 44, 125; Talamo 1987–1988, 89, 91, Figs. 115, 116; Cologne: Letta 1984, 97, 98, 111, nos. 37, 46, 182; Talamo 1987–1988, 78, Fig. 106.

23. See Nicholls 1979, 20–21, no. D1, Pl. Xb; Béal and Feugère 1981; Maguire et al. 1989, 226, no. 141. For hinge lids see Bíró 1994, 56–58; MacGregor 1985, 204.

24. Cf. Béal 1983a, 337–341, who classifies these objects as "objets circulaires divers et indetermines."

25. See Fremersdorf 1940; MacGregor 1985, 203–205; Bíró 1994, 57–58.

26. See S. Smith (glass) and B. Ault and L. Flusche (metal) in the forthcoming final report of the excavation.

27. See Chapter 3, p. 18. For nails used in the manufacture of couches see Béal 1991, 309–310, Fig.15; Nicholls 1979, Pl. Xb.

28. On residuality in these contexts see Peña 1998.

29. Rome: E. Talamo in Vetere et al. 1983, 66–69, no. 14 (2nd c.); Dacia: Virgili and Viola 1990, 110–111, nos. 220.9, 221.3, Figs. 34, 44, 47 (2nd c.). For boxes presumed to be of Egyptian manufacture and dated to the fourth–fifth century see Cairo: Strzygowski 1904, 171–175, Pls. XI–XIII; Weitzmann 1979, 332–333, no. 311; Loverdou-Tsigarida 1986, no. 16, Figs. 1–3; Albertoni 1991–1992, 368, Fig. 50; London: Longhurst 1927, 20; Albertoni 1991–1992, 360, 363–364, Figs. 44–46; Baltimore: Randall 1985, 90, 91, no. 135, Pl. 44; Albertoni 1991–1992, 361, Fig. 43. For diamond and triangular inlays see Abruzzo: Letta 1984, 104, nos. 93–96, Pl. VIIb (1st c. B.C.–A.D.). Rome: Virgili and Viola 1990, 111, no. 221, 3, Figs. 44, 47 (2nd c.); Corinth: Davidson 1952, 136, no. 959, Pl. 69 (not later than 3rd c.); Weitzmann 1979, 332, no. 311 (Egypt, 4th c.).

30. Albertoni 1991–1992, 343, Fig. 1.

31. See Stern 2000; Scranton et al. 1978, 68–69; Scranton and Ramage 1967, 141–146. The final report by Stern is forthcoming.

32. Cf. Egypt: Marangou 1976, nos. 76, 86, 143, 156, 165, Pls. 24, 26, 45, 47, 49; Leptis Magna: Joly et al. 1992, 213, no. 50 (3rd–5th c.). See also Randall 1985, 92–93, no. 142; Gonosová and Kondoleon 1994, 202–203, no. 66 (5th c.). An earlier painted example is from Murecine (Pompeii): Donati 1996, 152, 283, no. 44 (Flavian).

33. See Chapter 3, p. 35.

34. Weitzmann 1979, 100–101, 107, nos. 91, 98.

35. See Albertoni 1991–1992; Bonacasa Carra and Albertoni in Ensoli and La Rocca 2000, 353, 471–472, nos. 73–82; Donati 1996, 217, 308, nos. 121–122. Cf. Albertoni 1994, 161, Fig.1, 166, Fig. 3, for plaques from the southwest Palatine and the Antiquarium at Rome.

36. Similar basket-carrying putti appear on the Projecta casket. See Donati 1996, 261–261, no. 143.

37. Volbach 1979, 125, no. 210, Pl. 100 (4th c.). Cf.
    Loverdou-Tsagarida 1986, 330, no. 88, Fig. 53 (4th–
    5th c.).

38. See Lányi 1972, 103–106, 167, Fig. 61; Bíró 1994, 35–
    39, 93–97, nos. 387–441, Pls. XXXVII–L; 27–28, 74–
    75, nos. 64–87, Pls. X–XI; MacGregor 1985, 73–98.

39. The Brescia casket and the Cathedra of Maximianus pro-
    vide examples of boxes and furniture with straight rather
    than turned legs. Consular diptychs also depict unturned
    legs, either rectilinear or in the shape of animal legs,
    which would have been veneered if decorated with bone
    or ivory. See Volbach 1976, 77, 78, no. 107, Pl. 57; 93,
    94, no. 140, Pls. 72, 73; 32–34, nos. 8–11, Pls. 4, 5.

40. Cf. Nicholls 1979, 4, no. A6, Pl. IIIb; Gaul: Béal 1991,
    287–288, no. 15, Fig. 1.15; Cologne: Letta 1984, 97, 98,
    111, nos. 37, 46, 182, Talamo 1987–1988, 78, Fig. 106.

41. Schiering 1991, 162, Pl. 35a.

42. Cf. Ayalon and Sorek 1999, 60, Fig. 83 (Roman);
    Volbach 1976, 53, 57, 59, 60, 64–65, 93, 94, 99, nos.
    58, 66, 73, 84, 85, 140, 150, Pls. 31, 38, 42, 46, 73, 79.
    Spiral decoration appears on cylindrical elements identi-
    fied as knife handles as well. See Béal 1983a, 73, no. 74,
    Pl. XI. Furniture mounts with similarly irregular spiral
    decoration are common in earlier periods. Cf. Vindo-
    nissa: Letta 1984, 98, 107, nos. 43, 44, 125; Talamo
    1987–1988, 89, Fig. 115 (1st c. B.C.–A.D.).

43. Schiering 1991, 162, Pl. 55a. Cf. Béal 1981 and 1983a,
    141–145; Bíró 1994, 56–58, Fig. 32.

44. See Béal 1983a, 283–285; MacGregor 1985, 132–133.

45. Cf. Bíró 1994, 103, no. 553, Pl. LXIV; MacGregor
    1985, 137, 186–187, Fig. 101, 11 (antler).

46. MacGregor 1985, 135–136, Fig. 172a,b,d.

47. Murray 1941.

48. Carthage: Henig in Hurst and Roskams 1984, 190–192,
    nos. 77–82, Figs. 63–64 (6th c.–modern contexts);
    Saraçhane: Gill 1986, 260–261, nos. 506, 507, 509–513,
    Fig. N (7th c.–modern).

49. Weitzmann 1979, 330–332, no. 310. The late antique
    fashion for hairpins may be connected to the revival of
    hairstyles associated with Faustina the Elder and members
    of the Antonine family. See St. Clair 1996b, 150–151.

50. Walker 2000, 50–51, nos. 12–13; 69–70, no. 29; 74, no.
    33; 89, no. 50; 94, no. 55; 121–122, no. 78; 135–136,
    no. 87 (late 1st–4th c.). See also Weitzmann 1979, 288,
    no. 266 (4th c.). On a 4th c. mummy portrait from
    Saqqara preserved in Dresden (Albertinum Museum, no.
    Aeg.778), the deceased is depicted with three apparently
    bone hairpins arranged in a row.

51. See Eygun 1933, 152, 153, 159; Cochet 1855, 49, cited
    in Béal 1983a, 183, who also notes exceptions.

52. For the type see Marangou 1976, 108, no. 118, Pl. 40 (late
    Roman); Buitron and Oliver in Randall 1985, 70–71, no.
    80 (1st–2nd c.); Weitzmann 1979, 137–138, no. 115 (early

6 c.?). For Venus finials see Béal 1984, 58, no. 241 (with
    one hand over breast); Cappelli 1992, 131–132, no. 13,
    Fig. 64; Ward-Perkins and Claridge 1976, no. 71b,f.

53. Davidson 1952, 278–279. See also Béal 1983a, 20–23,
    201–202, no. 708.

54. Brownish stain on tips is common and has been attrib-
    uted to the use of hot oils or cosmetics into which the
    pins were dipped (Davidson 1952, 279), but the limited
    nature of the staining and the fact that many functioned
    as hairpins makes such an explanation problematic. The
    tips may simply be most vulnerable to staining from long
    burial underground.

55. Cf. Béal 1983a, 183–237; 1984, 49–59, with extensive
    parallels cited for most examples.

56. See Virgili and Viola 1990, 104–107, nos. 196–217,
    with most examples of unknown provenance or from the
    antiquities market. For Corinth see Davidson 1952,
    278–287.

57. For a discussion of types see Clarke 1979, 301–314. For
    an example of a bracelet constructed this way using jet,
    see Kleiner and Matheson 1996, 177–178, no. 137.

58. A number of Roman dolls preserve rings and bracelets in
    various materials. See Rinaldi 1956, 118–119. For a bone
    bust of a woman with a bone necklace see Virgili and
    Viola 1990, 104–105, no. 200 (Constantinian).

59. See Bíró 1994, 26–28, nos. 64–87, Pls. X–XI; Clarke
    1979, 313–314; MacGregor 1985, 112–113, Fig. 63;
    Lányi 1972, 167, Fig. 61.

60. Interestingly, however, at Corinth all catalogued bracelets
    are bronze or glass. See Davidson 1952, 262.

61. Recent studies of these grave goods are DeSantis 1994
    and Felle et al. 1994, 114–120.

62. Felle et al. 1994, 154. For a discussion of types see Clarke
    1979, 301–314.

63. Examples of dolls or their imprints in situ are collected in
    Felle et al. 1994, 115–116, n. 45. For an example from
    the tomb of a septuagenarian Vestal Virgin see Manson
    1978, 124–125, 338–40, no. 390; Mancini 1930, 353–
    369; Del Moro in Felle et al. 1994, 116, n. 45. Examples
    said to be from the catacombs, but without a secure con-
    text include: Salvetti 1978, 109–111, nos. 5, 6.

64. Manson 1978, 121–128, 332–348, nos. 386–404. The
    most famous example (2nd c.) is preserved in the collec-
    tion of the Capitoline Museum (Sommella in Vetere et
    al. 1983, 49–56, no. 10).

65. See Kanzler 1903, 4, nos. 116–119, Pl. XIII (Museo
    Profano), 6, Fig. 21 (Museo Gregoriano), 7, nos. 3–5, Pl.
    I (Museo Cristiano); Elderkin 1930, 472–475, Figs. 24–
    25; Morey 1936, 51–52, nos. A6–10, 1136–1140, Pl. II,
    and 55, no. A41, 1154, Pl. V (misidentified as furniture
    leg); Rinaldi 1955–1956, 104–129; Salvetti 1978, 109–
    111, nos. 5–6; Manson 1978, 130–131, 348–362, nos.
    405–432; Bordenache Battaglia 1983, 115–117, 133–

134, Figs. 9–10; St. Clair in Hostetter et al. 1994, 169; Donati 1996, 284–285, nos. 181, 182; Ostia: Ostia Museum inv. nos. 4319, 5242, 5243.

66. Manson 1978, 130–131, 363–370, nos. 433–450.

67. Ricci in Paroli 1997, 264, 265, Fig. 10, 23.

68. Hutchinson and Reese in Humphrey 1989, 566, 575–577, nos. 46, 47, Fig. 16. Cf. Sagui and Paroli 1990, 262, 264, Fig. 10.2, 3, 4, identified as intarsia.

69. See Chapter 2, note 45.

70. See for example the eleventh-century Venice, Bib. Marciana, cod.gr. Z479, fol. 36r, reproduced in Cutler 1985a, 38.

71. Cutler's close scrutiny of a large group of ivories has produced impressive evidence of the variety of tools employed in late antique and Byzantine ivory carving. See 1985a, 37–50; 1994, 79–152.

72. For the metal tools see the forthcoming final report by B. Ault and L. Flusche.

73. Becker 1999–2000, 10. See also MacGregor 1985, 30. In some cases the epiphyses were retained with the long bone and their shape exploited. See St. Clair 1995–1996.

74. See MacGregor 1985, 130, 134, Fig. 71m. (7th–8th c.).

75. Gaitzsch (1980, 72–98, 181–205) published saws and hammers from Roman contexts in a number of shapes and sizes.

76. For dice created from horizontal sections of bone with the cavity filled by a bone plug see MacGregor 1985, 130, Fig. 71e; Béal 1983a, 345–346, nos. 1228–1231, Pl. LIX.

77. Cf. Béal 1983a, 24–25, and Evely 1992, 8, who present detailed analyses of sawing procedures.

78. For similarly prefabricated strips on Byzantine boxes see Cutler 1985a, 35.

79. Cf. Béal 1983a, 23–27; Evely 1992, 7–8.

80. Cf. Stern 2000, 362.

81. See the forthcoming final metalwork report by B. Ault and L. Flusche.

82. Ibid.

83. For examples of center bits or scribing tools see MacGregor 1985, 60–61, Fig. 38; Hutchinson and Reese in Humphrey 1989, 593. For compasses see Petrie 1917, 60, Pl. 72.

84. It has been suggested that Romans also were familiar with the brace, a cranked shaft, which took interchangeable bits. See Hodges 1976, 117. For examples of Roman bits see Gaitzsch 1980, 19–36.

85. Mütz 1972, 29–30. See also MacGregor 1985, 58–59; Hodges 1976, 117–118; Hutchinson and Reese in Humphrey 1989, 560–61.

86. Frequently the matrix is longer than the object and sawn off so that no indentation is present on the finished object. For a description of the procedures associated with lathe turning see Béal 1983a, 30–34.

87. Similar evidence in bone, but not ivory, survives from Carthage (Hutchinson and Reese in Humphrey 1989, Fig. 68) and from Ashkelon (Wapnish 1991, 56; Ayalon and Sorek 1999, 17, Fig. 7).

88. Schiering 1991, 160.

89. The chambers to the south of the apsidal hall were deliberately buried, in the fourth century, perhaps before being finished. See Hostetter et al. 1994, 149–151.

90. On the Palatine in late antiquity see Augenti 1996, esp. 27–45. For the Vigna Barberini see Villedieu 1995; F. Chausson and E. Hubert in Royo et al. 1997, 79–85, 89–140. For the Schola Praeconum, which similarly went out of use ca. 430–440, see Whitehouse et al. 1982.

91. For burials within the walls see Meneghini and Santangeli Valenzani 1993. Burials at Palatine East are a continuation of the small cemetery to the south and west in the Vigna Barberini. See Rizzo et al. 1999. For burials around the Colosseum see Rea 1993, 77–80.

92. Caillet (1986) argues convincingly for Constantinople as the major carving center during this period. See also Cutler 1993, 176–182.

93. Recent scholarship is summarized by Hodges in Paroli and Delogu 1993, 353–363.

94. Especially valuable for this topic are the proceedings of three symposia: Paroli and Delogu 1993; Delogu 1996; Paroli 1997. See also and Ensoli and La Rocca 2000.

95. Carignani et al. 1990, 75–76. For the late antique and medieval history of the Celian see Pavolini 1993.

96. An overview of the site and its history is provided in Manacorda et al. 2000.

97. Ricci 1997. For the Middle Ages see Saguì and Paroli 1990.

98. Saguì and Manacorda 1995, with previous bibliography.

99. Manacorda et al. 2000, 86, 88. Cf. an ivory arm of a cross in low relief from the Velian Hill in Rome, dated to the same period (92).

Catalogue

1. Radiocarbon dating of both materials is discussed in Gibson and Southworth 1990.

2. For the stratigraphy of the site see Hostetter et al. 1991, 1994, and the forthcoming final report. On residuality in the late antique contexts see Peña 1998.

3. Similar evidence in bone, but not ivory, survives from Carthage and from Ashkelon. See Chapter 4, note 87.

4. In some cases the matrix is longer than the finished object and the end is sawn off, leaving no indentation on the object. For a description of the procedures associated with lathe turning see Béal 1983a, 30–34.

5. For comparable evidence of drill holes see Béal 1983a, 27. For examples of Roman bits see Gaitzsch 1980, 19–36. MacGregor (1985, 36–37) provides evidence for the use of tools resembling crown or trepanning saws for cutting disks from bone.

6. Petrie 1917, 60, Pl. 72.

7. For a discussion of prefabricated strips on Byzantine caskets see Cutler 1985a, 35–36.

8. Most recently see Bonacasa Carra in Ensoli and La Rocca 2000, 353–358. For intaglio in late antiquity see E. Rodziewicz 1995; Loverdou-Tsigarida 1986. Michaelides (1990) attributes an example from Cyprus to the second century.

9. Cf. Abruzzo: Letta 1984, Pl. VIIb (1st c B.C.–A.D.); Rome: Virgili and Viola 1990, 111, no. 221, 3, Figs. 44, 47 (2nd c.); Corinth: Davidson 1952, 136, no. 959, Pl. 69 (not later than 3rd c.); Egypt?: Weitzmann 1979, 332, no. 311 (4th c.).

10. Volbach 1976, 111, 112, 117, 118, nos. 176, 177, 179, 191, 193a, 194, Pls. 89, 90, 95, 96 (late antique).

11. Sackett 1992, 383, Pl. 317.12 (2nd c.).

12. Cf. Gaul: Béraud and Gébara 1986, 190–191, nos. C12–15, Fig. 4.6; Aosta: Talamo 1992, 85, Fig. 113; Chieti: Talamo 1992, 87, Fig. 114; Vindonissa: Talamo 1992, 89, 91, Figs 115–116.

13. Béraud and Gébara 1986, 193, nos. B44–57, Fig. 7, 10.

14. See above note.

15. Cf. Gaul: Béal 1986, 112–115, Figs. 2, 5, 6, 8; Béraud and Gébara 1986, 193, nos. A20–29, Fig. 6.4, 5; Italy: Talamo 1987–1988, 35, Fig. 22 (Rome) and 85, Fig. 103 (Aosta).

16. Cf. Nicholls 1979, 4, no. A6, Pl. IIIb. See also Gaul: Béal 1991, 287–288, no. 15, Fig. 1.15; Cologne: Talamo 1987–1988, 78, Fig. 106.

17. Cf. funerary couches: Nicholls 1979, 7–8, Pl. VIa; Talamo 1987–88, 78, 85–95, Figs. 106, 113–118 (1st c. B.C./A.D.). Late antique caskets are equally varied. See Randall 1985, 90–91, no. 135 (4th–5th c.).

18. Rome: Talamo 1987–1988, 260, Fig. 70 (see also 78, Fig. 106; 89, Fig. 115; 91 Fig.116; 93, Fig. 117); Cambridge: Nicholls 1979, 7, 12, Fig. 3, Pl. VIa. (1st c. B.C.–A.D.). For boxes see Randall 1985, 90, no. 135, 177, colorplate 44; Weitzmann 1979, 332–333, no. 311; Marangou 1976, 117, no. 169. Similar framing elements appear as integral parts of many late antique ivory diptychs and some caskets. See Volbach 1976.

19. Albertoni 1991–1992, 353–358, Figs. 19–40.

20. Cf. Egypt: Marangou 1976, 132, no. 267c, Pl. 67 (n.d.).

21. Cf. Vermeule 1989, Pl. 60 (Hellenistic?); Chieti and Rome: Talamo 1987–88, 87, Fig. 114, and 59, Fig. 69 (1st c B.C.–A.D.). The design is closely paralleled on the border of an ivory pyxis from the Sancta Sanctorum in the Museo Sacro of the Vatican, dated to the fourth century (Volbach, 1976, no. 90, p.70, Pl. 50). See also Gaul: Béal 1983a, 362, no. 1310, Pl. XIX; Egypt: Marangou 1976, 260h, 261h, 263h, p. 131, Pl. 67 (all borderless strips).

22. Cf. Egypt: Marangou 1976, 132, no. 265a, Pl. 67, where a similar technique creates a spiral pattern (n.d.).

23. Volbach 1976, 32–33, nos. 8, 9, Pls. 4, 5.

24. Petrie and Mackay 1915, 1, 50, no. 7 (4th c.).

25. Albertoni 1991–1992, 357–358, 360, 368–369, Figs. 38, 50–51. For the diptychs see Volbach 1976, 33–34, 35–37, nos. 11, 16, 18, 20, 21, Pls. 8, 9 (6th c.).

26. Cf. Pannonia: Bíró 1994, 27–28, 74–75, nos. 64–87, Pls. X–XI (bracelets); Gloucester: Hassall and Rhodes 1974, 73, no. 36i, Fig. 28 (furniture mounts).

27. Gill 1986, 229, no. 41, Fig. 298 (from a 10th c. context).

28. Cf. Great Britain: Hostetter and Howe 1997, 321, Fig. 147, no. 481g (furniture or casket mount, late Roman); Pannonia: Bíró 1994, 74, no. 71, Pl. I, 48 (bracelet); 97, no. 439, Pl. L (comb plate without incisions, late Roman).

29. Cf. MacGregor 1985, 93, Fig. 51 (both Roman and early medieval examples); Pannonia: Bíró 1994, 96, 185–186, nos. 425–427, Pls. XLVII–XLVIII, (Roman) with similar decoration.

30. For metallic backing on medieval caskets see MacGregor 1985, 199; Bíró 1994, 74, nos. 80–82, Pl. XI (bracelet, Roman). South Shields: Allason-Jones and Miket, 1984, 60–62, nos. 232–235. For metallic backing on combs see St. Clair and McLachlin, 1989, 101–102, no. 62; Castle Copse: R. Payne in Hostetter and Howe 1997, 312–313, no. 465, Fig. 145 (4th c.).

31. Gaul: Béal 1991, 303–304, Fig. 14. 55 (1st c. B.C.–A.D.). Cf. Rome: De Grossi Mazzorin and Minniti 1995, 372, 374, Fig. 2.3, 4 (1st c. A.D.); Chieti: Talamo 1992, 87, Fig. 114 (1st c. B.C./A.D.); Corinth: Vermeule 1989, Pl. 60 (Hellenistic). Albertoni 1991–1992, 358–359, no. 22, Fig. 39 (intaglio, 4th c.?); Volbach 1976, 34–37, 104, nos. 16–21, 161, Pls. 8–9, 82 (late antique).

32. Cf. MacGregor 1985, 97–98, Fig. 54.

33. Cf. Volbach 1976, 53, 59–60, 65, nos. 58, 73, 85 Pls. 31, 42, 46. Spiral decoration appears on cylindrical elements identified as knife handles as well. See Béal 1983a, 73, no. 74, Pl. XI.

34. Cf. Nicholls 1979, 11.

35. Davidson 1952, 128, no. 871, Pl. 64. Knife handles are often similarly topped with a knob (Saraçhane: Sackett 1992, 387, no. 99, Pl. 322 (Severan context).

36. Talamo 1987–1988, 89, Fig. 115 (1st c. B.C.–A.D.).

37. Cf. Volbach 1976, 53, 59–60, 65, nos. 58, 73, 85, Pls. 31, 42, 46. Spiral decoration appears on cylindrical elements identified as knife handles as well. See Béal 1983a, 73, no. 74, Pl. XI.

38. Saguì and Paroli 1990, 524, 525, no. 657, Fig. 160, 10 (second half of the 14th–15th c.).

39. Cf. Weitzmann 1979, 330–332, no. 310 (4th c.); Volbach 1976, 57, 64–65, 93–94, 99, nos. 66, 84, 140, 150, Pls. 38, 46, 73, 79 (late antique).

40. See Chapter 3.

41. Béal 1991, 303–304, Fig. 14.54; Cf. Pannonia: Bíró
1994, 93, nos. 387, 389, 390, Pls. XXXVII—XXXVIII.
Similar motifs decorate Roman combs (MacGregor 1985,
89, Fig. 50).

42. De Grossi Mazzorin and Minniti 1995, 372, 374,
Fig. 2.8.

43. Béal 1986, 112–113, no. 8, Fig. 4, and 1991, 303–304,
Figs. 13, 14 (1st c. B.C.–A.D.); Cf. Aosta: Talamo 1987–
1988, 85, Fig. 113 (1st c. B.C.–A.D.).

44. Cf. Nicholls 1979, 10, Fig. 1; Gaul: Béal 1986, 113–114,
Figs. 2, 5, 6; Béal 1991, 287–288, no. 2, Fig. 1.2.

45. Nicholls 1979, 4, no. A7, Pl. Va,c, Fig. 1. Cf. Cologne:
Talamo 1987–1988, 78, Fig. 106.

46. Cologne: Talamo 1987–1988, 78, Fig. 106; Vindonissa:
Talamo 1987–88, 91, Fig. 91; Lyon: Béal 1983a, 369,
no. 1320, Pl. LX (undated); Corinth: Vermeule 1989,
273, Pl. 60.

47. Weitzmann 1979, 330–332, no. 310 (4th c.); Volbach
1976, 57, 64–65, 93–94, 99, nos. 66, 84, 140, 150, Pls.
38, 46, 73, 79. Cf. Vindonissa: Talamo 1987–1988, 93,
Fig. 117 (1st c. B.C.–A.D.).

48. Engemann 1987, 174, Pl. 19.

49. Volbach 1976, 80, no. 111, Pl. 60.

50. Cf. Murecine (Pompeii): Donati 1996, 152, 283, no. 44
(Flavian); Egypt: Marangou 1976, nos. 76, 86, 143, 156,
165, Pls. 24, 26, 45, 47, 49; Leptis Magna: Joly et al.
1992, 213, no. 50 (3rd–5th c.). See also Longhurst 1927,
20; Albertoni 1991–1992, 360, 363–364, Fig. 46;
Randall 1985, 92–93, no. 142; Gonosová and
Kondoleon 1994, 202–203, no. 66.

51. Cf. Vetere et al. 1983, 67, 69, B3, B4, F3.

52. For the type see Loverdou-Tsagarida 1986; Randall
1985, 88, no. 144; E. Rodziewicz, 1995. For a hunting
scene in this technique see Weitzmann 1972, 27–28, no.
16, Pl. XIII.

53. Loverdou-Tsagarida 1986, 330, no. 88, Fig. 53 (4th–5th
c.); Volbach 1976, 125, no. 210, Pl. 100 (4th c.).

54. Cf. Graeven 1903, 6 no. 3. A maenad in the Virginia
Museum of Fine Arts clutches a disk divided into eight
sections (Gonosová and Kondoleon 1994, 198–199,
no. 64).

55. Cf. Volbach 1976, 87–88, no. 125, Pl. 66 (Murano Diptych, Ravenna, Museo nazionale, 6th c.?); 98–99, no.
149 (unknown provenance; Lyon, Musée des Beaux Arts,
6th c.?).

56. Saraçhane: Gill 1986, 229, no. 32, Pl. 295, Fig. a (ivory
and without attachment holes). Kenchreai: Isthmia
Museum (unpublished, without attachment holes)
(4th c.?).

57. Cf. Weitzmann 1979, 100–101, no. 91; Volbach 1976,
35–37, nos. 16, 18, 21, Pls. 8, 9.

58. Gaul: Béal 1983a, 141–145, and 1983b; Pannonia: Bíró
1994, 56–58, Fig. 32 (all late antique).

59. Gaul: Béraud and Gébara 190–191, nos. C12–15, Fig.
4.6; Aosta: Talamo 1992, 85, Fig. 113; Chieti: Talamo
1992, 87, Fig. 114; Vindonissa: Talamo 1992, 89, 91,
Figs 115–116.

60. Cf. Vindonissa: Talamo 1987–1988, 89, Fig. 115.

61. Randall 1985, 68, no. 72.

62. Gaul: Béal 1984, 20, no. 38 (1st c.?). For the pyxis shape
see Béal 1983a, 80–81, Type A VI, 2, Pls. XIV–XV; Béal
and Feugère 1991, 118, 119, Type 3, Fig. 4 (1st c., probably imported into Gaul).

63. Delos: Déonna 1938, 245–248, Pl. 79.668.5
(Greco-Roman); Gaul: Béal 1981, and 1983a, 141–145.

64. Cf. Gaul: Béraud and Gébara 1986, 193, nos. Fig. 6.4, 5.

65. Cf. Corinth: Davidson 1952, 196, no. 1497, Pl. 89
(Byzantine).

66. Cf. Olympia: Schiering 1991, 160, Fig. 55a (5th c. B.C.);
Gaul: Béal 1983a, 91, no. 103, Pl. XVII (possible furniture mount, 1st–3rd c.).

67. Bíró 1994, 108, 637–638, Pl. LXXVII.

68. Cf. Delos: Déonna 1938, 248, Pl. 79.668.5 (Greco-
Roman); Pannonia: Bíró 1994, 447, 450, nos. 97–98, Pl.
LII (Roman).

69. Delos: Déonna 1938, 245–248, Figs. 276–283, Pl.
7.666, 667 (Greco-Roman); Ashkelon: Wapnish 1991,
55 (undated). Cologne: Talamo 1987–1988, 78, Fig.
106. See also Bíró 1994, 105, no. 576, Pl. LXVII
(3rd c.); Saraçhane: Gill 1986, 227, no. 11 (7th—8th c.
context).

70. See Nicholls 1979, 5–6, no. A11, Fig. 1; Béal 1991, 311,
Fig. 16.

71. Gaul: Béraud and Gébara 190–191, nos. C12–15, Fig.
4.6; 1986, Aosta: Talamo 1992, 85, Fig. 113; Chieti:
Talamo 1992, 87, Fig. 114; Vindonissa: Talamo 1992,
89, 91, Figs. 115–116.

72. Rome: Ricci in Paroli 1997, 265, 267, Fig. 12, 2 (7th c.),
identified as pyxis lid. Cf. Nicholls 1979, 20–21, no. D1,
Pl. Xb (1st c. B.C.–A.D.); Maguire et al. 1989, 226, no.
141. For pyxides see Béal and Feugère 1991. For hinge
lids see Bíró 1994, 56–58; MacGregor 1985, 204.

73. Cf. Gaul: Béraud and Gébara 1986, 198–199, nos. F1–5,
Fig. 10, 8–9; Vindonissa: Talamo 1987–1988, 91, Fig.
116 (1st c. B.C.–A.D.).

74. Gaul: Béraud and Gébara 1986, 190–191, nos. C12–15,
Fig. 4.6. Vindonissa: Talamo 1987–1988, 91, Fig. 116;
Corinth: Davidson 1952, 136, no. 966, Pl. 69 (Roman).

75. Bíró 1994,104, 207, no. 586, Pl. LXIX (lid from a hinge
joint). Cf. Corinth: Davidson 1952, 220, no. 1702, Pl.
99, without a central hole, identified as a counter
(Roman).

76. Nicholls 1979, 7, A11b, Pl. 8b; Pannonia: Bíró 1994,
105, no. 587, Pl. LXIX, identified as hinge lid or spindle
weight (Roman); Ashkelon: Wapnish 1991, 56, identified
as buttons or whorls (n.d.); Knossos: Sackett 1992, 387,

no. E107, Pls. 318, 322, identified as button (late 2nd–early 3rd c.).

77. Cf. Knossos: Sackett 1992, 380, no. 10, Pl. 320 (identified as disk bead, Hellenistic); Gaul: Béal 1983a, 328, no. 1176, Pl. LV, but with different profile, identified as spindle whorl (1st–2nd c.).

78. Cf. Ashkelon: Wapnish 1991, 56, identified as buttons or whorls (n.d.).

79. Aosta: Talamo 1987–1988, 85, Fig. 113; Chieti: Talamo 1987–1988, 87, Fig. 114; Vindonissa: Talamo 1987–1988, 89, Fig. 115. Gaul: Béal 1983a, 321–330.

80. For hinges see Béal 1983a, 101–126. For the use of pigment see Bíró 1994, 106, nos. 592, 593, Pl. LXX.

81. Béal distinguishes two types, of which this is A XI, 1 (1984, 26, no. 58, Pl. 4). Cf. Béal 1983a, 101–126, esp. 105, 109, nos. 143, 170, Pls. XX–XXI (1st–2nd c.); Rome: De Grossi Mazzorin and Minnitti 1995, 372, 13; Settefinestre: Ricci 1985, 54, Pl. 10.6; Ostia IV 1977, Pl. 62, Fig. 511; Delos: Déonna 1938, 242–245, Pl. 78.644–651 (Roman).

82. Cf. Béal 1983a, Type A XI, 2, 118–119, nos. 278, 289, 290, Pl. XXIII. See also 1984, 27–28, nos. 69, 84, 88, Pl. 4.

83. See Chapter 3, pp. 16–17.

84. Béal 1983a, 183–219; 1984, 49–59. See also Bíró 1994, 30–35.

85. Gaul: Béal 1983a, 183–184, Type A XX, 1 (pyramidal summits), nos. 574–577, Pl. XXXIV (n.d.). He notes unpublished examples from recently excavated first-century contexts.

86. Cf. Corinth: Davidson 1952, 174, 278, Pl. 147b, for a similar uncatalogued small pin.

87. Gaul: Béal 1983a, 187, Type A XX, 4 includes this type. See no. 598, Pl. XXXIII (n.d.). Cf. Pannonia: Bíró 1994, 31, 77, 150, Type 1, no. 109 (1st–3rd c.); Ostia: Carandini and Panella 1973, 298, Fig. 1018, Pl. XCV (A.D. 80–90); Delos: Déonna 1938, 278, Pl. 717.4, 5, 8 (n.d.); South Shields: Allason-Jones and Miket 1984, 80–81, Type H, nos. 2.458, 468, 470, 471, 476, 479 (5th–7th c.).

88. Gaul: Béal 1983a, 185–186, Type A XX, 3, nos. 587–596, Pl. XXXIII (1st–3rd c.). Cf. Pannonia: Bíró 1994, 77–79, 151–153, nos. 114, 117, 119, 134–151 (n.d.); Ostia: Carandini and Panella 1973, 217, no. 879, Pl. LXXXVIII (first half of the 2nd c.); Troina: Militello 1961, 346, 359–360, Fig. 19, I (Roman); Corinth: Davidson 1952, 280, 287, no. 2386, 2387, Pl. 120 (1st–beginning 2nd c., and late Roman–Byzantine); Salamis: Chavane 1975, 168, 169, nos. 477, 480, 481, Pls. 47, 70 (2nd–3rd c.); Tarsus: Goldman 1951, 397, no. 13, Pl. 271 (150–50 B.C.); Britain: Crummy, 1979, Type I (A.D. 70–200/250); South Shields: Allason-Jones and Miket 1984, 80–81, Type H, nos.

2.452, 455, 463, 466, 472, 478, 478. The two examples illustrated are roughly fashioned (5th–7th c.).

89. Cf. Gaul: Béal 1983a, 187, Type A XX, 5, no. 602, a pin of unknown provenance with a trapezoidal head, "presque plate."

90. Gaul: Béal 1983a, 187–188, Type A XX, 5, nos. 601–608, Pl. XXXIV, no. 608, (A.D. 150–250). Cf. Ostia: Carandini and Panella 1973, 156 no. 790, Pl. LXXXV, and 1977, 66. no. 312, Pl. XLV (A.D. 225–250); Corinth: Davidson 1952, 174, Pl. 147, Fig. b (Roman) ; Conimbriga: Avila Franca 1968, 68, Type I, 5, no. 18, Pl. 1; Alarcâo et al. 1979, 127, 130, nos. 75–83, Pl. XXIX; Pannonia: Lányi 1972, 172, Fig. 66,4 (late antique). Crummy's Type 6 includes pins topped by a reel (1979, 162; 3rd–late 4th/5th c.).

91. Beckmann 1966, 42, Group III, type 54, nos. 49, 51, 54, 55, 75, 77 (2nd–5th c.).

92. Gaul: Béal 1983a, 199–200, Type A XX, 9, nos. 701–702, Pl. XXXV, with rounded bases (second half of the 2nd–3rd c.) He notes that the head becomes more elongated in later examples. Cf. Pannonia: Bíró 1994, 32, 86, 165, Type 2, VIII, no. 286 (undated); Conimbriga: Avila Franca 1968, 13, Type A XI, nos. 57–62, Pl. I; Alarcão et al. 1979, 127, 131, nos. 94 (5th c.)-96 (n.d.), Pl. XXIX; Corinth: Davidson 1952, 279, no. 2331, Pl. 119 (1st–2nd c.). South Shields: Allason-Jones and Miket 1984, 71–72, 87, Type B, nos. 2.335–345, and esp. 2.553 (5th–7th c).

93. Gaul: Béal 1983a 189–193, Type A XX, 7, nos. 612–628 (n.d.), 629–644, Pl. XXXIV (A.D.150–250). See also 209, n. 35. Cf. Virgili and Viola 1990, 107, nos. 214–216; Pannonia: Bíró 1994, 31–32, 78–85, 154–162, Types 2: I, II, V, nos. 152–174, 219–258 (1st–5th c.); Ostia: Carandini and Panella 1977, 393, no. 522, Pl. LXIII, (A.D. 80–90). Luni: Frova 1977, 587, nos. K2101, 2302, Pl. 3.11, 12, 14 (3rd–4th c.); Conimbriga: Alarcão et al. 1979, 128, 131, nos. 101–102, Pl. XXIX; Carthage: Hutchinson and Reese in Humphrey 1989, 570–571, nos. 3–16, Fig. 13 (4th–5th c.); Leptis Magna: Joly et al. 1992, 208–209, nos. Ao.5, 17, Figs. 219, 223 (3rd–5th c.); Britain: Crummy 1979, 161, Type 3 (A.D. 200–late 4th /early 5th c.); South Shields: Allason-Jones and Miket 1984, 68–71, nos. 2.289–334 (5th–7th c.).

94. Beckmann 1966, 23, Group III, no. 48; Conimbriga: Avila-Franca 1968, 86–87, nos. 105–108, Pl. II (5th c.).

95. The term "spherical" is applied more or less strictly by various authors (see Béal 1983a, 209, n. 35). It seems impossible to date this type based on the precise shape or size of the head. The suggestion that spherical heads appear later than elongated ones (Carandini and Panella 1973, 646–647) has not been substantiated.

96. Gaul: Béal 1983a, 196, no. 679, Pl. XXXV (end of the 2nd c.); Cf. Pannonia: Bíró 1994, 32, 80–83, 156–159, Types 2: III, IV, nos. 175–188 and 189–218 (1st–4th

c); Rome: Virgili and Viola 1990, 107, nos. 215, 216; Ostia: Berti et al. 1977, 35, no. 16a, b, Pl. VIII (second half of the 2nd c.); Carandini and Panella 1977, 393, no. 486, Pl. LX (A.D. 90–140); Carthage: Hutchinson and Reese in Humphrey 1989, nos. 6, 8, 9, Fig. 13, p. 571 (4th–5th c.); Leptis Magna: Joly et al. 1992, 208–209, no. Ao.8, Fig. 221 (3rd–5th c.); Conimbriga: Alarcâo et al. 1979, 131, no. 105, Pl. XXIX (5th c.); Avila Franca 1968, 69, Type VII, nos. 45–51, Pl. I; South Shields: Allason-Jones and Miket 1984, 68, no. 290 (roughly fashioned) (A.D. 600–700); Portchester Castle: J. Webster in Cunliffe 1975, 215, no. 81, Pl. 116 (end 3rd–4th c.).

97. Ostia: Carandini and Panella 1977, 66, 273, Pl. XLV, 312 (A.D. 200/225–240); Luni: Frova 1977, 409, no. CS1393, Pl. 199.13; Pannonia: Bíró 1994, 32, 86, 164, Type 2, VII, nos. 275–284 (4th c.); Lányi 1972, 172, Fig. 66,7 (late antique); (Pannonia) Britain: Crummy 1979, 161–162, Type 4 (A.D. 250–late 4th–early 5th c.).

98. Gaul: Béal 1983a, 193–199, Type A XX, 8, nos. 645–700 (nos. 678–700, 2nd–3rd c.), Pls. XXX, XXXIV, XXXV. Cf. Pannonia: Bíró 1994, 32–33, 86–87, 165, Types 2, IX, X, nos. 287–293 (late 3rd–early 5th c.); Ostia: Carandini and Panella 1977, 393, Pl. LX, 486 (A.D. 90–140); Luni: Frova 1977, 324, no. CM3442, Pl. 176, 6 (4th c.); Carthage: Hutchinson and Reese in Humphrey 1989, 571, nos. 17–19, Fig. 14 (4th–5th c.); South Shields: Allason-Jones and Miket 1984, 78, 87, 88, Type F, no. 2.443 ("onion"-shaped head), unclassified nos. 2.549, 562 with "pear shaped heads" may belong to this type (5th–7th c.).

99. Gaul: Béal 1983a, 201–202, Type A XX, 12, nos. 707–708, Pl. XXXVI (oval separately attached heads, n.d.). Cf. Virgili and Viola 1990, 107, nos. 212–13; Pannonia: Bíró 1994, 33, 87, 166–167, Type 3, II, nos. 299, 310, 312, 313, (3rd–4th c.); Corinth: Davidson 1952, 238, nos. 2300, 2301, Pl. 118 (1st–2nd c., 4th c., both with separate heads); Alexandria: Wulff 1909, no. 482 (4th–5th c.); Shurafa: Petrie and McKay 1915, 43, nos. 17, 18, 19, Pl. XLIX (3rd c. or later); Salamis: Chavane 1975, 171, no. 492, Pl. 48 (3rd c.); Leptis Magna: Joly et al. 1992, 208, no. Ao.5, Fig. 219 (3rd–5th c.); South Shields: Allason-Jones and Miket 1984, 82, no. 494 (cylindrical head).

100. Cf. Pannonia: Bíró 1994, 33–34, 87–88, 166, Type 3, II, nos. 307–309 (3rd–4th c.).

101. Gaul: Béal 1983a, 200, Type A XX, 10, no. 705, Pl. XXXVI (n.d.). Cf. Virgili and Viola 1990, 107, no. 210; Portorecanti: Capitanio 1974, Fig. 10c–d, p. 156 (1st c.); Ostia: Museum, inv. no. 5232 (2nd–3rd c.); Conimbriga: Alarcâo et al. 1979, 129, 132, no. 118, Pl. XXX (5th c.); Avila-Franca 1968, 81, Type B, I, 3, nos. 74–75; Corinth: Davidson 1952, 279, 284, nos. 2315, 2317, Pl. 118

(3rd–4th c.). Britain: Crummy 1979, 162, Type 5 (A.D. 250–late 4th–early 5th c.); South Shields: Allason-Jones and Miket 1984, 86, 87 nos. 2.526, 542, 543 (5th–7th c.); Portchester Castle: Cunliffe 1975, 215, nos. 82–84, Pl. 116 (end of the 3rd–4th c.).

102. Bíró 1994, 33–34, 88, 167–168, Type 3, III, nos. 314–323, with reels (4th c.).

103. Gaul: Béal 1983a, 203–205, Type A XX, 15, nos. 713–718, Pl. XXXVII (nos. 717–718, 2nd c.). Cf. Ostia: Carandini and Panella 1973, 156, no. 807, Pl. LXXXV (A.D. 235/40–250); Portorecanati: Capitanio 1974, 156, Fig. 10c,d,e, Fig. 266, tomb 205a (mid-1st c.) Salamis: Chavane 1975, 171 no. 493, Pls. 48, 70 (6th–7th c.); Cazeres: Manière 1966, 108–109, nos. 1, 3, 29, 60, Pl. II (end of the 1st c.); Ampurias: Almagro 1955, 115, no. 1, Fig. 74 (Claudian).

104. Styli: Corinth: Davidson 1952, 185–187, nos. 1365–1376, Pls. 83, 84 (Roman–late Byzantine periods); Delos: Déonna 1938, 254–255; Spindles: Conimbriga: Alarcâo et al. 1979, 48, nos. 127, 130, 131, Pl. X (Flavian). Dress pins: E. Saglio, "Acus" in DA, Figs.101, 102, 105. Cf. Salamis: Chavane 1975, 166–168; Pannonia: Bíró 1994, 42.

105. Gaul: Béal 1983a, 203–205, nos. 716, 719, Pl. XXXVII (n.d.). Bíró identifies two examples decorated along their shafts with a bead and reel motif as "unguentum sticks" (1994, 42, nos. 456–458, Pl. LIII).

106. Behel and Veysseyre 1996, 39.

107. Cf. Carthage: Henig in Hurst and Roskams 1984, 188, no. 32, Fig. 62 (4th c.); Hutchinson and Reese in Humphrey 1989, 574, no. 39, Fig. 15 with bead and reel (4th–5th c.); Corinth: Davidson 1952, 284, no. 2338, Pl. 119 with a series of reels (4th c.); Pannonia: Bíró 1994, 33–34, 88, 167–168, Type 3, III, nos. 321–323 with series of reels; South Shields: Allason-Jones and Miket 1984, 88, no. 561. See also 76, nos. 395, 400–403 with crudely fashioned grooves at the summits (5th–7th c.).

108. Davidson 1952, 283, no. 2305, Pl. 118 (1st–2nd c.).

109. Hutchinson and Reese in Humphrey 1989, 573, nos. 22–23, Fig. 14 (4th–5th c.).

110. Cf. Ostia: Ostia Museum, inv. no. 5229 (imperial). An undecorated flange supports a fourth- to fifth-century pinecone head from Carthage (Hutchinson and Reese in Humphrey 1989, 571 no. 21, Fig. 14).

111. Inv. no. 26511. See Virgili and Viola 1990, 107, no. 211.

112. Davidson 1952, 283–228, nos. 2308, 2310, 2312, Pl. 118 (1st–2nd c.).

113. Corinth: Davidson, 1952, 282, no. 2292, Pl. 118 (1st–2nd c.); Delos: Déonna, 1938, 282, Pl. 85. 726. Cf. Pannonia: Bíró 1994, 34, 90–91, 170, Type 3, IV, no. 355 with head separate from body (3rd–4th c.).

114. Rome: Antiquarium Comunale, inv. nos. 27657, 27043.

Cf. Virgili and Viola 1990, 107, nos. 207–208, both with flaring shafts; Corinth: Davidson 1952, 284, no. 2319, Pl. 118 (3rd–4th c.); Leptis Magna: Joly et al. 1992, 208, no. Ao.4, Fig. 218; Bíró 1994, 34, 90, 169, Type 3, IV, no. 341 (3rd–4th c.). Cf. South Shields: Allason-Jones and Miket 1984, 81, no. 493 (crudely fashioned, 5th–6th c).

115. Cf. Luni: Frova 1977, 324, no. CM7068, Pl. 178.20, head not incised (mid-4th c.).

116. Cf. Pannonia: Bíró 1994, 34, 90, 169, Type 3, IV, nos. 343–345 (3rd–4th c); Delos: Déonna, 1938, 279, Pl. 85.725.12 (Greco-Roman.).

117. Pannonia: Bíró 1994, 34, 91, 171, Type 3, V, nos. 360–362 (4th c.). Cf. Corinth: Davidson 1952, 284–285, no. 2330, Pl. 119, but with undecorated head, and perhaps fragmentary (1st–2nd c.); South Shields: Allason-Jones and Miket 1984, 82, 84, no. 508, without reel at neck (5th–6th c).

118. Bíró 1994, 34, 90, 170, Type 3, IV, no. 353 (3rd–4th c.); Corinth: Davidson 1952, 284, no. 2318, Pl. 118, with head resting on two reels (Roman).

119. Ostia: Carandini and Panella 1973, 298, Pl. XCV, Fig. 1020 (A.D. 80–90); Corinth: Davidson 1952, 283, no. 2299, Pl. 118 (1st–2nd c.); Pannonia: Bíró 1994, 33–34, 88–89, 167–168, Type 3, III, nos. 317, 320, 325 (late 3rd-4th c.).

120. Salamis: Chavane 1975, 50, nos.136, 137, Pls. 16, 62; Corinth: Davidson 1952, 189, 192, no. 1414.

121. Gaul: Béal 1983a, 222–223, Type A XXI, I, a, b. Cf. Virgili and Viola 1990, 107, no. 206; Ostia: Carandini and Panella, 1973, 298 no. 1020, Pl. XCV (Flavian); Ostia Museum, inv. no. 5276 (imperial); Luni: Frova 1977, II, 663, no. CS2252, Pl. 330, 4 (early medieval); Carthage: Hutchinson and Reese in Humphrey 1989, 571, no. 20, Fig. 14 (4th–5th c.); Henig in Hurst and Roskams 1984, 188, nos. 28, 29, Fig. 62 (5th–6th c.). Bíró 1994, 89–90, 169–70, Type 3, IV, nos. 335–340, 346–352 (3rd–4th c.).

122. Cf. Ostia: Carrandini and Pannella 1977, 393, no. 485, Pl. LX (late second–1st quarter of the 3rd c.); Delos: Déonna 1938, 279, Pl. 85.727,6 (Greco-Roman); Corinth: Davidson 1952, 195, 1484–1485, Pl. 89 (1st c.).

123. Cf. Egypt: Marangou 1976, 108, no. 118, Pl. 40 (late Roman); Buitron and Oliver in Randall 1985, 70–71, no. 80 (1st–2nd c.); Weitzmann 1979, 137–138, no. 115 (early 6th c.?).

124. Sackett 1992, 385, no. E 40, Pl. 315, 11. Cf. Pompeii: Ward Perkins and Claridge 1976, no. 71b, f (1st c.); Gaul: Béal 1984, 58, no. 241 (with one hand over breast); Cappelli 1992, 131–132, Fig. 64.

125. Cf. Corinth: Davidson 1952, 278, Pl. 148b.

126. Cf. Carthage: Hutchinson and Reese in Humphrey 1989, 573, no. 27, Fig. 14, (4th–5th c.).

127. Cf. Luni: Frova 1977, 409, no. CS1266, Pl. 203, 11 (n.d.).

128. Cf. Gaul: Béal 1983a, 206–207, A, XX, 18. Cf. Luni: Frova 1977, 663, no. CS2421, Pl. 330, 5 (early medieval), 324, nos. CM4939, CM4099, CM6528, Pls. 176, 9, 10, and 178, 19 (1st c.).

129. For a discussion of types and uses see Béal 1983a, 163; Chavane 1975, 103–105, nos. 314–321, Pl. 30.

130. See, for example, Davidson 1952, 173; Chavane 1975,103.

131. Pannonia: Bíró 1987b, 38, Fig. 7; 1994, 23–25.

132. Bíró states that large size is an important criterion for dress pins. However, she catalogues a small (L.0.044) example as such. It is broken at the top and is not certainly three-holed (1994, 23,74, no. 63). For double perforation types see Gaul: Béal 1983a, 171, Type A XIX, 8, no. 432; 1984, 44–45, no. 172; Corinth: Davidson 1952, 176–177, nos. 1258, 1260, 1261, Pls. 78, 79 (3rd–4th c.).

133. Béal 1983a, 173–174.

134. For single circular holes see Béal 1983a, 182, Profile Type 1.

135. For the various types see Béal 1983a, 182, Profile Types 9, 10; Bíró 1994, 23–25, nos. 57–61 (catalogued as dress pins).

136. Béal 1983a, 163–182; See also Pannonia: Bíró 1994, 48–49.

137. Gaul: Béal 1983a, 164–166, Type A XIX, 2, nos. 390–414; 1984, nos. 151–153. Cf. Pannonia: Bíró 1994, 49,101–102, nos. 513–520. Cf. Settefinestre: Famà in Ricci 1985, 70, Pl. 18.5 (3rd c.–modern); Luni: Frova 1973, 594, no. CS337, Pl. 1 68; Frova 1977, 324, no. CM7451, Pl. 178, 16 (second half of the 4th c.); Troina: Militello 1961, 360, Fig. 19b; Portorecanati: Capitanio 1974, 386, Fig. 310, with similar break (1st–2nd c.).

138. Gaul: Béal 1983a, 168, Type A XIX, 4, no. 420; Pannonia: Bíró 1994, 101, nos. 511–512. Salamis: Chavane 1975, 104, no. 316, Pl. 30 (1st–2nd c.)

139. Gaul: Béal 1983a, 169–170, Type A XIX , 6, nos. 423–428; Settefinestre: Famà in Ricci 1984, 70–71 Pl. 18.7 (late antique–early medieval); Ostia: Berti et al. 1977, 46, no. 65, Pl. X (second half of the 2nd c.); Carandini and Panella 1973, 229, Pl. 89, Fig. 898; 1977, 393, Pl. 59, Fig. 494 (end of the 2nd–first quarter of the 3rd c.); Corinth: Davidson 1952, 174, 176–177, nos. 1249, 1252, 1255, 1256, Pl. 78 (1st–2nd c.); Knossos: Sackett 1992, 386, nos. 83, 84, Pls. 315, 322 (later 2nd c.).

140. Cf. Gaul: Béal 1983a, 171–173, Type A XIX, 9, nos. 433–440 (pyramidal heads); Béal 1984, 45, nos. 159–160; Bíró 1994, 73, no. 59, Pl. IX; Settefinestre: Famà in Ricci, 1984, 70–71, Pl. 18.6 (late antique–medieval);

Albintimilium (Italy): Lamboglia 1950, 158, no. 173, Fig. 91 (A.D. 300–350); Conimbriga: Alarcâo et al. 1979, 81, 82, no. 315, Pl. XIII (2nd c.); Colchester: Crummy, 1987, 214, no. 111 (4th c); Knossos: Sackett 1992, 386, no. 20, Pl. 315 (mid-2nd c.).

141. Cf. Gaul: Béal 1983a, 173–174, Type A XIX, 10, no. 441; Pannonia: Bíró 1994, 73, no. 57, Pl. IX; Conimbriga: Alarcâo et al. 1979, 81–82, no. 307, Pl. XII (2nd c.); Corinth: Davidson 1952, 174, 177, no. 1262, Pl. 79 (late Roman).

142. Béal 1983a, 241. Bíró believes they were used for mixing paint on a bone paint palette (1994, 42). For ear scoops see Saglio in *DA*, "Auriscalpium"; Conimbriga: Alarcâo et al. 1979,146. For the medical use of metal examples see Guzzo 1974, 469, nos. 95, 96, Pl. 32.

143. Gaul: Béal 1983a, 241–242, Type A XXIII, 1 241–242, nos. 762–764, Pl. XLII; 1984, 63–63, nos. 248–250, Pl. 12; Pannonia: Bíró 1994, 42, 98 no. 454; Virgili and Viola 1990, 104–105, nos. 190–192; Ostia: Carandini et al. 1968, 46, no. 67a,b, Pl. X (150–beginning of the 3rd c.); Carthage: Hutchinson and Reese in Humphrey 1989, 574–575, no. 35 (4th c.); Corinth: Davidson 1952, 82, nos. 1336, 1337 (Roman), 1338 (1st–2nd c.), Pl. 184; Conimbriga: Alarcâo et al. 1979, 146–147,149, nos. 261–264, Pl. XXXV (late 1st–2nd c.).

144. Cf. Carthage: Hutchinson and Reese in Humphrey 1989, 574–575, nos. 35, 36, Fig. 15 (4th c.); Hurst and Roskams 1984, 188–189, no. 21 (4th c.).

145. Hutchinson and Reese in Humphrey 1989, 574–575, no. 36 (4th c.).

146. Gaul: Béal 1983a, 245–248, Type A XXIV, 2 a; 1984, 64, no. 253, Pl. 12; Pannonia: Bíró 1994, 42, 98, nos. 452, 453, Pl. LII; Knossos: Sackett 1992, 386, 388, nos. E75 (Hadrianic to mid-2nd c.), E120 (2nd–4th c.), Pls. 316, 321; Rome: Mocchegiani Carpano in Mele 1982, no. 7, Fig. 7 (4th c.); Carandini and Panella 1973, 298, no. 1029, Pl. XCV (A.D. 50–75); Corinth: Davidson 1952, 184, nos. 1328, 1329, Pl. 82 (1st–2nd c.).

147. See E. Saglio, "Cochlear" in *DA*; Riha and Stern 1982; MacGregor 1985, 181–183, Fig. 98; Pannonia: Bíró 1994, 44–45, 99, nos. 474–475, 477–478; Gaul: Béal 1983a, 249–252, Type A XXV, 1, nos. 780–793, Pl. XLIV; Knossos: Sackett 1992, 385–386, nos. E56 (Trajanic), E59 (Trajanic), E95 (2nd c.), Pls. 316, 321, 322; Rome: De Grossi Mazzorin and Minniti 1995, 372, Fig. 2, 5 (1st c. B.C.); Virgili and Viola 1990, 104–105, nos. 181–184 (n.d.); Settefinestre: Famà in Ricci 1985, 239, 240, Pl. 63.4–5 (n.d.); Leptis Magna: Joly et al. 1992, 210–211, no. Ao.37, Fig. 230 (3rd–5th c.), handle inscribed with ring and dot; Knossos: Sackett 1992, 388, no. E118, crosshatch design banded by reels (late 2nd–early 3rd c.), E46, bead decoration on handle (later

148. Martial XIV, 121, and Petronius XXXIII, 5–6, cited in Béal 1983a, 249 and 253 n. 2.

149. MacGregor 1985, 99–102. One disk pierced with holes survives from a fourth-century context at Corinth (Davidson 1952, 302, no. 2579, Pl. 124).

150. Hutchinson and Reese in Humphrey 1989, 582, nos. 72–73 (late 4th–early 5th c); Henig in Hurst and Roskams 1984, 190–191, no. 70, Fig. 63 (3rd c.).

151. Cf. Henig in Hurst and Roskams 1984, 190–191, no. 70, Fig. 63 (3rd c).

152. For a typological review of both types in the late Roman and medieval periods see MacGregor 1985, 73–96; Bíró 1994, 35–39.

153. Ricci in Paroli 1997; Manacorda et al. 2000, 62.

154. Cf. Luni: Frova 1973, 565, no. CM637, Pl. 139, 29 (6th–7th c.). See also Graeven 1903, 7–9, no. 4 (578). For a typological review of both types in the late Roman and medieval periods see MacGregor 1985, 73–96; Bíró 1994, 35–39.

155. Cf. Carthage: Henig in Hurst and Roskams 1984, 188, Fig. 61, 11 (before 500–540).

156. For fly switches and fans see Gill 1986, 251. For an ivory fan handle from the Roman period see Sintès 1996, 92, no. 75.

157. See Ault and Flusche in final report, forthcoming.

158 Cf. Colchester: Crummy 1987, 225, 227, nos. 246, 247; Gaul: Béal 1982a, 75–76, A IV, 2, no. 79, Pl. XII.

159. Saraçhane: Gill in Harrison 1986, 252, no. 382, Fig. 338.

160. Cf. Gaul: Béal 1982a for handles rectangular in section, 347–348, B II, nos. 1232, 1233, 1234, Pls. XII, LIX.

161. Saraçhane: Gill 1986, 251–252, no. 379, Fig. j (7th–8th c.).

162. Cf. Pannonia: Bíró 1995, 100, nos. 482, 483, Pls. LV, LVI, undecorated.

163. Gill 1986, 251.

164. Cf. Saraçhane: Gill 1986, 252, no. 387, Fig. 341, with ring and dot motif (12th c.?).

165. Roosters also appear as pinheads. See Bíró 1994, 92, nos. 376, 377, 379.

166. For the form see Gaul: Béal 1983a, 149, nos. 349–350, Pl. XIII; 1984, 40, no. 132; Knossos: Sackett 1992, 386, no. 81, Pl. 318 (baluster shape, Hadrianic to mid-2nd c.); Corinth: Davidson 1952, 192, nos. 1423 (Byzantine), 1426, 1428 (Roman), Pl. 86.

167. Cf. South Shields: Allason-Jones and Miket 1984, 43–44, no. 2.53 (6th c.); MacGregor 1985, 168, Fig. 88i.

168. A number of Roman dolls preserve rings, bracelets, and necklaces in various materials. See Rinaldi 1956, 118–11; Virgili and Viola 1990, 104–105, no. 200 (Constantinian).

169. Cf. Virgili and Viola 1990, 18, 27, 54.
170. For a discussion of types see Clarke 1979, 301–314. For
an example of a bracelet constructed this way using jet,
see Kleiner and Matheson 1996, 177–178, no. 137.
171. These assemblies included objects presumably associated
with the household of the deceased such as gaming
pieces, buttons, plaques, combs and articulated dolls.
Recent studies of these grave goods include: DeSantis
1994; Felle et al. 1994, 114–120.
172. See MacGregor 1985, 99–102.
173. See Chapter 4, pp. 48–49.
174. Cf. Salvetti 1978, 109–111, nos. 5, 6; Elderkin 1930,
472–475, Figs. 24, 25. For separate heads see Kanzler
1903, 4, nos. 116–119, Pl. XIII. It is not indicated if they
are broken at the base or were to be mounted on a body.
175. Larger bone disks were cut from the mandibles of cattle.
Some were composite, built up from several layers of
antler or bone. See MacGregor 1985, 135–136, Figs.
71q, 72.
176. For examples see MacGregor 1985, 130, Fig. 71.
177. See Bíró 1994, 61–63.
178. Cf. MacGregor 1985, 130, 132–137, Figs.71–72; Béal
1983a, 283–285. MacGregor 1985, 132–133.
179. Cf. Gaul: Béal 1983a, 295, 299, 319, Type A XXX III, 3,
nos. 977, 1033, Pl. L; 1984, 76, nos. 285, 287, Pl. 15;
Pannonia: Bíró 1994, 119, no. 844, Pl. LXXXIII;
Fishbourne (England): Cunliffe 1971, 146, nos. 5, 6, 7,
Fig. 67 (Roman).
180. For examples, including undecorated, in walrus ivory
that are probably blanks, see MacGregor 1985, 136–137,
Fig. 72.
181. For disks similar in size and decoration in antler and
bone dated to the medieval period see MacGregor 1985,
135–136, Fig. 72a,b.
182. Saguì and Paroli 1990, 550, no. 767, Fig. 164, 20.
183. Murray 1941.
184. Cf. Gaul: Béal 1983a, 321–322, Type A XXXIV, 2, nos.
1167, 1168, Pl. LIV; Pannonia: Bíró 1994, 119, nos.
838–844, Pl. LXXXIII (Roman); Rome: Ricci 1997, 264,
265, Fig. 10, 22 (7th c.); Morey 1936, 54, nos. A31,
1177, A32, 1150, A33, 1151, Pl. IV (3rd–4th c, identified as buttons); Carthage: Hutchinson and Reese in
Humphrey 1989, 581, no. 64, Fig. 20.66 (4th c); Leclerc
1982, 72–76, nos. 116–121, Pl. 7; Henig in Hurst and
Roskams 1984, 191–192, nos. 83–88, Fig. 64 (late
antique); Knossos: Sackett 1992, 384, no. E20a, Pl. 318
(Augustan); Corinth: Davidson 1952, 219, nos. 1691
(Roman), 1692, 1693 (late antique), Pl. 99; South
Shields: Allason and Miket 1984, 60–61, nos. 2.209,
2.212 (533–600) Conimbriga: Alarcâo et al. 1979, 180–
181, no. 217, Pl. LIX.
185. Gaul: Béal 1983a, 301–303, 319, profile Type 5, Type A
XXXIII, 5, nos. 1059–1069, Pls. LI, LIII; 1984, 77–80;

186. Pannonia: Bíró 1994, 112–117, nos. 707, 715–802, Pls.
LXXIX–LXXXII; Saraçhane: Gill 1986, 261, 521, Fig. P
(undated).
186. Gaul: Béal 1983a, 283–323, Types A XXIII and A XXIV
include these types; Pannonia: Bíró 1994, 110–112, nos.
683–706, Pl. LXXIX. Cf. Ricci 1997, 264, 265, Fig. 10,
17–18 (7th c).
187. For the type see Bíró 1994, 62–63, Fig. 40; Steiner 1939.
188. A similar process of disguising the cancellous core was
used for antler. See MacGregor 1985, 137–138, Fig. 73.
189. Carthage: Henig in Hurst and Roskams 1984, 190–192,
nos. 77–82, Figs. 63–64; Rome: Ricci 1997, 264, 265,
Fig.10, 20 (7th c).
190. Saraçhane: Gill 1986, 260–261, nos. 506, 507, 509–513,
Fig. N (7th c–modern);
191. Saguì and Paroli 1990, 550, no. 767, Fig 164, 20. Cf.
MacGregor 1985, 136, Fig. 72b (walrus ivory, medieval).
192. Béal 1983a, 322, no. 1169, Pl. LIV.
193. Cf. Gaul: Béal 1983a, 301–303, Type A XXXIII, 5.
194. Cf. Gaul: Béal 1983a, 303–305, Type A XXXIII, 6, Pl.
LII, 1073, 1089, 1094, 1096.
195. Cf. Gaul: Béal 1983a, 319, profile Type 7; Pannonia:
Bíró 1994, 111, nos. 689, 690, Pl. LXXIX.
196. Cf. Rome: Ricci 1997, 264, 265, Fig. 10, 20 (7th c).
197. Cf. Carthage: Henig in Hurst and Roskams 1984, 191–
192, no. 79, Fig. 64 (7th c. context); Saraçhane: Gill
1986, 260, nos. 506, 507, Fig. N (medieval context).
198. Cf. Carthage: Henig in Hurst and Roskams 1984, 190–
191, nos. 75 (6th c), 78 (modern context), Fig. 63.
199. Sparta: Dawkins 1929, 237 (7th–5th c. B.C.). See Schmid
1968; MacGregor 1985,129–132; Gaul: Béal 1983a,
345–346, 349–354. See G. Lafaye, "Tessera" in DA.
200. For examples see MacGregor 1985, 130–131, Fig. 71e;
Gaul: Béal 1983a, Type B 1, 345–346, nos. 1228–1231,
Pl. LIX.
201. See MacGregor 1985, 129–131, Fig.71a.
202. Cf. Rome: Ricci 1997, 264, 265, Fig. 10, 5–7 (7th c).
Carthage: Henig in Hurst and Roskams 1984, 191–192,
nos. 89–95, Fig. 64 (late antique); Corinth: Davidson
1952, 221–222, nos. 1747, 1748, 1751, 1752, Pl. 100
(1st c.–Byzantine).
203. MacGregor 1985, 129–131, Fig. 71a.
204. See Chapter 4, note 70.
205. Hutchinson and Reese in Humphrey 1989, 566, 575–
577, nos. 46, 47, Fig. 16 (4th c).
206. Cf. Carthage: Hutchinson and Reese in Humphrey 1989,
575–576, no. 46, Fig 16 (4th c.).
207. MacGregor 1985, 149–151, Fig. 78.
208. Cf. Pannonia: Bíró 1994, 61,108, no. 634, Pl. LXXVI;
Egypt: Maguire et al., 1989, 225, no. 140; Arles: Sintès
1996, 122, no. 106 (Roman); Corinth: Davidson 1952,
197, no. 1503, Pl. 90 (5th c. B.C.); Delos: Déonna 1923,
325, Pl. 92.813–815 (Greco-Roman).

BIBLIOGRAPHY

Acta Conciliorum Oecumenicorum. 1914–. Ed. E. Schwartz (Berlin).

Aiosa, S. 1997. "Ossi Lavorati da Leptis Magna: una rilettura," *Libya Antiqua,* n.s., 3, 139–148.

Akurgal, E. 1966. *Die Geburt der griechischen Kunst* (Baden-Baden).

Alarcâo, J., R. Etienne, A. Moutinho-Alarcâo, and S. da Ponte. 1979. *Fouilles de Conimbriga,* vol. 7, *Trouvailles diverses-conclusions générales* (Paris).

Albertoni, M. 1991–1992. "Lastrine di revestimento dall'antica via di Porta San Lorenzo," *Bullettino della Commissione archeologica comunale di Roma* 94, 341–392.

———. 1994. "Inediti frammenti di classicismo tardo-antico," *Bullettino della Commissione archeologica comunale di Roma,* n.s., 8, 160–167.

Albizzati, C. 1916. "Two Ivory Fragments of a Statue of Athena," *Journal of Hellenic Studies* 36, 373–402.

Allason-Jones, L., and R. Miket. 1994. *The Catalogue of Small Finds from South Shields Roman Fort,* Society of Antiquaries of Newcastle upon Tyne Monograph Series 2 (Newcastle upon Tyne).

Almagro, M. 1955. *Las necropolis de Ampurias,* vol. 2, *Necropolis romanas y necropolis indigenas* (Barcelona).

Amandry, P. 1939. "Rapport préliminaire sur les statues chryséléphantines de Delphes," *Bulletin de correspondance hellénique* 63, 86–119.

Amory, A. 1966. "The Gates of Horn and Ivory," *Yale Classical Studies* 20, 3–57.

Andronikos, M. 1978. *The Royal Graves at Vergina* (Athens).

———. 1984. *Vergina: The Royal Tombs and the Ancient City* (Athens).

Augenti, A. 1996. *Il Palatino nel medioevo: Archeologia e topografia (secolo VI–XIII), Bullettino della Commissione Archeologica Comunale di Roma,* suppl. 4.

Avila Franca, E. 1968. "Alfinete de Toucado Romanos de Conimbriga," *Conimbriga* 7, 17–93.

Ayalon, E., and C. Sorek. 1999. *Bare Bones: Ancient Artifacts from Animal Bones* (Tel Aviv).

Bacchelli, B., M. Barnera, R. Pasqualucci, and L. Saguì. 1995. "Nouve scoperte sulla provenienza dei pannelli in opus sectile vitreo della Collezione Gorga," in I. Bragantini and F. Guidobaldi, eds., *AISCOM, Atti del II Colloquio per lo studio e la conservazione del mosaico, Roma, 5–7 dicembre 1994* (Bordighera), 447–466.

Baer, N. S., B. Appelbaum, and N. Indictor. 1971. "The Effect of Long-Term Heating on Ivory," *International Institute of Conservation: American Group Bulletin* 12.1, 55–59.

Baer, N. S., N. Indictor, J. H. Frantz, and B. Appelbaum. 1971. "The Effects of High Temperature on Ivory," *Studies in Conservation* 16, 1–8.

Baer, N. S., and L .J. Majewski. 1970–1971. "Ivory and Related Materials: An Annotated Bibliography," *Art and Archaeology Technical Abstracts* 8.2–3, Supplement. Section A: Conservation and Scientific Investigations. Section B: Working Techniques, Forgeries, History.

Bailey, D. M., ed. 1996. "Little Emperors," in D. M. Bailey, ed., *Archaeological Research in Roman Egypt, Journal of Roman Archaeology* Supplementary Series 19 (Ann Arbor).

Bammer, A. 1982. "Forschungen im Artemision von Ephesos von 1976 bis 1981," *Anatolian Studies* 32, 61–87.

———. 1992. "Ivories from the Artemesion at Ephesus," in Fitton 1992, 185–204.

Barbier, M. 1988. "Le travail de l'os à l'époque gallo-romaine," *Dossiers histoire et archéologie* 126, 48–55.

Barnett, R. 1948. "Early Greek and Oriental Ivories," *Journal of Hellenic Studies* 68, 1–25.

———. 1957. *A Catalogue of the Nimrud Ivories: With Other*

Examples of Ancient Near Eastern Ivories in the British Museum (London).

———. 1982. *Ancient Ivories in the Middle East,* Qedem Monograph Series 14, Institute of Archaeology, Hebrew University of Jerusalem (Jerusalem).

Batiffol, P. 1911. "Les présents de Saint Cyrille à la cour de Constantinople," *Bulletin d'ancienne littérature et d'archéologie chrétiennes* 6, 247–264.

Battaglia, G. B., ed. 1983. *Corredi funerari di età imperiale e barbarica nel Museo Nazionale Romano* (Rome).

Béal, J. C. 1983a. *Catalogue des objets de tabletterie du Musée de la Civilisation Gallo-Romaine de Lyon* (Lyon).

———. 1983b. "Les ateliers gallo-romains de tabletterie à Lyon et à Vienne," *Latomus* 42.3, 607–618.

———. 1984. *Les objets de tabletterie antique du Musée archéologique de Nîmes,* Cahiers des musées et monuments de Nîmes 2 (Nîmes).

———. 1986."Eléments en os de lits gallo-romains," *Documents d'archéologie méridionale* 9, 111–117.

———. 1991. "Le mausolée de Cucuron (Vaucluse), 2. Le lit funéraire à décor d'os de la tombe no.1," *Gallia* 48, 285–317.

Béal, J. C., and M. Feugère. 1991. "Les pyxides gallo-romaines en os de la Gaule méridionale," *Documents d'archéologie méridionale* 4, 115–126.

Becker, M. J. 1999–2000. "Tanyards and Paupers' Graves in Ancient Rome," *Old World Archaeology Newsletter* 22.2, 8–15.

Beckmann, B. 1966. "Studien über die Metallnadeln der römischen Kaiserzeit im Freien Germanien," *Saalburg-Jahrbuch* 23, 5–100.

Bedwin, O. 1992. "The Animal Bones," in L. H. Sackett, ed., *Knossos: From Greek Colony to Roman Colony. Excavations at the Unexplored Mansion II* (London), 491–492.

Behel, M., and P. Veysseyre 1996. *Guide des Collections. Musée archéologique Saint-Romain-en Gal, Vienne* (Lyon).

Béraud, I., and C. Gébara. 1986. "Les lits funéraires de la nécropole gallo-romaine de Saint-Lambert (Frejus)," *Revue archéologique de Narbonnaise* 19, 183–208.

Berke, S. 1989–1990. "Geschnitze Klinentrile aus der Gräberfeld von Haltern," *Mitteilungen der Archäologischen Gesellschaft Steiermark* 3–4, 33–43.

———. 1991. "Das Gräberfeld von Haltern," in R. Asskampf and S. Berke, eds., *Die römischen Okkupation nördlich der Alpen zur Zeit des Augustus, Kolloquium Bergkamen 1989* (Münster), 149–157.

Bernard, P. 1967. "Ai Khanum on the Oxus," *Proceedings of the British Academy* 53, 71–95.

———. 1970. "Sièges et lits en ivoire d'époque hellénistique en Asie Centrale," *Syria* 47, 327–343.

Berti, F. A., Carandini, E. Fabricotti, C. Gasparr, et al. 1977. *Ostia II, le terme del Nuotatore, scavi dell'ambiente I, Studi Miscellanei* 16 (Rome).

Bertoletti, M., M. Cima, and E. Talamo, eds. 1997. *Sculture di Roma antica. Collezioni dei Musei Capitolini alla Centrale Montemartini* (Milan).

Bianchi, C. 2000. *Cremona in età romana. I letti funerari in osso* (Milan).

Bird, J., A. H. Graham, H. Sheldon, and P. Townend, eds. 1978. *Southwark Excavations 1972–1974,* London and Middlesex Archaeological Society and Surrey Archaeological Society Joint Publication 1 (London).

Bíró, M. T. 1985. "The Indian Ivory Comb from Gorsium," *Acta Archaeologica Academiae Scientarium Hungaricae* 37, 1985, 419–430.

———. 1987a. "Bone Carvings from Brigetio in the Collection of the Hungarian National Museum," *Acta Archaeologica Academiae Scientarium Hungaricae* 39, 153–192.

———. 1987b. "Gorsium Bone Carvings," *Alba Regia* 13, 1987, 25–63.

———. 1994. *The Bone Objects of the Roman Collection,* Catalogi Musei Nationalis Hungarici Series Archaeologica 2 (Budapest).

Blinkenberg, C. 1931. *Lindos, fouilles de l'acropole, 1902–1914, les petits objets* (Berlin).

Boardman, J. 1968. "Artemis Orthia and Chronology," *Annual of the British School at Athens* 58, 1–7.

———. 1978. *Greek Sculpture: The Archaic Period* (New York).

Boehringer, E., ed. 1959. *Neue deutsche Ausgrabungen im Mittelmeergebiet und im vorderen Orient* (Berlin).

Bommelaeur, J. F., and D. Laroche. 1991. *Guide de Delphes. Le site,* Ecole française d'Athènes, Sites et monuments 7 (Paris).

Bonacasa Carra, R. M. 1995. "Gli ossi lavorati del Museo Greco-Romano di Alessandria: aspetti e problemi del repertorio iconografico," in N. Boncasa, C. Naro, E. Chiara Portale, and A. Tullo, eds., *Alessandria e il mondo ellenistico-romano. Atti del II Congresso Internazionale Italo-Egiziano* (Rome), 279–282.

Bordenache Battaglia, G. 1983. *Corredi funerari di età imperiale e barbarica nel Museo Nazionale Romano* (Roma).

Branigan, K. 1977. *Gatcombe: The Excavation and Study of a Romano-British Villa Estate, 1967–1976, BAR* British Series 44 (Oxford).

Brize, P. 1992. "New Ivories from the Samian Heraion," in Fitton 1992, 163–172.

Bruckner, A., and E. Pernice. 1893. "Ein attischer Friedhof," *Mitteilungen des Deutschen Archäologischen Instituts* (Athen. Abt.)18, 73–191.

Cabrol, F., and H. Leclercq. 1907–1953. *Dictionnaire d'archeologie chrétienne et de liturgie* (Paris).

Cahn, H. A. 1972. *Bronzen der Antike: Tarentinische Skulpturen: Schnitzereien aus Bein und Elfenbein,* Sonderliste O (Basel).

Caillet, J. P. 1986. "L'origine des derniers ivoires antiques," *Revue de l'art* 72, 7–15.

Cameron, A. 1982. "A Note on Ivory Carving in Fourth Century Constantinople," *American Journal of Archaeology* 86, 126–129.

Capitanio, M. 1974. "La necropoli romana di Portorecanati," *Notizie degli scavi di antichità* 28, 145–445.

Cappelli, R., ed. 1992. *Bellezza e lusso: Imagini e documenti di piaceri della vita* (Rome).

Carandini, A., E. Fabbricotti, C. Gasparri Tatti, et al. 1968. *Ostia I, le terme del Nuotatore, scavo dell'ambiente IV, Studi Miscellanei* 13 (Rome).

Carandini, A., and C. Panella, eds. 1973. *Ostia III, le terme del Nuotatore.* 2 vols., *Studi Miscellanei* 21 (Rome).

———. 1977. *Ostia IV, Studi Miscellanei* 23 (Rome 1977).

Carignani, A., A. Gabucci, P. Palazzo, and G. Spinola. 1990. "Nuovi dati sulla topografia del Celio: le ricerche nell'area dell'ospedale militare," *Archeologia laziale* 10, 72–80.

Carnap-Bornheim, C. von. 1994. "Some Observations on Roman Militaria of Ivory," *Journal of Roman Military Equipment Studies* 5, 27–32.

Carter, J. B. 1985. *Greek Ivory Carving in the Orientalizing and Archaic Periods* (New York and London).

———. 1989. "The Chests of Periander," *American Journal of Archaeology* 93, 355–378.

Chaplin, R. 1971. *The Study of Animal Bones from Archaeological Sites* (London and New York).

Chavane, M. J. 1975. *Salamine de Chypre VI. Les petits objets* (Paris).

Cicerchia, E., E. La Rocca, and A. Somella Mura. 1976. "Avorio con scena dionisiaca dalla tomba Arieti," in E. La Rocca and A. Sommella Mura, eds., *Affreschi romani dalle raccolte dell'Antiquarium Comunale* (Rome), 29–31.

Clarke, G. 1979. *The Roman Cemetery at Lankhills,* Winchester Studies 3, pt. 2 (Oxford).

Clerc, C. 1915. *Les théories relatives au culte des images chez les auteurs grecs du II siècle après J.-C.* (Paris).

Cochet, Abbé. 1855. *La Normandie souterraine, ou notice sur les cimitières romains et les cimitières francs explorés en Normandie* (Paris).

Collini, A. M. 1983. "Considerazioni su la Velia da Nerone in poi," in K. De Fine Licht, ed., *Città e architettura nella Roma imperiale,* Analecta Romana Istituti Danici, suppl. 10 (Odense), 129–145.

Connor, C. 1998. *The Color of Ivory: Polychromy on Byzantine Ivories* (Princeton).

Cox, W. E. 1946. *Chinese Ivory Sculpture* (New York).

Craven, R. C. 1997. *Indian Art: A Concise History,* rev. ed. (London).

Crawford, M. H. 1974. *Roman Republican Coinage* (London and New York).

Crummy, N. 1979. "A Chronology of Romano-British Pins," *Britannia* 10, 157–163.

———. 1981. "Bone Working at Colchester," *Britannia* 12, 277–285.

———. 1983. "The Roman Small Finds from Excavations in Colchester, 1971–79," *Colchester Archaeological Report* 2 (Colchester).

Crummy, P. 1987. "Excavations at Culver Street, the Gilberd School, and Other Sites in Colchester 1971–85," *Colchester Archaeological Report* 6 (Colchester).

Cunliffe, B. 1971. *Excavations at Fishbourne 1961–1969 II: The Finds,* Reports of the Research Committee of the Society of Antiquaries of London 27 (Leeds 1971).

———. 1975. *Excavations at Portchester Castle* (London).

Currey, J. D. 1970. "The Mechanical Properties of Bone," *Clinical Orthopaedics* 73, 210–231.

Cutler, A. 1983. "Observations on the Production of Carved Ivory in Late Antiquity and the Early Middle Ages," in X. Baral, ed., *Artistes, artisans, et production artistique au Moyen-Age,* Rapports provisoires II (Rennes 1983), 936–986.

———. 1985a. *The Craft of Ivory: Sources, Techniques, and Uses in the Mediterranean World* A.D. *200–1400,* Dumbarton Oaks Byzantine Collection Publications 8 (Washington, D.C.).

———. 1985b. "The Elephants of the Great Palace Mosaic," *Bulletin d'information de l'Association international pour l'etude de la mosaique antique* 10, 125–131.

———. 1985c. "On Byzantine Boxes," *Journal of the Walters Art Gallery* 42–43, 32–47.

———. 1986. "Observations on the Production of Carved Ivory in Late Antiquity and the Early Middle Ages," in X. Barral i Altet, ed., *Artistes, artisans, et production artistique au Moyen-Age: Colloque international, Centre national de la recherche scientifique, Université de Rennes II, Haute Bretagne, 2–6 May 1983* (Paris), 936–986.

———. 1987. "Prolegomena to the Craft of Ivory Carving in Late Antiquity and the Early Middle Ages," in X. Barral i Altet, ed. *Artistes, artisans et production artistique au Moyen Age, Actes du Colloque de Rennes 1983* (Paris), 431–475.

———. 1991. "Barberiniana: Notes on the Making, Content, and Provenance of Louvre OA. 9063," in E. Dassman, ed., *Tesserae. Festschrift für Josef Engemann, Jahrbuch für Antike und Christentum* Ergänzungband 18 (Münster), 329–339.

———. 1993. "Five Lessons in Late Roman Ivory," *Journal of Roman Archaeology* 6, 167–192.

———. 1994. *The Hand of the Master: Craftsmanship, Ivory, and Society in Byzantium (9th–11th Centuries)* (Princeton).

Dabrowski, l. 1960. "Résumé des recherches archéologiques faites autour du Fort Kôm el Dikka," *Bulletin de la Faculté des Lettres, Université d'Alexandrie* 14, 39–49.

Daremberg, C. V., ed. 1877–1919. *Dictionnaire des antiquités greques et romaines, d'après les textes et les monuments* (Paris).

Davidson, G. R. 1952. *Corinth XII: The Minor Objects* (Princeton).

Dawid, M. 1980. "Bemerkungen zu zwei Relieffreisen aus dem ephesischen Elfenbeinfund," in F. Krinzinger, ed., *Forschungen und Funde, Festschrift B. Neutsch* (Innsbruck), 95–102.

Dawid, M., and P. G. Dawid. 1972–1975. "Restaurierungsarbeiten von 1965–1970," *Jahreshefte des Österreichischen Archäologischen Institutes in Wien* 50, Beiblatt, 524–558.

Dawkins, R. M. 1929. *The Sanctuary of Artemis Orthia at Sparta, Journal of Hellenic Studies Supplement Paper* 5 (1929).

De Cupere, B. 1994. "Faunal Remains at Sagalassos: Preliminary Results of the Archaeozoological Analysis," in Ayri Basim, ed., *Arkeometri Sonuçlari Toplantisi*, 24–28 May 1993 (Ankara), 225–235.

De Cupere, B., W. Van Neer, and A. Lentacker. 1993. "Some Aspects of the Bone-Working Industry in Roman Sagalassos," in *Sagalassos II: Report on the Third Excavation Campaign of 1992*, Acta Archaeologica Lovaniensia Monographiae 6 (Leuven), 269–278.

De Grossi Mazzorin, J. 1995. "La Fauna rinvenuta nell'area della Meta Sudans nel Quadro Evoluto degli animali domestici in Italia," in R. Peretto and O. De Curtis, eds., *Padusa Quaderni 1.Atti del 1 Convegno Nazionale di Archeozoologia, Rovigo 5–7 March 1993* ((Rovigo), 309–318.

De Grossi Mazzorin, J., and C. Minniti. 1995."Gli scavi nell'area della Meta Sudans (I sec.d.c.) L'industria su Osso," in R. Peretto and O. De Curtis, eds., *Padusa Quaderni 1. Atti del 1 Convegno Nazionale di Archeozoologia . Rovigo, 5–7 March, 1993* (Rovigo) 371–375.

Delogu, P., ed. 1998. *Roma medievale. Aggiornamenti,* Conference Proceedings, Rome, 1996 (Florence).

Déonna, W. 1938. *Le mobilier Délien,* Exploration archéologique de Délos, 18 (Paris).

De Santis, P. 1994. "Elementi di corredo nei sopolcri delle catacombe romane: l'esempio della regione di Leone e della galleria Bb nella catacomba di Commodilla," *Vetera Christianorum* 31, 23–51.

Desborough, V. R. d'A. 1972. *The Greek Dark Ages* (London and New York).

Devauges, J. B. 1975 "Compierre. Près du temple un atelier de tabletier," *Annales du Nivernais* 10–11, 18–23.

Donati, A., ed. 1996. *Dalla terra alle genti: La diffusione del Cristianesimo nei primi secoli* (Milan).

Donohue, A. A. 1988. *Xoana and the Origins of Greek Sculpture* (Atlanta).

Driesch, A. von den, and J. Boessneck. 1982. "Tierknochenabfall aus einer spaätromischen Werkstatt in Pergamon," *Archäologischer Anzeiger* 97, 563–74.

Driver, J. C. 1984. "Zooarchaeological Analysis of Raw Material Selection by a Saxon Artisan," *Journal of Field Archaeology* 11, 397–403.

Dunbabin, T. J. 1957. *The Greeks and Their Eastern Neighbours: Studies in the Relations between Greece and the Countries of the Near East in the Eighth and Seventh Centuries* B.C. (London).

During Caspers, E. L. C. 1979. "Westward Contacts with Historical India: A Trio of Figurines," *Proceedings of the Seminar for Arabian Studies* 9, 10–29.

Dzierzykray-Rogalski, T., E. Prominska, and M. Rodziewicz. 1969. "Refuse of Animal Bones from Kôm el-Dikka, Alexandria," *Etudes et travaux* 6, 173–178.

Eckinger, T. 1929. "Knochenschnitzereien aus Gräbern von Vindonissa," *Anzeiger für Schweizerische Altertumskunde* 31, 241–56.

Elderkin, K. 1930. "Jointed Dolls in Antiquity," *American Journal of Archaeology* 34, 455–479.

Engemann, J. 1987. "Elfenbeinfunde aus Abu Mena/Ägypten," *Jahrbuch für Antike und Christentum* 30, 172–186.

Ensoli, S., and E. La Rocca, eds. 2000. *Aurea Roma. Dalle città pagana alla città cristiana* (Rome).

Espinoza, E. O., and M. J. Mann. 1992. *Identification Guide for Ivory and Ivory Substitutes 2* (Baltimore).

Evely, D. 1992. "Towards an Elucidation of the Ivory Worker's Tool Kit in Neopalatial Crete," in Fitton 1992, 7–16.

Eygun, F. 1933. "Le cimitière gallo-romain des Dunes, à Poitiers," *Journal des fouilles du père De la Croix et du rapports du commandant Rothman. Mémoires de la Société des Antiquaires de l'Ouest,* 3rd ser., 11 (Poitiers).

Faust, S. 1989. *Fulcra. Figürlicher und ornamentaler Schmuck an antichen Betten, Mitteilungen des Deutschen Archäologischen Instituts* (Rom. Abt.) 30. Ergänzungschaft (Mainz).

———. 1992. "Beinschnitzereien von Betten in Genf," *Numismatica e antichità classiche* 24, 227–255.

Felle, A. E., M. P. del Moro, D. Nuzzo. 1994. "Elementi di 'correde-arredo' delle tombe del cimitero di S. Ipolito sulla via Tiburtina," *Rivista di archeologia cristiana* 70, 90–158.

Fink, J. 1967. *Der Thron des Zeus in Olympia* (Munich).

Fiocchi Nicolai, V., F. Bisconti, and D. Mazzoleni. 1999. *The Christian Catacombs of Rome* (Regensburg).

Fischer, J. 1990. "Zu einer griechischen Kline und weiterer Südimporten aus dem Fürstengrabhügel Grafenbühl, Asperg, Kr. Ludwigsburg," *Germania* 68, 115–127.

Fitton, J. L., ed. 1992. *Ivory in Greece and the Mediterranean from the Bronze Age to the Hellenistic Period,* British Museum Occasional Paper 85 (London).

Floriani Squarciapino, M., I. Gismondi, and B. Barbieri. 1958. *Scavi di Ostia. III. Le necropoli. Part I. Le tombe di età repubblicana e augustea* (Rome).

Fouet, G., and M. Labrousse. 1952. "Ivoires romains trouvés a

Saint-Loup-de Comminges (Haute Garonne)," *Monuments et mémoires publiés par l'Académie des Inscriptions et Belles-Lettres (Fondation Piot)* 46, 117–129.

Fremersdorf, F. 1940. "Römische Scharnierbänder aus Bein," *Vjesnika Hrvatskoga Archeolskoga Drustva* (Serta Hoffilleriana), n.s.,18–21, 321–327.

Freyer-Schauenburg, B. 1966. *Elfenbeine aus dem samischen Heraion* (Hamburg).

Frova, A., ed. 1973. *Scavi di Luni I: relazione delle campagne di scavo 1970–1971* (Rome).

———. 1977. *Scavi di Luni II: relazione delle campagne di scavo 1972, 1973, 1974* (Rome).

Gaborit-Chopin, D. 1978. *Ivoires du Moyen Age* (Fribourg).

Gaitzsch, W. 1980. *Eiserne römische Werkzeuge. Studien zur römischen Werkzeugkunde in Italien und den nordlichen Provinzin des Imperium Romanum, BAR* International Series 78, nos. 1–2 (Oxford).

Gatti, G. 1905. "Sepolcri e memorie sepolcrali dell'antica via Salaria," *Bullettino della Commissione Archeologica Comunale in Roma* 33, 154–188.

Gatto, L. 1998. "Riflettendo sulla consistenza demografica," in Delogu 1998, 143–156.

Gaugler, W. M., and P. Hamill. 1989. "Possible Effects of Open Pools of Oil and Water on Chryselephantine Statues" (Abstract), *American Journal of Archaeology* 93, 251.

Gianfrotta, P. A. 1986. "Rinvenimenti archeologici sottomarini," in G. M. De Rossi, ed., *Le isole pontine attraverso i tempi* (Rome), 213–222.

Gibson, M. T., and E. C. Southworth. 1990. "Radiocarbon Dating of Ivory and Bone Carvings," *Journal of the British Archaeological Association* 143, 1990, 131–133.

Gill, D. W. J. 1992. "Sources for Ivory in the Archaic, Classical and Hellenistic Periods," in Fitton 1992, 233–237.

Gill, M. V. 1986. "The Small Finds," in R. M. Harrison et al., *Excavations at Saraçhane in Istanbul* (Princeton), 226–263.

Goldfuss, H., and K. Bowes. 2000. "New Late Roman Bone Carvings from Halusa and the Problem of Regional Bone Carving Workshops in Palestine," *Israel Exploration Journal* 50, 185–202.

Goldman, H. 1951. *Excavation at Gözlü Küle, Tarsus I, The Hellenistic and Roman Period* (Princeton).

Gonosová, A., and C. Kondoleon. 1994. *Art of Late Rome and Byzantium in the Virginia Museum of Fine Arts* (Richmond).

Gonzenbach, V. von. 1950–1951. "Zwei Typen figürlich verzierter Haarpfeile," *Jahresbericht/Gesellschaft Pro Vindonissa,* 3–19.

Graeven, H. 1903. *Antike Schnitzerein aus Elfenbein und Knochen* (Hannover).

Graziosi, G. 1912. "Un monumento quasi ignorato della regione prima," *Bullettino della Commissione Archeologica Comunale di Roma* 40, 204–222.

Greifenhagen, A. 1930. "Bronzekline im pariser Kunsthandel,"

Mitteilungen des Deutschen Archäologischen Instituts (Rom. Abt.) 45, 137–165.

Groh, S. 1992. "Beinerne Möbelbeschläge aus Flavia Solva," *Fundberichte aus Österreich* 31, 51–56.

Guarducci, M. 1978–1980. "Antichi elephanti in Vaticano," *Atti della Pontificia Accademia Romana di Archeologia, Rendiconti* 51–52, 47–55.

Guide de Delphes: le musée. 1991. Ecole française d'Athènes (Paris).

Guidobaldi, F., C. Pavolini, and Ph. Pergola, eds. 1998. *I materiali residui nello scavo archeologico,* Collection de l'Ecole française de Rome (Rome) 249.

Guzzo, P. G. 1974. "Luzzi, localia S. Vito (Cosenza): Necropoli di età romana," *Notizie degli scavi di antichità* 28, 449–484.

Hackin, J. 1939. *Recherches archéologiques à Bégram,* Mémoires de la Délégation archéologique française en Afghanistan 9 (Paris).

———. 1954. *Nouvelles recherches archéologiques à Bégram,* Mémoires de la Délégation archéologique française en Afghanistan 11 (Paris).

Hägg, R., N. Marinatos, and G. C. Nordquist, eds. 1988. *Early Greek Cult Practice, Proceedings of the Fifth International Symposium at the Swedish Institute at Athens,* Acta Instituti Atheniensis Regni Sueciae 4, no. 38 (Stockholm 1988).

Hammond, L. 1995–1996. "A Laconian Lady in Missouri," *Muse* 29–30, 50–73.

Hassall, M., and J. Rhodes. 1974. "Excavations at the New Market Hall, Gloucester 1966–7," *Transactions of the Bristol and Gloustershire Archaeological Society* 93, 15–100.

Harrauer, H., and P. Sijpestein. 1985. "Ein neues Dokument zu Roms Indienhandeln: P. Vindob. G40822," *Anzeiger Akademie der Wissenschaften in Wien. Philosophischhistorische Klasse* 22, 124–155.

Hauser, O. 1904. *Vindonissa: das Standquartier römischer Legionen* (Zurich).

Haywood, L. G. 1990. "The Origin of the Raw Elephant Ivory Used in Greece and the Aegean during the Late Bronze Age," *Antiquity* 64, 103–109.

Heilmeyer, W. D. 1981. "Antike Werkstättenfunde in Griechenland," *Archäologischer Anzeiger* 96, 440–453.

Helbig, W. 1963. *Führer durch die öffentlichen Sammlungen klassicher Altertümer in Rom,* 4th ed. (Tübingen).

Henig, M. 1984. "Objects of Metal, Stone, and Bone," in H. R. Hurst and S. P. Roskams, eds., *Excavations at Carthage: The British Mission I, 1, The Avenue du President Habib Bourguiba, Salammbo: The Site and Finds Other than Pottery* (Sheffield), 182–193.

Hill, D. Kent. 1963. "Ivory Ornaments of Hellenistic Couches," *Hesperia* 32, 293–300.

Hodges, H. 1976. *Artifacts: An Introduction to Early Materials and Technology* (London).

———. 1992. "The Riddle of St. Peter's Republic," in Paroli and Delogu 1993, 353–363.

Hogarth, D. G. 1908. *Excavations at Ephesus: The Archaic Artemisia* (London).

Holdsworth, P. 1976. "Saxon Southampton: A New Review," *Medieval Archaeology* 20, 26–61.

Holliger, C., and C. Holliger Wiesmann. 1993. "Vier Totenbetten mit Knochenschnitzereien aus Vindonissa," *Jaresbericht/Gesellschaft pro Vindonissa,* 21–27.

Hostetter, E., and J. R. Brandt. 1999. "Excavations on the NE Slope of the Palatine Hill (1988–1994): A Summary," *Jäsenkirje. Suomen Klassillisen Arkeologian Seura ry* 2, 8–11.

Hostetter, E., J. R. Brandt, A. St. Clair, M. Parca. Forthcoming. "Complesso tardoromano sul versante NE del Palatino (1992–1993)," *Bollettino di Archeologia.*

Hostetter, E., and T. Howe, eds. 1997. *The Romano-British Villa at Castle Copse, Great Bedwyn* (Bloomington and Indianapolis).

Hostetter, E., T. N. Howe, and J. R. Brandt. 1990. "Palatino. Excavations of the Late Roman Buildings," *Bollettino di Archeologia* 3, 89–91.

Hostetter, E., T. N. Howe, J. R. Brandt, A. St. Clair, M. Parca, C. Gleason, and T. Peña. 1994. "A Late Roman Domus with Apsidal Hall on the NE slope of the Palatine: 1989–1991 Seasons," *Rome Papers. Journal of Roman Archaeology* Supplementary Series 11, 131–181.

Hostetter, E., T. N. Howe, J. R. Brandt, A. St. Clair, M. Parca, and T. Peña. 1993. "Complesso tardo romano sul versante NE del Palatino (1991)," *Bollettino di Archeologia* 19–21, 81–89.

Hostetter, E., T. N. Howe, J. R. Brandt, A. St. Clair, and T. Peña 1991. "Palatino. Versante nordorientale. Complesso tardoromano (1990)," *Bollettino di Archeologia* 9, 47–56.

Huls, Y. 1957. *Ivoires d'Étrurie* (Brussels and Rome).

Hülsen, Ch. 1890. "Miscellanea epigrafica," *Mitteilungen des Deutschen Archäologischen Instituts* (Rom. Abt.) 5, 287–304.

Humphrey, J. H., ed. 1989. *The Circus and a Byzantine Cemetery at Carthage* (Ann Arbor).

Hurst, H. R., and S. P. Roskams. 1984. *Excavations at Carthage: The British Mission I, 1, The Avenue du President Habib Bourguiba, Salammbo: The Site and Finds Other than Pottery* (Sheffield).

Ibrahim, L., R. Scranton, and R. Brill. 1976. *Kenchreai: Eastern Port of Corinth II* (Leiden).

Inan, J., and E. Alföldi-Rosenbaum. 1979. *Römische und früh byzantinische Porträtplastik aus der Türkei: Neue Funde* (Mainz am Rhein).

Inscriptiones Christianae Urbis Romae septimo saeculo antiquiores, nova series. 1922–1992. Vols. 1–10, ed. A. Silvagni, A. Ferrua, D. Mazzoleni, and C. Carletti (Rome, Vatican City).

Joly, E., S. Garraffo, and A. Mandruzzato. 1992. "Materiali minori dallo scavo del teatro di Leptis Magna," *Quaderni di archeologia della Libia* 15, 197–233.

Jordan, H., and C. Hülsen. 1907. *Topographie der Stadt Rom* (Berlin).

Jourdan, L. 1976. *La faune du site gallo-romain et paléochrétien de la Bourse (Marseille)* (Paris).

Kampen, N. 1982. "Social Status and Gender in Roman Art: The Case of the Saleswoman," in D. Garrard and N. Broude, eds., *Feminism and Art History: Questioning the Litany* (New York), 63–77.

Kanzler, R. 1903. *Gli avori dei Musei Profano e Sacro della Biblioteca Vaticana* (Rome).

Karageorghis, V. 1968. "Die Elfenbein-Throne von Salamis, Zypern," *Archaeologia Homerica,* 99–103.

Kenyon, K. M. 1948. *Excavations at the Jewry-Wall Site, Leicester* (Oxford).

Kiss, Z. 1973. "Les Ampoules de St. Menas découvertes à Kôm el-Dikka (Alexandrie) en 1969," *Etudes et travaux* 7, 137–154.

Kleiner, D. E. E., and S. B. Matheson, eds. 1996. *I Claudia. Women in Ancient Rome* (Austin, Tex.).

Klumbach, H., and U. Moortgat-Correns. 1968. "Orientalisches Rollsiegel von Mainzer Legionslager," *Germania* 46, 36–40.

Knigge, U. 1976. *Karameikos IX: Die Südhügel* (Berlin).

Kollwitz, J. 1963. "Alexandrinische Elfenbeine," in Klaus Wessel, ed., *Christentum am Nil. Internationale Arbeitstagung zur Ausstellung "Koptische Kunst," Essen, Villa Hügel, 23–25 Juli 1963* (Recklinghausen), 207–220.

Krzyszkowska, O. 1990. *Ivory and Related Materials: An Illustrated Guide,* Institute of Classical Studies Classical Handbook 3, *Bulletin* Supplement 59 (London 1990).

———. 1992. "Aegean Ivory Carving: Towards an Evaluation of Late Bronze Age Workshop Material," in Fitton 1992, 25–35.

Kunze, E. 1930. "Zu den Aufängen der griechischen Plastik," *Mitteilungen des Deutschen Archäologischen Instituts* (Athen. Abt.), 147–155.

———. 1959. "Olympia," in E. Boehringer, ed., *Neue deutsche Ausgrabungen im Mittelmeergebiet und im vorderen Orient* (Berlin), 263–310.

Kyrieleis, H. 1969. *Throne und Klinen. Studien zur Formengeschichte altorientalischer und griechischer Sitz- und Liegemöbel vorhellenistischer Zeit, Jahrbuch des Deutschen Archäologischen Instituts,* Ergh.24 (1969).

Lamboglia, N. 1950. *Gli scavi di Albintimilium, e la cronologia della ceramica romana. Campagna di scavo 1938–1940* (Bordighera).

Lányi, V. 1972. "Die spätantiken Gräberfelder von Pannonien," *Acta Archaeologica Academiae Scientarium Hungaricae* 24, 53–213.

Lapatin, K. 1997. "Pheidias ἐλεφαντουργός," *American Journal of Archaeology* 101, 663–682.

———. 2001. *Chryselephantine Statuary in the Ancient Mediterranean World* (Oxford).

Lauffer, S., ed. 1971. *Diocletians Preisedikt* (Berlin).

Leahu, V. 1975. "Cercetări Arheologice în necropola tumulară de la Romula," *Cercetari Arheologice* (Bucharest) 1, 191–216.

Leclerc, H. 1982. "Catalogue raisonné des objets en os et ivoire trouvée à Carthage par la deuxième équipe canadienne, saisons 1978–1979," M.A. thesis, University of Ottawa.

Lessing, E., and W. Oberleitner. 1978. *Ephesos, Weltstadt der Antike* (Vienna and Heidelberg).

Letta, C. 1984. "Due Letti funerari in osso dal centro italico-romano della valle d'Amplero (Abruzzo)," *Rendiconti della Pontificia Accademia romana di archeologia* 52, 67–115.

Liebowitz, H. 1977. "Bone and Ivory Inlay from Syria and Palestine," *Israel Exploration Journal* 27, 89–97.

Lipinska, J. 1966. "Polish Excavations at Kom el Dikka," *Etudes et travaux* 3, 181–185.

Longhurst, M. H. 1927. *Catalogue of Carvings in Ivory, Victoria and Albert Museum* I (London).

Loverdou-Tsigarida, M. 1986. *Osteina plakidia diacosmesi xilinon kyvotidion apo to christianiko* (Thessalonika).

Macchioro, S. 1988. "Il sondaggio stratigrafico nella sede centrale della Cassa di Risparmio di Modena (1985–1986). I materiali," in A. Cardarelli, ed., *Modena dalle origini all'anno mille. Studi di Archeologia e Storia I,* Exhibition Catalogue (Modena), 426–449.

MacGregor, A. 1985. *Bone, Antler, Ivory, and Horn: The Technology of Skeletal Material Since the Roman Period* (London and Totowa, N.J.).

———. 1989. "Bone, Antler and Horn Industries in the Urban Context," in D. Serjeantson and T. Waldron, eds., *Diet and Crafts in Towns: The Evidence of Animal Remains from the Roman to the Post-Medieval Periods, BAR* British Series 199, 107–128.

MacGregor, A., and J. D. Currey. 1983. "Mechanical Properties as Conditioning Factors in the Bone and Antler Industry of the 3rd to the 13th Century A.D.," *Journal of Archaeological Science* 10, 71–77.

Mack, S., and J. Menè. 1933. "L'industrie de l'os à Reims pendant l'occupation romaine. Essai sur la technique employée," *Bulletin de la Société Archéologique Champenoise* 3–4, July–Dec., 19–25.

Maguire, E. D., H. P. Maguire, and M. J. Duncan-Flowers. 1989. *Art and Holy Powers in the Early Christian House* (Urbana-Champaign).

Maiuri, A. 1938–1939. "Statuetta eburnea d'arte indiana a Pompeii," *Le arti* 1, 111–115.

Mallwitz, A. 1972. *Olympia und seine Bauten* (Munich).

Mallwitz, A., and W. Schiering. 1964. "Die Werkstatt des Pheidias in Olympia I," *Olympische Forschungen* 5 (Berlin).

Manacorda, D., M. S. Arena, P. Delogu, et al. 2000. *Museo Nazionale Romano. Crypta Balbi* (Milan).

Mancini, G. 1930. "Scoperta della tomba della vergine Vestale Tiburtina Cossinia," *Notizie degli scavi di antichità* 6, 353–369.

Mangin, M. 1981. *Un quartier de commerçants et d'artisans d'Alesia. Contribution à l'histoire de l'habitat urbain en Gaule* (Dijon, Semur-en-Auxois).

Manière, G. 1966. "Un puits funéraire de la fin du Iers. ap. J.-C. aux Aquae Siccae, (Cazères, Haute-Garonne)," *Gallia* 24.1, 101–146.

Manson, M. 1978. "Les poupées dans l'empire romain, le royaume du bosphore cimmerien et le royaume Parthe," Ph.D dissertation, l'E.P.H.E., Paris.

Marangou, L. 1969. *Lakonische Elfenbein-und Beinschnitzerein* (Tübingen).

———. 1976. *Bone Carvings from Egypt* (Tübingen).

Marazzi, F. 1998. "I patrimoni della chiesa romana e l'amministrazione papale fra tarda antichità e alto medioevo," in Delogu 1998, 33–50.

Marteaux, B., and M. Le Roux. 1913. *Boutae (les fins d'Annecy), vicus gallo-romain de la cité de Vienne* (Annecy).

Masson, M. E., and G. A. Pugacenkova. 1982. *The Parthian Rhytons of Nisa* (Florence).

Mastrocinque, A. 1991. "Avori intarsiati in ambra da Quinto Fiorentino," *Bollettino di archeologia* 10, 1–10.

Meiggs, R., and D. Lewis. 1969. *A Selection of Greek Historical Inscriptions* (Oxford).

Mele, M., ed. 1982. *L'area del santuario siriaco del Gianicolo* (Rome).

Melucco Vaccaro, A.1993. "Hierosolimam adiit (. . .) tabulas eburneas optimas secum deportavit," *Arte medievale* 7.2, 1–19.

Meneghini, R., and R. Santangeli Valenzani. 1993. "Sepolture intramuranee e pasaggio urbano a Roma tra Ve VII secolo," in Paroli and Delogu 1993, 89–111.

Michaelides, D. 1990. *Paphiaca I: A Personification of the Nile on a Bone Plaquette from Nea Paphos,* Report of the Department of Antiquities Cyprus, 159–167.

Michel, C. 1900. *Recueil d'inscriptions greques* (Brussels).

Militello, E. 1961. "Troina. Scavi effetuati dall'Istituto di Archeologia dell'Università di Catania negli anni 1958 e 1960," *Notizie degli scavi di antichità* 15, 346–360.

Miller, P. C. 1994. *Dreams in Late Antiquity* (Princeton).

Milojcic, V. 1968. "Zu den spätkaiserzeitlichen und merowingischen Silberlöffeln," *Bericht der Römisch-Germanischen Kommission* 49, 111–148.

Minns, E. H. 1912. *Scythians and Greeks* (Cambridge).

Moccheggiani Carpano, C. 1982. "Considerazioni sul versante orientale del Gianicolo," in Mele 1982, 25–35.

Monacchi, D. 1990–1991. "(Umbria) Aquasparta (Terni) Loc. Crocifisso: Scavi di un'area funeraria romana con rinvenimento di letti di osso," *Notizie degli scavi di antichità* 1–2, 87–145.

———. 1994. "(Umbria) Aquasparta (Terni) Loc. Crocifisso: Scavi di un'area funeraria romana con rinvenimento di letti di osso," *Notizie degli scavi di antichità* 1–2, 87–145.

Morel, J.-P. 1987. "La topographie de l'artisanat et du commerce dans la Rome antique," in *L'urbs: espace urbain et histoire. Actes du colloque international organise par le Centre National de la Recherche Scientifique et l'Ecole Française de Rome. Rome 8–12 mai 1985,* Collection de L'Ecole française de Rome 98, 128–155.

Morey, C. R. 1936. *Gli oggetti di avorio e di osso del Museo Sacro Vaticano* (Vatican City).

Murray, H. J. R. 1941. "The Medieval Game of Tables," *Medium Aevum* 10, 57–69.

Mütz, A. 1972. *Die Kunst des Metalldrehens bei den Römern* (Bâle and Stuttgart).

Nicholls, R. V. 1979. "A Roman Couch in Cambridge," *Archaeologia* 106, 1–32.

———. 1991. "More Bone Couches," *Antiquaries Journal* 71, 36–45.

Nielson, L., and K. Phillips. 1983. "Poggio Civitate (Siena): The Excavations at Murlo in 1976–8," *Notizie degli scavi di antichità* 37, 5–24.

Oliver, A. 1992. "Ivory Temple Doors," in Fitton 1992, 227–232.

Pagenstecher, R. 1913. *Expedition Ernst von Sieglin, II, part 3. Die griechisch-ägyptische Sammlung Ernst von Sieglin* (Leipzig).

Panciera, S., ed. 1987. *La collezione epigrafica dei Musei Capitolini* (Rome).

Panella, C. 1996. *Meta Sudans I. Un'area sacra in Palatio e la valle del Colosseo prima e dopo Nerone* (Rome).

Pantò, G., ed. 1996. *Il monastero della visitazione a Vercelli: Archeologia e storia* (Alexandria).

Paroli, L., ed. 1997. *L'Italia centro-settentrionale in età longobarda. Atti del Convegno Ascoli Piceno, 6–7 ottobre 1995* (Florence).

Paroli, L., and P. Delogu, eds. 1993. *La storia economica di Roma nell'alto medioevo alla luce dei recenti scavi archeologici. Seminario Rome 2–3 april 1992* (Florence).

Pavolini, C. 1993. *Caput Africa I: Indagini archeologiche a Piazza Celimontana (1984–1988). La storia, lo scavo, l'ambiente* (Rome).

Payne, H., and T. J. Dunbabin. 1962. *Perachora: The Sanctuaries of Hera Akraia and Limenia,* II (Oxford).

Peña, T. 1998. "Aspects of Residuality in the Palatine East Pottery Assemblage, in Guidobaldi et alii 1998, 5–19.

Penniman, T. K. 1952. *Pictures of Ivory and Other Animal Teeth, Bone, and Antler,* Pitt Rivers Occasional Paper on Technology 5 (Oxford).

Petrie, W. M. Flinders. 1917. *Tools and Weapons* (London).

Petrie, W. M. Flinders, and E. Mackay. 1915. *Heliopolis Kafr-Ammar and Shurafa* (London).

Petropoulos, G. A., ed. 1939. *Papyroites en Athenais Archaiologikes Hetaireias,* Pragmateiai tes Akademias Athenon 10 (Athens).

Pfeiffer, R. 1946. "The Measurements of the Zeus at Olympia," *Journal of Hellenic Studies* 61, 1–5.

Pietsch, M. 1983. "Die römischen Eisenwerkzeuge von Saalberg, Feldberg, und Zugmantel," *Saalburg-Jahrbuch* 39, 5–132.

Pipili, M. 1987. *Laconian Iconography of the 6th c. B.C.,* Oxford University Committee for Archaeology Monograph 12 (Oxford).

Poplin, F. 1974a. "Deux cas particuliers de débitage par usure," in *Premier Colloque international sur l'industrie de l'os dans la préhistoire, Abbaye de Sénaque, avril 1974* (Aix-en-Provence), 85–92.

———. 1974b. "Principes de la détermination des matières dures animales," in *Premier colloque international sur l'industrie de l'os dans la préhistoire, Abbaye de Sénaque, avril 1974* (Aix-en-Provence), 15–20.

———. 1977a. "Analyse de matière de quelques ivoires d'art," in *Méthodologie appliquée à l'industrie de l'os préhistorique, Abbaye de Sénaque, 9–12 juin 1976,* Colloque International du CNRS 568 (Paris), 77–94.

———. 1977b. "Utilisation des cavités naturelles osseuses et dentaires," in *Méthodologie appliquée à l'industrie de l'os préhistorique, Abbaye de Sénaque, 9–12 juin 1976,* Colloque International du CNRS 568 (Paris), 111–118.

Poulain-Josien, Th. 1966. "Etudes de la faune," in J. Allain, A. Cothenet, Th. Poulain-Josien, and M. Vauthey, "Un dépotoir augustéen à Argentomagus: étude de la faune," *Revue archéologique du Centre* 5, 17–39.

———. 1976. *L'étude des ossements animaux et son apport à l'archéologie,* Centre de recherches sur les techniques gréco-romaines 6 (Dijon).

Pugachenkova, G. A. 1948. "Tron Mitridata I iz Parfianskoy Nisy," *Vestnik Drevney Istorii* 1, 161–171.

Randall, R. H. 1985. *Masterpieces of Ivory from The Walters Art Gallery* (New York).

Ransom, C. L. 1902. "Reste griechischer Holzmöbel in Berlin," *Jahrbuch des Deutschen Archäologischen Institut* 17, 125–140.

———. 1905. *Studies in Ancient Furniture: Couches and Beds of the Greeks and Romans* (Chicago).

Rea, R. 1993. "Il Colosseo e la valle da Teodorico ai Frangipane: note di studio," in Paroli and Delogu 1993, 71–88.

Reese, D. S. 1985. "Hippotamus and Elephant Teeth from Kition. Appendix VIII (D)," in V. Karageorghis, ed., *Excavations at Kition VIII,* (Nicosia), 391–408.

———. 1987. "A Bone Assemblage at Corinth of the Second Century after Christ," *Hesperia* 56, 255–274.

———. 1992. "The Earliest Worked Bone on Cyprus," in *Report of the Department of Antiquities Cyprus*, 13–16.

Reese, D. S., and O. Krzyskowska. 1996. "Elephant Ivory at Minoan Kommos," in J. W. Shaw and M. C. Shaw, eds., *Kommos1/2. The Kommos Region and Houses of the Minoan Town* (Princeton), 324–326.

Rehm, A. 1958. *Didyma: Die Inschriften* (Berlin).

Reilly, J. 1997. "Naked and Limbless: Learning about the Feminine Body in Athens," in A. O. Koloski-Ostrow and C. L. Lyons, eds., *Naked Truths: Women, Sexuality, and Gender in Classical Art and Archaeology* (London and New York), 154–172.

Rhomiopoulou, K. 1973. "A New Monumental Chamber Tomb with Paintings of the Hellenistic Period near Lefkadia," *Athens Annals of Archaeology* 6, 87–92.

Ricci, A., ed. 1985. *Settefinestre. Una villa schiavistica nell' Etruria romana, III. La villa e suoi reperti* (Modena).

Ricci, M. 1997. "Relazioni culturali e scambi commerciali nell'Italia centrale romano-longobarda alla luce della Crypta Balbi in Roma," in Paroli 1997, 239–273.

Richter, G. M. A. 1966. *The Furniture of the Greeks, Etruscans, and Romans* (London).

Riha, E., and B. W. Stern. 1982. *Die römischen Löffel aus Augst und Kaiseraugst: Archaeologische und metallanalytische Untersuchungen,* Forschungen in Augst 5 (Augst).

Rinaldi, M. R. 1956. "Ricerche sui giocattoli nell'antichita a proposito di un'iscrizione di Brescello," *Epigraphica* 18, 105–229.

Rizzo, G., F. Villedieu, and M Vitale. 1999. "Mobilier de tombes des Vie–VIIe siècles mise au jour sur le palatin (Rome, Vigna Barberini)," *Mélanges d'archéologie et d'histoire de l'Ecole française de* Rome 111, 354–401.

Rockwell, P. 1991. "Unfinished Statuary Associated with a Sculptor's Studio," in R. R. R. Smith and K. T. Erim, eds., *Aphrodisias Papers* 2, *Journal of Roman Archaeology* Supplementary Series 2 (Ann Arbor), 127–143.

Rodziewicz, E. 1966. "Late Antique ivory and bone plaquettes in the National Museum in Warsaw," *Bulletin du Musée national de Varsovie* 7.2, 33–37.

———. 1968. "Small Greek Heads as Furniture Decoration," *Etudes et travaux* 2, 257–265.

———. 1969. "Bone Carvings Discovered at Kôm el-Dikka, Alexsandria in 1967," *Etudes et travaux* 3, 147–152.

———. 1974. "Greckie Wyroby z Koski Sloniowej Okresu Klasycznego" (Les ivoires grecs de la période classique), *Rocznik Muzeum Narodowego w Warszawie* 18, 59–110 (French and Russian summaries).

———. 1978. "Reliefs figurés en os des fouilles à Kôm el-Dikka," *Etudes et travaux* 10, 317–336.

———. 1992. "Remarks on Chryselephantine Statue from Alexandria," in G. Pugliase Carratelli, G. Del Re, N. Bonacasa, and A. Etman, eds., *Roma e l'Egitto nell'antichità classica. Atti del I Congresso Internazionale Italo-Egiziano (Cairo 6–9 Febbraio 1989)* (Rome), 317–328.

———. 1995. "On Stylistical and Technical Components of the Roman Coloured Bone Appliques from Egypt," in N. Bonacasa, C. Naro, E. C. Portalie, and A. Tullio, eds., *Alessandria e il mondo ellenistico-romano. Atti del II Congresso Internazionale Italo-Egiziano (Alessandria 23–27 novembre 1992)* (Rome), 405–411.

Rodziewicz, M. 1962. "A Bone Plaquette in the Shape of A Silenus Head at the National Museum of Warsaw," *Bulletin du Musée national de Varsovie* 3.3, 65–68.

———. 1976. "Un quartier d'habitation gréco-romain à Kôm el-Dikka (Sondage R, 1970–1973)," *Etudes et travaux* 9, 169–210.

———. 1984. *Les habitations romaines tardives d'Alexandrie à la lumière des fouilles polonaises à Kôm el-Dikka,* Alexandrie 3 (Warsaw).

———. 1991. "Opus Sectile Mosaics from Alexandria and Mariotis," in E. Dassmann and K. Thraede, eds., *Tesserae. Festschrift für Josef Engemann, Jahrbuch für Antike und Christentum,* Ergänzungsband 18, 204–214.

Romano, I. 1980. "Early Greek Cult Images," Ph.D. dissertation, University of Pennsylvania.

Rosenthal, R. 1976. "Late Roman and Byzantine Bone Carvings from Palestine," *Israel Exploration Journal* 26, 96–103.

Rossi, F. 1988–1989. "Brescia, via di S. Zeno, località Area Patrioti. Sepoltura a incinerazione di età romana," *Notiziario della Soprintendenza Archeologica della Lombardia,* 197–198.

Royo, M., F. Chausson, E. Hubert, M. Smith, M. A. Tomei, and P. Meogrossi. 1997. *La Vigna Barberini I. Histoire d'un site,* Etude des sources et de la topographie, Roma Antica 3, EFR/SAR (Rome).

Rudolph, W. 1988. "Workshops: Some Reflections and Some Pots," *Proceedings of the 3rd Symposium on Ancient Greek and Related Pottery. Copenhagen August 31–September 4 1987* (Copenhagen), 524–35.

Ruffo, M. 1994–1995. "Anagni (Frosinone) Località S. Cecilia. Indagini nel santuario ernico: il deposito votivo arcaico," *Notizie degli scavi di antichità* 5–6, 5–164.

Sackett, L. H., ed. 1992. *Knossos: From Greek City to Roman Colony. Excavations at the Unexplored Mansion II* (London).

Saguì, L. 1993. "Crypta Balba (Roma): conclusioni delle indagini archeologiche nell' esedra del monumento romano. Relazione preliminare," *Archeologia medievale* 20, 409–418.

———. 1998a. "Indagini archeologiche a Roma: nuove dati sul VII secolo," in Delogu 1998, 63–78.

———, ed. 1998b. *I vetri della collezione Gorga: un patrimonio ritrovato* (Rome).

Saguì, L., and D. Manacorda. 1995. "L'Esedra della crypta

Balbi e il Monastero di S. Lorenzo in Pallacinis," *Archeologia laziale* 12.1, 121–134.

Saguì, L., and L. Paroli, eds. 1990. *L'Esedra della crypta Balbi nel medioevo (XI–XV secolo)* (Florence).

Saguì, L., and A. Rovelli. 1998. "Risidualità, non-residualiltà, continuità di circolazione: Alcuni esempi dalla crypta Balbi," in Guidobaldi et al. 1998, 173–195.

St. Clair, A. 1995–1996. "Women in Context: Eight Statuettes from the Roman Period," *Muse* 29–30, 30–49.

St. Clair, A. 1996a. "Evidence for Late Antique Bone and Ivory Carving on the Northeast Slope of the Palatine: The Palatine East Excavation," *Dumbarton Oaks Papers* 50, 369–374.

———. 1996b. "Imperial Virtue: Questions of Form and Function in the Case of Four Late Antique Statuettes," *Dumbarton Oaks Pape* 50, 147–162.

St. Clair, A., and E. P. McLachlan, eds. 1989. *The Carver's Art: Medieval Sculpture in Ivory, Bone, and Horn* (New Brunswick).

Sakellarakis, J. 1979. *To elephantodonto kai i katergasia tou sta mykenäika Khronia* (Athens).

Salvetti, G. 1978. "Il Catalogo degli oggetti minuti conservati presso la Pontificia Commissione di Archeologia Sacra," *Rivista di archeologia cristiana* 54.5, 6, 109–111.

Salzman, M. F. 1964. *Industries in the Middle Ages* (London).

Saronio, P. 1990. "Cortemaggiore (Piacanza). Area SAIPEM. Necropoli romani," *Bollettino di archeologia* 5–6, 124.

Sautot, M. C., ed. 1978. *Le cycle de la matière, Os,* Exhibition Catalogue (Dijon).

Schäfer, T. 1989. *Imperii insignia, sella curulis und fasces: zur Reprasentation römischer Magistrate* (Mainz).

Schiering, W. 1991. *Die Werkstatt des Pheidias in Olympia II: Werkstattfunde, Olympische Forschungen* 18 (1991).

Schlumberger, D., and P. Bernard. 1965. "Ai Khanum," *Bulletin de correspondance hellénique* 89, 590–657.

Schmid, E. 1968. "Beindrechsler, Hornschnitzer, und Leimsieder in römischen Augst," in E. Schmid, L. Berger, and P. Bürgin, eds., *Provincialia, Festschrift für Rudolf Laur-Belart* (Basel 1968), 185–197.

———. 1972. *Atlas of Animal Bones: For Prehistorians, Archaeologists and Quaternary Geologists* (New York).

Schofield, L. 1992. "The Influence of Eastern Religions on the Iconography of Ivory and Bone Objects in the Kameiros Well," in Fitton 1992, 173–184.

Schwartz, J. H. 1984. "The (Primarily) Mammalian Fauna," in H. R. Hurst and S. P. Roskams, eds., *Excavations at Carthage: The British Mission I,1, The Avenue du President Habib Bourguiba, Salammbo: The Site and Finds Other than Pottery* (Sheffield), 229–256.

Schwarz-Mackensen, G. 1976. "Die Knochennadeln von Haithabu," in K. Schietzel, ed., *Berichte über die Ausgrabungen in Haithabu* 9 (Neuminster), 1–94.

Scranton, R. L., and E. S. Ramage. 1967. "Investigations at Corinthian Kenchreai," *Hesperia* 36, 124–186.

Scranton, R., J. W. Shaw, and R. Brill. 1978. *Kenchreai. I. Topography and Architecture* (Leiden).

Scullard, H. H. 1974. *The Elephant in the Greek and Roman World* (London).

Serjeantson, D., and T. Waldron. 1989. *Diet and Crafts in Towns: The Evidence of Animal Remains from the Roman to the Post-Medieval Periods, BAR* British Series 199 (Oxford 1989).

Shear, T. L. 1936. "Excavations in the Athenian Agora. The Campaign of 1935," *Hesperia* 5, 1–42.

———. 1937. "Excavations in the Athenian Agora. The Campaign of 1936," *Hesperia* 6, 333–381.

———. 1975. "The Athenian Agora Excavations of 1973–1974," *Hesperia* 44, 331–374.

Shenouda, S. 1973. "Alexandria University Excavations on the Cricket Playground in Alexandria," *Opuscula Romana* 9 (Stockholm), 193–205.

Simone, L. 1991. "Cascina Medaglia. Frammenti di letti funerari in osso," *Notiziario della Soprintendenza Archeologica della Lombardia,* 69–71.

Sinn, U. 1982. "Ein Elfenbeinkopf aus dem Heraion von Samos." *Mitteilungen des Deutschen Archäologischen Instituts* (Athen. Abt.) 97, 35–55.

Sintès, C., ed. 1996. *Musée de l'Arles antique. Collections archéologiques d'Arles* (Arles).

Stampolidis, N. 1992. "Four Ivory Heads from the Geometric/Archaic Cemetery at Eleutherna," in Fitton 1992, 141–162.

Steiner, P. 1939. "Römisches Brettspiel und Spielgerät aus Trier," *Saalburg Jahrbuch* 9, 34–45.

Stern, W. 2000. "A Decorated Bone Ring from a Cabinet or Chest and Workshop Procedures in the 4th c. A.D.," *Journal of Roman Archaeology* 13, 359–364.

Stevens, G. P. 1955. "Remarks on the Colossal Chryselephantine Statue of Athena in the Parthenon," *Hesperia* 24, 240–76.

———. 1957. "How the Parthenos Was Made," *Hesperia* 26, 350–61.

Stewart, A. F. 1990. *Greek Sculpture: An Exploration* (New Haven).

Stillwell, R. 1936. "Excavations at Corinth," *American Journal of Archaeology* 40, 21–45.

Strzygowski, J. 1902. *Hellenistische und koptische Kunst in Alexandria, Bulletin de la Société Archéologique d'Alexandrie* 5 (Vienna).

———. 1904. *Koptische Kunst* (Vienna).

Talamo, E. 1987–1988. "Un letto funerario da una tomba dell'Esquilino," *Bullettino della Commissione Archeologica Comunale in Roma* 92, 17–102.

———. 1992. "Contesti funerari della prima età imperiale

dall'Esquilino," in M. E. Tittoni and S. Guarino, eds., *Invisibilia. Rivedere i capolavori, vedere i projetti,* Exhibition Catalogue (Rome), 192–194.

Tarn, W. W. 1928. "Ptolomy II," *Journal of Egyptian Archaeology* 14, 348–60.

Thornton, J. 1981. "The Structure of Ivory and Ivory Substitutes," *American Institute for Conservation of Historic Works* 9, 174–177.

Tod, M. N. 1968. *Selection of Greek Historical Inscriptions* (Oxford).

Tournavitou, I. 1992. "The Ivories from the House of Sphinxes and the House of Shields: Techniques in a Palatial Workshop Context," in Fitton 1992, 37–44.

Vassy, A., and H. Müller. 1922. "Ebauches d'objets gallo-romains en os de Sainte-Colombe-lès-Vienne, Rhodania," *Congrès de Nîmes 710,* 1–14.

Vaulina, M., and A. Wasowicz. 1974. *Bois grecs et romains de l'Ermitage. Ossolineum* (Warsaw).

Vercoutter, J. 1962. "Un palais des 'Candaces,' contemporain d'Auguste," *Syria* 39, 262–299.

Vermeule, E. 1989. "Carved Bones From Corinth," in A. Leonard and B. B. Williams, eds., *Essays in Ancient Civilization Presented to Helene J. Kantor,* Studies in Ancient Oriental Civilization 47 (Chicago), 271–286.

Vetere, U., P. L. Severi, and R. Nocilini, eds. 1983. *Crepereia Tryphaena: Le scoperte nell'area del Palazzo di Giustizia* (Venice).

Vetters, H. 1981. "Ephesos Vorläufiger Grabungsbericht 1980," *Anzeiger de Österreichischen Akademie der Wissenschaften in Wien,* Philos.-Hist. Klasse, 118, 137–168.

———. 1982. "Ephesos Vorläufiger Grabungsbericht 1981," *Anzeiger de Österreichischen Akademie der Wissenschaften in Wien,* Philos.-Hist. Klasse, 119, 65–68.

Villedieu, F. 1995. "La Vigna Barberini (Palatino): Nouve Acquisizioni," *Archeologia Laziale* 12,1, 1995, 33–39.

Virgili, P., and C. Viola, eds. 1990. *Bellezza e seduzione nella Roma imperiale,* Exhibition Catalogue, Palazzo dei Conservatori, Rome, 11 June–31 July 1990 (Rome).

Volbach, W. F. 1976. *Elfenbeinarbeiten der Spätantike und des frühen Mittelalters* (Mainz am Rhein).

Von Bargen, F. 1994. "Zur Materialkunde und Form spätanatiker Elfenbeinpyxiden," *Jahrbuch für Antike und Christentum* 37, 45–63.

Wace, J. B. 1949. "Excavations on the Government Hospital Site, Alexandria: Preliminary Report," *Bulletin of the Faculty of Arts, Farouk I University of Alexandria* 5, 151–156.

Waelkens, M., ed. 1993. *Sagalassos II: Report on the Third Excavation Campaign of 1992,* Acta Archaeologica Lovaniensia Monographiae 6 (Leuven).

Waldstein, C. 1905. *The Argive Heraeum,* vol. 2 (Cambridge).

Walker, S., ed. 2000. *Ancient Faces: Mummy Portraits from Roman Egypt* (New York).

Waltzing, J. 1968. *Etude historique sur les corporations professionnelles chez les Romains, depuis les origines jusqu'à la chute de l'empire d'occident,* 4 vols. (Louvain, 1895–1896; reprint, Hildesheim-New York).

Wångstedt, S. V. 1968. "Demotische Steuerquittungen aus ptolemäischer Zeit," *Orientalia Suecana* 17, 28–60.

Wapnish, P. 1991. "Beauty and Utility in Bone: New Light on Bone Crafting," *Biblical Archaeology Review* 17.4, 54–57.

Ward-Perkins, J. B., and A. Claridge. 1976. *Pompeii 79,* Exhibition Catalogue, Royal Academy of Arts, 20 November 1976–27 February 1977 (London).

Weinberg, S. S. 1975. "Etruscan Bone Mirror Handles," *Muse* 9, 25–33.

Weitzmann, K. 1972. *Catalogue of the Byzantine and Early Medieval Antiquities in the Dumbarton Oaks Collection III: Ivories and Steatites* (Washington, D.C.).

———, ed. 1979. *Age of Spirituality. Late Antique and Early Christian Art, Third to Seventh Century* (New York and Princeton).

Wessel, K., ed. 1964. *Christentum am Nil. Internationale Arbeitstagung zur Ausstellung "Koptische Kunst," Essen, Villa Hügel, 23–25 Juli 1963* (Recklinghausen).

Whitehouse, D., et al. 1982. "Schola Praeconum I: The Coins, Pottery, Lamps and Fauna," *Papers of the British School at Rome* 50, 53–101.

Williams, C., and H. Williams. 1987. "Excavations at Mytilene, 1987," *Canadian Mediterranean Institute Bulletin* 9, 10–11.

Winkelmann, W. 1977. "Archäologische Zeugnisse zum frümittelalterlichen Handwerk in Westfalen," *Frümittelalterliche Studien* 11,92–126.

Wulff, O. 1909. Altchristliche und mittelalterliche, byzantinische und italienische Bildwerke (Berlin).

INDEX

acro-elephantine statues, 9

ajouré technique, 22

Alexandria, 34–36, 40

Amanishakhete (Queen), 30

American Academy in Rome, xi

animals: couchant, 21; as source: —of bone, 2–3; —of ivory, 4–5

Aphrodite Anadyomeme, 98

Apollonius of Tyana, 12

Aristophanes, 10

Ashkelon, 30, 36

Augustus, 11

aula, xi

Begram, 30–31

bits, twist or auger, 52, 58, 65

blanks: objects identified as, 58; sawing and shaping of, 51–52, 60

bone: cancellous *vs.* compact, 2; central medullary cavity of, 3–4; commonly utilized, 2–3, 111, 116–17; elasticity and tensile strength of, 1–2; as interchangeable with ivory, 18; as poor substitute for ivory, 1, 13; production of objects from, 16–17; size and shape of objects carved from, 3; softening of, 4; tanners as suppliers of, 50; veneer and, 3, 4, 42

bone carving: in Alexandria, 34–36; as craft and industry, 13–14; debris from, *26,* 58; as household skill, 199n. 50; material remains of, 17; in Olympia, 24–25, *25*; in regional centers, 36–37; in Sparta, 19–24

bone figure, Sparta, *20*

bow drill, 52, 65

boxes, 33–34, *34,* 66, 77

bracelets, 17, 48, 106

cancellous tissue/material, 2, 3, 86

Carthage, 36

carving tradition, continuity of, xii

catacombs, objects buried in, 17, 48, 107

cattle skeleton, *2*

chisels, 50–51, 52, 60

chryselephantine statues, xii, 9–10, 25–27, 200n. 2

Chrysostom, John, 11

Cicero, 9, 10

Clement of Alexandria, 11

Colchester, 37

combs, 104

compact tissue, 2, 3

consular diptychs, 33

context date, 57

Corinth, 36, 37

couchant animals, 21

couches, veneered, 41–42. *See also* funerary couch

counters, disk-shaped, 46, 111

Crypyta Balbi, 49, 54

cylinders, 43, 53, 64, 80

Cypselus, 10

Cyril, 11

dating of objects, 57

Delphi, 24

Demosthenes, 11, 12, 29

dentine, 4

dice: first- and second-century A.D. contexts, 44; late antique contexts, 46; size, shape, and decoration of, 113–14

Dio Cassius, 11

Diocletian, Edict of Maximum Prices, 9

Diodorus Siculus, 10

Diogenes Laertius, 11, 28–29

Dipoenus, 9, 15

diptychs: consular, 33; ivory, 11

dolls, articulated, 48–49, 108

domus, ix

doors, 10

dress pins, 99

Egypt. *See* Alexandria

elephant tusk, *4*

Endoeus, 9, 15

Ephesos, 19, 24

epiphyses, 50, 58–59

Etruria, 30

fashion, and ivory and bone industries, 11, 16–17, 31, 48

fibula plaques, 22

foramina, 2

foundry, 24

framing strips, 44, 66

funerary couch: from Aielli, 42; from Athens, *19,* 27–28; at Cambridge, *29,* 42; from Cologne, 42; as composite work of art, 18–19; from Cucuron, 42; decline in production of, 32–33; from Esquiline Hill, 42; Greek art and, 32–33; in Italy, Gaul, and Germany, 31; of Julius Caesar, 11, 32; production centers for, 31–32; from Saint-Lambert, 42

furniture: bone, ivory, and, 10–11, 16; industry in third century, 33; legs of, 28, *29,* 42–43, 69–70, 77; Palatine Hill objects associated with, 44–46; pulls, 106; remains from decoration of, 66; veneered couches, 41–42. *See also* funerary couch; mounts; veneer

gaming pieces, 46–47, 111

glassworking, 35, 43

Greece. *See* Olympia; Sparta

Hadrian, 10

handles: first- and second-century A.D. contexts, 44; late antique contexts, 47; types of, 104–5

Hasdrubel, 9

"heirloom" factor, 57

Herodes Atticus, 10

Herodian, 10, 11

hinges, 43, 53, 66, 80

hippopotamus, 5

hoarding of ivory, 9